The Folklore of the Black Country

The Folklore of the Black Country

by

Roy Palmer

Roy Palmer

Logaston Press

LOGASTON PRESS
Little Logaston Woonton Almeley
Herefordshire HR3 6QH
logastonpress.co.uk

First published by Logaston Press 2007

ISBN 978 1 904396 84 0

Set in Times by Logaston Press
and printed in Great Britain by
Oaklands Book Services, Gloucestershire

Contents

Acknowledgements

As always, I am deeply in debt to my wife, Pat, for tolerating my obsessions and for spending long hours listening to recordings and deciphering tunes, then producing manuscript copies suitable for publication.

I am also grateful to Frank Billingham, Rhoma Bowdler, Rev. Mark Bridgen, Inga Bulman, Jeff Carpenter, E.C. Cawte, Keith Chandler, Miss Rhoda Dawtry, George Dunn, Barrie Gavin, Rev. Colin Gibson, Bill Gwilliam, Mr and Mrs Hadley, Paul Hipkiss, Tom Langley, Charles Parker, Wesley Perrins, Steve Roud, Royston Slim, David Taylor, Mrs E.M. Turner, Max Vernon, Robert Wilks, Clifford Willetts, Lucy Woodall and Trevor Woodall, as well as to these institutions: Birmingham Reference Library, Black Country Living Museum, Cambridge University Library, Dudley Archives, Mitchell Library (Glasgow), National Library of Scotland, Sandwell Archives Service, Vaughan Williams Memorial Library (London), Walsall Local History Centre, Walsall Museum, William Salt Library (Stafford), Wolverhampton Archives and Worcestershire County Library (especially the Malvern Branch), Worcestershire History Centre and Worcestershire Record Office.

For communicating a recording from the Helen Hartness Flanders Ballad Collection of 'The Creation of the World' (item. No 700, D 30 A 14), and allowing me to publish a transcription of the tune (on page 268), I am indebted to Andrew Wentink, Librarian of Special Collections, Middleybury College, Middlebury, Vermont, VT 0573, USA.

For illustrations on the pages indicated I thank Ian M. Bott (from his book, *Wednesbury Revisited*), 4 (lower), 49 (upper), 194 (upper); Bob Clarke and Michael Reuter (from their book, *Stourbridge, Wollaston & Amblecote*), 206 (upper), 250; Dudley Archives and Local History Service, 82, 270; Janet Kerr, 137; Tom Langley, 71; Pat Palmer, 4 (upper), 31, 47 (upper), 73, 125 (both), 136; Ken Rock Collection, 255 (lower), 256, 257 (lower); William Salt Library, Stafford, reproduced by courtesy of the trustees, 7, 124, 253, 254; David Taylor (from his booklet, *Images in Wood*), 46 (both); Mrs Jane Tipton, 49 (lower); Estate of Edward Wadsworth/DACS © 2007, 6 (upper); by courtesy of Walsall Local History Centre, 11, 72, 88, 147, 204; by kind permission of the Vicar and Churchwardens of St Bartholomew's Church, Wednesbury © 2007, 170; Tom Whittingham, 53, Cliff Willetts, 141; Ned

Williams (from his book, *A Century of the Black Country*), 257 (upper); Wolverhampton Archives & Local Studies, 43 (both), 92, 249; Worcestershire Record Office, xiv, 145, 238.

Introduction

The Black Country has often been the butt of hostile comment. Even local people said: 'God made the Black Country but the devil put the iron and limestone together at Dudley'. Visitors were even worse, using phrases like 'Dante's Inferno' and 'Gehenna of hidden fires'. Little Nell — or rather Charles Dickens — found 'a cheerless region, where not a blade of grass was seen to grow'. Just a few years later the Scots stonemason and geologist, Hugh Miller, travelling from Wolverhampton to Dudley, saw to his right a verdant countryside, but to his left 'a barren wilderness of slag and shale, the debris of limekilns and smelting works and of coal and ironstone pits; and ... what seemed a continuous city of belching furnaces and smoke-vomiting chimneys, blent with numerous groups of little dingy buildings, the dwellings of iron-smelters and miners'.

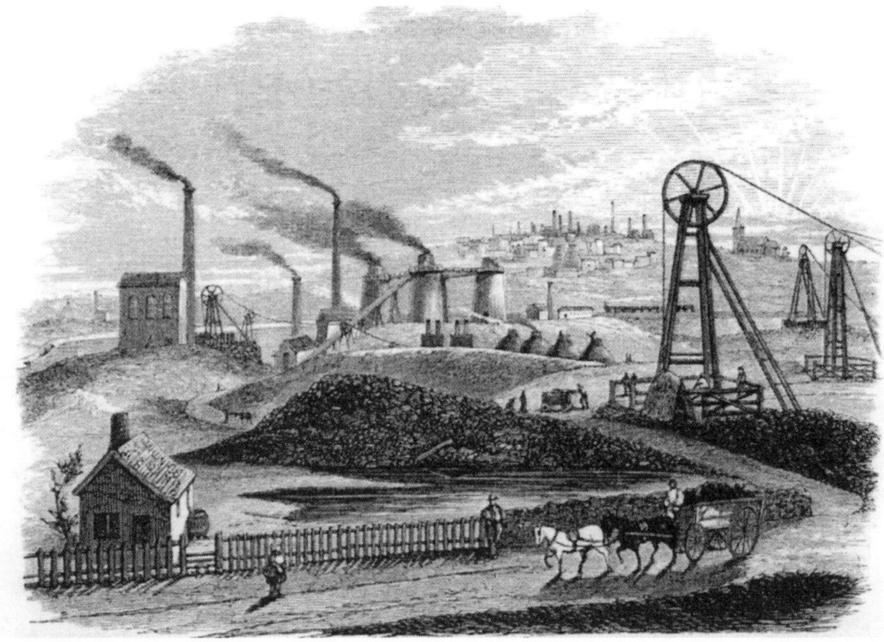

The 'Black Country', from Mrs Alfred Payne's book, Pits and Furnaces *(1869)*

Almost a century on, J.B. Priestley concluded: 'Industry has ravaged it; drunken storm troops have passed this way; there are signs of atrocities everywhere; the earth has been left gaping and bleeding; and what were once bright fields have been rummaged and raped into these dreadful patches of waste ground'. In 1951, more concisely, W.G. Hoskins wrote of a 'black, tormented Sahara'.

The inhabitants of the place fared little better. At the end of a working day, Disraeli observed, 'The plain is covered with a swarming multitude: bands of stalwart men, broad-chested and muscular, wet with toil, and black as the children of the tropics; troops of youth — alas! of both sexes — though neither their raiment nor their language indicates the differences; all are clad in male attire; and oaths that men might shudder at, issue from lips born to breathe words of sweetness. Yet these are to be — some are — the mothers of England!' At least he concedes: 'But can we wonder at the hideous coarseness of their language, when we remember the savage rudeness of their lives?'

Writing some forty years later, the journalist, J.A. Langford, claimed: 'The habits of a large part of the people, especially the inhabitants of the Gornals and Gospel End, are of a rude and barbarous kind'. For Priestley, too, the women of Gornal with their caps and shawls, going home from the brickworks, 'looked as outlandish as the place they lived in'.

Yet Gornal, like other villages and towns in the Black Country, was cherished by many. The antiquarian, John Noake, related in 1851 a memorable anecdote from 'the baleful region': 'Some years ago I was travelling through this district on the outside of a coach, and among the passengers was a poor girl who had been out at service, a long way off, for four or five years. On catching sight of some well-known object — no doubt the church tower — she suddenly clapped her hands together with the most ecstatic delight, and shouted out — "Oh, there's my dear Gornal!"' Such loyalty meant that Rowley Regis, itself by no means large, was perceived to consist of the five separate 'towns' of Cradley Heath, Old Hill, Blackheath, Rowley and Tividale, each with its own dedicated partisans. Even separate streets commanded allegiance. George Dunn, born in Sheffield Street, Quarry Bank, stayed there for most of a long life, and regretted that he could not finish his days there: 'It was a mean street but there was a lot of love in it, a lot of kindness'.

For all its power of creating an identity and attracting loyalty, the Black Country has never been an administrative unit. On the contrary, parts of it at various times have been in Shropshire and Warwickshire, as well as Staffordshire and Worcestershire. Currently it belongs mainly to the four metropolitan county boroughs of Wolverhampton, Walsall, Dudley and Sandwell. Its boundaries are therefore traditional or notional, and by no means universally agreed. The consensus would probably be the rough quadrilateral with Stourbridge and

Halesowen at the south-west corner, Wolverhampton at the north-west, Walsall at the north-east and Smethwick at the south-east. Simon Elmes offered a workaday but somewhat soulless definition in 2005: 'the heavily urbanised and industrialised area beyond the city of Birmingham to the west and north; formerly characterised by buildings blackened by smoke pollution'.

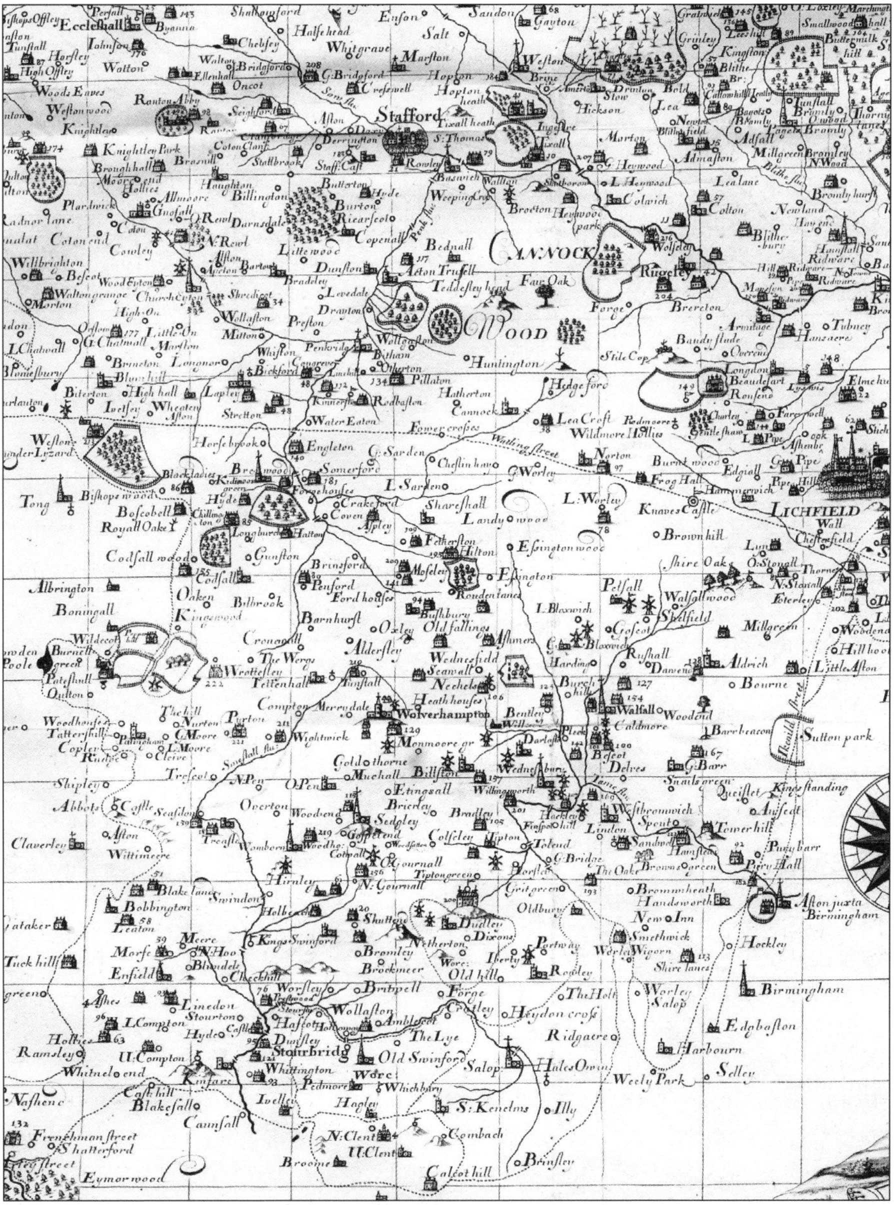

Map from Plot's *Staffordshire* (1686), showing, among other places, the area which was to become known as the Black Country

The last words echo the remark made in 1860 by Walter White that 'The name [of the Black Country] is eminently descriptive, for blackness everywhere prevails'. White's use of the term — his second chapter begins 'To the Black Country' — is alone enough to dispel the common belief that it was coined in 1868 by Elihu Burritt in his book, *Walks in the Black Country and its Green Borderland.* In fact the earliest use that I have seen is by the Coseley parson, William Ford Vance, who in 1853 wrote in his book, *Sermons: with A Voice from Mines and Factories*: 'With reason has the stigma of "The Black Country" been applied to this once fair portion of the soil of "Merrie England"; for black, in truth, it now is, alike in its appearance, and in the character of a large section of its inhabitants'. One has the feeling that Vance here, quoting in inverted commas, is using a recent coinage. It is entirely possible that previous references will come to light, but earlier writers would surely have used the phrase, had they known it. For William Hutton, the historian of Birmingham, writing at the end of the eighteenth century, 'Birmingham first took root in the black soil of Wednesbury, whose mines have emptied their riches into her lap'. Adolphe Blanqui, the French economist, visiting in 1823, made a similar observation: 'The riches and industry of Birmingham can be explained by the closeness of the plain of Wednesbury and Wolverhampton, which one could call, without metaphor, the plain of the Cyclops'. The Black Country formula, apparently had to wait for a couple more decades.

The folklore of the area has attracted writers since Robert Plot (1640-1696) in the late seventeenth century and Stebbing Shaw in the eighteenth. The subject, though, was only a small aspect of their books on the history of Staffordshire, and only in the next century was it systematically pursued, by G.T. Lawley and F.W. Hackwood. Lawley (1845-1935) worked for over fifty years as a traveller for W. Butler and Company of

A

HISTORY OF BILSTON,

IN THE COUNTY OF STAFFORD.

A RECORD OF

Its Archæology, Ecclesiology, Parochialia,

Folk Lore, and Bibliography.

WITH

COPIOUS EXTRACTS FROM THE PARISH REGISTERS.

BY

GEORGE T. LAWLEY

COPYRIGHT.

BILSTON:

PRINTED AND PUBLISHED BY JOHN PRICE, MARKET PLACE.

1893.

Springfield Brewery, Wolverhampton, until his retirement in 1920. He lived at Priestfield House, Ettingshall. He wrote extensively on the customs and superstitions of the Black Country, mainly in the form of newspaper and magazine articles, though he did publish in 1893 a volume entitled *A History of Bilston, in the County of Stafford. A Record of its Archaeology, Ecclesiology, Parochialia, Folk Lore, and Bibliography, with copious extracts from the Parish Registers.* He was also in touch with other folklorists such as Charlotte Burne and Robert Hope (see Bibliography), and he was a literary mentor to F.W. Hackwood, six years his junior.

By contrast with Lawley, to whose work he refers on a number of occasions, Hackwood (1851-1926), was born in Wednesbury, and taught there after training as a teacher at St Peter's College, Saltley. From 1878 until his retirement in 1916 he worked as headmaster in various primary schools in the Winson Green area of Birmingham, and from 1898 he lived in Handsworth. He nevertheless remained strongly attached to Wednesbury, where he served as a town councillor of 'independent Radical' persuasion. He supported the allotment movement and helped to create Wednesbury's Brunswick Park. He keenly supported the town's free library, institute, dramatic club, soccer team, and horticultural society. Starting in 1883 he published a stream of books: biographies, textbooks and teachers' handbooks, works on sport, food and drink, natural history and religion. Twenty-five volumes, often with limited print runs, covered the social history of Staffordshire and the Black Country. Some dealt almost exclusively with folklore, including *Staffordshire Stories, Historical and Legendary: a Miscellany of County Lore and Anecdote*; and *Staffordshire Customs, Superstition and Folklore*, the latter published only a few months before Hackwood's death. He also wrote on the Worcestershire sector: for example, *Oldbury and Round About in the Worcestershire Corner of the Black Country.*

F.W. Hackwood, after a drawing of 1915 by Robert Kemp

With surprising symmetry, two twentieth century writers, the brothers Jon and Michael Raven, from Wolverhampton, have also written extensively on the Black Country and its folklore. Their books are listed in my bibliography, and I am greatly indebted to them. Michael has been particularly generous with gifts of his works.

H.E. Palfrey (1874-1962)

Why am I seeking to add to the canon? The answer is partly because I have had the benefit of consulting some of the many books and papers in the Palfrey Collection in the Worcestershire Record Office. H.E. ('Harry') Palfrey (1874-1962), was born in Stourbridge and attended King Edward's School there. He ran a business in the Black Country and was a county councillor from 1913 until 1950, latterly as an alderman. Over forty years and more he amassed a large collection of Worcestershire and Black Country books and pamphlets, deeds and documents, maps and prints: 'my business journeys took me from Bournemouth to Aberdeen and I used to spend many happy hours in the second hand book shops'. In addition he assiduously read the local press and took cuttings on items of interest, which he pasted into scrapbooks. 'Dudleiana' runs to 29 volumes, covering the period from 1890 to 1955; 'Stourbridgeiana', 76 volumes, 1904 to 1956.

I have also had the inestimable advantage of in some cases lengthy conversations with people from the Black Country or closely connected with it. Of these, Lucy Woodall (1894-1979) of Old Hill, worked for over fifty years as a chainmaker, and had an interesting repertoire of songs, many of them learned at work. Tom Langley (1907-1980) was born at Chasetown and went to the King Edward VI School at Lichfield. At the age of seventeen he enlisted in the Grenadier Guards, but his main career was a twenty-year spell in the police, serving both in the Black Country and Birmingham. His Black Country roots ran very deep, and he was intensely interested in the tales and traditions of the area, culled both from his own experience and from the lore of his extensive family. One of his preoccupations was boxing. His father was a bareknuckle amateur and his grandfather a promoter of prize fights. His great-grandfather was a cousin of the Tipton Slasher, one of several fighters about whom Langley wrote books. He was a gentle, generous man, with an acute sense of humour.

George Dunn (1887-1975) spent nearly the whole of his long life in Quarry Bank. His grandfather, Benjamin Dunn, was an iron bundler; his father, Samson, a puddler, then an annealer. Like them, George worked in the iron trade, though as a chainmaker. He started work in 1900 and retired fifty-nine years later at the age of 72, having been employed mainly at the chain shop of Noah Bloomer and Sons in Oak Street, Quarry Bank. He had an invaluable fund of recollection and information. He came to the attention of the wider world only in his last years, both as a raconteur and a singer (see chapter 12). Fortunately, his rich accent and superb singing voice have been preserved for posterity on recordings.

The folklore of the Black Country as I have described it is part of social history, and by the same token of the past. The area is now post-industrial and multicultural, and it will be interesting to see whether new patterns of folklore emerge. Certainly, enormous interest in the past remains, as the success and continued expansion of the Black Country Living Museum demonstrates. The artefacts and buildings, the techniques and processes, have undoubted fascination, but the human spirit shines fully through only in the songs and stories, the customs and beliefs, the speech and humour, of Black Country men and women.

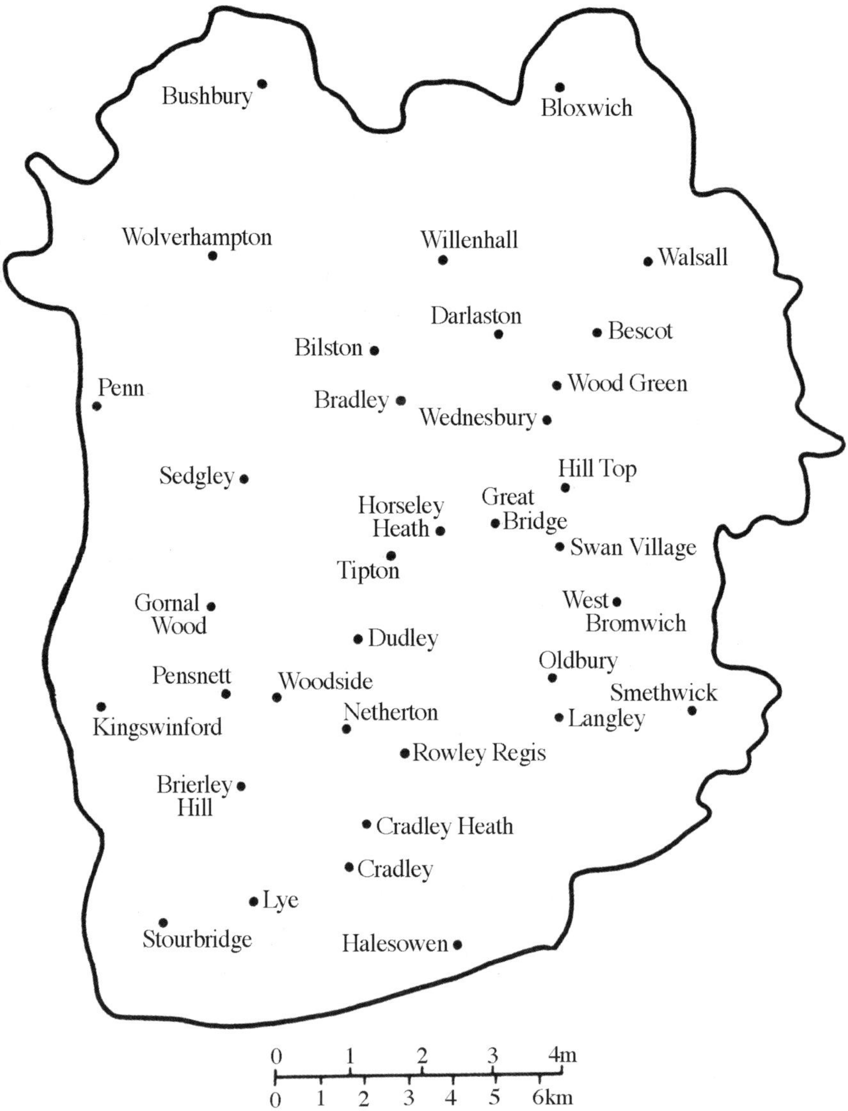

Outline map indicating the boundaries of the Black Country

CHAPTER 1

Strangers, Neighbours and Nicknames

'It was the custom to throw stones at strangers less than forty years ago', wrote Charles Hatton in 1945 of 'one of the toughest parishes in the Black Country'. A *Punch* cartoon of the late nineteenth century showed one Blackcountryman saying to another: 'Ay, Bill, 'ere's a stranger! Let's 'eave 'alf a brick at 'im!' G.T. Lawley described how at the same period boys and young men from Wolverhampton and other Black Country towns, including Bilston, organised 'mimic warfare' against their peers in neighbouring streets:

> The combatants met by mutual consent at some given spot, and after various passages of verbal warfare, champions were selected to fight for the honour of their respective streets. Sometimes as many as three or four pitched battles thus occurred in one night, and if the victory was indecisive it frequently happened that the whole of the opponents took the matter up and began fighting with sticks, stones and whatever weapons were handy. Then the weaker party had to seek safety in flight, pursued by the victors. The defeated party beat up their friends on the following night, and the same kind of hostilities again took place, ending by the flight of the weaker. These street fights used to last for several weeks, and often ended in serious injuries.

Rivals fortunately confined themselves to 'verbal warfare' on many occasions.

Dudley, Wednesbury and Wolverhampton all laid claim to being the unofficial capital of the Black Country. Wednesbury boasts that its name derives from that of Woden, though no convenient myth offers an explanation of how this came about. A verse of unknown provenance explains Wolverhampton's noble origins:

> A thriving town, for arts Vulcanian famed
> And from its foundress, good Wulfruna, named.

St Peter's Church, Wolverhampton (postcard dated 1913)

Wulfrun (or Wulfruna), benefactress of the local church, did not found Wolverhampton, but her name was joined with that of the manor of Heantune after she acquired it in 650. Well over a thousand years later, the original designation, in the form of Hampton, is still in use. Dudda, who gave his name to Dudley, is said to have built the first castle there. He was reputedly an ancestor of Lady Godiva. Perhaps he can be equated with the giant who lived on Castle Hill and had as his vassal another colossus based in Birmingham. When the latter became lazy and recalcitrant, the Dudley giant hurled a great stone

Dudley Castle (undated postcard)

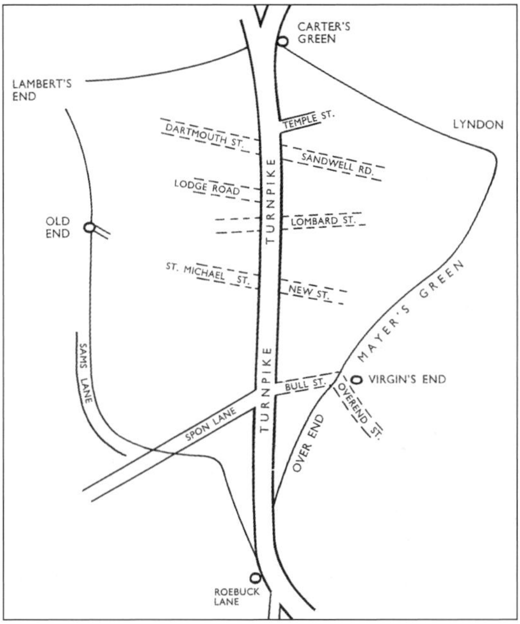

Map showing the original extent of common at West Bromwich

which killed him and wrecked his castle. Warstone Lane in Birmingham's jewellery quarter is supposed to mark where the missile fell.

Until the early twentieth century the people of Dudley had the generic nickname of 'muslins', after the rough jute cloth used to make bags in which nails were transported all over the world. The term faded from use when barrels were brought in to carry the nails. The 'throstles' of West Bromwich derived from the thrushes prolific on an expanse of waste land near the town prior to enclosure in 1802. Perceived foibles, characteristics or predilections were signalled in expressions such as:

Bilston 'balloons', from the non-existent flights promised by a publican in a scam to increase his trade.

Cradley 'bag-puddings', because of the alleged practice locally of boiling puddings in new (calico) stockings. (More recently, 'a pudding-bag street' was the term used in the Black Country for a cul-de-sac. Until the 1970s there was a Bag Pudding Street in West Bromwich).

Darlaston 'geese', from the local passion for eating roasted goose, the bird conversely being known as a 'Darlaston mon'.

Halesowen 'yelts', an unfathomable term which could derive from the ancient pronunciation of Hales.

Tipton 'slashers', after the nickname of a celebrated prizefighter (see chapter 9).

Walsall 'bowlegs', presumably connected with the local manufacture of saddles, which also accounts for the nickname of the soccer club's players as 'The Saddlers'. (From 1390 until 1488 the manor of Walsall belonged to the earls of Warwick, whose badge, the bear and ragged staff, remained in the town's emblem). An alternative suggestion is that so many steps were required to go up to the church, reputed to be the highest in Staffordshire, that the townspeople became bowlegged.

Wednesbury 'cockings', referring to the townspeople's passion for cock fighting (see chapter 10).

Wednesbury itself was dubbed 'tube town', thanks to the development there in the nineteenth century of new technology for forging iron pipes. West Bromwich once claimed to be 'the city of a hundred trades'; Darlaston, 'the city of nuts and bolts'. Less happily, Willenhall was 'umpshire' because of the crooked backs which resulted from the long years lock filers were bent over their work. 'There is a tale', wrote Harold Parsons, 'that public houses had holes cut into the wall behind the benches to receive the humps of the men when they came in for their pint'. Oldbury's title of 'the town of the four moons' came from four of the many furnaces which lit up the place at night. The Tipton moon on the other hand was the real thing, and generations of drunks were alleged to have tried to fish it out of one of the canals.

St Matthew's Church, Walsall: the steps are alleged to have caused the townspeople to become bandy-legged

Workers at James Russell's Tube Works, Bilston Road, Wednesbury c.*1910*

(Tipton, which boasted of being the Venice of the Midlands is still popularly known as Tip'on-on-Cut).

On the subject of the moon, George Dunn told me this story of the Gornal people:

> They were supposed to be so stupid that they thought the old jack-donkey had swallowed the moon. Zakel was out one evening with his donkey and he saw the moon reflected in a great big thing o' water they'd got in the back yard; and he says, 'Missus, look at this meoon. What's it doin' 'ere?' She says, 'Ooh, I d'know. It must be the Dudley meoon'. He says, 'It ain't', he says, 'it's in our big jorum o' water'. Well, at that moment the old jack-donkey was comin' by and he fancied a drink. So he drank from the water and at the same moment as he was drinkin' there came a cloud over the moon; and when old Zakel looked again the moon had gone. He says, 'Eh, come out, Sarah, and see this. Our old donkey's bin an' drunk the meoon'.

In addition, the Gornal villagers — like selected others, up and down the country — were said to have demonstrated their stupidity by taking the trouble to put a pig on the wall so that it could watch the band go by. The occasion is recalled in the name of an Upper Gornal public house, the Pig on the Wall. Perhaps the band in question is the one of which the tale is told that their drummer was so small that he couldn't see which way his colleagues went, and arrived at Ruiton by himself, still beating the big drum.

Not much to the credit of Darlaston was the story of a local man who, thinking himself under attack from a playful calf as he walked through a field, began to belabour the animal with his brawny fists. The calf bellowed with the pain, and attracted the attention of a nearby bull. 'Ah', said the man, goo on an fetch thee fayther, an I'll serve him the saame'. Much to his surprise, before he was ready to defend himself, the bull tossed him over the hedge into the next field. As he picked himself up he called out: 'Yah, yer coward. Why day yer call out time afore yo begun?'

Some of the qualities, real or alleged, of different places were expressed in rhymes which ranged from straightforward topography to considered insult. One of these runs:

> Walsall Town for bandy legs,
> Bilston Town for bulls,
> Hampton Town for fancy girls,
> And Sedgley Town for trulls [trollops].

A variant has:

View of Bilston, by Edward Wadsworth (1889-1949), from The Black Country: a Book of 20 Drawings, with an Introduction by Arnold Bennett

Sedgley Beacon (postcard, c.1904). The monument was erected in 1864

Walsall for bandy legs,
Baggeridge for nuts,
Bilston for dust and dirt,
And Sedgley for sluts.

The last place features again in:

The devil ran through
Sedgley, booted and spurred,
With a scythe at his back as
long as a swerd [sword].

The remarkable pronunciation indicated by the spelling of the last word reaches back to the time of Chaucer. The devil, so it is said, ran through Sedgley because even he wanted to minimise the time he spent within hearing of the extreme bad language of the nailers there. He is often evoked in the Black Country, thanks to the infernal qualities of the industrial landscape:

And the devil stood on Bradley Moor
And heard the forges roar;
Quoth he, 'I've heard a row in hell,
But none like this before'.

Bradley is pronounced 'Braidlee', in which form it appeared in the Domesday Book.

And again:

At Brierley Hill the devil made his will,
Then he staggered to Dudley Woodside,
Where he laid him down
And very soon doyed [died].

The devil, we suppose, expired in chagrin at discovering that the fires in the Black Country equalled those of hell. Another verse puts it:

When Satan stood on Brierley Hill,
and far around he gazed,
He said, 'I never shall again at hell's
flame be amazed'.

Detail from Bradley Ironworks, by Robert Noyes, 1817 (see also page 124). Is the woman in the foreground one of the workers, or has she just happened along?

According to another local saying, he made Gornal out of bits and pieces left over after the creation.

On the other hand, Cradley had the reputation of fighting the devil, probably because of its reputation for piety, with seven Free Churches flourishing at one stage. In a poem entitled 'Cradley Bag-puddings' Francis Perks of Stourbridge wrote:

They're the happiest people that on the earth dwell,
Altho' they reside near the precincts of hell;
For in purity they all that's good resemble,
The sight of Bag-Pudding makes old Nick tremble.

Even the allegedly satanic Brierley Hill had its supporters (see panel), though the expression, 'Go to Brierley Hill', may have been intended to banish an irritating interlocutor to a highly undesirable destination. It contrasts with another formula, usually addressed to children: 'Oh, you are too clever for this world. You ought to go to Walsall'. However, the exclamation, 'Well, I'll goo to Smerrick [Smethwick]', was simply intended to express amazement or indignation.

Of all the places in the Black Country, these, at least according to a traditional rhyme, were the least favoured:

> The Lye and the Waste and Careless Green
> Were the three worst places that ever were seen.

Until the early nineteenth century at least, 'the Lye' and its environs had a particularly bad reputation. 'There was not a single place of worship … most

A Ballad of Brierley Hill

There's many a mon'll tell yer, if yo listen to 'is tale,
There ain't a blessed thing round 'ere what's wuth a minute's look.
He sez there's no green fields about, no pleasant hill an' dale,
But it ain't what he cun see 'imself; he sid that in a book.

The tachers tellen 'im that tack when 'e's a little kid,
The fields we'n got am black as ink an' we'm as white as chalk.
Of course, we knowen better, but the truth from 'im's bin hid,
Ah could show 'im very diffrunt if ah tuk 'im for a walk.

There's as good trees in the Sautwells as yo getten in Hyde Park,
An' yo cor find better bluebells if yo look for hours and hours,
You can sit an' listen quietly to the throstle an' the lark,
But there's other things that tak the eye besiden trees an' flowers.

Look at all them stacks an' chimdeys, straighter than a tree an' 'igher,
Mekkin' clouds as good as any sailin' up there in the skies,
An' if he cor see no beauty in a cinder bonk afire
Then he wuz either born wrang or 'e's got no bloomin' eyes.

See the furness flames a-leapin' down the Level of a night,
While the cold canel is glowin' like the gold of man's desire,
An' tho' the lamps am douted an' the street's without a light,
There's enough light cums from up Round Oak to set the stars afire.

An' if 'e wants some music let 'im listen to the sound
Of the dinner bulls an' whistles; an' they'll gie 'im such a feast!
What with Noah 'Ingley's 'ommer an' the rolls all gooin' round,
An' the Earl's steel saw a-singin' when the wind is in the East.

There's many a mon in London town'll whisper in yer ear
That if he ever cum this road he'd quickly tak 'is 'ook,
For the place's got nuthin' in it; but the facts am pretty clear,
He never sid it for 'imself, 'e sid it in a book.

D.R.G., 1916

of the houses were of mud … There were no streets in the place; there were the Dark Lane, Fanny's Lane, Connop's Lane, the Dock and Crab Lane … Bull and badger baiting, and dog and cock fighting were favourite amusements of the people, and … men and even women fights were not uncommon'. So wrote a shocked R.G. Jones, and added: 'Very few of the inhabitants had not a fictitious name, and some of them most curious. Bogy, Dogham, Pig-hook, Wollam, Tar, Ding, Tacker, Twagg, and such-like names were once very common'. In 1854 John Noake, referring to the family nicknames of the area, mentioned 'the hereditary Tuckeys, Squirrels, Pongies, Stour-uns, Crabs, Old Crokers', and quoted 'an old ballad' on the subject. This was another of the poems of Francis Perks (see panel below), on the place of which William Hutton, the historian of Birmingham, wrote in 1782: 'The houses stand in every direction, composed of one large and ill-formed brick scoped into a tenement, burnt by the sun, and often destroyed by the frost. … We might as well look for the moon in a coalpit as for stays or white linen in the City of Mud'.

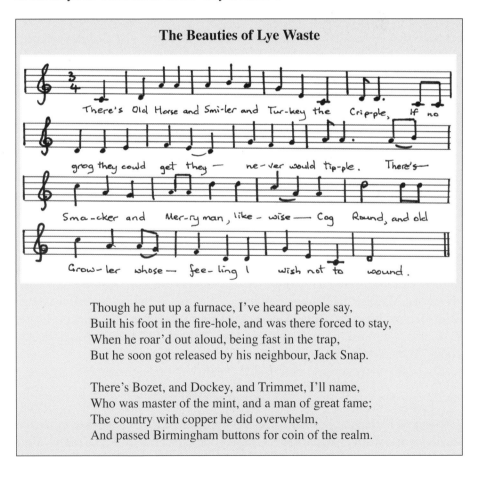

The Beauties of Lye Waste

There's Old Horse and Smi-ler and Tur-key the Crip-ple, If no
grog they could get they — ne-ver would tip-ple. There's—
Sma-cker and Mer-ry man, like - wise — Cog Round, and old
Grow-ler whose — fee-ling I wish not to wound.

Though he put up a furnace, I've heard people say,
Built his foot in the fire-hole, and was there forced to stay,
When he roar'd out aloud, being fast in the trap,
But he soon got released by his neighbour, Jack Snap.

There's Bozet, and Dockey, and Trimmet, I'll name,
Who was master of the mint, and a man of great fame;
The country with copper he did overwhelm,
And passed Birmingham buttons for coin of the realm.

There's Duggon and Guzzle, there's Bummers and Smarts,
They are dealers in cocktail and cranberry tarts;
This race of true Britons they're honest good fellows,
There ne'er was but one known to come to the gallows.

For which great lamentation the natives did make,
And vow'd the poor fellow was hung in mistake,
They said he was crucified, and shed many tears,
And from the day he was hang'd they now date their years.

They are industrious and fierce, in hard work they delight,
From four in the morning till eleven at night,
There's no men toil like them on this side the waves,
And their song is — true Britons shall never be slaves.

It is a pity that we shall never know the stories behind such nicknames. John Darby, Duke (1543), and William Seaveger, alias Wicked Will (1624), are recorded in the church register at Rowley Regis. The Sedgley records include:

Edward Wilkes, of Ettingshall, commonly called Eyenecked Wilkes (1674)
William Whitehouse, of Coseley, commonly called 'Great Will Whitehouse' (1675)
John Bradley, of Gospell End, commonly called 'Squire John' (1676)
Edward Fellow, of Sedgley, commonly called 'the Giant' (1678)
Thomas Tomlinson, commonly called 'Dobbin' (1679)

Other nicknames recorded in the same parish are Chapman John, Subtill, Kag, Sandy, Old Yeoman, Darke, Madge more leg, Honest William Gibbins, Old Feather, Old Doctor Glover, Old Suttle, Ye Old Earle, Little Oliver and Thin Ears.

The surname of Rudge was very common in Halesowen, and among the nicknames used to distinguish different possessors were Fake, Shett, Squeak, Trick, Trotter, Trumper, Turk and Turpin. The Hacketts of the town featured as Birdie, Harmates, Mardles and Mopnail. Other nicknames recorded from Halesowen were Blethus, Corjers, Dons, Dutch, Dyneys, Flays[Fleas], Hondrays, Jackie Flax, Kincking Ters, Liza Lightning, Liza Topcake, Moscows, Shamropcks, Todds, Tumantatum and Tupmuck.

There are many stories in the Black Country of people who are completely unable to recognise the official names of workmates and even family members. G.T. Lawley relates how the artist, Arthur Crowquill, when he was in Bilston on business during the 1840s with a steel toy manufacturer, happened to meet a small boy in the street and asked: 'What's your name, my lad?' The reply, 'Wait a bit, mister, while I goo an' ax me mother', caused Crowquill to fear that 'the paternity was doubtful, whereas it was merely a proof of the universal use of nicknames in the district, when not only children but wives frequently knew their fathers and husbands by their nicknames only'.

From the same period comes this account 'from a respectable attorney':

> During his clerkship he was sent to serve some legal process on a man whose name and address were given to him with legal accuracy. He traversed the village to which he had been directed from end to end without success; and after spending many hours in the search, was about to abandon it in despair, when a young woman, who had witnessed his labours, kindly undertook to make enquiries for him, and began to hail her friends for that purpose.
>
> 'Oi say, Bullyed, does thee know a man named Adam Green?' The Bull-head was shaken in sign of ignorance.
>
> 'Loy-a-bed, dost thee?' Lie-a-bed's opportunities of making acquaintance had been rather limited, and she could not resolve the difficulty.
>
> Stumpy (a man with a wooden leg), Cow-skin, Spindleshanks, Cock-eye, Pigtail, and Yellow-belly, were similarly invoked, but in vain, and the querist fell into a brown study, in which she remained for some time. At length, however, her eyes suddenly brightened, and slapping one of her companions on the shoulder, she exclaimed, triumphantly, 'Dash moy wig! Whoy he means moy feyther!' and then turning to the gentleman, she added, 'Yo should'n axed for Ode Blackbird!'

King Street, Darlaston, in 1903: a rather gloomy prospect

In Darlaston, thanks to the preponderance of a small number of surnames — Foster, Partridge, Wilkes and Williams — the alternative identification provided by nicknames was particularly widespread. A Liverpool businessman enquiring of a pub landlord there for a Mr Foster received this response:

> Now I wonder which on 'em it's as yo'm wantin'. Is it Gentleman Foster, or Jonah's Foster, or Billy Gunner Foster, or Ode Shade Tupty Foster, or Joel Tinny Foster, or Ode Wag Foster, or Tum Jorden Foster, or Ode Mouldy-yed Foster, or Ode Boggen Foster?

When none of these proved helpful the landlord thought again and added: 'Then it mun be Ode Jack Fox Foster yo' wantin' — he's a screwmaker'. This turned out to be the right man. Another Darlaston tale, much quoted but possibly apocryphal, concerns a man called Brewer who left the town for Walsall and sent a letter addressed:

> To Mr Wilkes, Darlaston, near Wednesbury,
> Not My Lord Wilkes,
> Nor Gentleman John Wilkes,
> Nor Soft Water Jack Wilkes,
> Nor They Wilkes,
> Nor Brick-end Wilkes,
> Nor Whackery Wilkes,
> Nor Dowker Wilkes,
> Nor Dragon Wilkes,
> Nor Hockey Wilkes,
> Nor Bullet Wilkes,
> Nor Darkey Wilkes,
> Nor Fagler Wilkes,
> Nor Tizzie Wilkes,
> Nor Dunty Wilkes,
> Nor Gallimore Wilkes,
> But Bacca Box Wilkes — that's the man.

It is claimed that the letter was duly delivered.

'Tom Brown' (Thomas Pinnock) attempted to explain some of these, and other, nicknames:

> Probably … 'Dunty' was short and squat. Perhaps 'Dragon' kept an inn with that sign, and 'My Lord' had an exalted idea of his own dignity. 'They' and 'Tizzie' would be substitutes for the scripture names Theophilus and Izreal. It may be a malicious slander, but Soft Water Jack is reputed to have earned the name by an avaricious scheme. He had affixed a range of spouting to the row of cottages adjoining his own, but

> took care to connect the down spout with a cistern on his own premises, and so in times of drought he drew a considerable tax from his tenants by selling back to them the stored accumulation of water from their own roofs. …
>
> Shake Tupty Foster's first name had nothing to do with that of our national playwright, but was merely a corrupted abbreviation of Shadrach. Another man got the nickname Clipper because he was suspected, rightly or wrongly, of clipping scraps of lead from roofs, spouts, or cisterns where property was left untenanted. Such names as Cab, Mouse, Rabbit, Foxy, Ode Nibbler, Rot, Duckface, and Jimmy Piggy would be given because of some fancied resemblance of feature or disposition to the various animals. A great many were bestowed because of what was odd or striking in personal appearance or manner. That is how we get such nicknames as Black Jack, Curly, Ginger, Long Jack o' the Bonk, Cock-eye, Four-eyes, Pegler, Dot an' Carry One, Trotter, Creeper, Wingy (a one-armed man), and Leggy (a very tall fellow). Soaker explains itself, Brassy would describe a man of illimitable cheek. Happy Jack, Warbler, and Whistling Ned are complimentary additions which carry their own explanation. Will Wag, Cheeky, Nancy Stepfine, Betty Patchwork, Sal Rag, Quiet William, Phoebe Stumper, and Fogy, bear evidence of satirical humour. A shrewd guess may be made at the miserly economy and close-fisted avarice in dealing which would earn such nicknames as Split-tater, Split-pay, Billy Pincher, Sal Screw, and Skin the Boone.

Phil Drabble claimed that seeking the origin of many nicknames was like chasing shadows, but he did find out how 'an old chap called Conquer Pudden, who used to be about the last jew's harp maker at Dunns Bank' acquired his: 'He and his brother always quarrelled about not getting fair shares of meat, and one of them said, "I'll conquer the mate, you conquer the pudden". And the name stuck to him for the rest of his life'. Drabble quotes a string of inexplicable nicknames such as Teddy Neddy from Bloxwich (real name, Somerfield), and at Lye Jim Dooker (Priest), a whole family called Mop Nails (Meredith), together with the Punches (Pearson), Pongoes (Taylor) and Bucks (Round). A Scotsman who moved to Old Hill in search of work found the vernacular so difficult that he took to responding when questioned with 'I dinna ken'. Local children converted this to Dinnercan, and then Dinnegan, which became the man's nickname. Sally Shortneck at Tipton was so called from the swiftness with which she swallowed pints of beer: 'There's no clack in 'er wazzin', people said ('There's no valve in her weasand — throat'). 'Get that down thi wazzin' is a common exhortation from a man to his mate, when handing him a pint of beer.

According to 'C.E.B.', writing in 1929 of Cradley Heath '60 years ago', one of the sights of the area was Benny Fiddler, landlord of the Bell Inn near Five

Ways. The nickname is unexplained, but the man was so fat that when he went to bed 'they wound him with a winch up through a trap door in the ceiling, chair and all'. At that time in Cradley Heath:

> If you inquired for, let us say, Thomas Jellicoe, who lived perhaps in Tibbett's Gardens, you would probably button-hole half-a-dozen people, who, though they knew everybody, had never heard of Thomas Jellicoe, and you would be fortunate if finally you found someone who knew that the man you wanted was 'Tommy Nobbler' who lived 'down the back', and the people who did not know Thomas Jellicoe would be equally surprised to learn that 'down the back' was correctly described as Tibbett's Gardens.

Dr Francis Maylett Smith, who worked from 1915 until 1933 as a general practitioner in a Black Country town which he disguises as Collier's Forge in his autobiography, had a similar problem with nicknames:

> A peculiarity of Collier's Forge was that about a dozen surnames did duty for some two-thirds of the population. Dunns, Cartwrights, Homers, Rayboulds, Priests, Shaws and Westwoods were among the most prolific family groups. As parents were generally unenterprising in choosing Christian names for their children, there were likely to be several Williams, Thomases or Georges in every group. This would have led to widespread ambiguity, and it was not uncommon to refer to some distinguishing mark, such as the person's trade, his residence, some well-known habit of his, or some physical defect. Thus, there might be 'William Cartwright at the crock shop', 'William Cartwright, bottom of High Street', 'William Cartwright with the squint' or 'William Cartwright who takes the Bible class'. Sometimes, for brevity, Christian names were dispensed with, and 'Crockshop Cartwright' or 'Bible Cartwright' would then be considered sufficient.
>
> In spite of these marks of identification, however, doubt might not be wholly dispelled. One day a woman came to the surgery and asked me to call at Cartwright's.
>
> 'Which Cartwright?' I asked.
>
> 'The one at the top'.
>
> 'What do you mean by that?'
>
> 'The one by the public'.
>
> 'Which public?'
>
> 'The one at the corner'.
>
> 'I'm sorry, I don't get you. Can't you give me his address?'
>
> 'It's next door to where you were attending that little boy'.
>
> 'I've been attending hundreds of little boys. Which street does he live in?'
>
> 'High Street'.

'What's the number of his house?'

'I don't know the number, but it's the man you talked to about the weather, when you were there last Thursday'.

'I talk to a lot of people about the weather'.

'Well, it's the man they sometimes call Stumpy Cartwright, but I don't suppose you know that yet'.

No doubt it would have been useful if Dr Smith could have consulted a directory like the telephone book issued in 2006 in the small village of Cedillo, in western Spain, which listed people under their nicknames such as 'Patata' (potato) and 'Chinita' (Chinese). The book was the idea of the mayor, Antonio 'Botines' (Booties) González, who explained that his mother bought him some boots when he was a little boy, and the heels clicked on the pavement, so his brother called him *botines*, which was later shortened to *boti*.

Even streets and tracts of land attracted the inventiveness and wry humour of coiners of nicknames such as Brandy Row, Bugs' Gutter, Cabbage Stalk, Candy Field, Chitties Bit, Dan's End, Duck Hole, Down the Spout, Graveyard, Hell Hole, Hell House, Hell Lane, Idle Alley, Lawyer's Walk, Little London, The Mop, Mouse Sweet Lane, Paint Cup Row, Paradise, Pig Street, Pigsty Park, Quality Square, Ragman's Row, Rodney Market, Round's Folk, Shaw's Leisure, Six Foot Road, Snakey Lane, Spittle's Fold, Spout Lane, Stewkins, Tackeroo and Tinker's Bush. Bilston alone boasted Firing Irons, five Never Sweat Meadows, Mince Pie Piece, The Nimmins and Rawbone's Crofts. The poet writing over the initials, D.R.G., reflected at length on the quirks of local nomenclature in 'A Little Song on Place Names':

These little names with magic spell,
Our curious minds in bondage hold,
But who is there the tale can tell,
Their wonders to our ears unfold?
Did e'er the primrose star with gold
The ashy slopes of Primrose Hill?
Is the next Hill so very Old?
Is there a Heath at Cradley still?

Did badgers sport across Brock moor?
Or harts seek shade in Woodside cool?
Did the rash urchin trace the spoor
Of bucks and does to far Buckpool?
Did ever fairies make a stool
Of mushrooms growing on the Green?
Or old King Sweyn with sceptre rule
The ford that can no more be seen?

Was e'er stone quarried in that Bank
That leads the Mount Pleasant adown?
Did ever man of princely rank
Meet death near Tipton? Did some clown
Make merry as he strolled from town
Along the slopes of Merry Hill?
Was it some mighty man called Brown
Threw up the Hills that stand there still?

Did the red-berried holly grow
Around some squire's hall of yore?
Did winds in winter then lay low
The Round Oak standing at his door?
Did that same wind with angry roar
And final blast bring to an End,
Strewing its sails about the floor,
The Windmill, farmer Giles' best friend?

Did e'er against the skies' bright blue
On Gossy Bank, the gorse flower flame?
Can no one tell where Tackeroo
And old Bughole each got its name?
Did that vain man e'er rise to fame
Who called his pet creation Lye?
Though, after all, was he to blame
If the place failed to please his eye?

CHAPTER 2

Speech and Humour

'Ter start everythin' off, God med the wairld. Mind yo', 'e couldn't see ennythtin' 'cuz it wuz all dark, soo 'ed sed, "let's a sum light", an' the light cum, an' 'e wor 'arf plaised wi' it...'.

Black Country dialect does not go back to *Genesis*, though it does share some features with the English of Shakespeare, and even that of Chaucer. The translation quoted is by Kate Fletcher, who as a child, both at home and at school, was taught that her local dialect should be avoided. She nevertheless spoke it with friends. Then, as a nurse in Wolverhampton's Royal Hospital during the Second World War, she found patients who were unable to communicate with her colleagues, most of whom came from outside the area. When she responded to an elderly man's request, 'Cost thee gi' me a clane onkercher?', he delightedly remarked: 'Thee bist th'onny one wi enny sense rahnd 'ere, bay yer?' She then found herself interpreting for a foreign doctor baffled by statements such as: 'Ah cor gutter slape cuz me too [toe] ay arf gi'n me sum ommer'. In later life, Kate Fletcher published not only vernacular versions of parts of the Old Testament but also her own poems in Black Country dialect.

Perhaps one should speak, not of dialect, but of dialects, in the Black Country. Certainly, there were and are different accents. Phil Drabble contrasted the 'sing-song lilt of Cradley Heath' with the 'gruffer broadness of Gornal' and the 'less pleasant twang of "Worsall"'. Pronunciation in Blackheath, Old Hill and Cradley Heath was such that 'strangers only understood the conversation of natives with difficulty'. Again, 'You can go through "Hamp'on", through "Bilsun", across "Dersy Bonk", around "Blue Button", up the "Dark Lerne", through the "Coppy", up the "Duck Hole", and across the "Bonky Bonk", down "Blewmfield", to "Tippon", and onward through "Dudley Ood Side" to "Quarry Bonk", finding in every district a peculiar "twang" of its own'. The last two comments date from 1920s, yet at the beginning of the twenty-first century a young man from Wolverhampton in all seriousness told a researcher:

> If you go to Broierley 'ill you can't understand a bloody word, can't understand what they're saying 'alf the toim, because they're even broader than what we are. Many a time I bin over there, asked for directions an' gone, "OK, mate, cheers", an' gone on to the next person an' ask 'im.

As with many dialects, while pronunciation remains marked, distinctive grammar and vocabulary have become attenuated. A verse from West Bromwich ('Brammidge') juxtaposes the affirmative and negative forms of a series of verbs:

> I bin and I bay, I was and I wort,
> I have and I hate, I con and I cort,
> I will and I wo, I dew and I doe,
> I sholl and I short, I must and I mo.

One could draw up a complete table of verb conjugations in different tenses (see panel for some examples). Indicating pronunciation is more difficult, and different writers on the subject have adopted a bewildering variety of different conventions.

Present tense
To be
I bin, thee bist, he/her bin, we bin or we'm, yo bin or yo'm, they bin or they'm
To be able
I con, thee cost, he/her con, we/yo/they con
To do
I du, thee dust, he/her duz, we/yo/they dun
To have
I've, theest, he/her has, we han or we'n, yo han or yo'n, they han or they'n
To see
I see, thee seest, he/her sees, we/yo/they see-en
To will
I wull, thee wut, he/her wull, we/yo/they wun

The widespread use of 'thee' was encapsulated in the tongue-twister: 'Thee cosn cuss like thee couldst cuss, cost?' (You can't swear as you could swear, can you?). A series of short exchanges could have run: 'How bist?' 'How bist *thee*?' 'How *bin* yer?' 'How bin *yo*?' 'Bay yo gooin?' 'No, I bay. Bist thee?' 'Why wusnt let her goo?' 'Cos I wo'.

Another feature was the formation of the plural of verbs in the present tense by the addition of 'en' to the singular. This produced forms such as we/yo/they callen, knowen and tellen. Nouns, too, had plurals in 'en': for example, brock (badger), broken; fleas, flen; folk, folken; house, housen; place, placen; sty, styen. In other cases, though, an ending in 'st' became 'sses', as in breakfast, breakfasses; breast, bresses; fist, fisses; nest, nesses; twist, twisses; vest, vesses; wrist, wrisses. A well-known couplet ran:

> Four ghosses, sitting on posses,
> Ating crusses for their breakfusses.

As early as 1846, F.D. Palmer, on a tour of the Black Country with the artist, Arthur Crowquill, noted at Darlaston that 'The dialect of the mining vicinity prevails here with unsophisticated hardihood', and provided this illustration:

> A huge bony-cheeked girl was sauntering under the hedgerow a short distance from the town. A grim, flannel-jacketed swain, of the earth-diving species, walked on the other side of the bank, and ogled her betimes with amorous ferocity.
>
> 'What brings yo he-ar?' said the lady.
>
> 'Whoi! Our gaffer hanna coom to tha pit yit', said the snub-faced admirer. 'Sh'on I goo alung with thee, Bess?' He added (with affecting modulation of voice, and a corresponding 'dowk' of the head).
>
> 'Au, chap, if thee loikst!' was the gracious permission.
>
> 'Well, wench, we-ar bist gooin to?'
>
> 'Noo wear!' Returned the hob-nailed Venus of Darlaston.

Almost a century later (in 1942) a more substantial (and more sympathetic) passage illustrates the continued vigour of the local vernacular (see panel overleaf). Attempts at phonetic representation of pronunciation vary widely from one author to another.

The vernacular vocabulary current in the Black Country was extensive, and a full glossary is given on pages 28 to 30. Much is now gone or obsolescent, but some two-thirds is still known to older people, and one third remains in use, in conversations, in anecdotes and stories,

Life in Bilston, drawing of 1846 by Arthur Crowquill

'Onds on yer Yed

Until recent years, it was a very common sight to see on the highway girls with a donkey, the latter laden with long bags of 'lily white sond' obtained from the quarries of Ruiton, Upper Gornal, which they hawked from town to town, crying as they went, 'Any lily white sond?' — this produce being used largely at that time by housewives for scouring purposes.

The bishop, having held a confirmation in Gornal, a lady who had several daughters, being convinced of the value of her own confirmation and that of her girls, … tried to bring the light to a woman who was in the habit of calling on her weekly with 'lily white sond'. This person was by name Molly Stubbs. 'Well, Molly', said she, 'ow bin yer?' 'Oh, tidy, missis, I bin. Never better. Ow bin yow?' 'All right, Molly, but I want to ax yer a question. 'An yer ever bin confirmed?' 'Lors, missis, why, what's that? I never 'eerd on 'im afore'. 'Why, 'ad the bishop's 'onds on yer yed. Becos, if yer dow, yow'm bound to goo to 'ell'. 'Yow dow say so, dun yer — and whatever's a bishop?' 'Why, a mon what preaches in a tub at church on a Sunday, and wears big, lawn sleeves'. 'Good gracious, missis! I never 'eerd talk of such a thing afore. But what's 'e put 'is 'onds on yer yed for?' 'Why, to convart yer, to be sure, and tak yer to 'eaven'. 'Well, that's a easy way o' dooin' it, and I wish 'e'd put 'is 'onds on my yed. But 'ow bin I gooin to 'ave it done?' 'I dow know, without yow goo to Dr Brown's, the Vicar o' Dudley, and preps 'e'll dew it as well as the bishop'. 'Dun yer think soo? Then dom'd if I dow goo and get 'im to dew it. I wants to goo to 'eaven, I does, as well as anybody else'.

Accordingly, on the following Monday, Molly put on her best bonnet and dressed herself in what she called her best 'Sunday shoot' [shirt], and walked to Dudley, calling at Dr Brown's. [Dr J.C. Browne was vicar of St Thomas's, Dudley, from 1845 until 1870]. Knocking loudly at the door, she said, 'Is the doctor a-whum?' 'He is', replied the servant, 'do you wish to see him?' 'In coorse I does. I cum on purpose'. The servant then bade her walk into the library, and she would fetch the doctor. 'Good morning, my good woman', said the doctor. 'Good marnin. Bin yow the man what bishops the women? Cos if yow bin, I'm come to be bishoped'. 'You mean confirmed, I suppose', said the vicar. 'Ah! I mean confarmed or bishoped or whatever yer call it. 'Onds on yer yed, yow know'. 'Yes, I see, but it is necessary that you should be examined'. 'Now, none o' that, Mr Vicar, I'm quite well, and dow want no physic, and what's more, I bain't a goin to ha' none'. 'Oh, I mean by examining, asking a few questions'. 'Oh, dun yer? Then why dai yow say so at fust. Yow con ask as mony questions as yow'm a mind, and I con answer um'. 'I am very pleased to hear it', returned the vicar.

'Now, how many commandments are there?' 'Why, three, to be sure. Yow know that, dow yer?' 'No, indeed, I do not, my good woman. I always thought there were ten'. 'Then yow oughten to ha' known better nor that, for yown bin a parson at Dudley, to my knowledge, a good mony 'ears, ai yer?' 'Oh, yes, you are quite right, but that is nothing to do with it. I must tell you there are ten commandments'. 'Then I tell yer it ai the truth, for I've lived at Gornal five-an-forty 'ears, and I say there is but three, and I ought to know'. 'Well, well', replied the doctor, 'perhaps you will tell me what they are'. 'In coorse I wull, if yow dow know. Why, they'n Aister, Whitsuntite and Sedgley Wake!'

It is needless to say that the astonished vicar did not recommend his ignorant visitor to the bishop for the next confirmation.

and even in poetry. It is said that at Oldbury the chain store, Toys R Us, is known as Toys Am We. Some words become clear as soon as the ubiquitous vowel transpositions are appreciated, as in aive (heave), saft (soft), sond (sand), wrostle (wrestle) and yarbs (herbs). A great many words, once in common use nationally but which then became archaic, survived in the Black Country. They include dout (put out), glede (cinder), helin or illin (book cover), liquor (grease), orts (leavings), rate (to scold) and risles (pea sticks, from the Anglo-Saxon, *hris*, meaning brushwood). In addition, there was a huge fund of lively local terms (some, of course, shared with other areas): adjectives like clammed (starving hungry), cracky (infirm), frit (frightened), gain (clever), lungeous (violent in play), nesh (susceptible to cold) and waxy (angry); nouns such as ballys (bellows), don-hand (expert), fix-gig (foolish person), gomerill (silly fellow), gullet (passage between two houses), hobble (difficulty), hontle (handful), megrims (facial contortions), nogman (noodle), raker (large lump of coal), rodney (idle wastrel) and skerrick (small piece); verbs like bezzle (drink greedily), croodle (crouch), hull (throw), ivver-ovver (hesitate), lamp (beat), moach (steal), siden (tidy), snape (snub) and yawp (bawl).

Black Country miners and ironworkers were at times extraordinarily inventive, both in dialect and standard English, with a great variety of variations on certain terms (see panel below).

dead: cheated the doctor, croaked his last, downed his tools, gone stiff, gone to grass, gone to pot, hopped the twig, jed as Methusalem, jed enuff, sure, pegged out, petered out, took his hook, turned up his toes

drunk: beery, bin in the sun, a bit gone/overcome/peart/wet, done up, a drop too much, drunk as a pig, fresh, flushed, fuddled, groggy, just so-so, muddled, muggy, over the line, quite gone, reelin/starin/staggerin drunk, to swilker [be unsteady], top heavy, upset

a fight: a bout wi fisses, a brogell, a randan, a rumpus, a scramble, a set-to, a shindy, a sloggin match, a tay party [signifying of poor quality], a wrostle

unwell: all overish, a bit offish, cor do nothin, gooin ter grass/pot, I bay right, off me aitin an drinkin, off me tommy, out of sorts, ready to be measured for a wooden suit, sick an saded, under the mark, wake as a cat

Black Country speech is studded with a wealth of powerful and pithy phrases. 'Rattlin like a bibble [pebble] in a can', which means chattering noisily, contrasts with 'gabblin like a guse [goose]'. However, 'Yo wantin to ate yer goose afore it's a goslin' is roughly equivalent to the standard saying about chickens before they are hatched. A rather more elaborate piece of wisdom is: 'Some men bin like Bils'n coalmines: theer's good stuff in 'em if you could ony get 'em dry but they'm allus soaked'. More laconically, 'Actin Dan'l [Daniel]' signifies keeping one's own counsel.

The expression, 'As lucky as Dicky Cox', not only seems to have been confined to Sedgley, but the story behind the simile is long forgotten. The same is true of some of the allusions in some of the many sayings peculiar to Netherton, which M.H.W. Fletcher noted in 1946:

> Er's got a mouth like old Shuck Amos, and earsen like a parish-evern.
> Er's one o t' white ens' chickens from Rowley: er never lays astray.
> Er was gooin round and round like Johnny Hayes's bell cases.
> E's like one o Sammy Whitehouse's pigs, e's little but e's got t'brade [breed] in im.
> E waants a drap o comfortin wairter, whom-brewed.
> Thee cost put t'best saddle in t'world on a cart-oss but e woh win t'Derby.
> Theer's no cadent to goo all round Warsal to get t'Dudley.
> Theer's no cadent t'tak eggs t'Bonny Haden's ommer t'crack um.

Some of the expressions recorded by Fletcher show the whimsical, almost surrealistic, sense of humour often found in the Black Country. One man remarks: 'I should ave spoke t'thee last night but thee wast out of sight afore I sed yer'. Again: 'The furst time e 'it it e missed it, the second time e 'it it in the same plaice, … an th' blacksmith 'it 'im on th' yead with 'is ond ommer an sent 'im whom'. An impeccable but lunatic logic lies behind this exchange between two elderly women:

First woman: 'Ah wish Ah knew wheer Ah was a-gooin to die'.

Second woman: 'What good'd that do yer?'

First woman: 'Well, Ah sh'd nivver goo theer'.

The same kind of whimsy occurs in snatches of repartee such as this:

Husband: 'I cor get me tay bottle in me pocket, me wench'.

Wife: 'Then pour a drap out, yer fule'.

And this:

Wife: 'Whatst back from thee wairk already for?'

Husband: 'Well, I'll be blowed. Thee knowst, I terned round ter light me pipe in the wind and I've forgot ter tern round agen'.

Unsurprisingly, the subject of work frequently arises in such anecdotes. For example, when an employer complains: 'I told yer to build a chimney an yo'n built a well', the offending worker replies: 'Ar, we'd got the plans upside down'. Again, a miner called Sammy is seen looking all round, and when he is asked what is missing, answers that he has lost his wescut (waistcoat). His mates join in the search, until one of them points out that Sammy still has the waistcoat on. 'Well I'm domned, so I 'ave', he said. 'If you 'adn't a tode me I should a gone wum without it'.

Harold Parsons believed that there was a 'cruel streak' in Black Country humour: a story dating from the time of the depression of the 1930s supports his view. An unemployed man filling time by walking along a canal tow-path hears a cry for help, and sees a man struggling in the water who shouts: 'I'm a-drowndin. Save me!' 'Oh ah', says the unemployed man, 'What's your name, then?' 'Abner Edwards. I'm drowndin. Help me!' 'Oh ah! Where d'you wairk?' 'Stewart and Lloyds. I'm a-drowndin. Save me!' 'Ah, and yo can bloody well drown. I'm a'ter your job'. He makes his way to the factory and asks the gateman: 'Abner Edwards wairk here?' 'Ah, but he ai come this morning'. 'I know. He's a-drowndin in the cut. Can I have his job?' 'No. Yo'm too late. We'm just set on the bloke what shoved 'im in'.

A similar callousness comes from this tale from the Enoch and Eli canon: One night — a pay night — Enoch had to work overtime unexpectedly. He asked Eli to call in and let his missus know he'd be late home. When Enoch got to the house he said: 'Enoch woh be comin home till late, and he asked me to tell yer. What about a bit, then, while we'm waitin?' 'We-ell ...'. 'Come on, I'll give thee a fiver'. 'No...'. 'I'll mek it a tenner, then ... fifteen ... twenty'. At this, she agreed, and they went upstairs. Eli left after a while, and Enoch came home much later. ''Ello, luv. Did Eli tell thee I'd be late?' 'Ar'. 'And did he give yer me wages?'

The story is not typical of the Enoch and Eli (or Aynoch and Ayli) stories, which are usually fairly light-hearted. They combine simple-mindedness with unexpected shrewdness, and preserve situations from the past as well as featuring innovative elements. They are still widely loved, and widely told. The two characters sometimes appear singly, though more usually together. In a single instance, one features as the son of the other. Some of these tales follow:

Infant Scholar
Enoch's granddaughter wins a place at Oxford, but becomes pregnant there, and eventually has to come home to have the baby. Enoch proudly takes the baby out in its pram and meets Eli, who remarks:''E looks a bright little chap'. ''E ought to', says Enoch, ''e's 'ad two terms at Oxford'.

A Short Way with Nails
Aynoch was making a fence when Ayli went past. Aynoch put 'is 'and in 'is pocket, brought out a nail and ommered it in. The next two 'e took out, 'e throwed away, then ommered the next un in. 'E went on like that, and Ayli asked why he was throwin' 'alf the nails away. 'Becos the yeds am on the wrong road'. 'Yer fule, goo round t'other side and ommer 'em in from theer'.

A Good Living

Aynoch had a car, which he sold to Ayli for £100. Afterwards he regretted it, and the next time he saw Ayli he said: 'Ay up, Ah'll gie yo £120 for that car back'. So Ayli sold it back to him, but then was sorry to have parted with it, and bought it back for £140. After a while Aynoch again had second thoughts, and went to offer Ayli £160 for the car. 'Ah'm sorry', said Ayli, but Ah've sold it to another chap'. 'Yo've spoilt a good livin for both on we', said Aynoch.

A Motorbike Accident

Aynoch bought a motorbike. 'E was tryin' it out one day when 'e saw Ayli, and 'e says: 'Ayli, what d'yer think on er?' Ayli says: 'Er looks a good un'. Aynoch says: 'Gerr on the back, an' I'll give yer a ride'. So off they went. After a while, Anoch asks: 'All right, Ayli?' 'No', 'e says, 'the cold wind ai 'alf gerrin down me chest'. Aynoch stops an'says: 'Gerr off, an' put yer overcoat on back to front and I'll fasten it up at the back. That'll protect yer chest a bit'. Off they went again, and after a mile or so Aynoch shouts: ''Ow is it now, Ayli?' But Ayli wor there. 'E'd fallen off. So Aynoch about turns and goes back. Presently 'e comes to a crowd of people, and there was poor Ayli lyin' on the floor. Aynoch asks: 'Is 'e 'urt much?' A chap answers: 'Ah doh know, but 'e ai spoke since we turned 'is yed round the right road'.

George Washington and the Privy

Aynoch and his son, Ayli, lived in a house with a privy at the bottom of the garden. The privy was made of wood, like a sentry box. Be'ind the privy was the canal. One morning, Aynoch called his son and said: 'Ayli, did yo push the privy into the cut last night?' 'No, ferther, Ah didn't'. 'Now, son', said Aynoch, 'I'll tell yer a story. Years ago in America there was a little boy called George Washington. One day 'is ferther noticed that a small apple tree 'ad bin cut down. 'E asked George if 'e'd done it. "Ferther", 'e said, "I cor tell a lie. I did cut it down". "Because you've told me the truth", said George Washin'ton's father, "I shall not beat you".

Now', said Aynoch, 'did yo push the privy in the cut?' 'Yes, ferther, Ah did'. And Aynoch gave Ayli a good 'idin'. After a while, Ayli complained: 'Ah cor understand it, dad. George's ferther did not beat 'im, because 'e told the truth. I told yo the truth, but yo beat me. Why?' 'Because', said Aynoch, 'there's a difference. George Washin'ton's ferther wor up the tree at the time'.

Enoch asks the Score

Enoch supported the Albion, known as the Baggies. One Saturday night after 'e'd been in bed a few minutes 'e got up and started dressing. 'Is wife asked what 'e was going to do. 'Ah'm gooin' down the road to ask Eli something'. Eli was in bed when Enoch knocked, but 'e put 'is yed through the bedroom window and asked what 'e wanted. ''Ow did the Baggies get on?' 'Drawed, nil-nil'. Enoch came 'ome and got into bed, but a few minutes later 'e got dressed and went up to Eli's again. This time 'e throwed some little bibbles [pebbles] up at the window. 'What d'yer want now?' asked Eli. 'Oh, I forgot to ask. What was the 'alf-time score?'

Enoch and the Neighbour's Fowls
Enoch moved house, and Eli asked 'im 'ow 'e liked it. 'The 'ouse is a treat but the bloke next door keeps a lot o' fowls and the cocks start crowin' about four o'clock in the mornin' and I cor get any sleep after that'. 'Well', says Eli, 'yo cor do anything about it. 'E's entitled to keep fowl'. Some time later, Enoch said to Eli: 'I've bought the fowls off 'im next door. They're in my garden now. Let 'em keep '*im* awake'.

Eli and the Pergola
Enoch said to Eli: 'I was comin' through the park this mornin' and I thought 'ow nice it'd be to 'ave a pergola there'. 'I agrees with yer', said Eli, 'but don't yer think it'd be better to 'ave two and breed from 'em?'

Aynoch and the Channel Tunnel
When the tunnel was mooted Aynoch went to London to offer his services. ''Ow'm yo gooin' ter do it?' asked the prime minister. 'Ah'll dig off Beachy 'Ead, but Ah wo 'ave to dig too far, cos ower kid's diggin' from the other side'. 'What if you miss 'im in the middle?' 'Yo'm easy, kid. Yo'll 'ave two tunnels instead o' one'.

There are also many briefer anecdotes featuring one or both of the characters. For example, Ayli pesters his missus to tell him what she wants on the family tombstone, and she eventually hands him a piece of paper with the words: 'Wife of the above'. After a long walk Aynuk and Ayli go into a country pub, order a pint apiece, and take out their sandwiches. 'You can't eat your own food in here', said the landlord. 'That's all right', says Ayli, 'we'll just swap over'. It seems that the two of them are immortal.

The jocular tales of the Black Country do not confine themselves to Aynoch and Ayli, though the sense of humour remains very similar.

Drowning the Puppies
Two women go to the seaside for a day. When they get there they want a bathe, but have no costumes. One said to the other: 'We sh'll be all right if we keep our bloomers on and keep our arms across our chests'. They set off down to the beach like that. A little lad who is passing says: 'Ay, missus, if yo're gooin' ter drown them puppies can I 'ave the one with a pink nose?'

Our Eynuck bay quite jed,
Nor never wull be;
O'd Eynuck bay forgot
Nor never con be.
Tek a sank around Blackyeth,
Or down the tump an' in t'O'd Hill;
Stond annunst the cross fer 'alf an hour,
Just watch the folken all goo by,
Yo'll see him theer as big as life –
O'd Eynuch, our Eynuck!

Our Eynuck left 'is mark,
Yo caw mistairke et, see?
His 'ommer prints bin 'ere
An' always wull be.
Just look in all the nailshaps,
Ef some bay theer that meks no odds;
See that ooman scuven up the gleeds?
That's 'er what fashions all the nails,
Yo'll bet her mon bay far away –
O'd Eynuck, our Eynuck!

Our Eynuck med big chain
('Is ooman med the small).
See them theer big anchors?
Eynuck med 'em all.
In Crairdley 'eath yo'll find 'im
Around any nailshap in the day;
Or ef et's night look in the pubs –
(Yo'll see um nustled 'gainst the church)
O'd Eynuch, our Eynuch!

No! Eynuck bay quite jed,
Nor never wull be.
O'd Enuch bay forgot
Nor never con be.
Hast ever sid a jew's harp?
He med um all by Rowley Church.
Stand atop Hawes Hill an' look adown,
See all them lights annunst the cut?
He used to puddle iron theer –
O'd Eynuck, our Eynuck!

J. Westwood

A Novel Way Home

A Black Country man and his son were employed at the same place, and used to go to work and return together along the canal. One night the son came home by himself and his mother said: 'Where's yer ferther?' He says, 'Well we was comin' along the tow path and all of a sudden, ferther says, "This footpath ain't 'alf muddy. I'm walkin' in the 'orse road". I ain't seen 'im since'.

A Vicar provokes swearing

A vicar was going to have a round of golf and he engaged a Black Country youth to carry his clubs. Before the lad started out from home his mother said, 'Now look 'ere, yo, yo'm carryin' the clubs for a clergyman. Now yo mind yer language, and none o' yer swearin''. 'All right, mother', 'e says. So off 'e went and got to the golf links. There was the vicar waiting at the first tee. The vicar put his ball down, made a mighty swipe at it, missed it, and dug out a lump of turf which went sailing through the air. The vicar shaded his eyes with his hands. He said to the boy, 'Where did that sod go?' He says, 'Ovver the bloody 'edge, an' yo' started it'.

The Drunken Farmer and the Sow

A farmer used to get drunk every night. One night as he started out his wife said to him, 'Yo come 'ome drunk tonight, and I s'll lock yo out'. He came home drunk, and she would not let him in. Looking through the window, she saw him stagger across to the pigsty and go in. After a time she relented, and went to fetch him. When she got to the sty, she found him lying by the sow, and she heard him say, 'I'm bin married to yo fer thirty years and I didn't know till now that yo'd got buttons on yer nightdress'.

An Unusual Meal

There was a Black Country chain-master called Billingham [whose works was in Oak Street, Quarry Bank]. 'E was a Liberal, an' despite bein' illiterate 'e was elected to the Parish Council. To celebrate 'is victory 'e decided to provide a free feed for all 'is men and their families. One of 'is men who was also called Billingham 'ad twenty-one children. 'E took them and 'is wife to the feast an' they ate a sufficiency, an' more. In the middle of the night the father 'ad to get up to be sick. Th' 'ouse was on a steeply sloping piece of land. The brew 'us was built underneath to save space, and there was a parapet in front of the door with some steps leadin' down to the road. Billingham leaned over this parapet to be sick an' then stood back for a while with 'is 'ead in 'is 'ands. During this time a pup which 'ad bin in the brew 'us came out and started making a meal of what it found. Billingham leaned over the parapet again an' saw the pup: 'Ah dunna remember atin' thee'.

Glossary

ackun acorn
Ah I
arout without
aud old
ah, ar yes
aive to heave, lift
asker newt

babby baby
bawm to daub, smear
bellock, belluck to bellow, roar
bibble pebble
bile boil (noun and verb)
blabbern to babble
blenchen to flinch
blob blister
bobowler large moth
boffomble, boffumble to confuse
bost to burst
breeze small coke
bug demon
bullyed tadpole
bunnyfire bonfire
backen to delay
belloil thrashing
bezzle to drink heavily
big-hour over an hour
blart to bleat, cry
blather, blether bladder
blether-yed fool
blob-mouth loose-tongued person
boffle to hinder
bonk little hill
bostin excellent
brodgel, brodgel, broggell row, scrimmage
buffet stool
bum clink weak beer

cade, cadled petted, tame, spoilt
cag-mag inferior meat
canking gossiping; crying of geese
chobble to crunch
clack Adam's apple; (as verb) to talk
clays claws
creachy ailing, delicate, inferior
crowning in hole caused by collapse of old pit shaft
caggy lefthanded
campling gossiping
chincuff whooping cough
chunder to talk loudly
clam, clem to go hungry
codge to patch up, bungle
croodle to croach, stoop
cunger, cowcunger cucumber

disannul to inconvenience
dowl down (soft hair)
drap drink (alcoholic)
draw cuts to draw straws (lots)
dishle o' tay cup of tea
dout, dowt to put out
drapper tree fuchsia
dummell dunce

'E husband or head of household
ess ash
eft newt

fairesses fairies
feke punch
flen fleas
franzy foolish
fairther, ferther father
fiz-gig fool
fod, fode yard, court, pavement in front of house

gain handy, skilful
gauk, gawk guy, ill-dressed person
glead, gleed, glede cinder, ember
Gornal cuckoo donkey
gratey, grawty dick groats and meat stewed together
gullet narrow passage between houses
gauby, gawby fool
gill-houter owl
gomerill simpleton
grate, grawt groat (grain)
grig, in **merry as a grig** lively
guggle windpipe

hefty dexterous
hontle handful
hillin, illin book cover
hull to throw

ift to heave, lift
ines lazy woman
ike to beckon, throw
ivver-ovver hesitate

jack-bannock minnow, stickleback
jack-squaler swift (bird)
jole large earthenware vessel; (v.) to knock
jubbur donkey
jack-bit elevenses
jed, jead dead
jollop medecine

keffle awkward fellow
kibbles small coals
kench to sprain, wrench
knivy mean, penurious

lamp to beat, thrash
lease, leaze glean
loff to laugh
lungeous violent
lather ladder
leaser, leasow, leasure, lezzer meadow
lommock awkward

maitrum matron (in hospital)
mandle mangle (in laundry)
mawkin guy, scarecrow; badly dressed woman
mouldewarp mole (animal)
mammock, mommack to pick at one's food
megrim, meegrum grimace
misken, miskin midden
mullock refuse, rubbish

nairun not one
nerker, nurker hedgehog; troublesome child
nisgul weakling
naunt aunt
nesh, nash soft, feeling the cold
nineter, nointer young tearaway
nogman ignoramus

ockerd awkward
odge to push
ongain, ungain clumsy, unhandy
oot? Will you?
ost to attempt, offer
owsen houses
ode, oud, owd old
omber, ommer hammer
ood wood; would
orts scraps, leftovers
ourn, owern my husband

pail to beat
pike pick (workman's tool)
pouk, powk stye on eyelid
puck picked
pash to hit hard
potch to forestall
proud tailor goldfinch

raker large lump of coal
rawm to over-reach
reeve to turn up
rantan fight
reasty, reesty rancid
rodney idle fellow; (as verb) to skulk, idle

sad heavy (e.g. of cake which fails to rise)
sawney simpleton
segs, seggs bulrushes; callouses
shommock foot; (as verb) to slouch
sike to sigh
skerrick scrap, tiny amount
sough, suff sewer, drain
sprag prop
steen large earthenware vessel
strollopin ungainly
swat sweat
sad-irons smoothing irons
scrobble tangle
shackler idler
siden out of the perpendicular; (as verb) to tidy
snape, sneap to snub
spottle to splash
squilt pimple
stodger very fat person
swale, sweale to gutter (e.g. of candle)
swilker to spill, splash

tabber to tap repeatedly
tank heavy blow
tantadlin tart cowpat
tind to light a fire
tittle to tickle
tranklements paraphernalia
tacky bonk pit bank
tan the land to walk quickly
tay tea; it isn't
tipe pit mound; (as verb) to tip
tommy, tummy food

urchin hedgehog
vargil mouth

wassel beer
whack-rowdy-dow weak beer, broth, tea
wrostle wrestle
wetched web-footed
wiouten without
wum home

yarbs herbs
yed head
Yethard Ned, Edward
yaup, yawp to shout loudly
yerrin herring

As one Blackcountryman put it, 'Why doh they spake plain English?'

CHAPTER 3

Churches and Parsons

Fairies in the Black Country? The idea may be difficult to accept, but the intervention of fairies or 'fairesses', to use the local vernacular, in the siting of at least three churches was once commonly accepted. In Saxon times a nobleman decided to celebrate his conversion to christianity by having a church erected somewhere near what is now Stow Heath Lane in Bilston. Fairies who frequented the spot, irritated by the intrusion, demolished by night any stonework put up by day. The would-be founder abandoned his plans, though on the Christmas Eve which followed, with malevolent spirits rendered powerless, bells were heard ringing and choirs singing 'Gloria in excelsis' far below the ground. The site, now forgotten, became known as Church Piece.

St. Matthew's, Walsall

The church of St Matthew at Walsall probably occupies the place of an Anglo-Saxon predecessor. Construction is said originally to have begun lower down, some distance away in what is now the suburb called The Chuckery. When masonry was repeatedly dismantled and moved to a different site, the people adopted this, believing that fairies were at work. As if in confirmation, the 'little folk' continued to frolic in their old haunts in The Chuckery. The curious word incorporates a version of the word 'church', and the whole story may have arisen because in mediaeval times a plot there bore the name of 'church grove field'. A similar tale of change is told of Sedgley, where building began in what was formerly Abbey Farm, in the present Ellowes Park, until the fairies' transfer of materials determined parishioners to build their church where it now stands.

Church construction often took place close to a well perceived to be holy, though the only instance in the Black Country seems to be St Giles's, Willenhall. The adoption of St Giles, patron of cripples, lepers and nursing mothers, may have indicated a belief that the well water was therapeutic. Some healing and holy wells are now memorialised in place or street names such as Spring Walk and Crosswells Road at Oldbury, Spring Hill at Penn, Springfield at Rowley Regis, and Spring Lane at Willenhall. Ladywell Close at Wombourne must be near the former site of Our Lady's Well, famous in the middle ages for its healing water, and a place of rural resort until at least the end of the nineteenth century. According to a Codsall tradition, sufferers from leprosy, after being blessed in the church by the priest, walked on a footpath down to the Lepers' Well, near Leper House Farm, to bathe in its healing, sulphurous water. The presence of a holy well beneath Sedgley Beacon is indicated by the name of Spring Vale. A sixteenth-century description unfortunately does not enable us to be more precise:

> To the south of Wolferhamptune ys a famous sprynge callyd Ladie Wulfruna's Sprynge, whershee usyd to come and washe. Yt ys ssaide yt ye ladie prayede for yt God woude endue yt with powers of no ordinarie virtu, inasmuche as yt itt hathe curyd manie, as itt were myraculouslie, healynge ye lame, ye weake, ye infirme, as manie ther bee can testyfie.

The disappearance of Wulfruna's Well is parallelled by those of St Boniface at Little Hill, Wednesbury, and St Augustine at Sandwell. Cruddley or Crudeley Well in Bilston was just off Lichfield Street near the entrance to Proud's Lane. (The latter took its name from a Major Proud who built a madhouse there in the eighteenth century). The well, with its reputation for miraculous healing powers, drew visitors in mediaeval times both from the locality and from farther afield. It bore the Latin inscription: '*Qui non dat quod habet,/Daemon infra ridet*' — 'Who does not give what he has [That is, make a contribution],/The demon laughs [at him] below'. Despite such warnings, the well's sanctity gradually lost credence, and by the early nineteenth century it was regarded simply as a source of water. In about 1830 it ran dry and was filled in, its feeder spring having disappeared into one of the local mineshafts.

There was a time when England was under curfew, and the verger 'e alluz 'ad to ring the bell at curfew time. 'E got the rheumatic and 'e couldn't walk to the church. 'E was in a pub and 'e asked one chap t' 'elp 'im to either go and ring the bell for 'im or tek 'im to ring it. 'Oh no, no, no'. 'E wouldn't goo in the church for all the tea in China by 'imself at dusk. The verger says, 'There's nothing in the church t' 'urt yer. The dead they never 'urt yer. It's the live people that'll 'urt yer, and yo needn't be afraid to goo into the church'. 'E got 'im in the right frame of mind and 'e says, 'I'll tell thee what I'll do. I'll tek thee on me back and I'll wait for thee, and when thee's rung the bell, I'll bring thee back'.

In the meantime — it was at a time when to live in England for the poor was very, very 'ard: they couldn't live without doin' summat such as to steal a sheep, and that was the ony road they could live, to stale a ship [sheep] or stale a deer or stale summat, they'd got to stale summat else they'd starve — so these two poachers they agreed to go one night, coincided with the very night as the verger couldn't goo and ring the bell. One says to the t'other, 'Now', 'e says, 'thee goo and catch a ship and bring 'im to the church, because this is the ony place where they doh search when they've missed a ship. Ah'll goo up in the belfry where Ah can get a good look at the countryside everywheer all round, and if there's any danger I'll let thee know and yo can dump the ship and mek the best o' yer road 'ome'.

So in the meantime it's a-gerrin' dusk at curfew and when the man in the belfry thought it was time for 'is mate to appear with the ship, it just coincided with the time when the countryman was a-bringin' the verger. 'E was a very big man and 'e was a-sweatin' and gaspin' when 'e was gerrin' towards the church door. The man in the belfry 'e thought 'is mate 'ad got a good big ship and 'e was a-puffin' and blowin' a-comin' up the drive. 'E couldn't see 'im, for the bad light in the trees on the road. 'E said to 'im, 'e says, 'Jack, is 'e fat?' The countryman 'e throwed the verger off 'is back and 'e says, 'Fat or lean, thee con tek 'im as 'e is'. 'E thought it was the devil.

Because of their use as burial grounds, churchyards were associated with death, and some were careful to avoid them at night. They inspired tales of ghosts (see chapter 6), and even of the devil, as George Dunn's traditional account (see panel above) shows. Lugubrious thoughts fostered by the sight of serried rows of gravestones and funerary monuments were reinforced by the messages of misfortune that they bore. Even without words, the tombstone in Tettenhall churchyard

Tettenhall Church (on a postcard franked 1930)

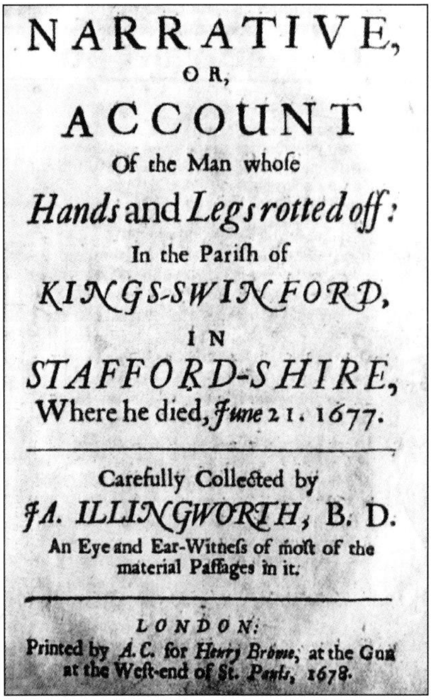

NARRATIVE,
OR,
ACCOUNT
Of the Man whoſe
Hands and *Legs rotted off*:
In the Pariſh of
KINGS-SWINFORD,
IN
STAFFORD-SHIRE,
Where he died, *June* 21. 1677.

Carefully Collected by
JA. ILLINGWORTH, B. D.
An Eye and Ear-Witneſs of moſt of the material Paſſages in it.

LONDON:
Printed by *A. C.* for *Henry Brome*, at the Gun at the Weſt-end of St. *Pauls*, 1678.

Illingworth's pamphlet of 1678

depicting a woman with no arms could reinforce a moral precept. The explanation emerged that the woman had worked on Sundays, and responded to reproaches by saying that she saw no harm in working on any day of the week. If there were, she hoped her arms would drop off. So they did, the following Sunday. The story is parallelled by that of John Duncalf of Codsall who stole a bible in 1677 from Miss Margaret Babb, just outside Wolverhampton. Taxed with the theft, he denied it, and swore that if he were guilty his hands would rot and drop off. They did, according to a full account of the incident written up by the local parson, James Illingworth, and published in London. A ballad printer took up the theme in 'A Warning for Swearers', of which three of the twelve verses run:

> In a small time he had his full desire,
> and what he of the Lord did then require,
> His hand-wrists rot away most wofully,
> His hands are dead, and black as black can be.
>
> The joynts of's knees do rot in the same sort,
> as several hundred people can report,
> That daily goes to see and take a view,
> and witness can, the same for to be true.
>
> Upon the ground he stinks, as he doth lie,
> none can endure for to stand him nigh,
> Lord grant that each good Christian may take care,
> how they themselves so falsely do forswear.

'Life! What is life? A shadow! Ten thousand accidents in ambush lie': so says the inscription on a cross in St Thomas's churchyard at Dudley which commemorates Helen Cosens, a former vicar's wife killed when the horse she was driving bolted and threw her into the road. Many epitaphs record Black Country miners who died in pit accidents: for these, see chapter 7. Among the earliest extant local epitaphs must be one in the south aisle of Wolverhampton parish church:

St Thomas's Church, Dudley, in a drawing of 1815

Here lyeth withouten miss,
The bodyes of Richard Tomkyns and his wife Alice,
Wch Richard on June y^{e} 2nd day
Towards heaven took his way,
In the year 1501.
His bodye and bones be laid under this stone,
Whose soul, sweet Jesus, have mercy upon.

The epitaph of Thomas Smith at St James's Church, Lower Gornal, tells us:

Under a wheel I lost my life
No time to get away
Now I must moulder in the dust
Until the judgement day.

He died in 1871, aged 37. The mood here is resigned, the words matter-of-fact. Earlier in the century this epitaph from the Providence Baptist Chapel at Coseley went even further:

You that are young prepare to die,
For I was young, though here I lie;
Remember death, for it is good –
The rose may wither in the bud
(James Turley, died 1829, aged 25).

There is rather more humanity in:

> I lived a virgin all my days
> My chief delight was in God's ways
> But now I've run my virgin race
> I hope with God to find a place
> (Rushall, St Michael: Sarah Meriden, aged 82).

And:

> Here lie the remains of a worthy old queen,
> As perfect a companion as ever was seen;
> At the Level she dwelt in every one's heart
> Till death at her majesty levelled a dart.
> Kings, princes, and peasants, at his summons must fall,
> For death, the great leveller, levels us all
> (Dudley, St Thomas's: Jane Pitt, died 1779, aged 67).

A more combative tone is adopted in the inscription at Bloxwich:

> To the memory of Samuel Wilks, late of this parish, locksmith, who died 6th November, 1764. Reader! If thou art an inhabitant of Great Bloxwich, KNOW, that the dust beneath thy feet (when overseer of the poor of this parish) was imprisoned in thy cause, because he refused to surrender thy rights, and to submit to an arbitrary mandate, by which it was intended

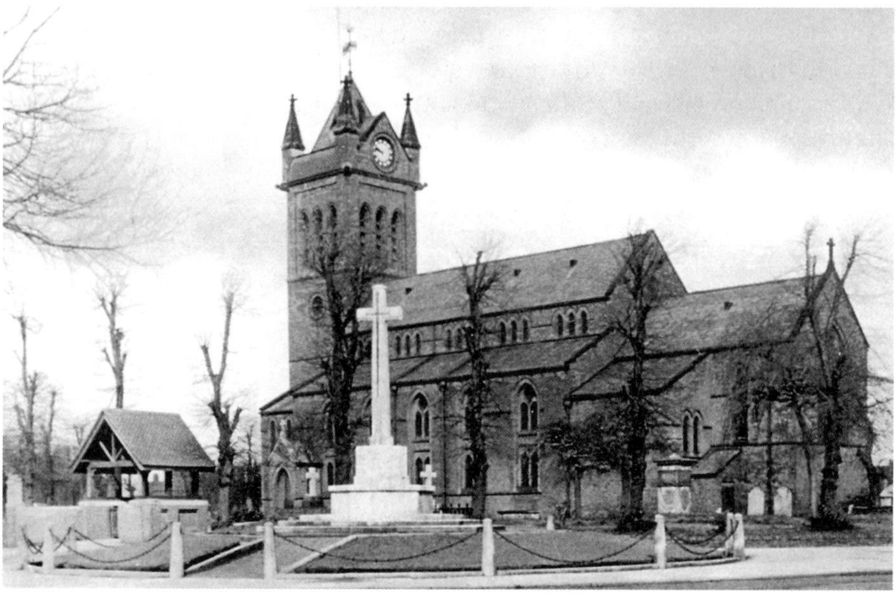

All Saints' Church, Bloxwich

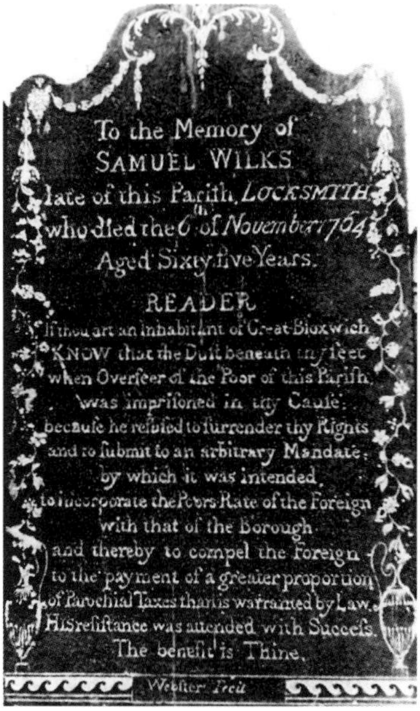
To the Memory of
SAMUEL WILKS
late of this Parish, LOCKSMITH
who died the 6th of November 1764
Aged Sixty five Years.
READER
and to submit to an arbitrary Mandate;
by which it was intended
with that of the Borough
and thereby to compel the Foreign
to the payment of a greater proportion
The benefit is Thine.
Webster Fecit

Tombstone of Samuel Wilks at Bloxwich

to incorporate the poor-rates of the foreign with those of the borough, and thereby to compel the foreign to the payment of a greater proportion of parochial taxes than is warranted by law; his resistance was attended with success. The benefit is thine.

A similar sense of grievance lies behind the epitaph written for himself by one of three men buried in Brierley Hill churchyard after being hanged for stealing. Their names were Lay, Naylor and Pearson. The last of these, known as Joe Merry, was betrayed by a friend he had trusted. He composed this verse, which is highly unlikely to have been inscribed:

Mourn not for me my children dear,
I am not dead but sleeping here;
Pray for my enemies, be not with them at strife,
For they were resolved to take away my life.

Richard Wilkes, another who wrote his own epitaph, was in a different category altogether. Willenhall-born and Cambridge-educated, he became a clergyman and preached in Wolverhampton. Then, 'disappointed in his expectation of preferment, he retired from the church, and began to practise physic at Wolverhampton in the year 1720'. So wrote William Pitt in his *Topographical History of Staffordshire,* not in the least surprised that a parson should at will turn himself into a doctor. Nor were Wilkes's contemporaries. He was 'a friend to the poor, to whom he always gave gratuitous [free] advice as a physician, and pecuniary aid'. His ministrations were not limited to the poor, and his visits as a doctor to the houses of the gentry helped to gain him access to their archives for his work as an antiquary. He died in 1760, and the epitaph which he wrote some years earlier and described as 'a true picture from the life' appears on his monument in Willenhall Church:

Here reader stand awhile, and know
Whose carcase 'tis that rots below.
A man's who worked by reason's rule,
Yet sometimes err'd and play'd the fool;
A man sincere in all his ways,
And full of the Creator's praise;

Who laugh'd at priestcraft, pride, and strife,
And all the little tricks of life;
Who lov'd his King, his Country more,
And dreadful party rage forebore,
He told nobility the truth,
And wink'd at hasty slips of youth.
The honest poor man's steady friend,
The villain's scourge, in hopes to mend;
His father, mother, children, wife,
His riches, honours, length of life,
Concern not thee; observe what's here,
He rests in hope, and not in fear.

As well as his own, Wilkes wrote an epitaph for Charles Phillips, an itinerant violinist, who died in 1732. It can be seen on the wall of the porch at Wolverhampton parish church:

Exalted soul! Whose harmony could please
The love-sick virgin and the gouty ease;
Could jarring discord, like Amphion [lyre-player of Greek antiquity], move
To beauteous order and harmonious love;
Rest here in peace, till angels bid thee rise,
And meet thy blessed Saviour, in the skies.

The actor, David Garrick, was impressed enough by this to learn it by heart. Dr Johnson, to whom he recited it, said 'I think, Davy, I can make a better', and, 'almost extempore', offered:

Philips, whose touch harmonious could remove
The pangs of guilty power or hapless love;
Rest here, distress'd by poverty no more,
Here find that calm thou gav'st so oft before;
Sleep, undisturb'd, within this peaceful shrine,
Till angels wake thee with a note like thine.

Many epitaphs were much less high-flown than these, though their identification is often suspiciously vague, which makes one wonder whether they are apocryphal. From 'a Wolverhampton churchyard', and dating from 1690, comes this:

Here lies the bones
Of Joseph Jones,
Who ate whilst he was able;
But once o'erfed
He dropt down dead,
And fell beneath the table.
When from the tomb
To meet his doom,
He rises amidst sinners:
Since he must dwell
In heav'n or hell,
Take him — which gives best dinners.

Equally irreverent, despite its being recorded from 'a stone in a local churchyard' in the diary of a Wesleyan and Radical, Benjamin Leadbetter (born in Dudley in 1784), is:

Below lies for sarten
Honest old Hartling,
And snug behind un
His fat wife, a wide un.
If another you lack,
Look down and see Jack;
And farther, a yard,
Lies Charles, who drank hard;
And near than un is Moggy,
Who never got groggy.
Like Charles and her father,
Too abstemious that rather,
And therefore popped off
In a tissicky cough.

Matthew Wilkes, a locksmith who lived at Bloxwich in the mid-nineteenth century, was reputedly commemorated in the churchyard with this verse:

Here lies the body of poor old Matty,
Better known as Matty Watty.
The devil he lived, the devil he died,
And we'll leave the devil to belt his hide.

The tradition of unorthodox epitaphs lingered at least until the mid-twentieth century. When John Thomas Edwards, a 'virtuous vagrant' well known in Cradley Heath, died in 1951, a local collection saved him from a pauper's grave. Cyril Parkes, businessman and county councillor, wrote this epitaph:

Here lies the body of John Tom,
No more jail from now on,
40 times behind prison walls,
And still commands respect by all.
A pauper's grave should have been his lot,
But 'No, John Tom, you're not forgot'.

John Tom rests in peace in Old Hill cemetery. Not so some of the dead of a century or more earlier. Until the Anatomy Act of 1832 authorised the supply of corpses for dissection, few specimens were available to medical students learning their trade as doctors. Before then, the bodies of hanged criminals were one of the legitimate sources, since judges had the power as a final indignity to order the dissection of those executed. When Abel Hill was hanged at Stafford in 1820 for the murder of Marie Martin, his corpse, by direction of the judge, was sent back to the scene of the crime at Bilston, and publicly dissected by a local surgeon, Mr Best. Afterwards Best preserved and articulated the skeleton, which he showed to the curious.

John Tom

The opening in 1828 of Birmingham's medical school created a new demand for cadavers. A man called 'Brummagem' Booth organised a gang of body snatchers or 'resurrectionists' who, sometimes in collusion with gravediggers, sextons and even undertakers, disinterred freshly-buried corpses which were then taken to Birmingham by horse and cart, often under the cover of goods for market. An adult corpse was worth four guineas, at a time when a skilled worker earned thirty shillings a week at most, and a labourer, nine. Some Black Country graveyards, easily accessible from Birmingham, such as West Bromwich All Saints, Tipton St Martin's and Walsall St Matthew's, were particularly vulnerable. The 'diggum-uppers' and their associates inspired hated and fear. A local rhyme claimed:

Here in eighteen twenty-five
A mon's wuth mower jed than alive
If yo doh believe this dyin' truth
Have a word wi' Brummagem Booth.

Since, according to rumour, a Wednesbury sexton known as 'Ode Picks', helped body snatchers, an elaborate trick was played on him. A carefully costumed charade, featuring the devil, convinced him that hell yawned, whereupon he reputedly said: 'Good Mister Devil, do forgive me this once! I've been bell-ringer, psalm-singer and amen-dinger at the old church for forty years! If you'll let me off this time, I'll never rob another stone, nor steal another bone!' More practical measures to deter body snatchers included placing large, heavy stones over new graves. At Bilston, watchmen were paid to keep vigil over graves for several weeks after an interment, until corpses were no longer suitable for dissection.

Interest in Black Country graveyards stretched to body snatchers well beyond the immediate area. A Londoner, Ben Crouch, features in the story of one incident at Wolverhampton. Crouch was the son of a carpenter at Guy's Hospital in London. He soon learned that the rough coffins made by his father for the poor went to funerals and the grave without their occupants, who had been sold to resurrectionists. During the wars with Spain and France Crouch combined working as a civilian supplier to the troops with scouring battlefields for the dead so as to remove their teeth (which could be sold at a good price for conversion into false dentures). Back in England after 1815 he did well enough as a body snatcher to be able to buy a hotel in Margate, though the business failed when the source of his wealth came out. Charles Dickens based on him the character of Jerry Cruncher in *A Tale of Two Cities*.

According to the story, which Tom Langley had from a great aunt, on Christmas Eve in 1836, Ben Crouch and a doctor took a corpse from a cemetery near the Fighting Cocks beer house in Dudley Road, Wolverhampton. (The establishment became well known enough to give its name to the whole district, but later was demolished to make way for a supermarket). Crouch and the doctor who was his accomplice travelled in a two-seater gig, the corpse wrapped in a greatcoat and propped up between them. The night was bitterly cold, and they stopped at the Fighting Cocks for a drink, leaving the gig and its occupant in the yard. Those inside knew Crouch's reputation, and also his appearance, 'heavy, hulking, tallish', and manner, 'rude, coarse, offensive'. When the prize fighter, Bill Perry — later to become famous as the Tipton Slasher — happened to walk in, he was quietly put in the picture. He slipped out and took the place of the corpse, just before the diggum uppers went out to resume their journey to Birmingham. As they travelled along part of what is now Wolverhampton New Road the doctor, perhaps sensing something amiss, felt one of the corpse's hands. 'It feels rather warm', he remarked. Crouch felt the other hand. 'It does and all', he said. 'Ar, an' yo'd feel warm if yo'd bin wheer Ah bin this last wik', came a voice from the corpse. The doctor jumped down and fled. Crouch struck out at the corpse, but was knocked senseless. Perry drove back to the Fighting Cocks and stabled the horse, but left Crouch in the gig, where he recovered consciousness the following morning, stiff with cold. The stolen body, restored to relatives, was re-buried beneath a substantial granite slab. Late in life, Perry

10 GUINEAS REWARD.

Whereas, early on Sunday morning last, some evil disposed Persons did steal and carry away the

WEATHERCOCK

from off the

STEEPLE.

Any Person giving Information so that the Offenders may be apprehended, shall upon Conviction receive TEN GUINEAS REWARD over and above what is allowed by the Association for the prosecution of Felons. And as more than one were concerned, if either will impeach his Accomplice or Accomplices, they shall receive the above Reward, and every endeavour used to obtain a free Pardon.

Willenhall,
July 24, 1827.

THOMAS HINCKS,
JAMES WHITEHOUSE,
Chapel Wardens.

used to recall: 'Ar, Ben said 'e'd 'ave me up afower they put me down, ar, and sell me afower Ah was cowd, but 'e's bin down a good many 'ears and 'ere Ah still bin'.

Back to churchyards. Darlaston people were alleged to scatter corn in theirs, in an effort to lure the weathercock to fly down. When, in mocking imitation, neighbours at Willenhall took to strewing corn in front of their own church, some Darlaston men scaled St Giles's steeple and stole the weathercock. Not until many years later did it come to light again, hidden in a coal pit.

Other troublesome worshippers were sometimes to be found among the singers and instrumentalists who provided the music, both in church and chapel. A west gallery was installed for such musicians in Wolverhampton's parish church as early as 1610. There was another at Wednesbury. Bilston's Providence Chapel had two galleries, with singing led by a string band. In 1828 at the Meeting Lane Chapel in Stourbridge singers threatened to leave when instruments were banned, unless they might retain a bass viol. As a result, 'it was resolved that the singers should be indulged, and the instrument granted on the following conditions. That they shall bear all the expense of keeping it in repair. That it shall not be used in any other place than our Chapel'. The last condition no doubt alluded to the singers' normal place of practice, in the club room of a neighbouring inn. The bass viol obviously gave good service, since it was not replaced until 1856, when a new instrument cost £3 10s. By this time the chapel, having sold its old site to the Oxford, Worcester and Wolverhampton Railway, had moved to a new building in South Street.

West gallery singers favoured repetitive treatments of words, which sometimes produced unintentionally amusing breaks in the lines of hymns. For example, 'And take thy pilgrim home' became:

And take thy pil-
And take thy pil-
And take thy pilgrim home.

Similarly:

O turn my pi-
O turn my pi-
O turn my pious thoughts to thee.

A Blackheath chainmaker called Joseph Parkes (born in about 1820) wrote hymns with this kind of arrangement, but suffered when tastes moved on.

Charles Perry, a former nailmaker who died in 1907 at the age of 95, had memories of music at Lye Church:

> There was no organ in those days. I usually played the piccolo, but I learnt to play two or three instruments. One of our best singers was a one-legged chainmaker, who used to walk from Brierley Hill. He did not have crutches, but used one big staff, with which he hopped along as fast as you could comfortably walk. He got over stiles as well, and how he did it I don't know. …
>
> As well as helping as church cleaner I used to ring the bell now and then. The proper bellringer was a blind man named Bennett, who also cleaned the clock. He was quite a character. In the morning he used to go round to wake the people up. At every group of houses he would play his fiddle, and cry the hour and the weather, like this: 'Four o'clock and a fine morning'. Very few people had clocks, and the church bell was rung at five in the morning and eight at night to tell them the time.

The vicar at Lye, Rev. Hudson, who had formed the band in which Charles Perry played, put forward a bizarre claim to have the right to mine clay and coal on the church site, and he set about having a shaft sunk. He desisted, though, in the face of vigorous protest, and moved elsewhere. Parishioner power ensured that until 1871 parsons at St Leonard's, Bilston, were elected, not appointed. The same applied at Willenhall, except that voting was limited to those who

St Leonard's Church, Bilston; and Rev. Charles Leigh (incumbent, 1871-1909), the last vicar there to be elected by parishioners

William Moreton, known as 'Old Mowton'

owned inherited land. Their choice had to be approved by the lord of the manor and the dean of Wolverhampton. In 1759 it fell on Rev. William Moreton, an illegitimate son of George IV, and a passionate follower of blood sports, including cock fighting. Only after thirty-six years of wrangling and litigation was his appointment confirmed. He could not afford to pay the lawyer, who sequestered his living and 'paid him a small weekly sum for the rest of his life, which he passed very much in the public house, a little in the poor tenement he called home, and very little in the pulpit'. Nevertheless, Moreton was popular, and the derogatory rhyme which alludes to him came not from parishioners but outsiders:

A tumbledown church,
A tottering steeple,
A drunken parson
And a wicked people.

A similar verse from Walsall seems to give a point of view from inside:

Our new church, our new steeple,
Our proud parson, our poor people.

Autocratic parsons did not necessarily incur the disapproval of their congregations. Rev. J.H. Thompson, incumbent at Cradley in the second half of the nineteenth century, walked with sticks after an accident, and was inevitably known as 'Tummy-Tew-Sticks'. He would inspect for cleanliness the hands of boys going into the school. Dirty hands would be hit with one of his sticks; clean would be rewarded with a gobstopper. Adults wearing false hair or eyebrows, make-up or conspicuous dress, either inside or outside the church, would be sternly reprimanded.

The deference implied in people's acceptance of such rebukes was not universal. A very different impression comes from the description by Benjamin Leadbetter of a penitential session in Dudley parish church in 1849, during the incumbency of Dr J.C. Browne:

> The church was crowded on Sunday morning to see a man doing penance in consequence of a sentence passed on him. It was performed in the presence of a large congregation, assembled from all parts of the district — the majority of whom were of the lower order. Some persons of more respectable positions had evinced great anxiety to procure pews and seats, and on the opening of the church doors a rush took place, and every part

> of the church was instantly filled. The screen was occupied by bargees, who sat astride; the capitals of the column had human occupants; and in other parts struggling and fighting arose for a good view of the penitent, a man called Smith, a gardener and fiddler, whose offence was having slandered Mrs James. The Minister on coming to the service was saluted with the shout, 'Speak up, old boy', accompanied by a chorus of laughter.
>
> The sermon was interrupted by the breaking of windows by the mob outside the church, by cat-calls, whistling, and other unseemly noises, and a dog fight in the building later divided the attention of the congregation with the ceremony of penance. The arrival of Smith the fiddler was at length announced by a tremendous uproar, which put an end to the sermon. He was received with three hearty cheers and the most discordant applause of his friends, many of whom were smoking tobacco. The crush was so bad that Smith had to be put in the churchwarden's pew. He waved over his head the paper containing his recantation, and was welcomed with one cheer more, after which a broom, hassock, pieces of pew, etc. were thrown in all directions, aimed at the head of the clergyman. Smith, at the conclusion, was carried on the shoulders of several of the mob to the Plough Inn.

Rather more seemly ceremonies were spread through much of the year. The ritual of clipping the church — joining hands to encircle it — took place until the 1920s on Shrove Tuesday at Cradley, the result of a revival of seventy or eighty years earlier. The hymn, 'We love this place, O God', featured in a short service, usually accompanied, wrote a participant, 'by the howl of the wind and the swishing of the rain'. A further revival on Mothering Sunday ran for a few years in the 1950s at St Peter's, Darby End, Netherton. For the most part, church clipping in the Black Country seems to have died out during the early nineteenth century. According to G.T. Lawley it took place at Easter:

> The children were assembled in the schoolroom and marshalled by the beadle and other parish officers, in procession, and then proceeded to the church. When the head of the procession arrived there, the first child turned her back to the building, the second then took her right hand, and so every child in succession until the building was surrounded, when they sang the hymn commencing 'Round about thy temple, Lord'. The procession then re-formed and was marched back to the schoolroom, where they were regaled with tea and buns, and after that engaged in simple and harmless amusements.

Among a set of fifteenth-century misericords is St Matthew's Church at Walsall is one showing a man carrying flowers in what can be presumed to be a Rogationtide procession. At Rogationtide (the three days preceding Ascension Day) parish bounds were beaten, with pauses for prayers, hymns and read-

Fifteenth-century misericords from St Matthew's Church, Walsall. Top: man with flowers who could have been taking part in a Rogationtide procession. Lower: A figure seated on a dragon and playing a stringed instrument with a bow. The carvings are said to have come from Halesowen Abbey

ings from the bible. Under the east end of St Matthew's is an archway which provides a porch to the crypt entrance and also gives access from the south of the churchyard to the north. According to David Vodden 'when the church was extended to the limit of the churchyard, an arch was needed to ensure the retention of a Rogationtide processional route all round the building'. The practice of pausing beneath a substantial tree for Rogationtide readings gave rise to street names such as Gospel Oak Road (and public house) in Tipton and Gospel End Road in Sedgley. A problem with Gospel End Village was that people took the first two words literally, and believed that all those living beyond were ungodly. In 1985 at the age of 80 Archie Butler remembered Rogation Days at Holy Trinity, Heath Town, when 'the children walked in the nearby allotments and blessed the crops, and many amusing remarks were quietly made when viewing old Ted Haywood's spring onions'. A detailed description of the Oldswinford parish bounds dates from 1733 (see panel overleaf). The bounds were important

Passage beneath the east end of St Matthew's Church, Walsall

Sedgley Church (postcard, c.*1904)*

because they determined where tithes were paid. Disputes on the subject could lead to considerable animosity. One wonders how many of the place names and of the physical features mentioned have survived to the present.

On Ascension Day at Sedgley until the 1890s the choir sang at dawn from the top of the church tower hymns including 'Hail the day that sees him rise'. Considerable numbers turned up to hear, then attended a communion service starting at 5 a.m.

Until at least the 1950s, early in May, in the week before the Sunday School Festival at St James the Great's Church at Gornal Wood, hundreds arrived at the churchyard to scrub and whitewash gravestones and to deck them with flowers. The custom dated back to the 1840s, and perhaps earlier. Something similar is reported some thirty years earlier from Ruiton, before the anniversary of the Congregational Sunday School. Neighbours keenly competed for the honour of achieving the most attractive gravestone. Chapel and Sunday School anniversary celebrations and outings were highlights of the year until well within living memory.

Where chapels had outings, the Church of England had wakes, prayer vigils originally, but long since turned into secular entertainments. They usually took place on or near the day of a church's patron saint, though in some cases other dates seem to have been arbitrarily chosen. They are considered in detail, along with the fairs they came to resemble, in chapter 10. F.W. Hackwood wrote that the approach

Oldwinsford Parish Bounds as recorded in 1733

The bounds against Kingswinford begin by the river side in Mr. Dudley Brittle's meadow, over against Low Lunt, all which meadow but about the upper fourth part is in Oldswinford, the first X [mark] which marks the bounds against Kingswinford is on Gray's Bank, near Scut's Gutter, which runs up to the Level Leasow, which is Paul Rogers', and so by the ditch and Widow Allchurch's garden and house to the X on Amblecote Bank, thence round Whittimore by the gutter side and through Mr. Raybould's ox leasow to the gutter mouth meadow, and thence round the west side of Bendy Coppy and the east side of Bendy lands, which are in Oldswinford parish, and so to the Phimbriel Leasow, at the corner of Brittle Lane, then by the north hedge of the Platts Leasows, which are Mr. Henzeys, to the Stower side over against Woolaston Coppy, where the boys sometimes cross the water and go along by the river side to the X at Oldford, at the bottom of Dividale, where the bounds end against Kinswinford and begin against Kinfare [Kinver] and run up to the X at the Newwood Gate, about which there is a dispute between Kinfare and Oldswinford. The Kinfare people say their bounds reach to the green path to the corner of the piece of ground at Oldford, and accordingly make their X by the green path. The people of Oldswinford say the ditch without the wood is the extremity of Kinfare bounds, and accordingly make their X near the ditch at the Wood Gate, from the Gate or green path the bounds run to the X at the south corner of the Wood over against the Ridge, and thence along the Ridge top to Mr. Haycock's farm, thence to the X at Wm. Parr's gate, then over the Hill to the corner of Norton's piece, where the bounds begin against Pedmore and to the X near the top of the Slough Ditch, and crossing that along the green trig to Chapman's gate, then across the moor, and up Hobson's meadow to the Lane over against the south hedge of Job Raby's garden in Upper Swinford. There was a dispute many years between the inhabitants of Oldswinford and Pedmore concerning their bounds upon the Hill before Parr's Farm. The Oldswinford parishioners made a X at Parr's Corner, but in the year 1730 it was agreed between the Rectors and some of the inhabitants of the two parishes that the bounds should be as they are above described. Then we go from the south hedge of Job Raby's garden and and cross the road and along the Lane to Mr. Spencer's ground and down by the south hedge to Jas. Boucher's meadow, and so to Jno. Orford's meadow, and along by the west hedge to the ground called Noman's Land; thence up to the Longcroft and along by the east side of the Hides, which leads to the top of Hob Green, so down by the watercourse of Hob Dingle to the tayl of Woolscoat Pool and along by the south edge of Brookal or Harts Meadow to Sensal Well, thence up the vally of Sensal Close to the X 10 or 12 yards on the north-west of the stile leading to Fosent and by the hedge side, then along the pathway of Newbrough's Sensal to Fosent and along Mr. Hill's five acres to the Little Meadow and down to the foredraught to the great meadow across Ludlee Road to the Lower Meadow, and from the gate streight along the footpath to the corner of Pargiter's meadow hedge and down to the lower corner of that piece where we make the X against Halesowen Parish and go up the north side to the X in the upper furlong, so into the Pikes and up the footpath into the Broad Image and so to the X at Oldnal

Gate and along the lane to Mr. Hill's house, so down the Well Leasow and down the Dingle of the Oldnal Leasow wich is Mr. Edwd. Badger's to the Brickill Close down by the dingle side to Saltbrook, from thence along the Stower side to the Lye Forge, from thence to the first place in the bounds above mentioned.

of the wakes gave 'the signal for a vigorous campaign of house-cleaning, of white-washing and re-painting, repairing and renovating, … all in the expecta-

Wednesbury's Leabrook Chapel Sunday School Anniversary, 1920s

The banner of St. Luke's Church School, Cradley Heath, carried in procession (undated photograph)

tion of visitors from far and near'. A special wake brew of beer would be made, and 'no caller, however slight the acquaintance, but was made welcome to as much as he could eat and drink'. An alternative to the Gornal woman's three commandments quoted in chapter 2 were the four seasons of 'Chrissmus and Aystertite, our waake, and Whissuntite'.

> Here lies an old ringer, beneath this cold clay,
> Who rang many peals both serious and gay.
> Through majors and trebles with ease he could range,
> Till death called the bob, and brought round the last change.
> (Henry Sedgwick, beadle and ringer, died 1838, aged 59
> [St Matthew's Church, Walsall]. The same epitaph was used for
> John Ashton, ringer, died 1857 [St Bartholomew's, Wednesbury])

CHAPTER 4

Weddings and Funerals

'Putting the beans to bile' meant in Black Country vernacular to have the banns of marriage read. The phrase, 'going with someone', indicated an engagement, as in the reported comment: 'Our Liz goos wi that lanky good-fur-nuthin, but if her marries him her'll ha' to keep him, sure as housen'. Another expression warned against 'marrying the miskin [midden] for the muck and getting pisoned with the stink on it'; that is, marrying for money and being unhappy as a consequence. Perhaps even this would have been better than one of the curiously-named 'knobstick weddings', when a parish paid a sum of money to a man as an incentive to marry a women he had made pregnant. One of perhaps many such cases occurred at Oldswinford in 1738, when Richard Jones was promised 3s. 6d. if he would wed the unfortunate Elizabeth Ellits.

Another sad pair feature in the account of a wedding in 1877, given to Cliff Willetts by his mother, the bride:

> She worked as a chainmaker in a shop at the corner of Lyde Green and Bridge Street, Cradley, with some other twelve women and girls. At about 11 a.m. she stopped work. She put her hammer and tongs in the bosh, a cast-iron receptacle where they were put to cool. She put her arms in the bosh, fifthy water of course, and dried them with her sweat cloth. She then wiped her face with the sweat cloth. She put on a shawl and fastened it with a safety pin. She put on her cloth cap and put a hat pin through to keep it on. She discarded her chainmaker's apron and put on a clean white pinafore. She couldn't change her hob-nailed shoes, as she only had one pair. As she walked out of the shop, she informed her workmates she wouldn't be long. She returned about an hour later, her friends having no idea where she had been. When they commented she had been a long time, she calmly showed them her wedding ring and remarked: 'Well, yo cor get married in five minutes, cor yer?'

> She had met her groom outside the Cradley Parish Church. They didn't even arrange for any witnesses. They waited until a woman came along to put flowers on a grave and later a man came along and they asked them to go into the church with them. They left the church and after a thank-you to their two witnesses, whom they didn't even know, they made their way back to their respective chain shops and started to work. When questioned as to why they didn't at least have a drink to celebrate the auspicious occasion, the bride replied they couldn't afford it, as the church fees had cost enough. When further questioned as to why they didn't have at least a wedding embrace, she calmly replied, 'We day have time for that saftness, as we had to goo back to work'.
>
> As she nearly always ended the reminiscence of what she described as the happiest day of her life, she said, 'I had to work till 9 that night instead of 8. That was my honeymoon'.

Those with rather more latitude exercised great care over the ceremony. The month of May was avoided as unlucky; so were Wednesdays and Fridays. On the other hand, Whitsuntide was favoured; so was Tuesday. The colour green for the bride's dress aroused particular revulsion: 'If yo'm gottner no other frock but ner green un to be married in, doh yo goo to church, that's all, or yo'n loosener yor mon afore lung if yo dun'. So said the wife of a collier overheard by G.T. Lawley in Bilston, where the custom lingered of handing the bride a pair of white gloves to symbolise virginity. A groom not only wore a buttonhole of bachelor's button, perhaps a final affirmation of his single status, but had some of the flowers stuffed in his pockets.

For the bridal party on its way to the church to meet a funeral cortege was, not surprisingly, a bad omen. On the other hand, for a bride to see the groom after midnight on the wedding eve, until the couple met in church, was dire. This is Tom Langley's narrative of his great aunt, Emma, who was born in 1848 and lived in Tipton:

The marriage ceremony, from an eighteenth-century woodcut

Wedding party at the Cottage Inn, High Street, Kingswinford, 1900. The groom was Fred Caddick, pig killer, and the bride, Alice Whittingham

> It's an owd belief in the Black Country that if a woman oo's gettin' married saw the bloke 'er was going to marry after midnight on the marriage day 'er'd be far better jed than 'ave 'im. The women'd look anywheer and they'd go to bed early the night afower they got married so they wouldn't see 'im. My great aunt 'appened to wake up about 'alf past one in the mornin' and 'er looked through the window. It was a bright, moonlight night, and oo should be comin' out o' me grandfather's pub over the road but this bloke 'er was goin' to marry, and 'er watched 'im turn into a devil. But it was too late. 'Er got married next day, and I might tell yo 'er *did* marry a devil as well. 'Er 'ad twenty-five 'ear on 'im and at the finish 'e passed on. 'Er went upstairs and laid 'im out, and when 'er come down 'er said 'er prayers. It went summut like this. 'Er says: 'Well, Lord, I ain't a-goin' a-grumble. Yo'm took 'im at last, but if yo'll excuse me sayin' so, yo'm bin a bloody long while about it'. 'Er says: 'Them twenty-five 'ear might ony bin a few minutes to yo up theer, but they bin a lifetime to me down 'ere'. 'Er suddenly thought 'er might be lookin' in the wrong direction so 'er looked down and 'er says: 'God 'elp yo if yo've got 'im'.

According to a strong Black Country belief, a married women if she wished to remain loyal to her husband should never remove the wedding ring from her finger once he had placed it there. If the ring were to wear out or be damaged it had to be carefully preserved once the husband replaced it with another. A local saying claiming, 'As your wedding ring wears it will wear away cares', implied that a marriage improved with time.

Left: Branks, or Scold's Bridle, from a sheet of illustrations from Plot's Natural History of Staffordshire *(1686). The device would have been secured at the back of the head, and at the front the tab marked 'e' would have been inserted in the mouth*

The reverse could, of course, be the case, and devices like the branks or scold's bridle and the ducking or cucking stool came into play. It is fair to say that on occasion the humiliating ritual was used against men, but women were the main victims. The antiquary, Robert Plot, wrote with great enthusiasm in 1686 of the 'artifice' of which there was an example at Walsall:

> For correcting of *Scolds*, which it does too so effectively, and so very safely, that I look upon it as much to be preferr'd to the *Cucking-Stoole*, which not only endangers the *health* of the *party*, but also gives the

A ducking stool as depicted in an eighteenth-century woodcut

> *tongue* liberty 'twixt every dipp; to neither of which this is at all lyable: it being such a *Bridle* for the *tongue*, as not only quite deprives them of *speech*, but brings shame for the transgression, and humility thereupon, before 'tis taken off.

Records show the expenditure at Walsall of 6d. in 1662 'For getting ye cucking stool out of ye town brooke' (which may indicate the device's unpopularity), and at Bilston of 10s. in 1695 'For a new ducking stoole for ye parish' (which may indicate repeated use). As late as 1924 F.W. Hackwood noted that 'Tradition refers to the rotting and rusty remnant' of a ducking stool 'lingering in a cattle pond near the old manor house of Wednesbury'.

Nevertheless, as Thomas Pinnock pointed out, in the Black Country 'among the lower class of ironworkers, miners, and brickmakers there lingers the old tradition of the superior rights of man, and the meek women of the class acknowledge the authority claimed by uniformly speaking of the husband as "our master". One of the rights which years ago used to be tacitly allowed was the privilege of administering correction to negligent or cantankerous spouses'. Pinnock, writing in 1893, went on to describe the case of a man living near Wednesbury some forty years earlier who 'had the misfortune to be tied to a veritable virago, who was the curse of his life'. He 'succeeded in moderating her behaviour by occasional thrashing, which she no doubt richly deserved', but he then turned Methodist, and 'abandoned wife-beating along with some other evil habits'. However, his wife saw the conversion as giving her impunity to taunt him with no fear of the consequences, until at last, in despair, he went to his church and resigned, then went home, after which:

> He locked and bolted the door, and reaching down a supple cane which had done similar service in days gone by, he quietly but sternly told his wife he was going to give her what she had been so long asking for. The woman laughed in his face, told him he daren't lay a finger on her, for if he did she would go straight to the parson, and he would be called before the church meeting and expelled. Then she fairly danced round the house in an ecstasy of tantalising revelry. But when the husband quietly told her he had already given up his class and left the church, she sank on her knees and a most pitiful state of terror, imploring mercy, and promising reformation if only he would forgive her this once.

Pinnock approvingly comments that 'his plan effected an almost perfect cure of the chiding wife', but adds that 'a man who habitually, or with undue severity, corrected his spouse would call down upon himself the condemnation of the whole neighbourhood'. Straw would be strewn in front of an offender's door, and if he were in any doubt as to its significance he would be told: 'Well, after a thrashing there's generally plenty o' straw'. The next step in the case

> A little boy said to his father, 'Dad, in this book it says that a man and his wife who are always quarrelling are leading a cat and dog life'. 'Yes', said the father, 'that's what they call it'. 'I can't understand it, Dad. Look at our cat and dog on the hearth. They don't quarrel'. 'No', said the father, 'they don't now, but yo tie 'em together and see what 'appens'.

of a squabbling couple, would be for villagers to 'set themselves to make the locality "too warm" for the obstreperous couple. And, as one means to the end, what is called a marrow-bones and cleaver band, but what is really a collection of old pans and kettles beaten by neighbours with pokers and sticks, would perform a noisy serenade underneath the windows, whenever the "differings" of husband and wife became audible to outsiders'.

If marital discord became unbearable, a couple could embark on the form of divorce — entirely outside the law, but widely believed to be legitimate — known as wife selling. The practice was well enough known nationally in the 1840s for Dickens to cause Edith Granger, a character in *Dombey and Son*, to remark: 'I suffered myself to be sold as infamously as any woman with a halter round her neck is sold in any market-place'. The ritual is seen here as degrading, but the wife's acquiescence would have been needed. There are a dozen or so recorded instances involving Black Country people, stretching over a period of some two hundred years.

The first of these is quoted by Hackwood from 'an old document relating to Bilston': 'November 1692. John, y^{e} son of Nathan Whitehouse, of Tipton, sold his wife to Mr Bracegirdle'. No more details are given, but in 1720 *Lloyd's Magazine* offered a fuller report from 'an old town in South Staffordshire':

The sale of a wife as shown in a woodcut from a street ballad with that title, printed by J. Catnach of London, c.*1832*

> It appeared that the husband had set his affections on another woman, and his wife hearing of it, had very justly showed her displeasure in a variety of ways; whereupon the husband, who was a collier, took her to the market-place, and sold her to the highest bidder for five shillings. There was much excitement in the crowd which assembled to witness the act, and the affair ended with a good deal of drinking at the expense of the husband and the purchaser.

Further sales were recorded in Aris's *Birmingham Gazette* at Rowley Regis in 1745, and in the *Annual Register* at the Bell Inn in Birmingham's Edgbaston Street in 1773 (a date wrongly given by Hackwood as 1733). In the latter case, Samuel Whitehouse of Willenhall sold his wife, Mary, for one guinea. Then followed a gap of almost half a century before the account of an event at Bilston in 1819 which G.T. Lawley reprinted, without indicating the source, in a newspaper article of 1921. It is worth quoting in full:

> It was announced by the bellman on a Saturday in May, 'Jimmy the Grinder' would put up his wife to auction in the Pig Market to the highest bidder, and that gentlemen in search of a partner were requested to attend, as the said 'Moll' was good-looking, young, and could cook, wash, bake, etc. The announcement, delivered in the broad dialect of the district, and embellished with various humorous additions which the fancy of the bellman or the auditors suggested on the spur of the moment, was greeted with laughter from the crowd, which, following the 'crier' from street to street, and receiving fresh accessions of numbers at every stand he made, at last contained nearly all the resident roughs (male and female) of the town, while the comments and criticisms uttered made a perfect babel. Having accomplished his mission and 'cried' himself till he could cry no longer without being moistened, the bellman resorted to his favourite pub, where, accompanied by a few choice spirits, and plentifully supplied with ditto by the liberality of his attendants, he retailed for their edification as much as he knew (and more) of the causes of the proposed divorce from bed and board of the said Moll, all of which information was soon filtered through various channels to the lady gossips of the place, and was soon as common as the air they breathed, and quite as fresh as the beer they usually consumed.
>
> On the day appointed, the local market place was tolerably full of men, women, and children, all assembled to partake directly ot indirectly in the various humours and incidents of the scene. Though so great a crowd would on these occasions be brought together that a stranger would have naturally concluded that the annual wake was in progress, yet it is doubtful if one of the number had the least idea that the proceedings were outside the law. Indeed, such care was taken in carrying out the formularies which custom had sanctioned as to give a sort of legal force to the proceedings. In the first place the husband was bound to buy a new halter,

which on the morning of the sale he tied round his wife's neck, as we see a butcher deal with a calf or a horse which he is taking to market for sale. Holding the end of the rope he next proceeded to drive her through the nearest toll-gate, where he paid toll for her at the usual rate charged for a cow, a horse, or a pig. In some instances the husband had been known to drive the unfortunate wife through three toll-gates and pay the toll in each instance, to make the proceedings more binding. During this perambulation the husband and wife were accompanied by a noisy crowd of admirers, with whom husband and wife frequently exchanged remarks, not always in the choicest English, and frequently of the most immodest nature. Sometimes the husband and three or four supporters were armed with sticks, which they were not slow in using whenever the crowd grew too demonstrative, or encroached upon the royal road they had to travel. Another necessary formality was the strictness with which the husband kept to the time, arriving at the market place as near the hour announced as possible, and generally as the church clock was striking the hour. Their arrival was greeted with a tumultuous shout from the assembled crowd, followed by jeers, laughter, coarse wit, and filthy language, such as the humour of the situation either suggested or provoked. In the centre of the market place a chair and table had already been provided, or if they were not available a substitute was found in inverted tubs or anything handy, and on these the woman and her husband stood, the observed of all observers: while in front stood perhaps the intending purchaser, who was generally known beforehand to the principal parties concerned, and between whom and the woman glances of mutual understanding passed.

The next necessary formality was that the husband should act as his own auctioneer, and knock down his wife in public, as he may have done dozens of times in the privacy of his own castle. Having mounted the rostrum, and called for silence, which was not easily obtained, the husband began to describe the conditions of sale, but the cries and jeers continued, until at last the men with the cudgels, who had formed round the platform as a guard, were obliged to resort to those wooden arguments which they plied with remarkable success about the ears of the nearest rowdies, who are amenable, as a rule, only to logic of that type. In the meantime the husband whiled away the time in drinking deeply from a large stone bottle, which had been filled with beer at the nearest public-house. Nor was he, perhaps, unneighbourly, but offered it to the woman, who in turn drank and handed it, without protest from her lord and master, to the intending purchaser in front. At last tolerable silence was obtained, and then the husband commenced. He narrated in choice idiomatic sentences the business they had to transact, enlarged on his 'Moll's' good and bad qualities, called attention to her 'points', her eyes, hair, teeth, etc., and incidentally alluded to certain reasons which had induced him to dispose of so capital and desirable possession. 'Her's as sound as a roach in wind an' limb; her con baake, an' wesh, an' brew'. 'Ah, thee bist reet', shouted a voice, 'an' her con drink a sup, Jimmy, yo' bet'. 'Ah', retorted the husband, laughing, 'her con do a tot full as well as the nex'. Her con mak' a suit o' clo's good's any snip'. 'An' con wear the britches', shouted a voice again from the crowd, a remark which was greeted with uproarious cheers. 'Her con swear like a trooper, an' fight like a game cock', continued the husband. 'Now, wot shan I say for her; who'll bid?' Somebody humorously offered a penny token, another suggested a 'joey' [6d. coin], a bid which tickled the fancy of the audience immensely, because the intending purchaser was known as 'Joey' among his neighbours. At last, after the crowd had been permitted to indulge their taste in chaff sufficiently, Joey, the intending purchaser, offered five shillings, and as there was no higher bidder, the woman was knocked down. Here the public proceedings terminated, but not so far as regarded the principals and their bodyguard. The latter, with their wooden arguments, had to clear a way to the nearest public-house for the heroes of the hour, through the press of jeering, laughing, swearing crowd, and it was not until many blows had been exchanged, and sundry phrenological developments produced upon the craniums of the most demonstrative, that the retreat was made. Having reached the inn, the final formalities were concluded. The end of the halter was transferred from the husband's to the purchaser's hand, the paper drawn up by 'a learned clerk' making the transfer duly signed, the halter as duly removed, and then the purchase money was spent in spirits and beer, the party drinking together as good humouredly as though no such thing as a divorce.

Inordinate interest accompanied the wife sales which continued sporadically throughout the nineteenth century (see table), and there were echoes even in the twentieth.

Date	**Place**	**Name**	**Price**
*c.*1823	Wednesbury: market place	Moses Maggs (Rough Moey)	3 gallons of ale
1824	W-- (?Walsall) market	Lydia Jones	10s., a quart of ale, paid the toll
1830	Dudley: market place	Moses Whitehouse	A gallon of ale
1837	Walsall: market place	Hutchinson, from Burntwood	2s. 6d.
1840	Stourbridge	Gibbon	2s.
1848	Bilston: market	Harry R	50s.
1849	Brierley Hill: via the Merry Hill turnpike		6d.
1853	Tipton		6d.
1859	Dudley		6d.
before 1901	Cradley		

Sally Lett, or, A Wife for Sale (A Bilston Ballad)

Ding-a-dong, ding-a-dong,
O, ha! O, ha! O, ha!
Ding-a-dong, ding-a-dong!

This is to gi' notice
That bandy-legged Lett
Will sell his wife, Sally,
For what he con get.

At twelve o'clock sertin
The sale'll begin;
So all yer gay fellers
Be there wi' yur tin.

For Sally's good lookin'
An' sound as a bell,
If you'n on'y once heerd her
You'n know that quite well.

Her bakes bread quite handy,
An' eats it all up;
Brews beer like a good un,
An' drinks ev'ry sup.

Her wears mon's breeches,
So all the folks say;
But Lett shouldna let her
Have all her own way.

Her swears like a trooper
And fights like a cock,
And has gin her old feller
Many a hard knock.

So now yo' young fellers
As wantin' a wife,
Come an' bid for old Sally,
The plague of Lett's life.

At twelve i' the mornin'
The sale'll begin;
So yo' as wants splicin'
Be theer wi' yer tin.

From a newspaper article of 1921 by G.T.Lawley

In January 1925 a Stourbridge newspaper carried an item about the recent death at Bilston of a woman who, many years earlier, had been sold by her husband to a lodger for sixpence: 'The details are that differences arose between the man and his wife. In the house was a lodger, who offered a "tanner" for her. The coin, it is stated, was thrown on the table, the bargain completed, and a receipt presented and signed'. In this case the formalities were abbreviated. Tom Langley, who died in 1980, passed on to me this family story: 'Now in 1853 my granddad, he saw a woman sold at Tipton, and she was sold for sixpence and the bids went up by a halfpenny. She was a poor little slip of a girl who'd been half starved. She was only twenty years of age and the chap who bought her he took her home and he said, "I'll soon put some flesh on 'er bones. I'll feed 'er on fat baacon". And he did. Now I can tell you this, that three of her children became school teachers'.

Wife sales were rare, and they attracted huge interest. Most marriages lasted, unremarked in some cases, until a memorial stone recorded a partnership of long duration. For example, in the chancel of the parish church at Darlaston a plaque commemorates the sixty-two years during which Walter and Joyce Wilkes were married. They died respectively in 1692 and 1705, aged 82 and 97.

Sometimes, though, the animosity of one partner towards another lingered even after death. A nineteenth-century businessman, 'Wily' Webster, insisted on this epitaph for his sharp-tongued wife:

Beneath this stone in deep repose,
Now in heaven — I suppose?
Lies one whose faith was ever strong,
A woman who could do no wrong.
She ran Ye Olde Antique Shoppe, Lye,
And me as well — but by and by
Her lusty lungs ran out of breath,
And quickly swooped the wings of death.
She lies — lip sealed — without a sound,
So if you'd hear my tale of woe,
To Ye Olde Antique Shoppe you must go.
It's only a walk of bare a minnit,
And what bargains galore you'll find within it,
So hurry on, dear tombstone scanner,
Come and hear my tale and spend a tanner.

The Lye councillors, distinctly unamused, had the stone removed, and left outside the churchyard. Webster, who was enjoying the publicity, paid for it to be replaced, but unknown local people took it away under cover of darkness, and smashed it in a nearby field. Another example of enduring bitterness comes from Tom Langley, who told me this in 1970, adding to the narrative of his great aunt's experiences (see above), after the death of her husband:

> 'Er lived twenty-five year after 'e'd gone, and 'er lived to see 'er family reared. When the little grandchildren used to get round 'er. They clustered round 'er and they'd say: 'Tell we a tale, grandmother, about we grandfayther as we never sin'. I suppose twenty-five years without 'im 'ad lent a bit of enchantment to 'er — 'er dae want to let 'im down — so 'er used to say: 'Ar, well, if 'e was no good 'e wor too bad'. 'Er said: 'There was ony one thing wrong with 'im, and that was two', 'er says, 'and both of 'em was the same. Whatever yer gid 'im it wor right, and when yo put it right it was bloody wrong. 'E could eat all right an drink all right and sleep all right but as soon as yo mentioned work 'e went all of a bloody tremble', 'er says.
>
> 'Never mind, 'e 'ad a gravestone as good as anybody'. But 'er didn't tell the grandchildren 'er wanted to put on it: ''E was a 'oly terror'. The parson wouldn't stand that. 'E said it sounded a bit ambiguous so 'er 'ad put on it: 'The angels got lonely, so they took 'im'. On Sunday mornin's when, like all the other women, 'er used to go out and scrub the gravestones, 'er'd be talkin' to 'erself and 'er'd say: 'Ar, the angels got lonely so they took 'im. I bet they bloody dee keep 'im long, neither'.

In a traditional story, Ayli's wife on her death-bed tries to select her successor:

> She says, 'Come 'ere, Ayli. I want to 'ave a word wi' yo'. 'What is it, m' wench?' 'Now', 'er says, 'doh yo forget Benny Simpkins down the road owes yo five bob'. 'E says, 'Ah sher forget, m' wench', and then looks round to th' audience 'oo were sittin' round the bedside, and then 'e says, ''Ark at 'er. Sensible to the last, ain't 'er'. And 'er says, 'Ar, and o' course we ae paid for last wik's groceries to owd gel Downton yet'. 'E says, 'Ah know. 'Er's a-wanderin''. And 'er says, 'Now, Ah sher be long 'ere but afore Ah goo, Ah want yo t' 'ev Widder Jones down the road. Ah've towd 'er just what yo like and 'ow yer like yer grorty puddin' cooked'. And 'e says, 'Well, Ah'm sorry, m' wench, to disappoint yer, but Ah'm med other arrangements'.

An intriguing contrast is provided in the story by Stanley Griffiths, of a man who changes his mind about committing suicide when he realises that someone else would inherit his wife. It concerns Jack Green, a 'foundry foreman who understood his men' and Joe Shaw, 'a good moulder in the foundry but a bad modeller of his own life'. The two men happen to meet when the latter is on his way to drown himself. Jack speaks:

> 'Wheerst gooen, Joe? To drownd theeself thee sest — right-o, I'll cum wi thee to see thee dust et proper, for like as not theest change thee mind, and that woe du', and coming to the canal continued, 'I sid um pull Sol Smart out o' the cut, jost ov ere an' he was jed enoo and blue with code, and when 'is missus sid 'im 'er said, "Fancy me ever makken a fuss uv a

thing like that", so if I was yo, Joe, I shud find sum waeter as is waerm, and ef we gozz down ter the Congraves [iron works], theer's a waerm pool theer, and the stroll un wear thee down a bit an et woe tak sur long to choke — an another thing — yo woe look ser bad when y' 'ome stiff.

'Yo bay a-counten on nobody greeven bin yer, Joe? 'cos the tears as'll be spilled fer thee woe mak a cupple o'dacent dewdraps, but thee missis mite be a bit sorry fo' thee, but why er shood God knows fer theest bin a varmint, Joe. Thy missis is a nice bit o' stuff, Joe, and why yer trated er ser bad I doe know, but when theest under the sod I inten's ter mak up to er meesel'. At this point the story is brought to an abrupt conclusion by the would-be suicide who, his gloomy project quite forgotten, pushes his tormentor into the canal instead of himself, a proceeding which fails to damp the latter's sense of humour.

From Black Dots *(1943), by S.A. Griffiths*

It would be a mistake to believe that Black Country people treated death light-heartedly. Colliers saw omens in a whole string of phenomena (see chapter 7). Others also believed in warnings. Hackwood quotes the case of a young woman called Louisa Benn, from Queen Street, Wednesbury, who in 1887 set off for Plymouth to travel as a passenger on the ship, *Kapunda*. Her mother immediately began having graphic dreams of a catastrophic shipwreck, in which her daughter was crying for help. She telegraphed the girl, who by then was on board, to return home immediately. The daughter, abandoning her luggage, which could not be removed from the hold, obeyed. The vessel sailed, and was lost, with great loss of life. Rather less dramatic signs of death were believed to include:

a cinder (known in Wednesbury as a 'coffin') flying out of the fire;
a child's marble rolling down the stairs;
a persistently howling dog;
a sparrow flying into a room;
a cradle being rocked with no baby in it.

It was a common belief in the Black Country that wearing a man's clothes within twelve months after his death would have unpleasant consequences for anyone doing so; and the ancient practice of informing the bees of a death in the family lingered until the twentieth century. According to a newspaper report of 1926 a Quarry Bank women had 'undying faith in the "three raps" which she hears at her bedroom door prior to the death of any member of the family'.

In his book on Sedgley, Hackwood related the story told to him by a Wolverhampton woman who was out with her mother in fields near Penn Road when she noticed a tall figure. 'Look, mother', she said, 'at that woman walking by your side'. 'I see nobody', her mother replied. 'It's only your fancy'. The figure disappeared, but next day the mother was taken ill, and the following day she died, at the time they had seen the figure in the fields.

A moribund person was thought to have a death sweat, death lice appearing in the hair, and finally a death rattle. If feather pillows were not removed the sick person would die in lingering agony. There was also a strongly held belief, recorded by Thomas Pinnock, that 'persons dying may have their parting agony prolonged by the unwillingness of their dear ones to "give them up"'. According to Phil Drabble, writing in 1952, 'It is considered that if the front door is closed between the time the coffin goes out and the mourners return, or if the horse drawing the hearse stamps the magical seven times, another death is inevitable within the year'. In 1985, Archie Butler, aged 80, remembered not a death sign but an ancient belief concerning a dead body. When a boy fell into the canal at Heath Town, near Wolverhampton, and drowned, the police placed a loaf of bread on the surface of the water in the expectation that it would come to rest above the body. The earliest recorded instance of such a practice was in 1586.

The unbaptised were denied burial in consecrated ground, so even public cemeteries had unconsecrated areas for the purpose, sometimes with separate entrances. Suicides were buried at a crossroads, with a stake driven through the body. The centre of Oldbury market place is believed to be the site of just such an interment. The practice was brought to an end in 1823, though suicides were still subjected to the indignity of burial at night, without any form of service. In 1929 workmen digging a trench at the junction of Gibbet Lane and High Park Avenue, near Stourbridge Cemetery, where there is now a traffic island, discovered a human skeleton some three feet down. This could have been the remains of a criminal gibbeted nearby, or of a suicide buried at the crossroads. The mystery remained unsolved, and the skeleton was 'disposed of'.

Another enigma came to light in about 1850 when the old church of Oldswinford was demolished. A coffin found with the remains of a lady fully dressed in antique costume contained a very large number of pins, blackened by age, both in the dress and strewed about. A century before that, a highwayman known as Rowley Jack, known for his penchant for fine clothes and horses, operated round Kinver, Rowley Regis and Dudley. One of his haunts was the forge of Abraham Fox at White Heath, which doubled as beerhouse and overnight accommodation for stagecoach travellers. The blacksmith's daughter, Rebecca, was Jack's lover, and she passed information to him on possible targets. Numerous attempts to catch Jack were fruitless, but in January 1754 watchers after midnight saw a lone rider dismount at the stables behind the smithy. Then Rebecca, dressed in male riding habit, came out of the house and went into the stables. The watchers shouted for the pair to come out, but instead, mounted on a single horse they galloped away. A search for the fugitives continued in the moonlight till dawn, but the flint-hard ground yielded no tracks to follow. From that day, no more was seen of either Jack or Rebecca. However, twelve years later members of a historical society were investigating the derelict, fourteenth-century Tividale Hall, when they came across a passage leading to underground

Entrance to the unconsecrated side of the cemetery at Oldbury, 1900

vaults. The way was blocked by a heavy fall of masonry, which was laboriously removed. Beyond were the skeletons of a horse, a man with tricorn hat, riding coat, breeches and spurred boots, and a woman dressed in male attire. Jack and Rebecca's refuge had proved to be their tomb.

Until the early twentieth century, Oldbury retained the division of its cemetery into consecrated and unconsecrated ground, with each having a separate entrance. Another form of humiliation after death was the practice of bringing a suicide out of the house head first, in contrast with the normal practice of feet first. The poor dreaded the stigma of a pauper's funeral, and scraped together a few pence at a time towards the eventual cost of a coffin. Alternatively they subscribed to a sick and burial club (see chapter 13). As late as the 1920s, according to G.T. Lawley, poor people went from house to house begging money to pay to bury a child, a wife, a husband, so as to avoid the disgrace of a pauper's funeral. In earlier times the treatment of paupers was more liberal. Such a funeral, for Alice Beebee, at St Leonard's, Bilston, on 3 April 1717, incurred the expenditure of 10s. 6d., made up as follows:

ale and bread	3s.
for the grave	7d.
for the fees	9d.
for laying out and a cap	8d.
to William Stokes (for bell)	2d.
for forth-fare	4d.
for coffin	5s.

The forth-fare was pay given to men for carrying the body to the grave. Fees for carriers and bearers could be considerable when bodies, as in the case of Bilston, Pelsall, Wednesfield and Willenhall, had to be carried up to three miles to reach the consecrated ground of the mother church at Wolverhampton.

The workhouse system of the nineteenth century instituted a harsh regime for paupers, both in life and in death: 'Rattle his bones over the stones,/He's only a pauper whom nobody owns', wrote Thomas Hood. According to Lawley, 'In Bilston and Willenhall, as elsewhere locally, it was the custom for women to carry paupers who died in the workhouse to the grave, both male and female'.

The practice does not seem to have been recorded elsewhere. The Black Country was known for lavish expenditure on funerals. Lawley again writes:

> These funeral feasts were not confined to the families of well-to-do people: no poor family buried its dead without keeping open house (as far as their means allowed) for all their neighbours to eat and drink. Nor was this extravagance confined to eating and drinking, but in wearing apparel the same disregard of economy was observable — the chief ambition of the bereaved was to give the deceased a 'respectable' send-off, in which they tried to outrival each other, oftentimes causing subsequent destitution and suffering.

He concludes, though, that 'Fortunately the funeral feast, together with hatbands and silk scarves, and other outward symbols of simulated grief, have been largely swept away by a more enlightened public opinion, and now as a rule the dead are laid to rest in a quiet and reverent fashion appropriate to the mournful occasion'. Thomas Griffiths (aged 96) of Cradley Road, Netherton, recalled in 1926 how as a youngster he had seen old-style funerals at which bearers on horseback with long crepe streamers round their hats ceremonially led the hearse to the church.

A strange and unusual parody of such a ritual was recorded (and possibly witnessed) by Frederic Willett, one-time rector of West Bromwich. The hearse was followed by six men on horseback, but instead of crepe streamers they ostentatiously wore flowing, brightly-coloured handkerchiefs in their hats. The dead man, it seems, as an aged widower had married a young wife, then died after only a few weeks and left his entire estate to her. 'The mocking mourners', wrote Willett, 'were the dead man's sons by his first wife, and they expressed their anger at their father's will by insulting his funeral and jeering his young widow'.

Tom Langley had a curious story from his great aunt, who during the course of twenty-five years as a nurse had successively laid out various members of a particular family. 'They'd all died in that hospital and the last one to be laid out it was about midnight, and as she walked away she saw all the others who'd died: that was the mother, the father and an elder brother, gathered at the bedside. Now there was no mistake about that. My aunt wasn't given to imagination. She was able to take in all the details because she'd known all the family'.

CHAPTER 5

Birth and Health

'Weigh a new-born babby? I bay such a fule. Whoy, it ud doi, certain'. Such, until perhaps the 1930s, would have been the sentiments of many Black Country mothers. Indeed, some believed that a child weighed before it was twelve months old would not live out the year. Similarly, neither the hair nor nails of an infant should be cut before its first birthday. The mother had to trim the nails with her teeth. Most babies were delivered by neighbours and friends, or by unqualified local women who had acquired skill and experience in midwifery. There was a time during the 1930s at Cradley, for example, when, in the absence of qualified nurses or midwives, Mrs Hipkiss of Park Lane and Mrs Harper of Windmill Hill officiated at births, for a fee of ten shillings a time. Local midwives charged less than doctors and nurses, and they also helped with child care and household tasks. In addition, their record of cross-infection was lower, since patients provided their own dressings and cloths.

Mr and Mrs William Henry Guest with their son of the same name, who was born at Sedgley in 1909. Baby boys were initially dressed in the same way as girls

Formerly it was the custom for a first son to be given the same christian name as his father, but the notion arose that this could lead to the early death of the boy. G.T. Lawley knew of a family in which three sons died in turn, each successively named after the father. When a fourth son was born the father doggedly wished to continue as before but the mother in the end insisted on a change of name. She triumphantly claimed vindication when the child thrived.

Biblical names were widely favoured. F.W. Hackwood tells the story of a Wednesbury soccer team which included 'an Eli and a Job, a Daniel and an Amos, to say nothing of Benjamin, Joseph and Samuel', which in the 1870s travelled to Oxford to play a university XI. During the game the players repeatedly called to each other by name, which caused one of the undergraduates to remark: 'By Jupiter, these fellows have brought a team of prophets and patriarchs against our ungodly crew!' Biblical names are very well represented in the list compiled by Ken Walker from Black Country gravestones (see panel below).

In view of such exoticism, it is surprising that the relatively innocuous Valerie proved to be an obstacle when George Dunn's sister came to be christened in 1884:

> When she [her mother] took 'er up to Quarry Bank Church to be christened she told the clergyman: 'I want 'er named Valerie'. 'E says to mother: ''Ow d'yer spell it?' Mother couldn't read, not at all. After a bit o' talk 'e said: 'I think yer better tek 'er back an' bring 'er another day. I'll christen 'er then'. Of course, 'e expected mother to go an' find out 'ow to spell Valerie. There was nobody in Quarry Bank as could spell Valerie.
>
> When 'er took 'er back next time 'e says: 'I can't christen 'er if I can't spell 'er name'. So mother says: 'Oh well, I bay comin' up 'ere no more with 'er. Yo gotta christen 'er now. 'Er gotta be named summut', 'er says. 'Name 'er Mary Ann, yo can spell that, cor you?' 'Oh, yes', 'e says, 'I

Christian names found on Black Country gravestones

Abel, Abraham, Absalom, Adam, Algernon, Alpheus, Auldar, Balford, Caleb, Celestino, Dodo, Eli, Elihu, Elijah, Enoch, Ephraim, Esau, Ethelbert, Eutychus, Ezekiah, Ezra, Gaius, Gideon, Henzy, Hercules, Hezekiah, Hyla, Hyma, Isaac, Isidore, Ismail, Israel, Issacher, Jabez, Jasper, Joel, Kezia, Lancaster, Levi, Mandel, Mesach, Moses, Napoleon, Nathan, Nehemiah, Noah, Obediah, Octavius, Otto, Philander, Philemon, Pierpoint, Rastel, Sampson, Scarlet, Silas, Slaney, Sparry, Squire, Sylvanus, Tenison, Theophilus, Tiras, Titus, Truelove, Urban, Uriah, Verney, Warwick, Zaccarius, Zechariah, Zeri.

Adeline, Adie, Alberta, Aletha, Amplias, Arelia, Belle, Bertha, Clarice, Comfort, Damaris, Dresilla, Drusilla, Effie, Espellina, Ethedreda, Evelina, Eveline, Fanny, Felicia, Felishua, Hagar, Honor, Honora, Jennett, Keturah, Lavinia, Letitia, Lottie, Lucretia, Meme, Mercy, Milbroe, Mozella, Nesta, Obedience, Pearletta, Perthaner, Philander, Rispah, Ruhamah, Sabina, Sabra, Sidonia, Sidney, Shiprah, Tabitha, Theodosia, Thirza, Trissie, Truth, Urena, Zannie, Zibbiah, Zillah, Zipporah.

> can spell that'. And she was christened Mary Ann, but that never altered the name what 'er should've 'ad. When mother brought 'er back — they always shortened the name then — 'er was Vally. 'Er went all through life with that name.

For centuries, a child born out of wedlock, known in the vernacular as a 'by-blow', attracted fierce reprobation. A number of entries in the Sedgley church register are similar to this: 'John, son of Ann Jevon, spinster, begotten of her by John Tomlinson of Bromwich, in fornication. 19 Oct. 1607'. The Wednesbury register in 1718 bluntly labelled a child as 'bastard'; at Wolverhampton the rather kinder designation of 'son (or daughter) of the people', or 'creatura Christi' (child of Christ) was preferred. Stigma attached to such children until late in the twentieth century, though it then disappeared with surprising speed.

As well as to birth and death, customs and beliefs inevitably attached themselves to the normal routine of life. F.W. Hackwood observed that in the Black Country an odd itching of the nose was thought to show that the person was 'going to be kissed, cussed or vexed'. In 1926 an anonymous newspaper article dwelt at some length on the superstitions of the people of Cradley Heath, seen through the eyes of a sceptic:

> Perhaps their greatest superstition is that to commence work on a Friday brings bad luck. ... Good jobs have been turned down through this belief. Our representative had a chat on Monday with an enlightened resident of the High Street, who 'pooh-poohed' many popular fallacies. He has crossed knives, but has never fought; he has passed persons on the staircase, and has not met with ill-luck the same day; he has put boots on the table, and his good fortune has been just the same. On the other hand, he can recall the time when a black cat entered his home — quite uninvited — and instead of Felix bringing him good luck it caused him to suffer loss, for it appropriated a joint of meat and made free with a cutlet of fish. Some men, rather than meet a cross-eyed woman in the street, will make a wide detour, he states, but he has never acted so foolishly, because he has met many a female who, though she appeared not to be looking where she was going, proved to be of a most kindly disposition. Some persons, on meeting a white horse, consider this a favourable omen, and go as far as to turn coins in their pockets. There is one particular resident in Cradley Heath who declares he can always win a game of dominoes if he selects a 'head' in the spin of a coin and wins the lead in the game. Years ago it was a popular idea that if a bride took an old boot with her to church this would bring her luck for the rest of her life. Our Cradley Heath friend remembers on one occasion that an old boot was thrown at a couple returning from the church, but the missile struck the bridegroom over the eye, and he was disfigured for weeks. It is considered, he declares, that to see the new moon through a glass betokens misfortune.

> Some persons will only allow a male to let the New Year in, and he for choice must be dark. Many housewives, too, will not sweep the floors of their dwellings on New Year's Day until after twelve o' clock. They claim that if they do so before the afternoon that they will surely sweep the luck out with it.

As well as to general well-being, superstitious inhibitions and provisions applied specifically to health. J.Wilson Jones, who moved to Rowley Regis in 1921 at the age of five, wrote: 'As a child I knew every pit, every "bonk", cut, wharf and lane. ... My grandfather, born in 1834 only twelve years after the enclosure maps, was living. He spoke the true Black Country dialect and believed the old superstitions. The herbal remedies and charms mentioned in books upon Staffordshire make quaint reading, but in the home I lived among this belief and have been "victim" of many such "cures"'.

In the days when doctors were few, and in any case unaffordable to most, people had recourse to a range of unofficial practitioners such as 'wise' or 'cunning' men, charmers and herbalists. Wise men combined their role in health care with that of tracking lost property. Early in the sixteenth century churchwardens at both Wolverhampton and Bilston considered it entirely normal to consult wise men about things taken from their churches. In every community there would have been a trusted wise man. One of the techniques used to trace a stolen item was to take the front door key of the house involved, place it in a Bible on the eighteenth verse of psalm 50, and tie it. Two people then held the ring of the key on the first finger of their right hands, and repeated in unison the verse of the psalm. ('When thou sawest a thief, then thou consentedst with him, and hast been partaker with adulterers.') After the word, 'thief', they said the name of the suspect, and if the Bible moved, that person was held to be guilty. At Wolverhampton in 1878 a woman from Monmore Green was fined for assaulting a man who, she said, had 'turned the key against her'.

Despite an Act of Parliament of 1614 which forbade under pain of imprisonment the search for stolen property in this way, Richard Baxter (1615-91) could still write of the 'conjurers' or 'white witches', as he called them, 'that shew Men the Face of the Thief in a Glass, and cause the Goods to be brought back'. He mentioned one of them in his book, *The Certainty of the World of Spirits*: 'When I lived at *Dudley*, *Hodges* at *Sedgley*, two Miles off, was long and commonly accounted such a one: And when I lived at *Kederminster*, one of my Neighbours affirmed, that having his Yarn stolen, he went to *Hodges* (ten Miles off) and he told him, that at such an Hour he should have it brought back home again, and put in at the Window; and so it was: and as I remember, he showed him the Person's face in a Glass'. As well as falling foul of the law, such activity could prompt very serious allegations, and Baxter carefully

The Dudley Devil, drawn from a disintegrating photograph

added: 'I do not think that *Hodges* made any known Contract with the Devil, but thought it an effect of Art'.

Two centuries later, such fears were diminished, and Elijah (some say Theophilus) Dunn from Bumble Hole in Netherton — known as 'Devil Dunn' or 'the Dudley Devil' — operated freely as a tracer of lost property, a fortune teller and a charmer. In the 1840s, in response to a question from a Dudley schoolmaster as to what life would be like two hundred years later, he prophesied:

> So quickly in time wull they travel
> That there'll be no 'ere or there.
> They'll pass by the moon in a bullet
> And live on co'd cloud and 'ot air.

When in 1850 the Tipton Slasher (for whom, see chapter 9) asked what the future held in store for him, Dunn, evidently no respecter of persons, replied:

> Slasher, yoh'll stop as yoh started.
> Yoh'll get all yoh gi'ed in one goo;
> Yoh and yer pub will be parted,
> Tom Little will mek it cum true.

Tom Little is taken to mean Tom Sayers. Not only did the Slasher lose to Sayers in 1857 but he was left penniless, since he had sold his pub and all his possessions in order to back himself to win.

According to Tom Langley, half the people of Dudley were afraid to go to Dunn, and the other half were afraid to stay away. In the 1840s Langley's grandparents kept the Mine Borers Arms (now demolished) in Willenhall Street, Darlaston. When money started to disappear from a drawer, his great-grandmother not only consulted Elijah — 'whether or not he was christened Elijah is uncertain. All prophets in the Black Country are 'Lijahs' — but made sure everyone knew she was going to do so. Dunn laconically pronounced: 'Look long at the liquor and leave it alone, /Tomorrow's the time to take by your own', adding only: 'Leave five bob on the table as yoh goo out'. On returning to the pub, the landlady gave orders that no one was to touch the liquor bottles on the top shelf, and she kept her eyes on them until closing time. Next morning she looked behind them and found the missing money.

Dunn has a standard specific for toothache, a formula which, for the price of a shilling, he wrote on a piece of paper to be kept close to the sufferer's skin:

> Peter … sat … at the gate of Jerusalem … Jesus passed by … and said … What aileth thee, Peter? … Peter said … unto Jesus … My teeth ache … and are sore … I am unable … to stand or walk … Jesus said … Rise and walk, Peter … in the name … of the Father … Son … and Holy Ghost. …He that puts faith … in these words I now speak … his teeth shall never ache.

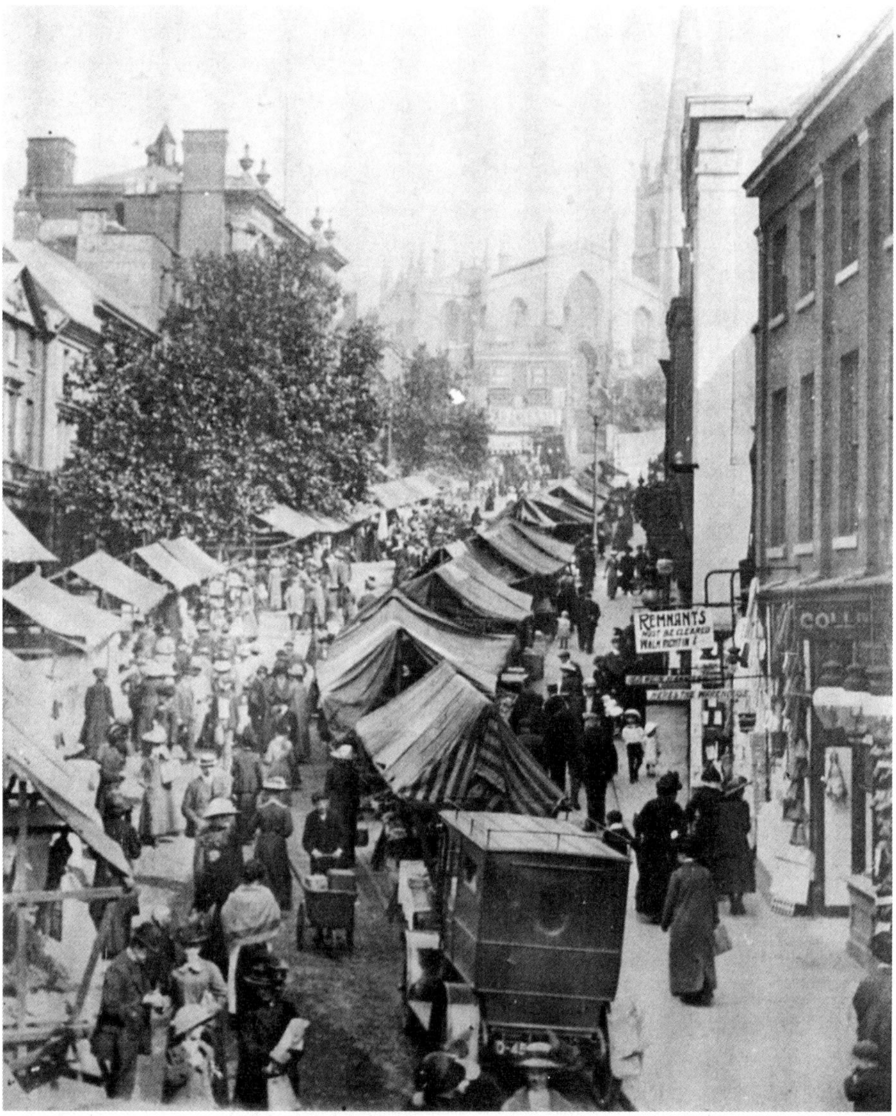

Walsall Market in 1914

Thanks to a widespread clientele, both local and national, drawn both from the poor and the well-to-do, Dunn made a good living, though in later life his income declined and he became simply a fortune-teller, working at Dudley Port. After he hanged himself at the age of 60 in 1851 he was buried in the churchyard at Netherton, where for many years his gravestone was regularly scrubbed. 'This was a service', writes Tom Langley, 'all Black Country mothers and wives did for their departed — only in this case he had no near relative, and no one ever saw it being scrubbed'.

There were, of course, many lesser known practitioners. The church register at Walsall tells us that Edward Briscow, quack doctor, of Gornal Wood, had a base child by Cath. Westwood in May 1706. In the mid-eighteenth century a box maker from Ettingshall called Thomas Poolton ran a sort of private lunatic asylum, and was challenged by a Bilston cobbler, S. P. (we do not have the full name), who put a notice in Aris's *Birmingham Gazette* accusing him of being 'a mere ignorant and illiterate Fellow, and undoubtedly … uncapable of relieving those Infirmities, or anything else'.

Walter White, describing in his book, *All round the Wrekin*, a visit to Walsall on market day in 1860 seems fascinated by the quack doctors there:

> … strangest of all was the sight of perhaps a dozen stalls scattered among the others, exhibiting an array of glass jars and bottles, some filled with bright yellow liquid, some with various kinds of worms, some with a green substance looking like a preparation of cabbage leaves, some with bullets. By each stood a glib-tongued orator, vociferating the virtues of

Walsall Market in 2007

> his vegetable medicines, extolling the efficacy of his pills (which I had taken for bullets), and pointing to the ghastly exhibition of worms as the consequence of neglect of his warnings and recommendations.

Some forty years earlier an old woman living in the Hen and Chickens Yard, Dudley Street, Wolverhampton, came to the attention of C.H. Poole, who did not, however, record her name:

> [She] did a 'roaring trade' in charming warts, painting black eyes, and prescribing for babies with the chin cough. One recipe for the latter was wearing a peppercorn necklace, accompanied by the recital of some ignorant jargon. For very bad cases a bit of hair cut off the cross on a donkey's neck; or drinking water in which a red hot cinder had been cooled, were considered efficacious. For quinsy, the patient was ordered to wear round the neck a thick bandage filled with pounded resin, and take two ounces of Epsom salts every morning until cured. Sufferers from rheumatism were directed to wear a powerful magnet in the pocket.

As late as 1893 Pinnock wrote that 'charms were used for every bodily ailment, from chilblains to apoplexy', and added that 'an experienced woman nurse, of competent skill and good general common sense, daily practises a number of charms on her patients, and for success in that branch of the healing

A mediaeval orchard and herb garden

art has a wide and honourable reputation'. Two celebrated quacks frequented Bilston Market. Doctor Dick (Richard Hill), originally an iron-worker, operated under the slogan: 'I'm Doctor Dick who cures you quick,/I've got a pill for every ill'. He claimed to have potions guaranteed to work off back rent and to cure wooden legs, and responded to sceptics by saying that the former referred to back strain rather than monetary matters, and that in the latter he was capable of removing, repairing and re-fitting a wooden leg. When he took to putting M.D. after his name he told the magistrates before whom he was summoned to appear that the letters stood for 'Money Down'. He nevertheless had to desist. Of his rival, Ode Texas (Nathaniel Catlin), who affected an American accent and wore a deerskin coat and stetson hat, Doctor Dick alleged that the nearest he had been to a red-skin was a tomato. Texas's painted wagon bore the legend: 'Dr Catlin, vendor of Secret Indian Cures for All Ailments', and he boasted that his herbs could cure anything from gout to a fractured skull. He later retired from market trading and set up a herbal stores in Bilston High Street.

Many wise men and women cut a wand or stick from a yew tree, and wielded it as a conduit bringing universal cure. In addition, people helped themselves and each other, drawing on a wide range of traditional wisdom and remedies. Herbs, grown in the garden or gathered in the wild, were taken in infusions — 'yarb tay' — or applied externally (see panel below).

Herbal Remedies

angelica apply roots to sprained limbs

bluebell (*Hyacinthoides non-scripta*) crush stalks and apply for sprains

bittersweet (*Solanum dulcamara*), also known as woody nightshade: thought to develop clairvoyance and second sight

camomile (*Chamaemelum nobile*) dried 'blows' (blossoms) used in poultices

coltsfoot (*Tusilago farfara*) dried flowers as infusion for coughs

comfrey (*Symphytum*) leaves applied as poultice to fractures and sprains

cowslip *(Primula veris)* drink water in which plants have been boiled for headaches, insomnia and nerves

dandelion (*Taraxacum officinale)* liquid from dandelion stalks applied to warts

eyebright *(Euphrasia)* infusion applied for all eye problems

heather *(Calluna vulgaris)* water, as hot as possible, in which heather had been heated, for aching feet

Coltsfoot

horehound *(Marrubium vulgare)* chest complaints
house eye green *(Sempervivum tectorum)*, also known as house leek: bathe with its juice a stye on the eye
ivy *(Hedera helix)* for itchy eyes, bathe them with water in which ivy leaves have been boiled
liverwort *(Anemone hepatica)* as an infusion of leaves and flowers, a mild remedy for indigestion and disorders of the liver
marsh mallow (*Althaea officinalis)* leaves, root, flowers, boiled in water and strained, for diseases of the chest such as coughs, bronchitis and whooping cough
mountain flax *(Linum catharticum)* purgative
mouse ear *(Hieracium pilosella)*, also called hawkweed: infusion, sweetened with honey, for whooping cough and lung infection
nettle *(Urtica urens)* infusion for anaemia, blood and skin disorders, urinary problems
raspberry *(Rubus idaeus)* infusion from leaves to ease pregnancy
Solomon's seal *(Polygonatum multiflorum)* ointment made from leaves for baldness and bruises
valerian *(Valeriana officinalis)* juice of fresh root for epilepsy and hysteria

Solomon's Seal

G. Denton's shop in Holloway End, Amblecote

A Mr H.T. Peplow of Round Hill, Sedgley, wrote to the *Black Country Bugle* in 1979 to say that he remembered herbalists at Wolverhampton to whom women went 'to buy for a few coppers a horrible-looking and nasty-smelling liquid which they drank hoping to end their latest pregnancy'. Far from being quack nostrums, though, herb remedies included time-honoured treatments traceable as far back as the ancient Greeks. They nevertheless fell into disuse, though as late as the 1930s there were outlets for herbs such as the shop of Mr G. Denton in Holloway End (now called The Holloway) at Amblecote. 'Dentie

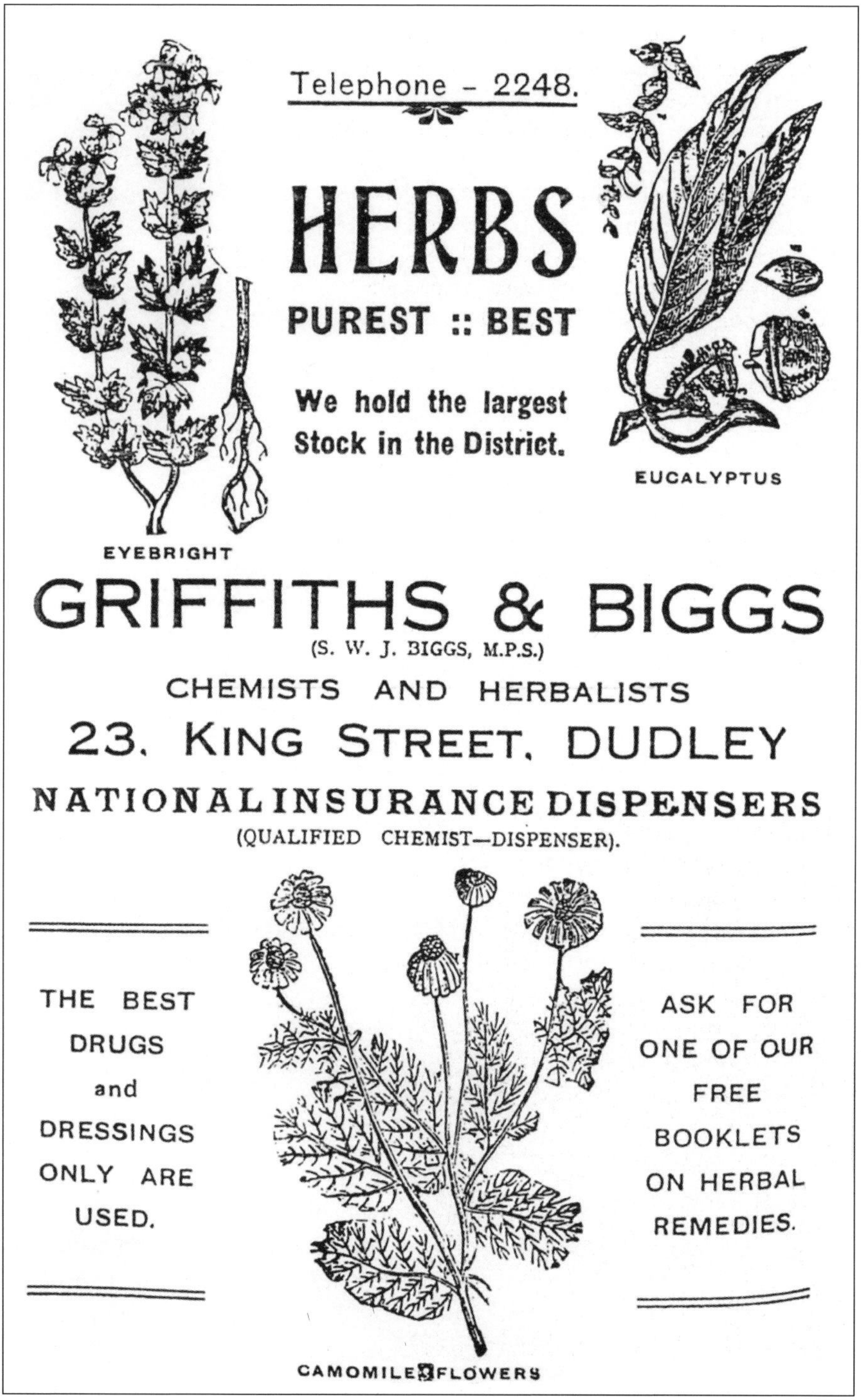

Telephone - 2248.
HERBS
PUREST :: BEST
We hold the largest
Stock in the District.
EUCALYPTUS
EYEBRIGHT
GRIFFITHS & BIGGS
(S. W. J. BIGGS, M.P.S.)
CHEMISTS AND HERBALISTS
23. KING STREET. DUDLEY
NATIONAL INSURANCE DISPENSERS
(QUALIFIED CHEMIST—DISPENSER).
THE BEST DRUGS and DRESSINGS ONLY ARE USED.
ASK FOR ONE OF OUR FREE BOOKLETS ON HERBAL REMEDIES.
CAMOMILE FLOWERS

An advertisement of 1948

the little pill mon', as he was called, because of his short stature, also travelled to markets with his wares, which included Watson's Matchless Cleanser. As late as 1940, directories show that there were still a score of herbalists' shops in the Black Country, including four each in Walsall and Wolverhampton. By the end of the decade, though, only three remained, two in Walsall and one in West Bromwich. Although herbal remedies have now returned to every High Street, thanks to health food shops, there is concern that traditional recipes may be lost. As a result a number of prestigious organisations — Kew Gardens, the Natural History Museum, Chelsea Physic Garden and the Eden Project — and an ethnomedica group of British herbalists have begun to record them, with 3,000 so far listed.

Other folk remedies consisted of a curious mixture of common sense and primitive magic. All sorts of substances were involved, from pieces of coal to bags of hot salt. Animal parts used included mole's and rabbit's feet. There were down-to-earth items such as cold tea and raw onion, and wildly optimistic rituals and incantations (see panel). The degree of desperation sometimes involved is illustrated by the claim of J. Wilson Jones's grandfather, born in 1834, to have 'cured an ulcerated stomach by swallowing little live frogs'.

Home Treatments

ague take broth made of dock leaves and stewed feet of rooks
asthma alleviated by eating raw carrots
boils apply hot bread poultice
black eyes and bruises apply ointment made of crushed carrots and resin
bleeding apply spider's web
chest infections breathe smell of hot tar
coughs rub goose fat on chest and back, and wear brown paper next to skin for three days (according to Philip Solomon, 'it always worked'); alternatively, swallow mustard and melted butter or apply mixture to chest and again cover with brown paper; take mixture of butter, sugar and vinegar; put demerara sugar between slices of turnip and swallow a tablespoon of the resulting juice three times a day
cramp go to bed with five corks in a bag and say 'Goodbye to cramp'; or recite this formula:

The devil is tying a knot in my leg.
Mark, Luke and John, I beg
Crosses three now make to ease us,
For the Father, Holy Ghost and Jesus.

croup give child broth made from frogs; or hold a pigeon to its throat, then cause the bird to die of starvation
diarrhoea drink, four times a day, a quarter of a cupful of milk into which nutmeg has been grated
earache hold to the ear the centre of a boiled onion wrapped in muslin or a bag of hot salt; pour warm olive oil in the ear

hangover F.W. Hackwood delicately wrote in 1924: 'The colliers and forgemen who indulged too heavily in malt beverages were wont to seek the rectification of a disordered system by doses of a concoction made from powdered snails'

impotence eat fresh carrots over a period of several months

infections eat mouldy bread

influenza and indigestion eat burnt toast; suck a small piece of coal

mumps walk round a well three times with eyes closed and chant: 'Mumps, go away'

nose bleed put a cold key down sufferer's back

quinsy apply goose fat to the throat with a feather

rheumatism keep new potato in pocket for a year; place nettles under bed-sheet; apply to the affected area, says Philip Solomon, a mixture of turpentine (one wine glass), crab vinegar (two wine glasses) and a raw egg

sore throat eat a small lump of butter, coated with sugar; gargle with mixture (after straining) of cayenne pepper (one dessert spoon), salt (one teaspoon), warm vinegar (half pint), boiled water (halt pint) which has cooled

stings press half a raw onion for five minutes to affected area

stye (called 'pouk' in the Black Country) rub nine times with gold wedding ring to 'swayne' it away; rub with scrap of stolen beef; apply juice of house leek

toothache wear on thread round neck a tooth previously extracted, preferably from a person now dead; wear mole's right or left paw, depending on which tooth is causing pain

warts rub with piece of raw beef, later buried; tie with silken thread, circle seven times with right hand at full moon, say words of a charm; place shape of moon cut in an onion, and say: 'New moon, true moon, take this wart away'; rub with snail, which is then impaled on a thorn; apply washing soda; wet the warts for nine successive mornings with the sufferer's own fasting spittle

whooping cough pass sufferer nine times on three successive mornings before sunrise through bramble rooted at both ends, while repeating: 'Under the briar and over the briar,/I wish to leave the chin cough here'; take sufferer to different place for each of seven days to breathe different air and smells, one of which should be hot tar

For general well-being — or what might be called preventive medicine — people wore a hare's or rabbit's foot. As a tonic, Philip Solomon gives several Black Country recipes:

1. One ounce senna, half an ounce salts, quarter pound best chopped figs, two ounces caraway seeds: pour on pint of boiling water and strain when cold. Take a wine glassful every day.

2. Half teaspoon salts, juice of half lemon: pour on a little boiling water. Drink when cool.
3. Eat eight or nine one-inch squares of bread and butter, dipped in sugared milk.
4. Eat juniper or parsley boiled in water.

For difficult dilemmas there were various expedients. As a pebble was dropped into a bucket of water the question needing an answer was spoken aloud: an odd number of ripples in the water indicated a positive response, even, negative. Alternatively, thirteen pieces of paper, seven bearing the word 'yes', and six, 'no', would be put in a bucket. When water was added, the first piece of paper to rise to the surface would provide the appropriate answer. Such activities, if they still exist, are now merely children's games. Some of the remedies may well continue to have validity; others indicate the desperate search for health by people denied proper medical care.

CHAPTER 6

Witches and Ghosts

St John's wort (*Hypericum performatum*) was once enthusiastically grown in Black Country gardens in the belief that it repelled ghosts and evil spirits. Easier still, a person with bible and key held in the right hand could banish ghosts simply by reciting the Lord's Prayer. To avert any malign influence, horseshoes were fixed over the doors of houses and stables. 'Good housewives', wrote Thomas Pinnock in 1893, 'mark their bread loaves with a cross, and housemaids ensure a brisk kindling of a newly-lit fire by making the same sacred sign over the grate'.

Pinnock added this passage documenting belief in the devil, 'th' ode lad' in the vernacular:

St John's Wort

> While Satan is endowed by the popular imagination with a ubiquity scarcely less than omni-present, he is supposed specially to haunt the shafts and subterranean workings of disused mines. And though practically omnipotent, he is invoked by the following absurd spell. A crust of bread and cheese placed inside a hat, with a crossed knife and fork (always an ominous sign), and over this the recitation of the Lord's Prayer backwards. You will to this day find people who are prepared to make the oath that when as boys they had tried this spell on a pit bank on dark nights, and had been brave enough to peep down the shaft, they had seen the very form of the evil one glaring at them from the depths below.

C.H. Poole reports an instance of the contrary belief that the Lord's Prayer 'back'ards' caused the devil to retreat. In a Bilston pit candles were mysteriously disappearing every night, and a careful watch failed to reveal the thief. A wise man called 'Old Nicholls' was called in. He concluded: 'Well, lads, don't be afeared, but it's the devil as steals the candles, 'cos it's awful dark where he is, an' candles 'll come in useful to him'. He advised 'the fearsomest chaps among yer' to go down the pit and confront the devil, armed with a bible and tinder boxes — a detail which must date the story to a considerable time back. The group of colliers went down the pit, then waited a long time in the dark. At last they heard strange scratchings and movements. The protective recitation began, but as soon as a light was struck the thieves were revealed, in flight: a pack of rats.

When a ghost troubled miners in a Bilston pit during the late eighteenth century they sought advice from a cunning man known as White Rabbit. He advised them to go down the mine at midnight, led by one of their number with a bible in his right hand and a key in his left. They were to repeat together the Lord's Prayer, first forwards, then backwards, alternately with: 'Matthew, Mark, Luke and John,/ God bless the errand we've come on'. The procedure failed to work. One of the party, suddenly realising that the leader was left-handed, called: 'Caggy, put the buik in yer *right* 'ond'. The man did so, and the apparition vanished.

Wednesbury colliers returning home

Bilston was also the scene, in 1620, of a case of pretended witchcraft and demoniacal possession. William Perry, aged 13, who became celebrated as 'the Bilston boy', under the alleged influence of witchcraft inspired by the devil, foamed at the mouth, vomited pins and needles and went into convulsions. He accused Joan Cox, 'a woman ill thought of and suspected for such things', of bewitching him, and she was put on trial at Stafford. Thomas Morton, the bishop of Lichfield, followed the proceedings, and formed doubts as to the boy's veracity. He persuaded the judge to adjourn, and to allow him to question the boy. The bishop tried him out by reading in Greek the first verse of the first chapter of St John's gospel, which in English caused the boy to feign convulsions. The devil understood all languages, argued the bishop, and since the boy had not reacted to the Greek he could not have been possessed. Perry, having confessed the imposture, appeared at the next assizes himself, but was discharged into the care of the bishop, and reportedly became a very honest man. Joan Cox was exonerated.

Rather less powerful than the devil, but still terrifying, were the 'bugs' or frightening creatures (the word 'bogey' is related) which manifested themselves in lonely places, to the affright of belated travellers. Place names like Bug Piece, Bug Hole (near Willenhall) and Buggins Lane (near Moseley Hole) attested to such encounters. Thanks to Joshua Vernal a curious account of the activities of one 'bug', based on 'a newspaper cutting, probably the [? Birmingham] "Post", about 1859', has survived (see panel below).

The Uffmore Bug

Between Northfield and Halesowen there was formerly two moors, both now enclosed; one was called Hellsmoor, and the other Uffmoor. There was a lonely farm house upon Uffmoor, about sixty years ago, which was the terror of the whole neighbourhood, for it was said to be haunted, and the people of the house were in league with the evil one. If any women went there their dresses were torn, their bonnets were pulled off by some mysterious means, their shawls were snatched from their shoulders by unseen hands, and all the bedevilments of witchcraft were practised upon anyone who entered the house.

These proceedings raised so much fear that the magistrates and clergy of the adjoining parishes thought it quite time to enquire into the truth of these alleged events. A girl in the house was first examined. She declared herself bewitched by an old man, well known in the neighbourhood. She declared that by various mysterious arts he had obtained the mastery over her. He had made her go to Halesowen Church, and say the Lord's Prayer backwards during the service; as she was returning a black bird, with a very long neck and enormous legs, jumped on to her shoulder, and told her that he would always be near to help her, and that she could do anything she wished to do. She then showed some of her powers to the examiners. The lookers-on fled away, and the magistrates and clergy could not make out the nature of her tricks — people said they were too frightened and left the examination rather hurriedly. The people now believed in the witchery more firmly than ever; and the house was avoided by all.

The owner of the place used to go in his cart to London at regular intervals. He was a sullen and reserved man who seldom spoke to people and who appeared to avoid them as much as they avoided him. Things remained in this state for a long while, till at last a boy out of mere curiosity ventured near the house, where he saw lights. This excited his curiosity still more but as he crept nearer he heard strange and unearthly noises, bump! bump! bump! which quite shook the ground. This was rather too much for his courage, and he rapidly decamped; but another night he went again yet closer to the house though the same noises still went on and on. Looking through a small grating, he saw in the cellar two men working a stamping press making base money. This fully explained the reason for the house being haunted, for no one would then go near it, and they could thus work there undisturbed. The gang were convicted and transported for life.

According to a jibe which acquired wide currency, the name of Halesowen derived from Hell's Own, thanks to the devil's keeping his hounds there. His huntsman, Harry-ca-Nab rode out on stormy nights on winged horses which breathed out fire and brimstone to hunt the great boars of Feckenham Forest or the wild bulls of the Lickey Hills. To see huntsman and pack would bring bad luck at best, death at worst. An alternative idea is that Harry-ca-Nab is in fact Old Harry, the devil himself. Perhaps an echo of the wild hunt tradition was the belief that on certain nights in winter months the devil and his imps hunted over Romsley Hill near Halesowen, with the result that local people rigorously avoided the place after dusk.

According to G.T. Lawley, at the end of the eighteenth century Bilston people felt that special efforts were needed to ward off the evil influence of demon or witch at Christmas time. They drew a chalk line at the end of every street or lane, with a cross at either end. Others fixed two straws in the shape of a cross to the lintel of their doors on Christmas morning.

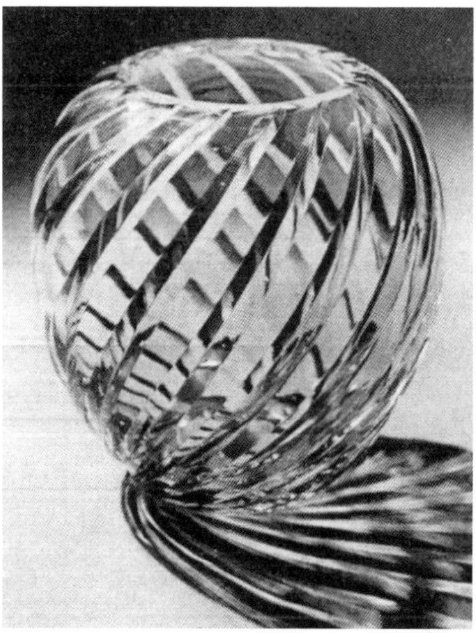

Witch sphere

More permanent protection was provided by the coloured glass spheres and miniature walking sticks hung inside a house window to keep at bay the evil eye, witches, and — latterly — even germs. Such items were surreptitiously made by glassworkers at Stourbridge, who called them 'friggers', and threw them, suitably wrapped, over the glass works' wall to an accomplice, warned by a whistle, who waited at a pre-arranged spot and time. Such works invariably had high walls and gates, thanks to the tax on glass repealed only in 1840. There was a ready sale for friggers, always unofficially.

One man at Bradley had a different safeguard, a strand from the rope used at the hanging of Abel Hill (see page 40) which he always wore round his neck to prevent being bewitched. Thanks to the fear they generated, witches were treated with great respect. An exception occurred in the case of Joseph Orford, an Oldswinford nailer, who in 1687 was in court 'for being a common disturber and for charging Thomas Barnes a person of good repute with being guilty of witchcraft, and that he hath boasted that he would have the said Barnes and his wife duckt for witches, and he would procure John Johnson a drummer to be present at the doing to make it more sport'. On the other hand, Nell Nicholls, who lived during the 1820s in Hell Lane (later re-named Ettingshall Lane) between Bilston and Coseley, was thought to be able to turn herself into a white rabbit, and in that form to go round the houses of neighbours to eavesdrop on their conversations. She was reputedly caught in that guise by Billy Moore's terrier, and then eaten, and thus she disappeared from the scene. At the same period, a wizard called Kat Rhodes was 'feared and respected by every thief' in Hell Lane. Sometimes people mastered their fear sufficiently to attempt countervailing magic or to break a witch's power by drawing her blood. At least two such cases reached the courts. In 1856 John Noake described how at Stourbridge 'a woman named Wassall charged a Mrs Cartwright, a poor woman afflicted with paralysis, with threatening to do her some bodily injury':

> The defendant alleged that the affliction under which she was suffering was caused by the complainant, who had bewitched her; and that when she begged her to remove the spell, complainant told her it had been upon her for twelve weeks, and it should continue six weeks longer. Finding entreaties vain, the defendant made use of some idle threat, which led to the summons. A 'charm' was shown to the court, which the deluded creature had worn by the advice of a 'wise' man to remove the spell; it was a small black silk bag, containing pieces cut out from the prayer book and the bible, and some hair, evidently from a cat's back, The bench endeavoured to assuage the fears of the poor woman, and told her not to impute her affliction to the evil machinations of anyone, at the same time severely lecturing the complainant for practising such deceit upon an ignorant and afflicted fellow-creature.

According to Thomas Pinnock, every parish had a witch. He 'distinctly remembers the feelings of horrified disgust (concealed through fear of her evil eye) with which, as a boy, he used to reply civilly to the passing greetings of a short, hunchbacked, bearded old woman, harmless and decent enough, but declared to be a witch, and by the name of Old Molly Buggibow, dreaded, feared, and conciliated by most of the villagers'.

Save for their appearances in fancy dress form at Hallowe'en, witches have been long gone from the Black Country. Ghosts, also thought at times to have connections with the devil, have enjoyed a longer reign, which is still not over. Some have attempted to take advantage of people's fears for their own purposes. Early in the nineteenth century a series of sightings of a ghost at Bilston coincided with thefts of poultry. Sam Jackson, refusing to be intimidated, decided to keep watch over his precious ducks. Many years later he gave a pithy account — worth quoting for its dialect value alone — of what happened (see panel below).

The Ghost of Big Piece

Some o' yo chaps remembrin, I dussay, as how before the railway was cut that a ghost was sed to walk in the Pig Piece, un every time it come sombrys fowls or ducks wun missin'. Soo puttin' this un that together I guessed that the ghost un ther thief won one un the saame. I had sum rare fat ducks in my own pen, an' as I waanted 'em for me own atin' I maade up me mind ter keep a sharp eye on 'em; soo I waatched two-three nights till daylight, but sid no sign of the ghost. Howsumever, I went down the gardin one night wi' a good sized cudgel, for I felt somehaw as summut was a-gooin' ter happen. It was a putty dark night, just the sort o' one uz a fowl staler was likely to fix on, an' hidin' meself close to the hole in th' 'edge I waatched un waited. Shure nuff, somewheer about ten er clock I sid a light muvin' about in ther field un sed I to meself, yander's either the ghost or a Jack o' Lantern; I wunder wot he's up ter now. As ge got nearer an' nearer I maade out that the light was that from a can'le, un' I guessed th' ghost carried it ter fritten off folks, as a sort a mak' believe.

One minit I sid the light, un' the nex' it was gone, on'y to come agen. Whoever it was he was makkin' fer th' 'ole in ther 'edge, an' I own up I got a bit uneasy, a bit took aback like, un I doh mind sayin', a bit afeard. But I pulled meself tergether, and says to meself: 'Hode tight, Sam, thee'st come ter see some fun, soo it wo' doh to be 'bashed now'. Just then the can'le went out fer good, an' then I heered somebody a-crawlin' through ther 'ole. Soo I got a tight ho'd o' ther cudgel, un in a gruff v'ice I called out, 'Who bin yo theer?' A big grunt o' surprise followed, un then the chap shouted, 'I'm o'd Nick, un I come to fatch o'd Bill Joones, fur his time's up'. 'Well', I says, 'I'm right glad thee's come, fur I'm o'd Nick's gaffer', in a disguised v'ice. 'Ger out', says O'd Nick, 'I ha' got no gaffer'. 'Hasn't, begom?' seys I. Wi' that I up wi' me stick un ketched him a tidy wipe on his yed.

Bless ye, he dae half yowk. Yo cud a heered 'im a mile off ommost; so I drapt on him like a lood o' bricks, an' knocked nearly all the wind out on him. 'Let me up, let me up', he roored like er mad bull, in his nat'ral v'ice; un then I knowed shure nuff it was o'd Shropsheer from down the church fode [fold]; soo I ged him another lick on ther yed, an' then went off whom loffin' fit ter split.

I dae see Shropsheer for two-three days after, un when I did ketch sight on him he'd got a lump on his foreyed as big as a tater, an' two black eyes, reg'lar beauties. I doh think I ever sid wus; no, I doh think I ever did. They wun all the colours o' ther rainbow, un half down his faace. He looked as ef he'd got a pair o' black goggles on fer certain shure. 'Hello!' I says, innercent like. 'Wheeriver hast got them eyes from. Hast tumbled through the bedroom winder thinkin' it was the front door?' 'Why', ses he, growlin' like a bear wi' a soor yed, 'I was takin' a shot cut across the Big Piece the tother night thinkin' o' nuthin' p'tic'lar, when some devil or other hit me across me yed wi'out sayin' by yer leaf, un drapt me on ther groun' like er log'.

'An' he dae miss his aim ayther, that's a downreet fact', ses I. 'Dost know who did it?' 'I on'y wish I did', ses he, wi' a oath. I'd settle his hash, I'm dashed if I wudner'. 'Sarve him right, too', ses I, 'lookin' at him sympertbisin', for he was a sorry objec', un I wished for a bit I hadn't hit soo hard. 'Yo doh ketch me in the Big Piece after dark in a hurry agen', ses he. 'Yo con bet yer boots on it', an' fer wonce I think he tode the truth'. 'But wot wast dooin' in the Big Piece after dark wen there's soo many ghosts about?' I axed, as mild as butter. 'Thee wasn't after ducks, wast?'

O'd Shropsheer started, an' fur a minit or soo he wondered ef I knowed summat about it, but I wor to be had. Then he swore like a trooper, turned on his heels an' wrostled off, soo I know'd I'd touched him in a soore plaace. When he was out o' sight I loffed like a good un; un I dae goo down the garden agen at night for many a wik, for ducks an' fowls won a sight saafer than they won before, an' it was me as knowed the reason why. But I dae let on, soo o'd Shropsheer never knowed till his dyin' day who maade that lump on his foreyed, un blacked his eyes that bad that his own mother wouldn't a knowed him from Adam till he spoke.

I suppose that if everyone showed the same common sense and resolution as the narrator here, there would be no ghost stories, though we might be the poorer without them. The White Hart in Corporation Street at Caldmore, near Walsall, has been an inn since 1813, though the building dates back in part to about 1540. In 1870 a sword and what seemed to be a mummified arm came to light behind a chimney. The sword could well have dated from the time of the Civil War, when George Hawe, a fervent

The White Hart at Caldmore, Walsall, after a painting of 1910 by Dixon. The inn was said to be linked by a tunnel to St Matthew's Church

royalist, entertained Queen Henrietta Maria and was later fined £212 for doing so by the winning side, the parliamentarians. As for the arm, this was a 'Hand of Glory', said local people, a magical torch made from a dead man's hand which had the power of casting into a deep sleep anyone against whom it was directed. With it a burglar, for example, could make a family insensible while he removed their treasures. It emerged, though, that the arm, that of a child, had been surgically removed, and injected with formaldehyde for preservation as a medical specimen. Moreover, a surgeon had lodged at the inn for a period of time in the 1860s. The rumour then circulated that the arm came from a young girl who killed herself in the mid-nineteenth century in the White Hart, then haunted the place. In 1950 the landlord found the print of a tiny hand in the dust on a table in a locked attic of which only he had the key. From the same room he heard the sound of disembodied footsteps. Since 1965 the arm has been in Walsall Museum, and it seems that the strange happenings at the White Hart have come to an end.

The so-called Hand of Glory

The powerful emotional effect of violent death perhaps conditioned people into expecting that victims would not rest quietly. Wallington House at Wallington Heath, near Bloxwich, was formerly a coaching inn called the King's Arms. A stagecoach passenger detained there in the 1790s by a blizzard was brutally murdered for the sake of a roll of silk, and also mutilated. Afterwards on stormy nights

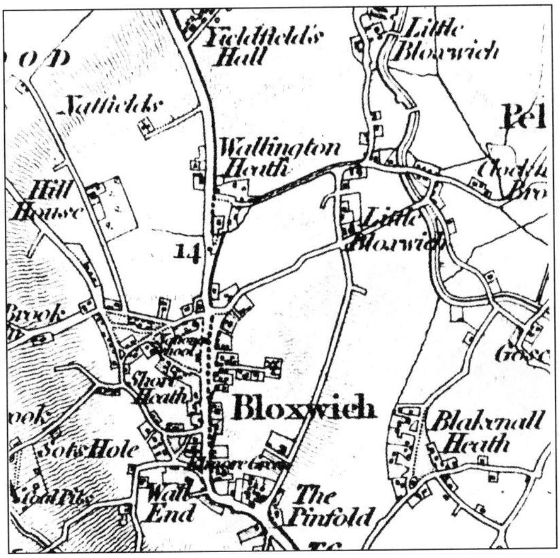

Map showing Wallington Heath

— including as recently as 1993 — she took to appearing, quietly weeping, under a tree opposite the building. Within living memory, some Bloxwich people were reluctant to pass that way in bad weather. Inside the inn, the woman's silhouette, found etched on a wall, resisted all attempts by painting or plastering to remove it.

The Swan Inn in Castle Street, Dudley, had the reputation of being the 'most haunted house in town'. It was built on the foundations of a nunnery whose former inmates, outraged, perhaps, that their holy place had become a common alehouse, persisted in making appearances there, and then faded away through the walls. In 1984 Sarah Craig described other cases of phantoms which passed through solid walls. As a 17 year-old she was walking home to Darlaston Green with another girl from a New Year's Eve fancy dress ball they had attended at Wednesbury. In Sparrows Forge Lane (which has now become Park Lane) they saw a man with top hat, knee breeches and swallow-tailed coat whom they took to be another returning reveller. Then the figure turned abruptly and walked through a cinder wall. Immediately afterwards the girls saw a friend approaching from the opposite direction, but she had neither seen the man, nor would she believe their story. On 7 January a wall at her workplace collapsed and killed her. A neighbour revealed to Sarah the tradition long held in her family that a gentleman of time long past had fallen from his horse and died at the very place where the two girls had seen the apparition.

During the Second World War Sarah, by this time married, was one

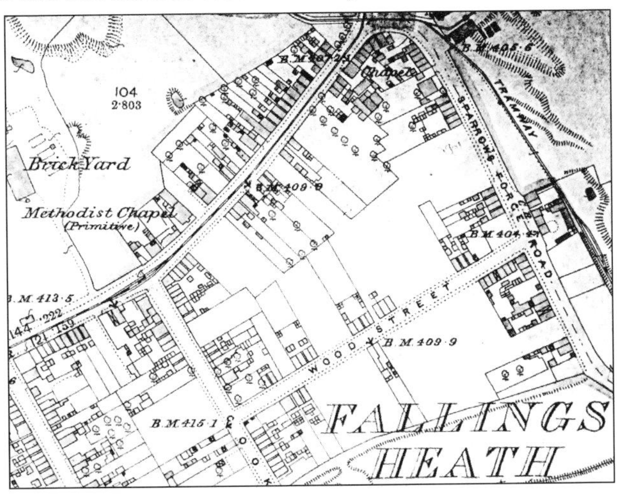

Map showing Wood Street and Sparrow Forge Road

day waiting for her husband to come home on leave from the army. He arrived pale and shaken, having walked the route she had taken many years earlier, and told her that he had seen the figure of 'an old-fashioned man' disappearing through the wall at the spot she so fearfully remembered. Of her husband's two companions, one had also seen the apparition; the other, the man's nephew, had not. Shortly afterwards, again on a 7 January, the nephew was killed in London by the collapse of a wall weakened by bombing.

During a much earlier time of trouble, on 8 November 1605 at Holbeach House, near Kingswinford, several Gunpowder Plotters including the notorious Catesby met their deaths, either from injuries caused (ironically) by gunpowder which exploded as they tried to dry it before an open fire, or from wounds inflicted by members of the posse which surrounded the house, or from a combination of the two. One might think that such dramatic deaths would have left ghostly traces. Not so; but two conspirators executed two months later may have done so.

Stephen Littleton, owner of Holbeach, and Robert Wintour, from Huddington Court in Worcestershire, slipped away before the posse closed in. They hid in a succession of cottages, barns and outbuildings, including the Old Paddock Croft in what became the present Barnett Lane in Kingswinford. There on a cellar beam Wintour left in poor Latin this despairing inscription:

> *R.W. Vestiga Nulla Restorsum. Valete ac plaudite.*
>
> (Footprints left behind. Fare you well and give your applause).

In another hiding place the fugitives were discovered by a drunken poacher, whom they had to shut in so as to make their escape. At Rowley Regis they took refuge in a yeoman farmer's barn, before moving to Hagley, where in Hagley House they thought themselves safe. A cook there, John Finwood, aware of the hue and cry, became suspicious of the great quantities of food sent up ostensibly for a single lady. He contacted the authorities, who descended on the place and arrested Littleton and Wintour. The pair were executed in London in late January 1606.

Some four hundred years later a tall figure with flowing cloak and cockaded hat was repeatedly seen in a hardware shop in Barnett Lane, which may occupy the site of the house where the hapless plotters hid. One November night a customer saw the 'phantom cavalier's' features so clearly on a wall in the shop that he thought he was looking at an advertisement for fireworks featuring a portrait of Guy Fawkes. As a result of the publicity which followed further accounts of 'strange phenomena' in Barnett Lane were found, dating from the 1870s and earlier.

Haden Hall, near Old Hill, where a mansion of some kind has stood since the eleventh century, also has disturbing reverberations from the past. An underground passage was said to link the building's cellars with Hales Abbey, some two and a half miles away. A young monk from the abbey, a member of

Haden Hall

the Haden family, attempted to use it to run away with Elaine or Eleanor of Hayseech Mill, with whom he had fallen in love. The couple were caught in the tunnel and walled up there, alive. After the savage punishment, Elaine, the miller's daughter, dressed in white, haunted the parkland round Haden Hall in search of her lost lover.

Another deeply unhappy spirit lingers at the hall, that of Ann Eliza Haden, who died in 1876 but for the next hundred years at least was from time to time seen peering out through an attic window. Ann's father was 57 years older than her mother. When he died his widow was married again, to Rev. George Barrs, curate during the first forty years of the nineteenth century of Rowley Regis Church, and renowned for sermons which had congregations in tears and penitents eager to acknowledge their sins. Obsessively determined to ensure that Haden Hall stayed in his family's possession, to prevent her marrying, Barrs kept his step-daughter in strict confinement in the attic which she later haunted.

The children of Alfred Barrs. His step-daughter, Anne Eliza Haden, is second from the left

Astonishingly, Haden Hall has a third dismal tale, that of a governess whose illegitimate son died, ostensibly from an accidental fall, though people hinted that the boy had been murdered. A medium claimed that his unhappy spirit lingered in the banqueting room.

More tales of misfortune are reported from Charlemont Hall, a seventeenth-century building demolished in the late 1940s, near West Bromwich's Holy Trinity Church. In the nineteenth century it was the residence of on ironmaster and coal owner, W.H. Dawes. At his Bromford Colliery three lads were asphixiated by choke-damp when they walked into disused workings which should have been fenced off. At the inquest Dawes managed to shift blame to the chartermaster, to whom he had sub-contracted the running of the pit. The man's house was attacked by relatives of the dead boys, and his sister drowned herself near Spon Lane in a pool which she afterwards haunted. She also appeared at Charlemont Hall, signalling a death in the family there by pointing a spectral but imperious finger at the clock.

At some stage a Bilston family called Price lived at the hall. After stealing lead from the roof of Tipton Church to cover the engine house at their works, they were dogged by ill-fortune: children died young, and the head of the family committed suicide. The last to live there was Madame Jones (so titled because she was Belgian), the widow of a former Wednesbury town clerk, Thomas Jones. One Thursday night, not long before Christmas, she was reading in bed and the room became icy and she sensed a presence near her. Then the figure of a woman in white took shape at the foot of her bed, and afterwards slowly faded. The temperature returned to normal. Madame Jones, a strong-minded woman, composed herself to sleep, though not before noticing the time: 11.30. A few days later she received a black-edged letter from a relative in Belgium bearing the news that her sister had died that Thursday night, soon after 11.

The Black Country, it seems, has many reminders of female victims. Dorothy Beaumont died, perhaps in childbirth, at Dudley Castle during the siege of 1646. The Parliamentary commander of the town garrison allowed her funeral cortege to go to the parish church, but her husband was forced to remain in the castle. Dorothy proceeded to haunt the place as a 'grey lady', last seen in 1987. A different story identifies the ghost as being that of an old woman who lived in the keep and hanged herself from the battlements, or alternatively was killed as a suspected witch by a gang of youths who tied a rope round her neck and threw her off the top. She was then buried outside the walls of St Edmund's Church, where the castle offices now stand.

A ghost scare at Halesowen dates back to December 1927, when a young couple sitting on a stile at night in fields near Olive Lane, Combeswood, heard muffled footfalls pass and re-pass, then heard the beating of wings. The woman fled, and the man followed after searching in vain for what might be causing the sounds. Next day he contacted the owner of the small, ruinous building close to the stile, a Mr Whorton, who told him its story. In February 1878 a miner called Joseph Harris, apparently driven by intense jealousy, battered to death

Dudley Priory and Castle, drawn by Arthur Crowquill, 1846

his wife, Amelia, and his two small daughters, in the cellar at what immediately became known as 'the Murder House'. Families which subsequently moved in quickly moved on because of strange happenings, including the recurrent sound of inexplicable footsteps. The place was demolished, and the materials used to build a rough shed for some twenty pigeons. When the birds several times 'became scared and fluttered about like things possessed', their keeper decided to keep vigil one night, with a roaring fire to keep him company. He too, heard footfalls which came and went, and then without warning a powerful gust of wind blew off the substantial door and carried it some yards away. The deaths inspired at least one song, of which only the first line, 'Joseph Harris did the murder in a house near Olive Lane', was later remembered. The fate of the victims (buried in one grave in Blackheath churchyard) aroused grief and anger, and the Murder House was long shunned after dark as being haunted. Perhaps the young people of 1927 somehow stumbled across reverberations of events and emotions of fifty years earlier.

Equally bizarre, not to say farcical, were a series of happenings at Lower Gornal, where in 1879 Rev. J.Y. Rooker, vicar of St James's Church, was wounded by a gunshot from an unknown assailant, whose motive remained unclear. The churchyard, where the attacker had been seen 'performing all sorts of strange antics' was shunned after dark, save by a group of young men who, vigilante-style, decided to protect the vicar and his family. On the first night of their watch they failed to recognise in the dark one of their number who came late, and had to run away to avoid being manhandled. Then the parson himself was seized by a man who shouted: 'You have come to kill the vicar, have you?

I've sworn to take your life, you villain, and I'll do it quick'. Fortunately, someone shone a light before the threat was carried out. The ludicrous aspect of these events failed to dispel the belief that the churchyard was haunted, and two years later *The Daily Telegraph* commented:

> To show the kind of superstition which exists, it may be stated that a woman a few nights ago called at the vicarage, and requested the Rev. Mr Rooker to permit her to cut a turf four inches square from a particular grave in the churchyard, in which she alleged was a young man, who could not lie at ease in his grave in consequence of a guilty conscience. She stated that if the turf were put under the communion table, and allowed to remain four days, all ghosts would disappear, and be laid at rest for ever.

There is no record of whether the remedy was adopted or proved efficacious. G.S. Tyack, who lived in Penkridge, picked up the turf cutting ritual in his book, *Lore and Legend of the English Church* (1899), but I have not seen any other instance of it. There may be a connection with the miners' belief that a man suffering from choke-damp should be treated by cutting a square of turf and placing him face down with his mouth over the hole, and so allowing the earth to draw the gas.

St Edmund's churchyard at Dudley once had the reputation of being haunted, and many shunned it at night. Especially feared was the ghost of Edmund Croaker, a public executioner buried there in the eighteenth century. A young man made a bet with his friends that he would go into the churchyard and sit on Croaker's grave as midnight struck, leaving a dagger stuck into the ground as a token that he had been there. Next morning he was found dead, apparently of fright: with his dagger he had pinned himself to the ground through his own coat tails, and no doubt believed himself in the grip of some unearthly power.

Rather more widely spread were stories of Spring-heeled Jack. Originally this was a generic name in Victorian times for any street robber who ran away very fast after striking, but it eventually came to refer to a kind of supernatural Superman of thieves, who could leap from roof to roof or from steeple to steeple. He was feared in the latter guise throughout the Black Country, though he may

Spring-heeled Jack, 1838

have ended merely as a sort of bogey figure with which parents frightened children into going to sleep.

There is a more modern sort of ring to some of the many reports of peculiar phenomena in Wolverhampton's Grand Theatre, such as poltergeist-style activity in the upper circle bar, where glasses are turned over, drawers opened and cash registers rung when no one is there. Rather than a poltergeist, some have suggested these were the spirits of actors who had performed in the theatre returning after death to play practical jokes. A mysterious scent of lavender by the orchestra pit is ascribed to the wife of a mayor of Wolverhampton who died there from a fall. One would have thought that such an event could hardly have escaped the local press. Perhaps the grandest of the Grand's ghosts is that of a Mr Purdy who was the general manager in the 1920s. After his death until the 1950s at least he returned to the theatre, a small man with great dignity, wearing cloak and top hat. He exudes an air of helpfulness, and if he is politely asked to go away he does so.

These phantoms of the theatre must qualify as workplace ghosts, of which there are many elsewhere, particularly in coal mines, which are described in chapter 7. Underground, too, is the blacksmith heard blowing his fire and striking his iron beneath Barnford Hill, two miles south of Oldbury. A smith worked in the Lomey Town shoeing forge in Whitehall Road for at least a century until it was pulled down in 1927. As late as some fifty years earlier than that, some fifty horses could be seen lined up outside at two o'clock in the morning, waiting for attention to their shoes. The smithy acquired the reputation of being haunted, thanks to stories such as this:

Barnford Hill

> A former owner, who used to get his beer in the evening from a neighbouring pub often found upon his return all his gleeds scooped out of the hearth. On one occasion he caused a local sensation by saying in a beerhouse that he saw a ghost picking up the white hot gleeds and putting them into his mouth. Crowds assembled with the hope that the 'fire-eating ghost' would return, and it is thought that they saw him hovering in the distance. ... There were few houses in the neighbourhood compared with its present congested state, and at the back there were plough fields.

The same intense interest which caused crowds to assemble in the hope of seeing a ghost arose, again in 1927, at Stourbridge, where a figure, 'seven feet in height, with the form of a beautiful woman dressed as a nurse', started to appear in the grounds of the sixteenth-century Manor House, New Street, punctually at 11 p.m., 'causing onlookers to go icy cold'. One witness, 'a well-known townsman', provided a detailed description for a *Stourbridge Gazette* reporter: 'She was wearing patent shoes, white stockings, white apron, and a big blue cloak over her shoulders and a blue hat. I saw her as plainly as I see you now, and until that moment I was a firm disbeliever in ghosts. ... I fell on my knees and was about to speak to her, but my brother and another man, who were watching in a distant corner, ran away. At this the apparition vanished'. The crowds which assembled in the hope of seeing the ghost were such that police officers had to be deployed to control them. The furore eventually died down, amidst speculation that the apparition must have been some sort of practical joke. If so, those responsible were never identified.

Tom Langley heard tell of a phantom road with a farm at the end, near Combes Lane at Halesowen, which people noticed in passing, then failed to see when they went that way again. He himself encountered a similar phenomenon at Chasetown: 'I've experienced that. I saw a lane once but this lane didn't exist. I can remember as a lad seeing it and wondering what was down this lane. Yet the next time you pass there *is* no lane there. It has gone, and that lane was there three hundred years ago'.

Inevitably, there were Aynoch and Ayli stories of ghosts. Tom Langley contributed this in 1970:

> Did you ever 'ear talk of Aynoch when 'e went in the haunted house? Well, this is supposed to be true. This house was only pulled down in the last ten years at Dudley. 'E said 'e'd stopped there in that 'ouse all night, and they locked 'im in. 'E laid 'imself down on a bench and 'e went to sleep. About two o'clock in the mornin' 'e was woke, and a voice says: 'There's on'y me and yo 'ere'. Aynoch, 'e says: 'Ar, and yo'll be on yer bloody own as soon as I can get this other shoe on'. 'E says: ''Ow did yo get in 'ere?' And the voice says: 'Through the wall'. 'E says: 'Well, out o' the road, Ah'm gooin' out the same way'. At any rate 'e did get out and 'e started to run. 'E'd got through Wednesbury, Tipton, Darlaston — 'e was still goin' strong, and all at once 'e got out on the open road towards Oakengates in Shropshire, and there was a hare got in front of 'im. As you know, a hare'll run in a straight line in front of anything that's approaching 'im. There was old Aynoch leggin' it, and the voice said: 'I'm still with yer, Aynoch'. So old Aynoch says to the 'are: 'Get out the road and let some'dy run as con'.

CHAPTER 7

Miners

Colliers they get gold and silver,
Nailers they get nought but brass.
Who d'you think would have a nailer
While there's plenty of collier lads?

So ran a song sung in the Black Country (and, with variations, elsewhere). Miners did enjoy periods of high wages but they often experienced great hardship, and their work was frequently hazardous. The antiquity of mines in the area which became known as the Black County is attested by old workings with names like 'Danes' Shafts' and 'Delves', a Saxon term meaning deep hole or pit. The earliest documented references to coal mining are from 1271 and 1291, both from the manor of 'Seggesley' (Sedgley), and the latter date is shared by Oldswinford. In 1307 the abbot of Hales was granted the lease of a coal mine at Coombs Wood, Halesowen. Further mentions occur in 1315 (at Bradley) and 1380, 1401 and 1418 (all at Bilston). In 1538 the antiquarian, John Leland wrote 'That sea coles abounde nere to Wolverhampton and Wednesbyrie'. (Sea coal was so called because it was transported by ship whenever possible). Some fifty years later William Camden, another antiquarian, observed: 'The south part of Staffordshire hath coles digged out of the

A Bilston Chap (sweetheart), by Arthur Crtowquill, 1846

Colliers at New Hawne Pit, Halesowen, c.*1900*

earth, and mines of iron, but whether to their commodity or hindrance I leave to the inhabitants who do and shall better understand it'. By this time a dozen pits were turning out coal at 2s. 4d. per ton, a price which held for another hundred years or more. When Dr Robert Plot travelled round the area for the purposes of his book, *The Natural History of Staffordshire* (1686) he found that the number of collieries had tripled, and some of them, from seams 'ten, eleven and twelve yards thick' were 'affording' as he put it, up to 5,000 tons of coal a year. Among the pits he visited was one at Bilston which had been in production since 1490.

By 1800 some 5,500 Black Country miners were digging a million tons of coal annually. They spent twelve hours (6 a.m. to 6 p.m.) down the pit, six days a week, but were paid for a total of only 66 hours, since they stopped at the coal face for a 'drink hour' each day. Despite periods of depression in the coal trade in 1815-23, 1826-33 and 1838-43 the industry grew in the Black Country, and new pits proliferated. Near Blackheath alone there were sixteen, the names of some of which pointed to the fields and woods where shafts had been sunk: Birchyfield, Brickbat, Cakemore, Causeway Green, The Lifter, Long Meadow, Lower Holt, Nine Apostles, Oark Hall, Ramrod Hall, Richard, Speedwell, Titford, The Valencia, Whiteheath and Wolf.

In 1874 over 37,000 miners were at work in Black Country pits, but this was a high point before a long period of inexorable decline. Only three big collieries, Baggeridge, Hamstead and Jubilee, remained in 1943, and they employed some

Baggeridge Colliery, c.*1911*

2,500 men. The first of these, of which the first shaft was sunk in 1900, survived into the era of nationalisation until 1968, but its closure brought to an end deep mining in the Black Country.

Mining was organised on what was called the butty system, and this continued into the twentieth century in the case of the Earl of Dudley's pits. The owner of land beneath which coal was to be dug leased it to a tenant in return for a royalty, normally an agreed sum per ton brought to the surface. The tenant, usually an ironmaster, paid for shaft-sinking and for most of the equipment installed. In turn the tenant contracted an agent, known as a chartermaster or butty, who organised the work and paid the miners. Walter White wrote: 'In Staffordshire the man who directs the work of the mine is called the butty; he employs a subordinate whose title is doggy. The feeling that prevails between them and the miners is far from affectionate'. During his tour 'all round the Wrekin' in 1860 White talked to Tipton miners, one of whom told him: 'A butty loike fair-play! ... Ye wunna find one in this country [district]. Bless ye! The butties all hangs together; an' if one ha' got anythin' agin a man he tells t'others, an' there ain't no work for a poor feller in all the country'. The miner went on to explain how wages were paid:

> Ye see ivvery butty keeps a public-house, and we must go there o' Saturdays to be paid, and there he keeps us waitin'; and some gets tired o' waitin', an' begins to drink, an' mebbie they drinks three or four shillin' afore we gets our money. Then sixpence is stopped from ivvery man all round ivvery week, 'cause, ye see, ivvery man is expected to drink a quart at pay-time whether he wants to or no. Then if a new man have bin took on at the pit, a shillin' is stopped from he for fut-ale [paying the

> footing], an' sixpence a-piece is stopped from all the rest on us for that. And so, ye see, wi' them sixpences, and what we drinks while we be kept waitin', there's some on us ain't got much to take out o' sixteen shillings a week.

White, who also heard forthright opinions on tommy shops, added: 'Suppose, reader, that you are possessor of a mine or furnaces, and employer of a host of work-people, and that you establish a shop at which they can buy their groceries and chandlery wares, and you will understand what is meant by a Tommy-shop. Taking advantage of the liberty of the subject to ascend to the gallows, or gravitate to perdition, the keepers of Tommy-shops used to compel their people to buy at the shops whether the wares were lower in quality and higher in price than elsewhere, or not; and so mercenary was the spirit in some quarters that customers were shamefully and systematically plundered'. (The word, tommy, though it was pronounced *tummy* in the Black Country, did not mean stomach, but food. It may originally have referred to a loaf of bread distributed to the needy on St Thomas's Day, 21 December).

Summing up, White concluded that 'a state of chronic ill-feeling prevails', and quoted, suprisingly, perhaps, for a middle class Victorian who might well have considered it blasphematory, a parodic *Miners' Catechism*:

> Rehearse the articles of your belief. I believe that my master, being set over me is at liberty, in his own opinion, to tyrannise over and cheat me by every means in his power; that he employs his butty to help him in so doing, and he again the doggy to assist in abusing and swearing at me; and that for all purposes of bullying and over-reaching, these three are one.
>
> What is your duty to your master? My duty to my master is chiefly to slave for him and cringe to him from morning till night: to give up my life and strength in his service, and expect nothing but ill-usage in return.

The Black Country historian, George Barnsby, angrily concluded: 'The chief object of the butty system was to obtain coal at the cheapest cost, and pits were worked in an unskilful way to the neglect of discipline and safety precautions'. In addition: 'The masters led a determined resistance to any legislative proposal for safety, inspection, or control, and it has been documented that this was invariably supported, and often instigated, in the name of the Earl [of Dudley]. The Earl stood above the law and this immunity was fully utilised. … Thus the Earls of Dudley, far from using their immense influence to ameliorate social and economic conditions were an active, and in some respects a decisive influence, in perpetuating dreadful conditions'.

The earliest recorded death in a pit of a Black Country collier seems to be that of Humphrey Mattocks of Bilston, in 1392. Church burial registers, beginning in the mid-sixteenth century, might reveal more, though they by no means always included the deceased's profession and manner of death. The laconic entry, 'killed in a coal pit', occurs in a number of instances, sometimes with additional details. For example, at Rowley Regis:

> 1695. Henry Sheldon of Tividale, killed in coale pit in Tipton Parish.
> 1803. Henry son of John and Mary Edmands. He was killed in a coal pit near Brierley Hill. His cloathes were caught in a hook or something of that kind, of the skep, which took him up a considerable way, at length his clothes tore, and he held by his hands till being unable to hang any longer, he fell and spoke no more.

At Sedgley:

> 1658. Alexr. Parke, collier, kill'd in Colepits at Dudley.
> Robt. Aston, of Etinhsole [Ettingshall], kild in the Colepits.
> 1662. Blind John Elwell, of Etingshole, kild in a colepitt.
> 1685. Andrew Nicklin, collier, and Edward Robbinson, collier, were killed by the damp [?firedamp] in a colepit.

At Bilston:

> 1725. Richard Allons … was killed in a colepit near the Portway Road. He was aged abt. 43 years.
> 1735. Thomas Teese, a collier, killed by a fall of coals in Wolverhampton cole pit.

Work underground in the thick seams of Staffordshire, 1860s

A Bilston colliery, 1810

1756. Jane Rowley. She was landing coals at ye pitt-eye, and ye board on which she stood broke. N.B. Ye landing board stands over ye pitt-eye [mouth], so that on breaking of this board she fell to the bottom of ye pitt, and was so much bruised that she died soon after.

1758. John Blewer. He was going down into a colepitt in ye work belonging to Mr. Gibbons, of Ettinghall, and ye rope broke, by wch accident he fell to ye bottom of ye pitt and was killed.

1766. John Jones. He was killed in a coalpitt by a fall of coles.

1764. George Whitehall. He was killed by a fall of coals in a colepitt.

In the nineteenth century gravestones and memorials started to appear with epitaphs commemorating miners' deaths at work. At High Ercal pit four young miners were going down the shaft in the cage (introduced for greater safety) when the rope, later found to have been weakened by contact with hot ashes, broke. In Brierley Hill churchyard their epitaph (now gone, but, fortunately, recorded) read:

Cornelius Plant Turner, aged 27 years;
Daniel Plant Turner, aged 22 years;
John Thompson, aged 21 years;
Thomas Dimmock, aged 18 years;
Colliers, who died August 23rd, 1815.

The coal pit rope asunder broke; we fell, and dead we lay;
Our sudden ends warn you, my friends, to work while yet 'tis day.
When blooming youth is snatched away by death's resistless hand,
Our hearts the mournful tribute pay which pity must demand;
Let this vain world delude no more; behold the gaping tomb,
It bids us seize the present hour; to-morrow death may come.

A young miner who died in 1820 has this epitaph at West Bromwich:

Farewell my tender parents dear,
Beneath this stone I lie here.
The coals all burst round my head,
And forst me to my death-bed.

At St Mary's Church, Bilston, is a plaque 'Erected to the brethren of St Mary's Miners Guild in memory of Brother Thomas Briggs who with seven fellow sufferers was killed in a coalpit at West Bromwich by an explosion of firedamp, Aug. 13th 1844'. Some of the many commemorations of individual miners have been sought out by Ted Walker. They include:

William Donaldson, died 1870, aged 19:
And when he did descend the pit
His daily bread to earn
On he went with little thought
He never should return (All Saints, Bloxwich).

John Tibbitts, 'who lost his life at Homer Hill Colliery May 17th 1877 aged 14 yr' (St Luke's, Cradley Heath).

David Hingley, 'who lost his life whilst working at the New Homeshaill coal pit. Dec.30th 1879 aged 21 yr' (Lye and Wollescote Cemetery).

John Davies, 'who was killed in Ashbourne Park Colliery Sept 29th 1885 aged 23 years' (Willenhall Cemetery).

William Thomas Little, 'who met his death while working at No.4 pit Hillsfield June 6th 1888 aged 26 yr' (Lye and Wollescote).

Richard Nightingale, died 1889, aged 31, 'killed at Hamstead Colliery' (Heath Lane Cemetery, West Bromwich).

William Cook, died 1889, aged 28 years, 'who lost his life … in a fall of coal at Bromley Peashall Colliery' (St James, Lower Gornal).

> 'William Adams of 15 Colley St who was burnt in thee [*sic*] Sandwell Colliery explosion and died 2 Nov 1894 aged 38 yr' (All Saints, West Bromwich).

> 'David beloved husband of Martha Evans of Gornalwood who was killed in no. 17 pit Pensnett Jan 2nd 1902' (St James, Lower Gornal).

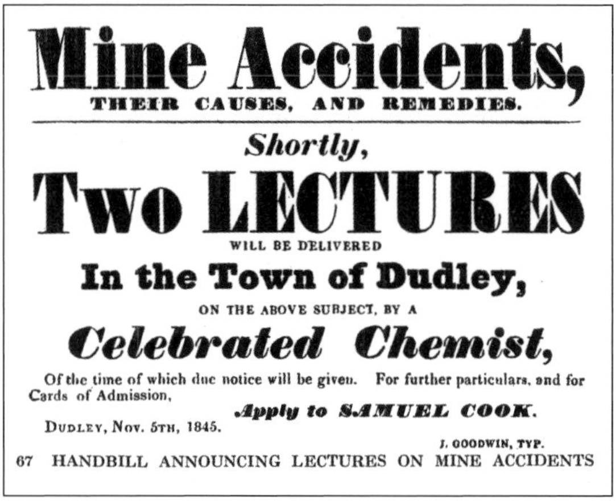

Handbill advertising talks at Dudley by Samuel Cook, 1845

According to an article of 1863 in the *Edinburgh Review*, such casualties in the Black Country were then running at about 800 a year, made up of 'accidents in the shaft, 150; explosions, 70; falls of the roof and of minerals, 400; miscellaneous below ground, 130; above ground, 50'. In addition to the attrition of individual losses there was an inexorable sequence of disasters which produced multiple deaths. These are a few examples from a long list: 1818: Bilston (15);1846: Rounds Green, Oldbury (19 deaths); 1853: Old Park, Dudley (11); 1856: Ramrod Hall, Oldbury (11); 1867: Homer Hill, Stourbridge (12); 1872: Pelsall Hall, near Walsall (22); 1894: Sandwell Park (4); 1908: Hamstead (26); 1923: Pensnett (4); 1929: Coombs Wood, Halesowen (8). Nor was this the end: in St John's Church at Walsall is a window to miners who lost their lives at work between 1873 and 1964. In addition to memorial inscriptions, miners were commemorated in printed ballad sheets such as 'The Sorrowful Lamentation of 36 poor Colliers, who were stopped up in a Coal Pit four days and four nights: fifteen of whom lost their lives, and twenty one were brought up alive, at Bilston, in Staffordshire, on Friday Sept. 17th, 1818'. The sheet which, somewhat unaccountably, was printed by S. Ashworth of Rochdale, begins with information in prose, then changes to verse:

> A most distressing accident happened at a Coal Pit at Bilstone, in Staffordshire, on Friday last. While the workmen were busily engaged in the Pit, the water from the Canal burst in upon them, and the roof at the same time giving way, they were in an instant buried in the ruins, together with eight horses, who were unfortunately drowned. Fifteen of the unfortunate men and boys lost their lives, and the rest were found in a miserable situation, but some of them are likely to recover.

The water is stated by the survivors to have burst in one side of the Pit, and gave the fifteen who lost their lives, timely notice to escape the danger, but they replied one to the other, it was nothing but cowardice to attempt to make their escape, and so they continued working till again urged to quit by the falling of some timber; but alas! Too late, for they were in an instant swallowed up. Persons were immediately employed to rescue them from their dreadful situation, when after working four days and nights, they succeeded in bringing up 21 miserable objects alive; the bones of their others were crushed quite flat, too horrid for description. They were all young men that lost their lives, leaving nine widows and sixteen children to lament their loss.

A HYMN
Composed for the Occasion, and Sung over them
Stay travellers and shed a tear
Upon the dust that's buried here,
Our death was awful — may it warn,
And caused all sinners for to mourn.

In prime of youth we were cut down,
And left our wives and babes to mourn,
A many hands our lives have lost,
It will be known whate'er they cost.

The Lord is true and just we know,
He will reward and here we do,
In many things we act amiss,
The scriptures say we're none of this.

We've left our wives and children dear,
For to lament our loss you hear,
In the arms of death we now do lie,
Our bodies are as cold as clay.

Weep not for us our children dear,
We are not dead but sleeping here,
Sleeping we are in silent dust,
Prepare to die, for die you must.

Great grief, O Lord, doth us assail,
Pity on our wives and children take,
Our eyes grow dim, our strength doth fail,
Our bones do now corrupt and waste.

One might have expected indignation, or at least questioning, but this is tear-jerking stuff, borrowing phrases often used in epitaphs, and it may have been intended to stimulate contributions to a charitable collection for the wives and children mentioned. Some years later the Dudley draper, Samuel Cook, did react angrily to another disaster (see illustration opposite), but then he was a radical and a Chartist.

As the nineteenth century wore on, coverage of pit disasters passed more and more from ballad sheets to newspapers. This was the case in 1869 when for

THE STAFFORDSHIER COLLIER'S
LAMENT.

God of my life, we now descend
To labour under ground,
While danger all our steps attend,
While darkness reigns around
The fiery damps thou canst control,
And stop our fleeting breath,
And cause that heavy fall of coal,
To crush us soon to death.

To face those horrid dangers
We brave men did descend
Unto our fellow sufferers
We did assistance lend
It struck their hearts with terror
And filled them with dismay
To see so many lifeless,
In death's cold arms to lay

Oh God our lives are in your hands
To spare or take away,
And to thy care we'll recommend
Ourselves through this day
From sudden death deliver us
And let thy will be done
I trust on God thou'lt let us see,
Once more the setting sun.

This was a dreadful accident
From all accounts we learn,
Their parents scarce could know their (own
They were so badly burnt
We hope the Lord received their soul
In Heaven for to dwell,
The sufferings we did undergo,
No mortal tongue can tell

Some go down to rise no more
To see the glorious light
Perhaps before the day is o'er
We enter deaths dark night
Parents mourn and children weep
For those that s laid below
Fathers and sons in deaths long sleep
Crushed by that fatal blow

With hearts so light we left our home
Upon that fatae morn
We little thought of our sad fate,
Before that night did dawn
Our lives were so uncertain
As you may plainly see
One moment we're in health & bloom
Next in eternity

O give us grace our Lord to see,
That all may there be well
Bless God when we descend the pit
'Tis not the pit of Hell.
Thou canst create thou canst destroy
Whatever thou thinkets best
If it is thy will this day we die
Then take our souls to rest

Their money Colliers dearly earn
They should protected be,
You well know a Collier
From dangers never free
The cries of wives and children
Was dreadful as we find
May God protect their lovely babes
Whom they have left behind.

The cries and groans of us poor men
Would cause your hearts to ache
And many did shed tears that day
For our poor Collier's sake
Whilst those poor mournful widow
Their hearts did ache with pain
To think that morn should be their las
They ne'er should meet again

Now their wives and helpless families
In sorrow are left behind
May the Lord be their protector,
And unto them prove kind
For grief is so distressing.
So piercing to the mind,
Each joy has fled, their father's dead
And those children left behind.

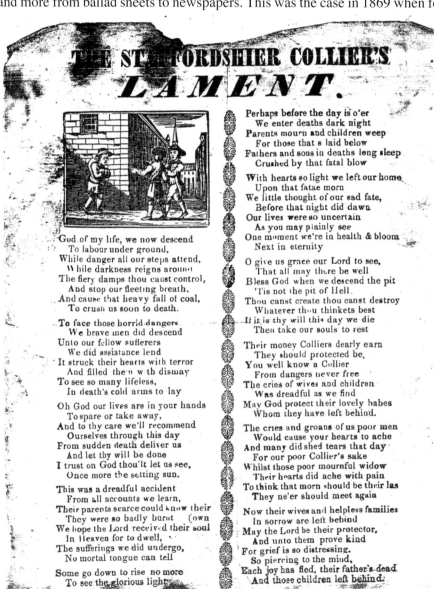

Ballad sheet: 'The Staffordshier Collier's Lament'

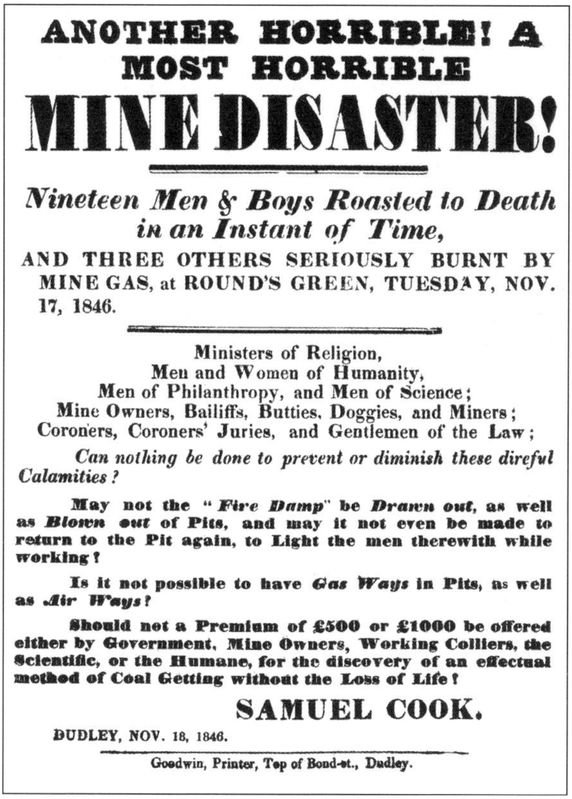

ANOTHER HORRIBLE! A MOST HORRIBLE

MINE DISASTER!

Nineteen Men & Boys Roasted to Death in an Instant of Time,

AND THREE OTHERS SERIOUSLY BURNT BY MINE GAS, at ROUND'S GREEN, TUESDAY, NOV. 17, 1846.

Ministers of Religion,
Men and Women of Humanity,
Men of Philanthropy, and Men of Science;
Mine Owners, Bailiffs, Butties, Doggies, and Miners;
Coroners, Coroners' Juries, and Gentlemen of the Law;

Can nothing be done to prevent or diminish these direful Calamities?

May not the "*Fire Damp*" be *Drawn out*, as well as *Blown out* of Pits, and may it not even be made to return to the Pit again, to Light the men therewith while working?

Is it not possible to have *Gas Ways* in Pits, as well as *Air Ways*?

Should not a Premium of £500 or £1000 be offered either by Government, Mine Owners, Working Colliers, the Scientific, or the Humane, for the discovery of an effectual method of Coal Getting without the Loss of Life?

SAMUEL COOK.

DUDLEY, NOV. 18, 1846.

Goodwin, Printer, Top of Bond-st., Dudley.

Handbill issued by Samuel Cook, 1846

up to six days the lives of thirteen men and boys hung in the balance in the Earl of Dudley's Nine Locks Colliery off Delph Road, Brierley Hill. (The name derived from the flight of locks — in fact, only eight — on the nearby canal). At about midnight on 16/17 March when a dam in old workings burst, a huge volume of water flooded into the pit and trapped the miners. Massive pumps installed on the surface raised 250 tons of water an hour but it was several days before levels in the flooded mine began to fall. After only thirteen hours the miners' lights ran out, but before that one of the men, David Hickman, wrote for each of them messages to wives and children which he put in an old tobacco tin. Another man had a watch, and could tell the time by opening the case and feeling the hands. As for the passing of the days, the miners could hear overhead the muffled thumps of the drop-hammer at Nine Locks Forge: 'When that stopped, as it did between the day turn and the night turn, we judged it was night, and then it was morning. … We knew [when] it was Saturday night because the Locks' hammer had come to a long stand'. Then, after five days, 'On Sunday morning we shouted, and we could hear voices. That was at about four o'clock in the morning of the day our deliverance was to be affected'. The ordeal went into a further day for some of the miners, all of whom in the end were recovered, twelve alive and one dead. After sharing a tiny amount of food, they had survived by chewing coal and sucking pieces of leather cut from their boots.

Despite the newspapers' extensive coverage of the crisis and the triumphant outcome, Rev. James White felt moved to write a 126-line poem, 'The Brierley Hill Catastrophe'. T. Jones, printer and bookbinder of Dudley Street, Brierley Hill, issued a different ballad by an unknown author:

Lines on the Brierley Hill Inundation

In Brierley Hill last March we hear,
How many hearts was filled with fear,
And many faces turned deadly pale,
While listening to a most dreadful tale.
Tears from their eyes in streams did flow,
As from their homes they forth did go;
Themselves the dreadful sight to see,
At Dudley's Locks Lane Colliery.

At the 'Wallows Pit' sad to relate,
Some thousands there did congregate;
To talk and think of men entombed,
Deep in that pit perhaps all doomed
To die, but willing hearts and hands combine
To work their friend from that fatal mine;
For thirteen miners' precious souls are there,
Shut in from friends, and light and air.

The waters bursting, caused a flood,
Which left them destitute of food.
Five dreary days and nights they passed,
In that deep mine, oh, what a fast!
Their drink was water, foul and brown,
To breathe close to it they lay down,
At times were singing, praying, crying,
With thoughts of home, of friends, and dying.

Hickman, brave man, while he had breath,
By praise and prayer prepares for death;
Hanley's religious soul doth praise
His God who lengthens out his days;
Taylor and Hunt both join in prayer,
And seem quite happy tho' imprisoned are.
Their wives and families prey on their mind,
But to their lot they are quite resigned.

Page says 'in heaven there still is light
Though round him reigns the darkest night;
Holden with grief was sore oppressed,
But in Christ at last found rest;
Skidmore did sleep much time away,
While some sing, others pray,
Sleep on brave man and take thy rest,
With grief thou art not now oppressed.

MINERS

Pearson and Son, brave boy was he,
To sit beside his father's knee,
His words have through the country ran,
'I'm but a boy, you are a man'.
Higgs, poor man his strength did fail,
Along the ground he scarce could crawl,
He prays for wife and children dear,
Commends them to his maker's care.

Skidmore his bread most nobly gave,
To Timmins his young life to save,
Embraced him close to keep him warm
And thus exposed himself to harm.
Taylor also, his bread did give,
To Sankey too that he might live!
Courageous man, long be you spared
Then meet in heaven your rich reward.

Hunt with the rest his bread did share,
When all was gone, how did they fare?
Why eating coal and chewing leather,
And hung'ring, thirsting, altogether.
Ashmore, poor man, his reason went,
And into shreds his garments rent.
Up the gate road he wildly fled,
And soon was numbered with the dead.

While in that pit they all remain,
Thousands of people crowd Locks Lane
Wives, Sisters, mothers too are there,
With haggard looks, disheveled hair.
Their tearful eyes, their pale blanched cheeks
Express far more than tongue can speak,
And many prayed that God would save,
Their husbands from a living grave.

As hour by hour both night and day,
The engines pump the flood away;
Plant with his men the shaft descend,
But choke-damp drives them back again.
They lime and water throw down there,
To kill the damp and clear the air;
All schemes are tried these men to save,
And bring them from a watery grave.

Thousands of hearts with grief was stirred
When hark! oh heavens a voice was heard!
From that deep mine the 'bond' to call,
When cheers burst from the lips of all,
The men again descend the shaft,
And take with them a floating raft,
The crowd in silence view the scene,
Well knowing what its use doth mean.

The bell upon the bank doth ring,
Soon to the top the men they bring;
Excited thousands rend the air
With cheers to see them safely there,
The people shout hurrah for Brown,
For Plant and Thompson who went down,
Risking their lives those men to save
From death and from a watery grave.

In garments warm they did attire,
And placed them close beside the fire;
Exhausted nature they soon restore,
To their homes they are conveyed once more.
To Church they went their prayers to rend,
To God, their maker and their friend;
Their lives in prayer henceforth be given,
And find at last their way to heaven.

Ye coal kings who do thus combine,
To raise from earth the precious mine;
Think of the words of Christ our Saviour,
And pay each man fair price for labour.
Defraud them not of time or measure,
Fair dealings a most precious treasure,
Cause not the fatherless to pine,
For parents lost down in the mine.

One thousand every year are slain,
Ten thousand more are also maimed;
While they their daily tasks fulfil,
Or are entombed as at Brierley Hill.
Their hours are long their pay is small,
Brothers on you we loudly call,
Help us to gain without delay,
Eight hours and five shillings per day.

The Nine Locks disaster was long remembered. The pit reopened but was eventually closed, though the head gear remained standing until 1918. One of the rescuers, Samuel Thompson, died only in 1926. Articles in local newspapers for the fortieth anniversary of the disaster in 1909 included an interview with a survivor, Thomas Sankey, who had been a boy at the time. Another, Joseph Pearson, told his story six years later. Further items appeared in 1919.

In his autobiography, *The Making of a Novelist*, David Christie Murray ('I was born and bred in the mining district, and was familiar with the heroism of the miners'), wrote a graphic account (see panel below) of how as a young reporter he was sent to Pelsall Hall Colliery, where in November 1872 twenty-two men died in an underground flood. The disaster was also commemorated in a ballad (see illustration on page 113).

With the Rescuers

I hired a horse at a livery stable at Walsall, and had him kept in readiness in the back yard of a beerhouse. ... It was a dreadful night, and not an easy matter for one unaccustomed to the place to find his way to the pit's mouth. The iron cages of fire that burned there in the windy rain and the dark impeded rather than helped the stranger on his way towards them. The feet of thousands of people who had visited the spot since the news of the accident was made known had worn away the last blade of grass from the slippery fields and had left a very Slough of Despond behind them. I was down half a dozen times, and when I reached the hovel where the rescue party had gathered I was as much like a mud statue as a man. Everything was in readiness, and the descent was made at once.

We were under the command of Mr. Walter Ness, a valiant Scotchman, who afterwards became the manager of her Majesty's mines in Warora, Central India. Five or six of us huddled together on the 'skip', the word was given, and we shot down into the black shaft, which seemed in the light of the lamps we carried as if its wet and shining walls of brick rushed upwards whilst we kept stationary. In a while we stopped, with a black pool of water three or four fathoms below us.

'This'll be the place', said one of the men, and tapped the wall with a pick.

'Yes', said Mr. Ness, 'that will be about the place; try it'.

The man lay down upon his stomach upon the floor of the skip and worked away a single brick, which fell with a splash into the pool below. Then out came another and another, until there was a hole there big enough for a man to crawl through. We had struck upon an old disused airway which led into the inner workings of the mine. One by one we snaked our way from the skip into the hole; and, whatever the miners thought about it, it was rather a scarey business for me. We all got over safely enough and began a journey on all fours through mud and slush five or six inches deep. Here and there the airway was lofty enough to allow us to walk with bent heads and rounded shoulders. Sometimes it was so low that we had to go snakewise. There was one place where the floor and the roof of the passage had sunk so that we actually had to dive for it. This seemed a little comfortless at the time, but it saved our lives afterwards. After a toilsome scramble we came upon the stables, and found there the first dead body.

It was that of a lad named Edward Colman, who had met his death in a curious and dreadful manner. He was sitting on a rocky bench, and at his feet lay a rough hunch of bread and meat and a clasp-knife. He had evidently heard the cry of alarm, had sprung to his feet, and had struck the top of his head with fatal force against a projecting lance of rock immediately above him. There had been a speedy end to his troubles, poor fellow, and he sat there stiff and cold and pallid, staring before him like a figure in an exhibition of waxworks.

The waters barred our further descent into the mine, but there was a belief that by breaking through the earthy wall of the stable a continuation of the old airway would be found. The experiment was tried with an alarming result. No sooner was the breach made than a slow stream of choke-damp flowed into the chamber, and the lights began to go out one by one. We scrambled back at once for our lives, and once past the pool were safe; the water effectually blocked the passage of the poisonous gas. I got but one whiff of it; but it gave me a painful sensation at the bridge of the nose which lasted acutely for some days. In all, our expedition had not lasted an hour; but it had proved to demonstrate the impossibility of saving a single life. …

There were two instances of escape at the Pelsall Hall disaster which seem worth recording. Every mine has what is known as an 'upcast shaft' – a perpendicular tunnel which runs side by side with the working shaft, and is connected with it at the foot by an airway which serves to ventilate the workings. When the first rush of water, breaking in from some old deserted working, came tearing down, a man and a boy were standing at the bottom of the downcast. They were carried on the crest of the wave clean through the airway, borne some distance upwards in the upcast, and were then floated on to the floor of a skip, where they were found insensible, but living, some hours later. No other creature was brought to bank alive.

Miners did not suffer in silence. Their defence mechanisms included adhering to various traditional norms, and organising themselves in collective actions such as demonstrations and strikes. Despite a reputation for recklessness, miners were acutely aware of potential dangers, which they attempted to counter with homespun expedients. Amy Lyons, the daughter of a one-time vicar of Wednesbury, describes in her book, *Black Country Sketches* (1901), a board in the town's Cockfighters' Arms on which was painted in big letters:

YE COLLIERS' GUIDE OF SIGNES AND WARNING

1st. – To dream of a broken shoe, a sure sign of danger.

2nd. – If you mete a woman at the rising of ye sun turne again from ye pit, a sure signe of deathe.

3rd. – To dream of a fire is a signe of danger.

4th. – To see a bright light in ye mine is a warninge to flee away.
5th. – If Gabriel's hounds ben about, doe no worke that day.
6th. – When foule smells be aboute ye pit, a sure signe that ye imps ben annear.
7th. – To charme away ghostes and ye like: Take a Bible and a key, hold both in ye right hand, and saye ye Lord's Prayer, and they will right speedily get farre away.

Lines on the Pit Accident at PELSALL.

Oh! list all you Christains as you 're passing by,
Its about those poor Colliers a mother and boy,
For all was commotion at every street door,
They rushed to Hall collery their hearts full and sore,
Some they are running they cry and they shout,
Our father is killed at Pelsall I doubt,
The water broke on them took them in suprise,
And stopped ventilation which cost them their lives.

Oh! do not weep mother our father will come,
For we are so happy when he is at home,
He is a poor Collier I can't make it out yet,
The reason he's stoping so long at the pit,
A 6 in the evening from his work he would go,
And we was so happy when his face he would show,
He'd call us his darling, play with us awhile,
So don't weep dear mother but give us a smile.

Hush, do not murmer, a secret I'll tell,
Your father, an angel in heaven doth dwell,
Although he was loving to his wife and child,
He'll not be returning, the thought drives me wild.
Its true he's a collier with twenty-one more,
Have gone to the angels on that distant shore,
So that is the reason that I weep and cry,
He has left me a widow, you an orphan boy.

He worked at Pelsall the place that you know.
You went with his dinner a short time ago,
Now you'll never ramble to that pit after him,
So think of the Colliers and poor little Jim,
So all take a wrning and do not long wait,
For death is a lurking close to our gate,
The hour and the minute we never can tell,
That we shall be summon'd above for to dwell.

Ballad sheet: 'Lines on the Pit Accident at Pelsall'

Of these warnings, Dr Plot, over a century earlier, mentioned one which was widespread in mining communities:

> We need go no further for an instance than the same town of *Wednesbury*, where the *Colyers* will tell you that early in the morning as they go to their work, and from the *Cole-pits* themselves, they sometimes hear the voice of a *pack* of *hounds* in the *Air*, which has happened so frequently that they have got a name for them, calling them *Gabriels hounds*, though the more sober and judicious take them to be *Wild-geese*, making this noise in their *flight*.

Of other signs of ill omen, according to an account of 1926, referring to the Halesowen area but no doubt applying further afield, 'there are many colliers who if they met a wooden-legged man, or a cross-eyed person, would refuse to descend the pit that day'. The writer added: 'There are innumerable superstitions associated with the collier, and many deaths are said to have been predicted in some strange manner'. One traditional way out of difficulty was adopted in 1911 (and no doubt on other occasions): 'The observation of the custom led to an action by the employers against the men concerned. These men proposed to take a holiday and, according to custom, one of them threw up a brick into the air, it being understood that if the brick came down they would absent themselves from work. The brick obeyed nature's laws, and the men took a holiday, and in due course appeared in court'.

Thomas Pinnock asserted that the devil himself was 'supposed specially to haunt the shafts and subterranean workings of disused mines' and could be summoned up by an 'absurd spell': 'A crust of bread and cheese placed inside a hat, with a crossed knife and fork (always an ominous sign), and over this the recitation of the Lord's Prayer backwards'. He continued:

> Besides the asssociation of the presence of the evil one in mines, there is a shadowy belief … that the spirit of any one killed in a pit hovers round the spot, at any rate until after the body is consigned to sacred earth. To this idea is doubtless due the custom of suspending work in a pit when a fatal accident happens. All the men engaged in that part of the workings come up out of the mine, and do not descend the shaft again until after the funeral.

According to John Noake, the custom of ceasing work in 'the Dudley coalfields' after a fatal accident dated 'from time immemorial'. The surviving colliers 'were allowed a certain sum of money to spend among themselves for drink, called "dead money". This was always spent at a public-house, and very improper scenes were often the result'. Writing in the mid-nineteenth century, he added:

> The general custom now is, that in the event happening as above, the *Field* (that is the proprietor of the colliery) provides the coffin, the *butty collier* (that is the principal man under the master of the colliery, and who engages the men, and is, in fact, the major domo of the works, although he himself is as black and as dirty as the colliers, but a little better dressed) pays the expenses of the funeral, such as the fees, eating and drinking, &c.; the widow is afterwards allowed a small sum per week from the *Field* (if the colliery continues long enough at work) for each child as long as she continues a widow.

Perhaps because of the dangers of their working lives, miners had the kind of zest for life observed by a visitor to a pit near Dudley in 1841: 'It is a fine sight to see the miners congregated at dinner, in a large dining hall cut out of the coal. There they sit, naked from the middle upwards, as black as blackamoor savages, showing their fine, vigorous, muscular persons; eating, drinking and laughing. They sit an hour, from one to two, and then resume their labours'. Or the sense of humour and love of high jinks revealed in this story told me in 1973 by Roger Hoole of Birmingham:

> Years ago there was a very hard-drinking parson who lived in the Wyrley or Essington area. One night, he was found lying dead-drunk in a ditch by colliers going to work. They picked him up and carried him down to the pit bottom and put him by the big fire which, in those days, was used to produce a draught, and thus to create ventilation. When the parson came to, he perceived the darkness and felt the heat of the fire, which was being stoked by a half-naked man. Because of his transgressions, he thought himself transported to hell, and broke into vehement prayers to his maker. The laughter of the miners eventually made him realise his mistake.

The anonymous author of the *Edinburgh Review* article quoted earlier emphasises Black Country miners' passion for enjoyment:

> A prize-fight, or a poaching adventure, has a charm for them that is irresistible. A wake, a fair, or a race empties the pits of all but the steadiest hands. No bribe would induce these votaries of pleasure to remain. The great difficulty of employers is to induce the men to go regularly to their work, especially when they are wanted, when the work is good and wages rise. Every Monday after pay-day is devoted by many to jollity. On such occasions the pit is said to be at 'play'.

Then he adds this curious and little-known passage:

> The pit-girls are not less fond of holidays than their fathers, and much they enjoy two days of saturnalia when, by immemorial custom, the field

> of labour is turned into a scene of general riot. On Easter Monday, the men roam about the colliery in gangs, and claim the privilege of heaving, as they call it, every female whom they meet, — that is to say, of lifting her up as high as they can, and saluting her in her descent. On Easter Tuesday the ladies have their revenge — and in their hands this strange horse-play acquires redoubled energy. Neither rank nor age are respected; not even the greatest of men, the manager himself, would be secure from attack; and those who will not enter into the fun must purchase exemption by a ransom proportionate to their station.

The writer, turning to sterner subjects, observes: 'The rate of wages is high, but is liable to considerable fluctuations; and the miner glories in his power of maintaining it by the combinations and strikes, which form so important a feature in the history of mining'. Many would see such actions as attempts to improve the conditions of life and work which for the majority of working people were, 'unspeakably bad'. They were faced, to quote George Barnsby, with 'the invocation of the Master and Servant Acts, importation of blacklegs, the use of courts dominated by employer J.P.s, and the calling in of military force'.

An encounter between soldiers and colliers protesting at the price of food is evoked in a song, 'The Brave Dudley Boys', taken down for the price of a shilling from the singing of a man breaking stones on the road between Tipton and Dudley in about 1850, but probably dating from the 1780s:

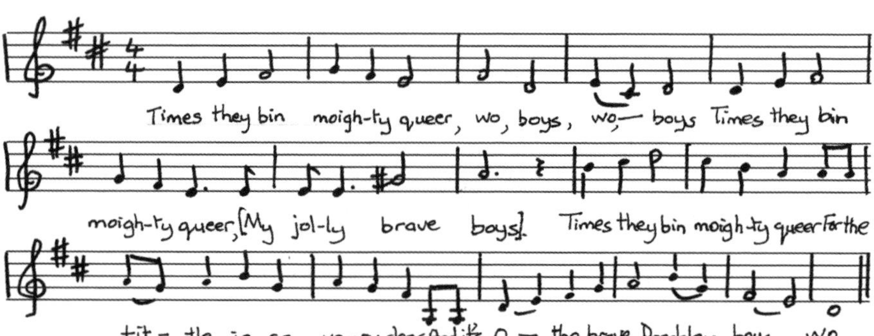
Times they bin moigh-ty queer, wo, boys, wo— boys Times they bin
moigh-ty queer, [My jol-ly brave boys]. Times they bin moigh-ty queer For the
tit- tle is sa ve-ry dear, And it's O — the brave Doodley boys, wo.

[Tune by Wilf Darlington, based on 'The Bold Benjamin']

We bin a marchin up and deown,
Fur to pull the housen deown.

Some gotten sticks, some gotten steavs,
Fur to be-at all the rogues and kneavs.

Then fur to mek the fittle chep,
We teks and burns it all of a yep.

But the Dragunes they did come,
And 'twas the devil tek the hoindmost wum.

We scrawn oop and deown the pits,
Fur we bin welly freeten oot a we wits.

God bless Lurd Doodley Ward,
For he knows these toims bin hard.

Fur he sent away them 'ere sojering men,
And we'en promised him faithfully never to riot again.

Could the sudden runaway loss of metre in the last line indicate tongue in cheek? Certainly, conflicts between colliers and the military during strikes, elections and various forms of political protest continued well into the nineteenth century. Black Country colliers led a march into Birmingham in October 1782 as another protest at food prices. The event may have inspired John Freeth, the Birmingham balladeer, to write, to the tune of 'The Staffordshire Fox Chase', 'The Colliers' March' (first published in 1790), which includes these verses:

Sworn to remedy a capital fault
And bring down the exorbitant price of the malt,
From Dudley to Walsall they trip it along,
And Hampton was truly alarmed at the throng.

Women and children, wherever they go,
Shouting out, 'Oh the brave Dudley boys, O';
Nailers and spinners the cavalcade join,
The markets to lower their flattering design.

Six days out of seven poor nailing boys get
Little else at their meals but potatoes to eat;
For bread hard they labour, good things never carve,
And swore 'twere as well to be hanged as to starve.

During the depression which followed the peace with France in 1815, the military quelled riots by out-of-work coal and ironstone miners. In June the following year a number of colliers hit on the novel idea of drawing the government's attention to their plight by dragging waggons of coal to London. Three teams of fifty set off on different routes, via Worcester, Birmingham and

Coventry, and Stourbridge respectively. According to the Staffordshire historian, William Pitt, 'they proceeded at the rate of 12 miles a-day, and received voluntary gifts of money, &c. on the road as they passed along, declining to *ask* alms: their motto, as placarded on the carts, being — "Rather work than beg"'. Alarmed at the prospect of the colliers' reaching London, the government sent magistrates who intercepted two of the parties, one at St Albans and the other near Maidenhead, and persuaded the men to desist.

> They were allowed the value of their coals, which were left to be distributed to the poor, and sufficient means were given to them to reach their homes. The conduct of these distressed men was most exemplary: they listened with the greatest attention to the advice of the Magistrates, and after obtaining a certificate of their good behaviour, returned with the waggons to their families and friends.

The third party, which must have been unsure of the way to London, was met by magistrates near Chester, with a similar outcome.

Protests were not always so peaceable. Colliers attmpting to resist wage cuts or short time working rioted in 1826 at Wednesbury and West Bromwich, in 1832, 1834 and 1842 at Dudley. In the latter year striking colliers marched down Dudley High Streeet and broke the windows of all the shops, save for that of Samuel Cook. In Wednesbury and round about, 300,000 miners 'marched to the pits still at work, compelling the remnant of their comrades to join in the strike by fetching them up in the skip, and then throwing them into any convenient canal or reservoir', writes F.W. Hackwood. Meanwhile:

> On Monday, miners stopped Lime and Coal pits at Walsall, compelling other workers to join them. The Walsall troop of the Staffs. Yeomanry turned out, augmented by troops of the 3rd. Dragoon Guards. Large number of colliers roamed about demanding food and money from all and sundry. Tuesday morning saw large numbers of colliers marching through Wolverhampton. On Wednesday and Thursday the pit-men visited Bilston and Princes End pits, bringing out workers and throwing into the canal all those who refused to join them. Bilston shops were raided and bread stolen. Ten thousand colliers met at West Bromwich (Spon Lane) and were addressed by the Chartists, who advised them not to return to work for less than Four Shillings per day. This meeting was followed by similar gatherings at Wolverhampton (Stafford Street), and large bodies of special constables were enrolled. Two companies of the 12th Foot and the Himley Troop of Yeomanry also stood by. 400 colliers threatened those working at Parkfield Colliery and work was stopped. The colliery-owner, Mr Underhill rode among the mob and later identified several of the miscreants. Eight were arrested.

As a result of these and other arrests, men received sentences at Stafford ranging from several months' hard labour in prison to transportation for life to penal colonies in Australia. Sporadic unrest continued through the 1850s and '60s. Colliers, using the black powder from their pits, blew up various buildings and also, at Old Hill in 1864, a blackleg. Tom Langley's grandfather, who worked at a pit in Tipton, was on strike in the 1860s: 'They would march with p'r'aps a band — my granddad played a fiddle — and they would march to other parts of the Black Country or just outside, and there they would beg. And that's how my grandfather came into Brownhills and Chasetown. They slept the night on Pelsall Common, and 'e came and got a job in the Cannock Chase pits, and 'e never went back again except for visits'.

Illustration from the Parliamentary commissioners' report of 1842

Langley's grandfather started work in the pit at Tividale in 1842: 'He's mentioned in the Shaftesbury Report, where it says: "James Baker was taking his little son, aged six years and ten months, in the dawn to the pit"'. The number of such children in Black Country pits, working as trappers (sitting in the darkness, opening and closing doors which regulated the air circulation) or pony drivers, was 'exceedingly large', according to the historian, T.E. Lones. Many paupers or orphans, virtual slaves 'wholly in the power of the butties', were bound apprentice 'for little or no wages' from the age of 7, 8 or 9 until that of 21. Lord Shaftesbury's efforts helped to bring about the Act of 1842 which banned females from working underground, and allowed males to do so only from the age of ten, unless they were already so employed.

Sheer necessity compelled parents to send their children to work. 'Times were very 'ard', said Langley in 1971. 'I 'ad a pal died recently, well over 80, and 'e told me that on 'is thirteenth birthday — 'is father'd been killed in the pit — 'is mother threw a pair of moleskins at 'im and said: "That's yer thirteenth birthday present. Down the pit yer go and earn some money"'.

At least girls were spared from pit work in the Black Country, according to the conventional wisdom. Yet both J. Wilson Jones and Tom Langley knew old women who had worked underground. The latter said: 'I remember the harness of one of the women who used to crawl on all fours with her brother, dragging tubs along; and the harness used to hang on the wall'. There is no dispute that women worked on the surface, the bank. The 'pit Sals' or 'bonk girls' received the skips or baskets of coal as they came up the shaft. The anonymous writer of 1863 in the *Edinburgh Review* seems to have taken quite a shine to them:

> This is heavy and dirty work, and the pit-girls who are engaged in it, with their shabby dresses tied grotesquely about them, and their inverted bonnets stuck on the top of their heads, seem not less sordid. But before the philanthropist draws his conclusions, let him see them on a Sunday (we wish it were an equivalent phrase to say at church), with clean persons, bright complexions, sparklng eyes, and dressed out in the cheap finery which now-a-days levels all distinctions of costume.

He continues:

> If the reader desires to see a specimen of the pit-girls, he need not travel to the Black Country for the purpose. In the fruit season they come up in gangs to gather the contents of the suburban wilderness of summer fruits, which are grown for the consumption of voracious London.

Amy Lyons, writing some forty years later, is less enthusiastic, but she gives a detailed description of the bonk girls' appearance:

> Their dress consisted of a piece of coarse sacking with a hole cut at the top, to put over their heads, and two holes cut in the sides for their arms to go through. This was tied firmly round the waist by a piece of cord or thick string. Under this was a short petticoat, coming to just below the knees, and they wore thick woollen stockings and heavy hobnailed boots. On their heads they wore the same kind of head-gear as the men – round, pudding-basin shaped hats. Some of the women wore cast-off coats of their husbands or brothers, and, with short clay pipes in their mouths, they looked more like men than women.

Pit bank wenches, Wednesbury, from a postcard of c.*1910*

Men and boys at the New British Iron Company's New Hawne Pit, 1 August 1872, photographed by Arthur Clarke of Stourbridge

Pit girls and miners alike are long gone in the Black Country. For all the dirt and danger they met, for all their desperate struggles for a decent wage, miners never lost their reputation as the elite troops of the industrial revolution, the aristocrats of labour. As a result hey were celebrated in such songs as 'Jolly Joe the Collier's Son', printed in 1818 by Henry Wadsworth of Moor Street, Birmingham, and circulating orally for a century afterwards:

Come all you colliers in this row, who delight in a bonny lass,
Who loves to drink good ale that's brown, that sparkles in the glass
My parents they do frown on me, and say I am to blame,
For keeping Rachel's company, who liveth in Mash Lane.

When I rose up one morning at the dawning of the day,
I like to hear the small birds sing, see the lambs to skip and play;
I took a walk to Oldbury town round by the Bilston hill,
And there I spy'd my own true love with Jack of Armlow mill.

I hid myself behind a shade a distance from where they were;
He gave her kisses one, two, three, not knowing I was there;
I boldly stepped up to them, saying, Rogue, what hast thou done?
I am jolly Joe, the collier's son, so you must either fight or run.

Hold your hand, dear Joe, she said, and no more of that let's have.
I will be thy servant, slave and wife till we both go to one grave.
Then to the church young Rachel went right sore against her will,
So maidens all, pity my downfall, by Jack from Armlow mill.

CHAPTER 8

Metalworkers

Wilkinson Primary School at Bradley (pronounced Braidlee), near Bilston, stands on the site of John Wilkinson's blast furnace, erected in 1766 for the purpose of smelting iron ore with coal. 'Iron Mad' Wilkinson (1728-1808) was celebrated in a ballad which G.T. Lawley suggests was written by John Freeth, the Birmingham balladeer:

Ye workmen of Bradley and Brymbo draw near,
Sit down, take a pipe, and my song you shall hear;
I sing not of war, or the state of the nation,
Such subjects as these produce naught but vexation.
Derry down, derry down.

But before I proceed any more with my lingo,
You shall drink my toast in a bumper of stingo;
Fill it up and, without any further parade,
John Wilkinson, boys, that supporter of trade.

May all his endeavours be crowned with success,
And his works, ever growing, prosperity bless;
May his comforts increase with the length of his days,
And his fame shine as bright as his furnaces blaze.

That the wood of old England would fail, did appear,
And though iron was scarce because charcoal was dear,
By puddling and stamping he cured that evil,
So the Swedes and the Russians may go to the devil.

Our murdering cannon too frequently burst,
A mischief so great he prevented the first;
And now 'tis well known they never miscarry,
But drive all our foes with a blast to Old Harry.

Now let each jolly fellow take hold of his glass,
And drink to the health of his friend and his lass;
May we always have enough stingo and pence,
And Wilkinson's fame blaze a thousand years hence.

After Wilkinson's death there was a widespread belief in the neighbourhood of Bradley that he would return to visit his works. On the seventh anniversary several thousand people assembled at Monmore Green, near Wolverhampton, in the expectation that they would see him again come riding by on his grey horse. During his life, though, Wilkinson did not please all the people all the time. In 1790 he is said to have lined up twenty-four of his own cannon outside the works' gates at Bradley in readiness for a mob which threatened to attack.

Nor was Wilkinson the only pioneering ironmaster of the Black Country. In the previous century the redoubtable Dud Dudley, one of the eleven illegitimate children of Edward Sutton, fifth Baron Dudley, smelted iron ore with coal instead of charcoal at Cradley, Himley and Dudley. He claimed the achievement in his book, *Dud Dudley's Metallum Martis*, printed in London at his own expense in 1665, but gave no details. As a result some experts have been suspicious but the current consensus accepts that he produced iron, though perhaps of inferior quality.

John Wilkinson (left) and a detail of the Bradley Ironworks (right) from a painting by Robert Noyes, 1817

Part of the memorial to Dodo (Dud) Dudley in St Helen's Church, Worcester, Dudley died in the city's Friar Street in 1684. The signs in the centre are reproduced on the right and are astrological in nature

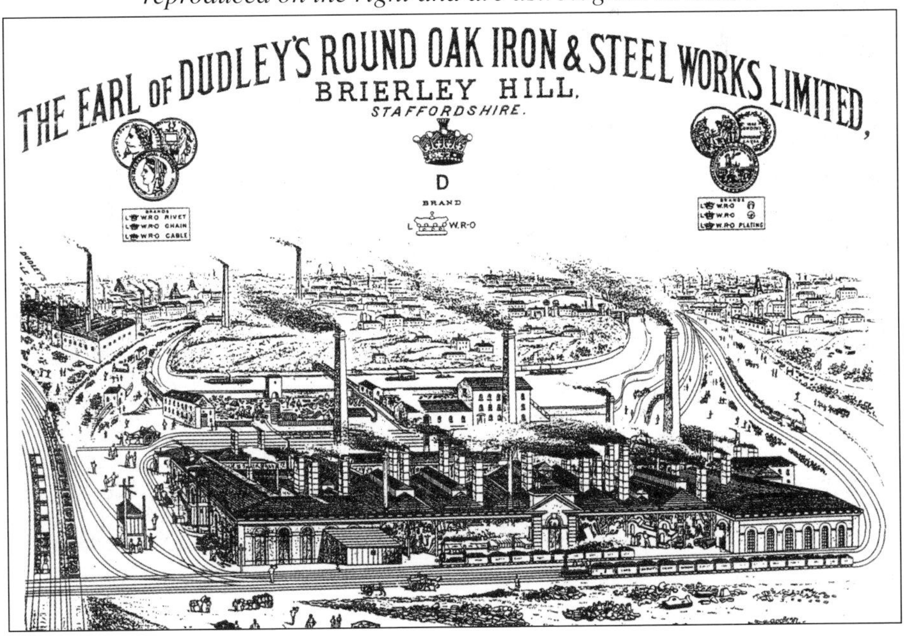

Wilkinson's works at Bradley failed to survive the squabbles of his legatees and the slump of post-1815. It closed in 1830, but others flourished. The famous Round Oak iron (and later steel) works at Brierley Hill opened in 1857 and remained in the Dudley family until nationalisation in 1951. Even after that people still called it 'the Earl's', until it closed in 1979. Another long-lived works was that of the New British Iron Company at Corngreaves, near Halesowen, which operated from 1810 until 1894. During the 1860s the day there began at 5 a.m. with a house prayer which mentioned some of the many different kinds of skill represented among the workpeople:

God bless the one that's started here
By men of faith, of zeal and prayer,
May Corngreave's Works the birthplace be
Of many yet that know not Thee.

Let shinglers, puddlers feel Thy power
When here – the sacred praying hour,
At morning dawn. O Spirit, strive,
And let thy work, great God revive.

May rollers and roll turners, too,
And furnacemen, the path pursue –
The path of love the Saviour trod,
To lead our souls safe back to God.

Smiths, fitters, engineers, unite,
And come well armed into the fight;
Let faith and prayer your weapons be,
Fight till poor sinners are set free.

May millwrights, moulders, each be brought
To love the Saviour as they ought;
Who gave His life their hearts to win,
And waits to wash their souls from sin.

Come patternmakers, be in time,
May God this day your souls incline
To give up sin, and start for Heaven,
And get the joy of sins forgiven.

Great God of Love, each foreman bless,
And guide them through this wilderness
To Heaven, where all the Saints shall meet,
And cast their crowns at Jesu's feet.

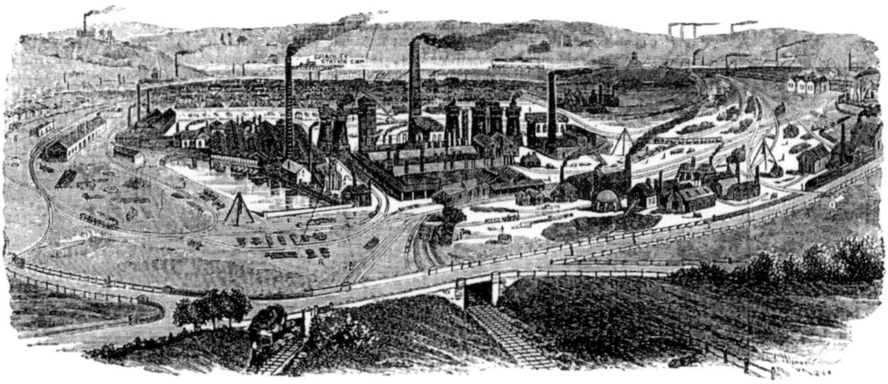

Congreaves Iron and Steel Works, c.*1880*

To this litany of iron workers one could add the lorimers (spur makers) of Walsall, the makers of traps of all kinds (including, until it was outlawed in 1827, the infamous man trap or 'iron wolf') of Wednesfield, the buckle-makers of West Bromwich and the locksmiths of Willenhall, the awl makers of Bloxwich; but most numerous in the Black Country, as early as the beginning of the seventeenth century, were the nailers of Rowley, Dudley, Old Swinford, Halesowen and West Bromwich. A persistent story attempted, with variations, to explain the advent in the area of the slitting mill, a device which cut from a sheet of iron the rods (previously separated by hand) which were needed for nail making. According to the Staffordshire historian, Stebbing Shaw, writing at the end of the eighteenth century, a man called Brindley 'went into Germany, and there acted the part of a fool, and by this means obtained this excellent machine, which has been so serviceable, and brought so much money into this country'.

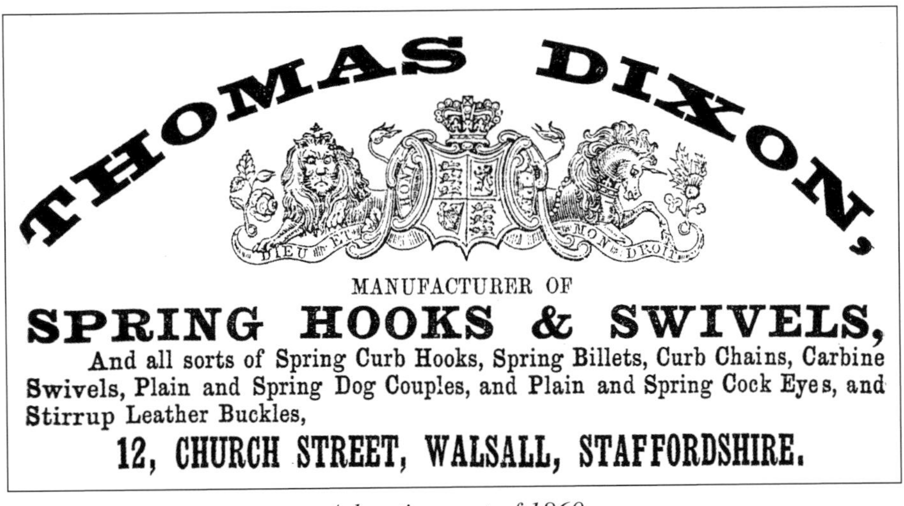

Advertisement of 1860

A different version names the feigned fool as a flute-playing Richard Foley (whose first wife was called Alice Brindley), and has him ingratiating himself into a works in Holland to obtain details of the device. Alternatively, Foley conducts his industrial espionage either in the Urals or in Sweden, his cover provided by fiddle playing, and returns with the desired information. Then, unable to make his new machine work, he is obliged to visit his complaisant hosts for a second time, and at last succeeds in building a slitting mill. The story was given wide currency in the nineteenth century by figures as diverse as S.T. Coleridge and Samuel Smiles.

Richard Foley, from Nash's History of Worcestershire *(1787)*

Richard Foley undoubtedly existed. He was born in Dudley in 1580, the son of a nailer, and followed his father's occupation. He prospered, and became mayor of the town in 1616. Ten years later a mill which he leased at Hyde, a mile from Kinver, was using water power for slitting rods. In fact, though, the earliest English slitting mill was working in Kent in 1590, and Foley's skill was in organisation and management, not fiddle-playing and subterfuge. He died at Stourbridge in 1657 and was buried in the town's St Mary's Church, having founded a dynasty of iron masters — and mistresses, too, for as well as his sons and sons-in-law his six daughters were also involved.

Thanks to Foley's introduction of the slitting mill, 'The nailer', wrote W.H.B. Court, 'the most typical figure of Black Country society from the days of Queen Elizabeth almost down to those of Queen Victoria, increased in numbers with the slow but sure expansion of trade'. People in other districts took up the work. After 1830, though, the introduction of machine-made nails inevitably reduced demand for the dearer, hand-wrought variety. The nailers' circumstances were made worse by their dependence on middlemen, known as 'foggers', who not only supplied rods and received the finished nails, but also ran 'tommy' shops (as did the miners' butties of the previous chapter). The main character in David Christie Murray's novel, *A Capful o' Nails*, delivers this indictment of the system:

David Christie Murray

Here's the fogger's game wi' the Black Country nailer. To begin with, he's got three sets o' weights: a light set to sell with, a heavy set to buy with, and another set to show th' inspector when he comes on his rounds. He's forbid by law to keep a tommy shop, but there ain't a fogger in the countryside as hasn't got a relation in that line o' business. We're forced to buy bad and dear, or woe betide us. When we buy for a certain size o' nail, they sell us rods too thick for use, and charge us for changing them. They give us light weight, to begin with, and they lighten light weight till you've got sixpenn'orth for ninepence. When it comes to sellin' the nails, they use the heavy weight, and they tek twelve hundred for a thousand. They're not contented to take the wool, but they shave hide and all, and some of us are bound to 'em, soul and body.

The government's Truck Act of 1831 proved to be an ineffectual attempt at reform, and twenty years later striking nailers — men, women and children — at Lye carried the coffin of 'Tommy Tuck' through Brierley Hill to Dudley, and on to Stourbridge:

> This procession, consisting of mourners and bearers, all dressed in black, with long scarves and hat bands and a numerous following, halted at the Horse Shoe Inn [in Dudley], and placed a coffin containing an effigy of 'Old Tommy Tuck' on the public footway outside. A tall middle-aged man, with a good voice, who acted as the officiating minister, then gave out, verse by verse, from a large black book, a hymn beginning with the words:
>
> Old Tommy Tuck is dead and gone,
> And buried at the Lye;
> He is a loss to many a mon,
> But then we need not cry,
>
> Which was sung in fair style, to the tune of the 'Old Hundredth' by the mourners and bearers, and those of the crowd who were able to join in. They sang some six verses of this doggerel, and made a short prayer and a collection for 'funeral and other expenses', the mourners and bearers meanwhile playing their parts with proper decorum. One of the men

THE

STAFFORDSHIRE NAIL-MAKERS' HUMBLE PETITION.

We Nail makers are in great distress,
  Employ we cannot find,
Thousands are by want compell'd
  To leave their friends behind.

What parent can behold his child
  With tears in either eye,
Petition for a little bread,
  Which ah! he must deny.

Each morn brings on our sorrow fresh
  Which makes us dread the light,
We cannot on our pillows sleep,
  Thus we spend a restless night.

And when the morning light appears
  Our children round us fly,
Regardless of our nightly grief
  To us for bread they cry.

They cry to us with meagre looks
  Which makes our hearts to ache,
Then oh! to us a trifle give,
  For these poor children's sake.

The mother she sits weeping,
  She raves and tears her hair;
When she beholds her children dead
  For they were her only care.

Their altered looks she does behold,
  Like death appears in view;
With weeping eyes to heav'n she ries
  Good Lord what shall we do.

Our visit now to you kind friends,
  We hope you will excuse,
And as we have explain'd our case,
  We trust you'll not refuse.

For he that giveth to the poor,
  But lendeth to the Lord,
So now kind friends on us bestow
  Whate'er you can afford.

The reason of our being out of employment is in consequence of the Machines and Foundries,—They will cast and cut more Nails in one day than 100 men can make in a week.—Our master, (Mr Woodhall, in Tipton) failed and 100 men were thrown out of employment. We being so many in number were forced to leave our homes, our Parishes being so much oppressed, could not give us employment, there being 500 out of employment there at this present time.

Good Christians, a small Trifle will be received by us with sincere gratitude.

N. B. P ease to keep this clean till called for.

Woodward. Printer, Tipton.

'The Staffordshire Nail-makers' Humble Petition', sheet printed by Woodward, Tipton

> was dressed as 'Molly Tuck', to represent the disconsolate relict of the deceased, and was satirically referred to as 'Chief mourner with a very large family of children'. This man wore a big black crape bonnet, and a shawl on the back of which was pinned a white paper announcing that he was 'Old Tommy Tuck's Widow'.

During the same strike, in 1852, nailmakers, adopting tactics used by local miners, publicised their cause by dragging a ton of coal the thirteen miles from Halesowen, where many of them worked, to Bromsgrove, when many nailmasters lived. The coal, donated by Thomas Attwood (a native of Halesowen, founder of the Birmingham Political Union for Public Rights, Chartist and MP), was sold in Bromsgrove for the benefit of the strike fund. The march was celebrated in a song, 'The Nailmakers' Strike'. Ten years later, another strike: another song. The dispute, caused by the continuing truck system and a proposed reduction in rates of pay ran for 16 months, with 13,000 workers involved in Old Hill, the Lye, Halesowen, Rowley and Dudley. One of their number, J. Knowles of Lye wrote a ballad (see panel below) on the subject, much of it devoted to a detailed dialogue between a man and his wife on their household running costs. He died in 1903, aged 82, and his words were taken down in 1932 by Howard Hill, also of Lye, from his mother, Knowles's daughter.

The Nail Maker's Lamentation

Come near my friends while I begin my true but mournful song.
I will be very careful lest I should speak too long.

Chorus
Oh the discount, oh the discount. With it we can't agree.
For twenty shillings we will have before at work we'll be.

I am a poor nail maker, the truth I will tell you,
I toil and labour all the week, I know it is my due.

And when Saturday evening comes and I've my money got,
I take it very careful home and say this is the lot.

My wife then casts a look at me and with a pitiful eye,
'Is that all?' mournfully she says, and then heaves a deep sigh.

And then says, 'Come sit down, and help to put it out'.
It almost bewilders my brain, and then I do walk out.

'But wait a moment, stop and see what has got to be said,
And do not send me sorrowing so soon down to my grave.

'You know there is our coal and gleeds for the house and shop fire,
Likewise the mending of the tools and changing of the iron.

WORKMEN'S PRICES,

AGREED UPON AT A GENERAL MEETING OF THE TRADE,

TO TAKE PLACE AUGUST 19, 1848.

Dudley, August 15th, 1848.

Rose & Flemish Tacks.

	s.	d.
4oz, 5 }	0	6½
6	0	6¾
7	0	7
8	0	7½
10	0	7¾
12	0	8¼
14	0	8
16	0	9½
18	0	9¼

Rose, Flatpoints and Clasp.

	s.	d.
1¼lb	0	10
1½	0	11
2	1	0½
2½	1	2½
3	1	3¾
3½	1	5¼
4	1	7
5	1	10
6	2	1
7	2	4
8	2	7
9	2	10
10	3	1½
11	3	4½
12	3	7½
13	3	10½
14	4	1½
16	4	7½
18	5	1½
20	5	7
22	6	1
24	6	7
26	7	1
28	7	6½
30	8	0
32	8	6
36	9	5
40	10	4
45	28	6
50	28	3

Long Rose 1d Fine 2d per m. more.

Plain Brads, 2d per m less.

Bill'd Brads, 1d per m less

Long Bill'd Brads, 1d per m more

Spikes.

	s.	d.
2s....4in.	28	0
2s6d 4½	27	6
3s4d 5	27	0
5½in	26	9
6, 7 }	26	6
Larger	26	3

Fine Spikes 6d per cwt more.

Cross head do. 6d pr cwt more

Fine X Head Spikes 1s per cwt more.

Drawing.

	s.	d.
45....3½	28	6
55....4	28	0
75....4½	27	6

Pound Nails.

	s.	d.
16lb 6d	32	0
18	31	6
20	31	2
28...8d	30	4
30	30	0
45 10d	28	6
48	28	3
50	28	0
60 20d	27	6

Sheathing.

	s.	d.
14 2in	29	3
16 2¼	29	0
22 2½	28	9
28 2¾	28	6
36 3	28	3

Long Clasp.

	s.	d.
7...2	2	5½
8...2⅛	2	8½
9	2	11½
10...2¼	3	2¾
12...2½	3	9
14	4	3
16...2¾	4	9
18	5	3
20	5	9
22...3¼	6	3
24	6	9
28	7	8½
32	8	8
36....4	9	7
45	11	8

Fine Clasp.

	s.	d.
1½	1	3
2	1	4
2½	1	5½
3	1	7
3½	1	8½
4	1	10
5	2	1
6 2in	2	4
7 2¼	2	7
8 2⅜	2	10
9 2½	3	0½

Fine Clout Spanish Hobs Flats & Trunk.

	s.	d.
5oz	0	8
6	0	8¼
7	0	8½
8	0	8¾
10	0	9¼
12	0	9¾
14	0	10
16	0	10½
18	0	11
1¼lb	0	11¾
1½	1	1
1¾	1	2
2	1	3
2¼	1	3¾
2½	1	4¾
2¾	1	5½
3	1	6½
3½	1	8¼
4	1	10
5	2	1
6	2	4
7	2	7
8	2	10
9	3	0½

Round Trunk, 1½d pr m more

Tip Nails.

	s.	d.
1¼	0	10¾
1⅜	1	0
1½	1	1
2	1	2
2¼	1	3¾
3	1	5½

Countersunk 1d m more.

Clout.

	s.	d.
1½	0	11
1¾	0	11¾
2	1	0½
2¼	1	1½
2½	1	2¾
3	1	3¾
3½	1	5¼
3¾	1	6
4	1	7
5	1	10
6	2	1
7	2	4
9	2	10½
10	3	2
12	3	8½
14	4	3
16	4	9
18	5	3
20	5	9
28	7	9
40	10	9

Woolding, 6d per m more.

Countersunk Clout.

	s.	d.
4½	2	0½
5	2	2
6	2	5
7	2	8
9	3	3
10	3	6½
12	4	1½
14	4	7½
16	5	2
20	6	2
24	7	2
28	8	2
30 to 36	32	0
larger	31	6

Battins.

	s.	d.
4, 5 }	0	5
6	0	5½
8	0	6
9	0	6¼
10	0	6½
14	0	8
16	0	8½
18	0	9
1¼lb	0	9½
1½	0	10½
1¾	0	11½
2	1	0½
2¼	1	1½
2½	1	2¾
3	1	4¼
3¼	1	5
3½	1	6
4	1	8
5	1	11½
6	2	2½

Fine Battins.

	s.	d.
4, 5 }	0	6
6	0	6½
8	0	7
10	0	7½
12	0	8¼
14	0	9
16	0	9½
18	0	10
20	0	10¾
1¼lb	0	11¾
1½	1	0¾
2	1	1¾
2¼	1	2¾
3	1	5½
3¼	1	6½
3½	1	7½
4	1	9½
5	2	1
6	2	4½

Clasp Round and Welch Hobs.

	s.	d.
14	0	8¾
16	0	9
18	0	9½
1¼lb	0	10
1½	0	11
1¾	0	11¾
2	1	0½
2¼	1	1¼
2½	1	[illegible]
3	1	3¾
3¼	1	5¼
3¾	1	6
4	1	7
5	1	10
6	2	1
7	2	4
8	2	[illegible]
9	2	11
10	3	2
12	3	8¼

Clinkers, 1d per m more.

Fine Hobs, 2d per m more.

Ox & Bell Hobs 6d per m more.

Dog and Uglies.

	s.	d.
12	4	[illegible]
14	4	7½
16	5	2
18	5	8
20	6	[illegible]
22	6	8
24	7	2
28	8	2
Larger	31	6

Bills.

	s.	d.
8	0	3½
12	0	4
16	0	4½
1¼lb.	0	5¼
1½	0	6
2	0	7½
2½	0	9
3	0	10

Hob Rivets.

	s.	d.
8	0	7¼
10	0	7½
12	0	8½
14	0	8¾
16	0	9¼
18	0	9½
1¼ lb.	0	10
1½	0	11
2	1	0½
3	1	3¾
4	1	7
5	1	10
6	2	1
7	2	4
8	2	7
9	2	10
10	3	1
12	3	7
14	4	0½
16	4	6½
18 to 28	31	6
Larger	31	0

Round Heads.

	s.	d.
8oz	0	8¼
13	0	9½
16	0	10
1⅛ lb.	1	0
2	1	1½
2½	1	3½
3	1	5
4	1	8½
[illegible]	1	11½
6	2	[illegible]
7	2	6
8	2	9½
9	3	1
10	3	4
12	3	10
14	4	4

Gate Nails.

	s.	d.
16lb 2in	5	0
2[illegible] 2½	7	3
32....3	9	0
40....3½	11	0
48....4	13	0

Fine Tray and Kent Hurdle.

	s.	d.
1[illegible]....2in	4	1
14	4	7
16....2¼	5	1
1[illegible]	5	7
20....2½	6	1
22	6	7
25....3	7	4
[illegible]0....3½	8	7

Fine Cooler & Essex hurdle to 25 lb. 10d. over Rose.

Larger 1s. per m. more than Rose.

Cooler.

	s.	d.
18....2 in	34	3
22....2¼	33	3
26....2½	32	6
30....2¾	32	3
36....3	32	0
40....3½	31	6

Best Rose Sample & Hurdle.

	s.	d.
8	2	10
9	3	1
10	3	4½
12	3	10½
14	4	4½
16	4	10½
18	5	5
20	5	11
22	6	5
24	6	11
26	7	5
28	7	10½
32	8	10
36	9	9
40	10	8
45....4in	29	6
60....4½	29	0
80....5	28	6

Fine hurdle 2d. more.

Rag Nails 2d. per m. more than best rose

Long Horse.

	s.	d.
4	3	0
5	3	2
6	3	5
7	3	8
8	4	0
9	4	4
10	4	8
11	5	0
12	5	4
14	6	0
16	6	8
18	7	4
20	8	0

Fine and countersunk 3d. per m. more.

Lath Hooks 6d. per m. more than Rose.

Tenter Hooks.

	s.	d.
1¼	1	4
1½	1	5
1¾	1	6
2	1	7
2½	1	9
4	2	3
5	2	6½
6	2	10
7	3	1½
8	3	5
9	3	8½
10	3	11½
12	4	6
14	5	0
18	6	0
20	6	6
24	7	6
28	8	6

Larger 3d. per lb advance.

Round Billed 2d. per m more

Tiling Hooks.

	s.	d.
6	2	11
7	3	3
8	3	7
9	3	10½
10	4	1½
12	4	9

Fine tucker 1s. per m. more

Glaziers.

	s.	d.
14oz	0	8
1[illegible]	0	8½
1¼lb	0	9½

Sash.

	s.	d.
4oz	0	5

Mop Nails.

33s. per cwt

Fine Mop.

5in. 24 to a lb.
5½....22 ....
6 ....20 ....
34s per cwt.

Back Nails.

	s.	d.
2in	33	0
2½	32	0
3	31	6
3½ & larger	31	0

Fine Knee.

3½ to 4in 30 6

Larger 30s cwt

Slender Clench.

3d. per m. more than Rose.

Rose Clench.

2d. per m more than Rose.

Fine Wherry.

	s.	d.
[illegible]oz	0	11
1¼ lb	0	11½
1½	1	1
2	1	3
2½	1	4½
3	1	6½
4	1	10

Scupper.

	s.	d.
5	2	0
6	2	3
7	2	6
8	2	9
9	3	0
10	3	3
12	3	9

Bermudas 6d per m more than Rose.

Yield.

6oz	32lb.
8	36
12	40
16	42
1¼	43
2	44
2½	45
3	46
5	48
7	49
8	50
9	51
11	51½
12	52
15	52½
16	53
20	53½
22 & larger	54

DUDLEY: PRINTED BY THOMAS DANKS, HIGH-STREET.

List of Workmen's prices, 1848

'My hommer and my steady, too, must be pared, if not steeled;
My bore and hardy must be done or I cannot make good nails.

'Out of repair our bellows are, and mended they must be,
And eightpence for the trerron, for it must snouted [iron plated] be'.

'The house rent you know must be paid or else the bums will come,
And then if payment can't be made the goods will soon be gone.

'I have no money for your club, and that's a sad affair.
What can we do when sickness comes? We can't live on fresh air.

'Well, don't be impatient now, for I have not yet quite done.
The shoe maker he must be paid, or shoes we shall have none.

'Our clothing has got very bare, over and underneath;
Our children want some things to wear, they must not catch their death.

'There's also butter, sugar, too, tea, candles, soap and flour,
And there's nor meat or garden stuff in such a house as ours.

'Now what's twelve shillings to cut up to pay so many things?
It would make a lawyer's head turn grey to try to meet two ends.

'It's just the thing I thought before I came to sit me down:
There's nothing left for Sunday dinner but a dark look or a frown.

'Could you not try to bring me more to help to pay my way?
You see I've done the best I can, not half enough to pay'.

'It's all the money I have had from the warehouse, you must know:
I should be glad to give you more if I knew where to go.

'There is two shillings from a pound they are about to take,
And then, however shall we live? It makes my heart to ache.

'When I think of my children dear I cannot send to school,
Being brought up in ignorance in this enlightened land.

'I cannot tell. I wonder why our masters do not see
How miserable and wretched, too, we poor nailers must be.

'Our masters must stand at God's bar, a just account to give,
For keeping back the labourer's hire which he ought to receive.

'Then do not be discouraged: there is no room to doubt.
We shall have twenty shillings by firmly standing out'.

So now my poem I conclude, hoping that each will strive,
Both masters and their workmen all to gain a heavenly prize.

Visitors to the Black Country constantly remarked on the nailers' struggle. Walter White in his trip 'all round the Wrekin', published in 1860, reaches Rowley Regis, where 'the click-click, and thump-thump of hammers in nearly every house, make us aware of having arrived among the nail-makers'. When he asks why no men are involved, one of the women tells him: ''T ain't work as pays for men, and 't ain't much better than clemmin' for women'. His informant adds that she has to work extremely hard to earn a shilling a day. In fact, between 1851, when there were some 19,000 nail makers in the Black Country, with men and women equally represented, and 1891, numbers fell by almost two-thirds, with women a majority of those still working. Women usually wore — and this applied until the 1920s — black boots, woollen stockings, a long black skirt, plaid shawl and a man's cap. Men typically had a red and green check shirt, brown corduroy trousers with a broad leather belt, and heavy boots.

STRIKE

Of South Staffordshire & East Worcestershire

HORSE NAIL MAKERS.

AN APPEAL.

Fellow Workmen,

We, the Horse-Nail Makers of Dudley, Old Hill, Halesowen, Cradley, Lye Waste, and District, are now out on Strike for an advance of 3d. per 1,000.

This advance is admitted to be reasonable and just by the employers themselves, and yet they refuse the same. Our wages have been reduced from time to time until it is impossible to earn a living when fully employed, our average earnings being from 12/- to 14/- per week of 60 to 70 hours. Should the advance be obtained, we should not then be able to earn more than from 14/- to 16/- per week. Surely this sum is far too small for a practical workman, and even too little to support our wives and children.

On these grounds we ask your sympathy and support. We have a small Union, and have recently joined the Midland Counties' Trades' Federation, but, unfortunately, the larger proportion of our men are not entitled to benefit, not having been members long enough; at the same time the Federation have already contributed **£10** towards the men out, with a promise of help from week to week should the same be required.

Subscriptions will be thankfully received by the authorized Collector, whose Book bears the initials—**M. O. T. F.**; also by Mr. J. Willets, 4, Princes Street, Netherton, near Dudley, or by the Secretary to the Federation, Mr. R. Juggins, 60, New Street, Darlaston, from whom all information can be obtained.

May 25th, 1889.

Strike notice of 1889.
This strike lasted for ten weeks

'The total extinction of the trade', wrote F.W. Hackwood in 1889, 'will not be a matter of much regret; for it is an industry that has never brought either profit or renown upon any locality in which it has been seated'. Nevertheless, it lingered. In 1913 there were three or four nailers still working in Oldswinford, with no doubt similar numbers in other places. In 1914 a newspaper reported a nailer, aged 90, still at work near Dudley with his 'olifer' (or oliver, a heavy hammer worked by a treadle): 'He must be pretty nearly the last of his race, though less than 40 years ago the "tap, tap" of the hammer on the nail-head could be heard persistently in Dudley and adjoining districts'. As a small boy in 1909 or 1910 Walter Taylor watched his grandfather at work in Halesowen, and over sixty years later recalled: 'The rat-tat-tat of the olivers when hammering

Mrs Brettle of Lye, aged 66, still making nails in her home workshop, 1928

on the hot iron on the anvil I can still hear, the long stroke and thud of the first blow, followed in rhythmic pattern by the staccato taps as the nail was made, and intermingled with the tinkle of the forceps as they tapped the mechanism that prevented the hot iron sticking in the die'.

In the 1920s those still working in the trade were almost exclusively women. On the annual outing of one firm, Sargeant, Turner, of Lye, in 1920 — they went to the Admiral Rodney at Martley, then to hopyards at Suckley and Knightwick, and stopped at the Dog in Harvington on the way back — the participants were all women, their average age 65. They were still engaged in making clout, clasp and cooper's nails. Some of the heavier nails, such as those for prison doors, were made in domestic nailshops until the early 1950s. Now, machine-made nails have taken over completely, and the old hand craft can be seen only in such places as the Avoncroft Museum of Buildings near Bromsgrove, and the Black Country Living Museum at Dudley.

The same applies to work with chain, nailing's younger cousin, the last firm making hand-wrought chain, Lloyd's of Brierley Hill, having closed in 2006.

A group of Cradley Heath chainmakers, drawn by Harold Piffard in the 1890s

Chain shop from Cradley Heath now preserved in the Avoncroft Museum of Buildings, Bromsgrove, Worcestershire

Yet this was once a strong industry, which was capable of rewarding its workers with a decent living, as well at times of reducing them to squalor. Cliff Willetts, a chainmaker for fifty-four years (starting in 1911 at a weekly wage of 10s., less 6d. for insurance), had this to say about his fellow-workers:

> Their genius, and that is not an exaggeration of terms, was unlimited. A man could take a piece of iron of 2" diameter and with only hammer, fire and anvil, would turn it into a swivel, a shackle, a ring, a hook or anything the trade desired. Give these men, who had no apprenticeship or [theoretical] experience, a drawing on a piece of paper, and they would, after a few moments study, work out sizes, shapes and produce the article. I could only marvel at their outstanding qualities and I was inevitably drawn to the conclusion that they were like poets, born not made. To have known such men is a great privilege. They were men whose skills made the Black Country famed and respected throughout the world. We shall never see their likes again, for the machine has replaced them. To see these men at the end of the day cast their eyes along what they had made, whether it be anchors, hooks, swivels, shackles or chain, was an unforgettable memory. They surveyed their handiwork and with a deep sense of pride would say, not with their lips but with their hearts, 'I made that'. No machine can speak that language.

One of those men was George Dunn, born in Sheffield Street, Quarry Bank, in 1887, who started work as a chainmaker a decade before Cliff Willetts. His grandfather, Benjamin, was an iron bundler, and his father, Samson, a puddler, then an annealer. George, long before he left school, earned a penny a week for spending half the two-hour lunch break each day 'a-blowin'' — pumping the bellows in one of the many backyard chainshops in Quarry Bank. When he left school in 1900 he found a full-time job as a blower at Judge Holloware in Cradley Heath, working from 6 a.m. to 6 p.m. with half an hour for breakfast and an hour for dinner, except on Saturdays, when work ended at 1 p.m., with only a break for breakfast. This amounted to 59 hours, for which he received 3s. 6d. — a rate of less than a penny an hour. In 1904, having learned the rudiments of smithing from his father, George moved to the newly established chainshop of Noah Bloomer and Sons in Oak Street, Quarry Bank. He started at a wage of ten shillings a week, which rose by 1913 to eighteen. He judged this too little to be married on, and gave notice to leave, whereupon the firm raised his wage to £1 a week. George stayed on for a further 46 years, until 1959, the last ten of which he was superintendent of the proof house. The strain appropriate to any chain's specification was exerted in the proof house, and any defects revealed at this stage had to be put right at the expense of the workers who made it.

George Dunn (right) re-visiting Noah Bloomer's chainshop in 1973

I recorded George Dunn's memories during a series of visits to his retirement bungalow in Quarry Bank between 1971 and his death in 1975 (which came only a year before the closure of Bloomer's). They provide a vivid and invaluable picture of life as a smith ('chainmakin' is a sort o' smithin''), starting over a century ago:

> Most o' the work was big work. It required a team of two or three, or even four. When I told you we made some three inch, every link'd be above 'undredweight. Well, it took about four men to do that job. If you 'adn't got somebody to take yer in an' give you a job to work with 'em, it was 'earth fillin'. Every chainmeker'd got an 'earth, with a fire in the middle on it. That's where 'e made 'is chain. Yo' filled th' 'earths. The fires were made o' cokes, an' yo' did that. If you'd got a minute or two to spare, and somebody o' yer own age were workin' there, yo'd goo an' do 'is job for a link or two. Let 'im 'ave a rest. 'E wouldn't mind at all. Whenever you got a chance to use the 'ammer yo' would. Eventually you would attain the skill to do the job.
>
> It was all the rule of thumb, when the iron was weldable; and there's other times when the temperature 'as risen when they'd gotta be very careful, because it'd smash, it'd pulverise, like breadcrumbs. If 'e [the chainmaker] brought 'is link out weldable, but wanted threshin', 'e'd say to the strikers: 'Come on, quick, 'it it, 'it it, *'it it*'. If it'd gone over when 'e brought it out, an' it'd pulverise: 'Light, light, light. Oooh, you bloody fool'. Yo' can almost feel it when you'm a-workin' it. The good iron, it's meant to stretch. It stretches an' 'owds, but th' 'ard iron, it's brittle, an' when yo' put the weight on it, it cracks. If it's good quality iron when you bring it out, it's like toffee. That is the secret of a good workman.
>
> Some o' the chainmakers in the very big chain, they employed three men beside themselves. That made the fire up into a team. The chainmaker, *'e* employed the strikers. The striker's name, prior to this last war [1939-45], *'is* name was never in th' office, never until it 'ad to be Pay As You Earn. 'E paid 'em what 'e liked; what they worked for. The pit was the same: the butty. That's 'ow it was.

George Dunn remembered nailmakers at Quarry Bank, few in number because 'they'd changed over to chainmakers'. Outworkers — often women — in both cases collected rods from the employers and returned the finished article. So far as the chainmakers were concerned:

> If they'd got 'undredweight of iron they'd gotta return 'undred an' four pound o' chain. Eight pound less than the 112. When they were working this iron up, workin' it into chain, they were as careful with it as gold. … When they took their 'undredweight o' chain in, if it weighed 'undred pound, it were four pound short, see. They'd get fourpence knocked off. For years an' years it was two and threepence 'undredweight for bare

sevens. Now there was lots o' girls an' women down Sheffield Street as made bare sevens. Bare sevens was the most popular size for selling. It was the most popular size to mek. If they were a pound short they'd gotta pay a penny a pound for that. If they got hundred and six pound in, they got 'a'p'ny a pound for that [i.e. on each of the two extra pounds]. That was the meanness o' the masters. It's true. They used to work all sorts of hours. Sheffield Street was alive at ten o'clock wi' chainmakers, ten o'clock at night.

After they'd worked till ten o'clock at night, if they'd got nine bob a week clear they were lucky. So much so that they used to go out on it if they could get a job in the factory. They dae get no more theer, but it wasn't so laborious. It's 'ard job makin' chain.

Lucy Woodall at work in 1972

Fortunately, there are recollections from the 'amazons of the chainshops' themselves, who as early as 1891 made up almost half the workforce, and eventually came to predominate. Lucy Woodall of Old Hill, the daughter of a woman nailmaker, left school in 1912 on her thirteenth birthday, a Friday, and started work the following Monday as an apprentice chainmaker. She encountered the usual initiatory tricks: being sent for a nine-inch foot rule or 'a left 'onded sponner', finding her tongs had been heated ('to make you jump') or the rock (handle) of her bellows plastered with mud. As for the work:

Four shillin' a week. Seven o'clock till seven o'clock. Two o'clock on a Saturday. Well, when you start first they get you doin' a bit o' blowin' for one of the others to kind o' break yer in a bit. And then after that you start tryin' to turn a link and then you go on to shuttin' a link.

You was glad to do it. There was no work really in them days. I had to do six month, you know, at that four shillin', and then the next month I 'ad a rise — five and six. 'Course, I 'ad to do two years as apprentice. Then the next twelve months I 'ad nine shillin', but they gave yer stint work for that nine shillin'. Well, when you'd done that stint, if you did any extra, that was put on one side every day and you was paid piece work on that little bit. Well, sometimes I should 'ave two shillin' or half a crown and I

> should be in 'eaven. And then after you'd done your apprenticeship you 'ad piece work — different sorts, different sizes.
>
> There was one or two started, like, at the same time as me. And one of 'em, I remember 'er. The boss 'ad an order come in for No.6 — and that was about eight link to the foot, I think. 'Er says, 'Ah bay a-bloody mekin' that', 'er says, 'Ah s'll a to mek a bloody ton to weigh 'undredweight'.

The women sang as they worked, sometimes with appropriate actions, and as a result Lucy acquired a fund of tear-jerking narrative ballads such as 'Break the news to mother', 'The volunteer organist', 'Inside a whitewashed hospital', 'I lost the sunshine and roses when I lost you' and 'Come again Christmas, old friend of us all' (see also chapters 12 and 14). She also sang:

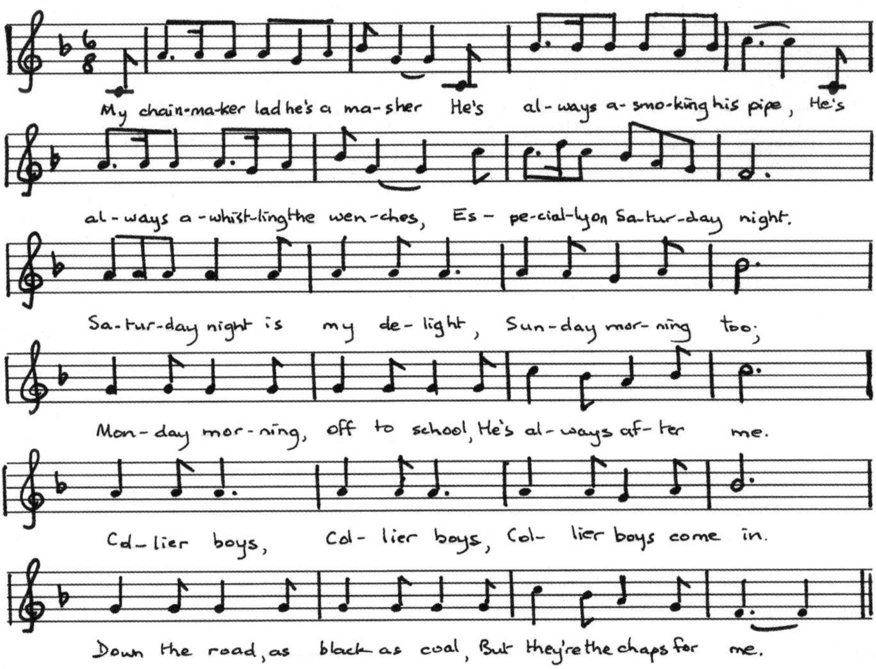

The appeal of the camaraderie of the workplace and the satisfaction of craftsmanship kept Lucy at work in various chainshops for sixty years and one month, until her retirement in December 1972. By this time she had become the last woman hand chainmaker. One Prince of Wales once visited the place where she was working. Her verdict on him was, 'Not so bloody naace [nice] as my chap' — a miner. She died in 1979.

A song, 'Holly Ho', which she knew only in part, has a verse relating to the strike of women chainmakers which took place at Cradley Heath in 1910. Their cause received considerable publicity the previous year, when at a sweated industries exhibition at Earl's Court, London, an 18-year-old woman made chain

Women chainmakers on strike in 1910 leave a theatre in Cradley Heath after being given bread. The photograph, treasured by Cliff Willetts for over fifty years, shows, somewhere in the crowds, his mother (see page 51)

at a hearth specially brought from Cradley Heath. A placard informed visitors that she received 3s. 3d. for making a hundredweight of chain, that she made two hundredweight a week, and out of her 6s. 6d. she had to pay 2s. for fuel. A Miss Julia Varley, of the Birmingham Women Workers' Federation, explained: 'I have paid about 500 visits to Cradley Heath and its women workers, and my heart bled at the sights I saw, and the life histories of these poor people, which I heard'. The nameless Cradley Heath woman added: 'It used to be better, but one woman would take work at a lower price to get it, and then the others had to come down to a similar sum or go without work, and so the price was gradually reduced to its present low state'.

Such disunity must have been overcome because in 1910 women chainmakers from Cradley Heath and elsewhere went on strike in an effort to compel employers to pay the rates newly agreed by the chainmaking trade board. They received the support of such figures as Julia Varley (1871-1952), who had herself begun work at the age of thirteen as a sweeper in a Bradford woollen mill, C.H. Sitch, who in 1918 became M.P. for Kingswinford, and Mary Macarthur (1880-1921), who was prominent in the Women's Trade Union League, the National Anti-Sweating League and the National Federation of Women Workers.

The strikers had their own anthem, to the tune — there is an irony here — of 'Men of Harlech', 'Rouse Ye Women':

Through years of uncomplaining,
Hope and strength are waning —
Your industry, a beggar's fee —
And meagre fare was gaining.
Now a Trade Board is created,
See your pain and dearth abated,
And the sweater's wiles checkmated,
Parliament's decree.

(Chorus)
Rouse, ye women, long enduring,
Beat no iron, blow no bellows,
Till ye win the fight, ensuing
Pay that is your due.

At length the light is breaking,
The sweater's throne is shaking,
Oh do your part with all your heart,
A sweeter world is making!
Stand together, strong and splendid,
In your union till you've ended
Tyranny, and with toil blended
Beauty, joy and art.

Two women nailmakers in a rare moment of leisure, c.1900

The song mentioned earlier, 'Holly Ho', is rather more down to earth and lighthearted. It was sung up to the 1970s by male chainmakers at work, especially on pay days. In some workshops each man had his own verse, which he would bring in at an appropriate time, and the rest would 'bost out' with the chorus. The source here was Joe Mallen, himself once a chainmaker, and later a publican (see chapter 9), recorded in 1958 by Elizabeth Thomson, and by me in 1971.

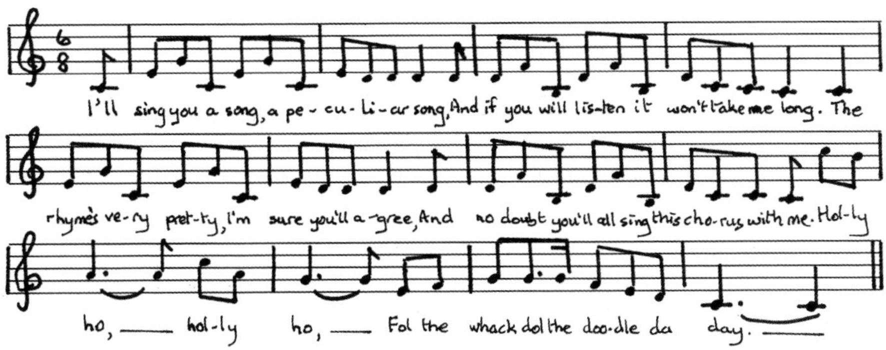
I'll sing you a song, a pe - cu - li - ar song, And if you will lis-ten it won't take me long. The
rhyme's ve-ry pret-ty, I'm sure you'll a-gree, And no doubt you'll all sing this cho-rus with me. Hol-ly
ho, — hol-ly ho, — Fol the whack dol the doo-dle da day. —

Now I said to my sweetheart the other day,
'What dost thee want for thy birthday?'
She snswered, 'Diamonds', so straight there an then
I gid 'er the ace, king, quuen, jack and ten.

The lady chainmakers they'm all gone on strike,
The bosses they think they can pay what they like.
They work 'em so hard by night and by day,
And for it they get such rotten pay.

Now I dreamed that I died and to heaven did go.
'Where did you come from?' they wanted to know.
Now I says, 'From down Cradley', and how they did stare:
They said, 'Come right in, Joe, you'm the first bloke from there'.

Now me and Phil Drabble*, we'm all right, you see,
And when we go out we go on the spree;
Now whether we win or whether we lose,
We'm allus ready for a damn good booze.

Cradley St Luke's is a very fine team,
They look very smart in the white and the green.
They went down to Worcester to play for the cup,
And it wor very long before they got Worcester done up.

My brother bought a cow, but then poorly it fell,
So we fed it on rum, just to make it get well;
And just like the silk-worm that gives us the silk,
That cow gave my brother hot rum and milk.

I bought me a chicken from town yesterday,
I thought that for me a nice egg it would lay.
Well, early this morning I had a great shock,
The fowl says, 'I can't lay an egg, I'm a cock'.

* Once well known in the Black Country as a writer and broadcaster.

CHAPTER 9

Pubs, Prizefighters and Pigeons

Makers of heavy chain, we are told, sweated so much at work that some would swallow twelve pints of beer a day, not counting any social drinking in the evening. Others spending long and strenuous hours in hot, dusty and sometimes dangerous mines and foundries looked for similar restoration. The liquid consumed may not have been the good quality 'fours' or 'fives', recalled by George Dunn, and costing four or five pence a quart, but the 'bum clink' sold at a half penny a pint when it was on the point of going off. At Netherton, according to M.H.W. Fletcher, in the single area of Bumble Hole, there were ten

Ox roasting in the yard of the Golden Cross at Halesowen, c.*1900. The inn later became a cinema called the Cosy Corner, then a factory making dresses. In 1958 Halesowen's first Woolworths took over the site*

public houses 'beside "wobble shops", where a low proof of beer, three times stronger than present day ale, was sold at twopence a bucket'. Wobble was the third 'shut' or product of a brew, the first of which was ale, the second, beer. Iron workers spurned the barrel of barley water which employers provided, and preferred to slake their thirst by sending our for a bucket of wobble.

In about 1860 a travelling Irish entertainer called Brian Kelly performed a monologue in Dudley pubs which mentioned over seventy of the town's establishments (see panel below).

Dudley Inn Signs

A *Star* was shining brightly when I came to town this morning, and I saw a *Green Man* who was about to kill a *White Swan*, when an *Angel* appeared on the scene and told him to take it to the *Cowshed* for safety, but instead of doing so he placed it behind a *Bush*, where a *Brown Lion* called him into the *Peacock*. The *George* wishing to bring them back mounted a *White Horse*, and taking up the *Cross Guns*, he followed and killed them. Fetching his *Wagon and Horses* he drove to the *Priory* where he presented them to the *King and Queen*, much to the pleasure of *Sir John Peel*, and all who were at the *Court House*. Just then I felt hungry, and having a *Bird in Hand*, I bought a *Hen and Chickens*, and had them cooked, and having a *Barrel* with some beer in it I enjoyed myself proper. After that I caught sight of *Shakespeare* with a *Hammer* in his hand, who said he was going to put the *Three Horseshoes* on the *Black Horse* so as to go hunting after a *Fox*, but when he got to the *Blue Gates* they were locked, so fetching some *Cross Keys* he soon gained admittance, and by the light of the *Seven Stars* he caught a *Blue Pig* and a *Falcon*, a *Green Dragon* at the *Beehive*, a *Dolphin* and a *Greyhound*, throwing them into a *Locomotive* which was passing, he rode home and milked a *Red Cow* in his *Field House Cottage*.

Feeling tired, I went to have a nap in a *Quiet House*, when I heard the *Legs of Man* approaching, and jumping up I saw the *Duke of Wellington* and the *Duke of York* before me, who commanded me to place the *Crown* on the *Queen's Head*, and give the *Plume of Feathers* to the *Prince of Wales*, and the *White Roses* to the *Highland Laddie*. They gave me a *Parrot*, a *Cross* for the *Dudley Arms*, and then I went to the *Old Inn* for a drink. After that, I went round to see the *Wrexham* and watched the *Welsh Go By*. The next thing I saw was the *Oddfellows Arms* robbing some *British Oak* out of a *Miners' Arms*, so I shifted them off with a *Malt Shovel*, and having a *Coach and Horses* with me, I drove round the *Wren's Nest*, where I was chased by a *Griffin*, but eventually received a splendid *Salutation* in the *Gipsy's Tent* from the people who were building the *Round House*. While I was looking at the *Old Windmill*, a *Grand Turk* asked me to have a drink, so we went into the *Junction Inn* where he sang *Britannia* rules the waves. I now saw a *Hearty Good Fellow* eating a *Swan*, and I fainted and fell into the *Earl of Dudley's Arms*, who rang the *Bell*, and told the waiter to go to the *Hope* and fetch some water from the *Cottage Spring*. Feeling better, I climbed a *British Oak* where I found *Three Crowns*, so I went to *Belle Vue* to spend them, and received a *Rose and Crown* for my efforts.

The White Swan public house (demolished in 1937) at the junction of Bath and Dudley Streets, Walsall. Three other pubs, the Duke of York, the Green Man and the Paul Pry, were within a distance of 125 yards

In 1909 one pedestrian, as he walked a half-mile stretch of road between Brierley Hill and Dudley, counted three public houses every minute, and there were five of them at Five Ways, Brierley Hill. A check of *Kelly's Directories* for 1928 (the year in which Samuel Millichap gave his account of Stourbridge rough house: see below) showed some 1,500 public houses in the Black Country, over 1,100 in the Staffordshire areas, the rest in Worcestershire. As well as pictorial signs some displayed boards with welcoming rhymes such as:

If you be hungry or a-dry,
Or your stomach out of order,
For sure relief, at the Round of Beef,
For both of these two disorders.

The Old Red Cow
Gives good milk now.

If you go by and thirsty be,
The fault is yours and not on me.
Fixed here I am and hinder none,
Refresh and pay and travel on.

Doorway of Crooked House (Glynne Arms), Himley, as shown in an undated postcard

Good malt makes good beer.
Walk in, you find it here.

These were in Dudley, the last two at the Traveller's Rest in Hall Street and the Malt Shovel respectively. At Brierley Hill, allegedly bearing out the truth of the saying, 'The nearer the church, the further from God', the Beehive Inn, which stood in the nineteenth century immediately by the churchyard gates, bore this message:

In this hive we're all alive,
Good ale makes us funny.
So if you're dry come in and try
The virtue of our honey.

One rector, a Mr Hooton or Wootton, took to sample the 'honey' after services, and became so fond of it that from time to time he had to be wheeled home in a hand-barrow. The Crooked House Inn at Himley, formerly known as the Glynne Arms, is well enough known not to need a rhyme, but in 1927 it inspired a song by Alfred Tyrer (with music by Charles Love):

Go and take a social glass and prove it is no fable,
That a marble rolls uphill when placed upon the table;
You try to walk but your legs go wrong; you find you can't get farther;
You seem to be reeling, it's quite a funny feeling, and one that knocks
you rather.

Pubs, paramount centres for the community's social and sporting activity, as well as relaxation and recreation, were often cherished over many centuries — not without an eye to commercial benefit. The Greyhound at Bilston has been in business since 1450. The Stone Cross at West Bromwich takes its name from the mediaeval wayside cross which stood close by until 1894. At the Old Star and Garter, Wolverhampton, King Charles I was entertained by local royalists after his victory at Hopton Heath, near Stafford. A Mr Henry Gough is said to have turned up with the gift to the king of a heavy purse of gold, saying: 'May it please your majesty to accept *this*; it is all the cash I have by me at present, or I would have brought more'. The contents turned out to amount to

Stone Cross Inn, West Bromwich, advertising its 'Fine home brew'd ales'. This building was demolished and replaced in 1932

£1,200. Gough was thereupon offered, but declined, a knighthood. The royal bedchamber, carefully preserved, proved an attraction to visitors for at least three hundred years afterwards. A rather wry tale concerning a Bilston pub appeared in 1871 (see panel overleaf).

Star and Garter Inn, Wolverhampton, and King Charles's bed in 1846, after drawings by Arthur Crowquill

The deeds of eccentric or outstanding customers often lived on in taproom narrative. At the Rising Sun Inn, Overend, Cradley, Bill Jones, nicknamed 'Billy Brawn' because of his great strength, was also notable for the great 'curtain'

What o'Clock, Mr 'Ooley?

Early in the present century, when Bilston was a long straggling village with one main street, which formed a part of the mail-road from London to Chester and Holyhead, the Bull's Head (advertised for sale Lady Day, 1870) was the principal inn of the place, and a well-known hostelrie on the old Irish route. It was naturally and almost as a matter of course, the house at which the town worthies were wont to meet, drink good wholesome home-brewed ale out of the Staffordshire black glazed pots, smoke their long Broseley pipes, and talk over the politics of the day and the tittle-tattle of the neighbourhood.

One bright summer's eve, while thus pleasantly engaged in the modest smoking-room (coffee rooms had not as yet come into existence), a gentleman rides up to the door, followed by his servant with saddle-bags. There is, of course, great curiosity amongst the assembled guests to know who the stranger may be; and from the communicative valet they soon learn that he is an Irish officer *en route* to London. They become immediately desirous of his company amongst themselves, both for society and news' sake; but the gentleman unsocially keeps his own room upstairs. So that at last, driven to desperation and perchance somewhat pot-valiant, one of the company, Mr. Edward Woolley of Stonefields, a screw-maker (*i.e.* of iron screw for wood), sends up the servant with his chronometer, to ask the Irishman if he can tell what time it is by an English watch. Great anxiety ensues as to the result. Presently the servant returns with his master's compliments, and he will be down directly with the watch and an answer.

A great shuffling of feet is heard overhead; and by and by appears Milesius, followed by his body-guard bearing a tray with a watch and a brace of pistols on it. He unhesitatingly announces that he is come to challenge the owner of the watch, and hopes he will have the 'dacency' to claim it and take up one of the pistols. (To the servant:) 'Take the watch round, John!' 'Is it yours, sir?' The old doctor, Moss, was the first thus addressed; and amongst others present were Messrs. Price and Bushbury. 'No, sir!' was the invariable answer from each put to this crucial test. At length it comes to the owner: 'Is this watch yours, sir?' 'No, sir!' 'Well then, John, since no one will own the watch, put it in your pocket; and as we do not appear to have fallen among 'jintlemen', bring out the horses, and we'll ride on another stage'.

The tale of course soon got abroad, and to the end of his career poor Woolley, or rather ''Oolley', as he was more generally called, was accosted with 'What o'clock, Mr. 'Oolley?' Only within a year or two of his death, while riding along quietly in his carriage, a young urchin thus annoyed him; and in getting out to make a dash for him, poor ''Oolley' was upset and grievously injured: so that he had good cause long to remember the loss of his 'family turnip', and his prestige of Quixotic combativeness.

Staffordiensis

beard which covered his chest. His most spectacular party piece consisted of raising a heavy table with his teeth until it touched the ceiling. 'Many a visitor lost money in a wager on this feat', said a report of 1925, which continued:

> One day someone wagered Billy £5 that he could not drink 12 quarts of beer straight off. He took on the bet and won the money. It is also said that on another occasion he wagered to drink a bucket of pig wash [swill], and won that bet also. A farmer in the neighbourhood had a large black horse which had proved so intractable that nobody could be found to manage it. It was being sold cheap, so Billy Brawn decided to buy it. Shortly afterwards the neighbours saw him astride the horse, which he rode straight from the farm to the Rising Sun. He did not stop at the door, but drove the horse straight into the passage, and thrust its head over the bar.

Landlords, too, made their mark. A Mr Albert Head, writing in 1982 of the period some sixty years earlier, recalled that of the sixteen pubs within a short distance of Five Ways at Cradley Heath, many were better known by the name of the landlord than that of the pub: Joe Bennett's (Railway Hotel), Tommy Evan's (Four Ways), Tom Farmer's (Royal Oak), Benny Fiddle's (Bell), Jasper's (Swan), Joe Mallen's (Old Cross Guns), Billy Plough's (Plough and Harrow), Llew's (New), Tommy Webb's (Bull's Head) and Charlie Wright's (Five Ways). Of these, Joe Mallen (1891-1975) was by far the most prominent. After working for some years as a chainmaker, at the age of 30 he took on the Old Cross Guns and proceeded to indulge his passion for fighting cocks and Staffordshire dogs. His prize 'Stafford', Gentleman Jim, which drew 'dog men' from miles around to the pub, took part in wholly illegal fights staged in the cellars. Mallen, who also organised cock fights, rejoiced in his rascally reputation. He was extremely shrewd, and deferred to none. When the Earl of Dudley brought a dog to be appraised, Joe asked: ''Ow much did yer pay furrim?' 'Ten pounds in London'. 'Well, for the fust start, he ate [ain't] no Stafford, an' the second, he ate wuth ten pence, let aloon ten pounds'. According to Tom Langley, after Gentleman Jim died Joe Mallen and his wife arranged 'a slap-up funeral ..., and when they got as far as the taxidermist

Joe Mallen in 1972

they took 'im in there and 'ad 'im stuffed'. After that he sat on the counter at the Cross Guns. 'There were some queer characters among the dog-fighters', Langley added, 'for the simple reason that in a twisted sort of way they loved the dogs. I remember one — Podgy, we called 'im — and every time 'is dog got bit it was 'im oo 'owled, not the dog. 'E felt the pain. But Podgy was a glutton for punishment. 'E never pulled 'is dog out o' the ring'.

Samuel Millichamp, landlord over a period of fifty years of a series of pubs in the Black Country, including the Burnt Tree Tavern at Tipton, told the *Stourbridge Gazette* in 1928: 'Dog fights were also staged in the taprooms at many houses, and I have seen lots of them end with their owners stripping to the waist and fighting each other in the same room when a dispute arose. Those were the days when taprooms often resembled a slaughterhouse, in so far as blood was concerned'.

Millichap also recalled rat pits, 'Years ago ...one of the greatest assets of the Black Country publican': 'I had one when I was at the Golden Lion, Daisy Bank. It was in the club room, and at times there were as many as thirty rats in the pit when the dogs were put in. A lot of money changed hands in bets, and there was often a ratting competition for which the stake was a good supper'. A rat pit was in fact a cage, some three to four feet in diameter and of a similar height. The winner of the contest was the dog which killed the most rats in a given time. If two dogs killed an equal number the prize would go to the smaller, and it followed that a tiny but lethal terrier would be worth its weight in gold. Hackwood observed 'There were many ... rat-killing arenas in and

'Billy ... killing 100 Rats in five minutes and a half', c.*1825*

around Oldbury sixty years ago' (i.e., 1855), and quoted the kind of notice which would be posted in a pub's window: 'At the ---- Inn, Oldbury, a Rat-killing Leger will take place on Saturday, November 1, when the Proprietor will give £1 10s. if there are ten dogs at 2/6 each. If over ten dogs all money added. Heats, the best of three; final, the best of five'. In 1850, when an Oldbury man called Bashford matched his dog against another from Darlaston, so many spectators turned up that the event had to move to a street in West Bromwich. The police moved in an arrested the principals, who were later heavily fined by magistrates in Handsworth. The law seems to have overlooked the more modest displays on Sunday afternoons in Chapel Square at Monmore Green, when Norman Evans for the amusement of onlookers used to release rats which his dog, Barney, would quickly kill.

The rats used on these occasions would previously have been caught, often on farms, by people such as William Kelly, from Blakenhall, near Wolverhampton. 'Hairy' Kelly, the 'rot ketcher', caught over ninety rats on one farm during the First World War. Many he killed and saved the tails to show the farmer. A large number he kept, alive, inside his shirt. When the farmer agreed to pay only for those killed, 'Hairy' opened his shirt and said: 'All right. Have 'em back'. The farmer paid. 'Hairy' kept the live rats for killing later, not by dogs, but by himself, with his teeth. As late as 1930 an *Express and Star* reporter joined people on the back lawn of a public house to watch 'one of the strangest exhibitions imaginable' (see panel overleaf).

Some pub activities were rather more sedate, including the meetings of friendly societies which are described in chapter 14. The smokers of churchwarden pipes had a club at the Portway Tavern in Rowley Regis devoted to their pastime. A picture of 1910 shows the landlord, Tom Bishop, among them; in the background is a model of the inn made of England's Glory matchboxes. A similar club at the Heath Tavern in Cradley Heath had strict rules:

1. All members must smoke their own pipes.
2. No member shall swear during the club hours.
3. No member to call a brother a liar.
4. Dumb insolence is not allowed.

Offenders paid fines, which were collected by an usher who went round with a bowl and a truncheon. All members had to doff their hats as they entered the club room. A chairman called them to order with a gavel. The formality no doubt seems ludicrous, but it can be understood in a context where the slightest dispute could lead to a vicious fight, and often did.

Such fights, both improvised and organised, often took place in pubs, a number of which were run by practising or retired fighters. Indeed, until the 1930s 'belloil [a thrashing] and blood for supper' provided a frequent attraction in Black Country pubs. A century before that, Dick Evans, a barefist pugilist, kept a pub on Hell Lane (now Ettingshall Road) in Bilston called the Marquis

'Hairy' Kelly, Rat-fighter

'Hairy' Kelly, 1930

A man was going to kill a rat — with his teeth. The expectant little crowd was grouped round a large table with a nail in the centre of it. Standing nervously by the table was a rather unshaven little man, with bright, almost hypnotic eyes, and a broad, thin-lipped mouth.

As he stood by the table he opened the mouth of a small bag and drew out a large, quivering rat. He held the rat up to look at it, and it squealed almost as though it knew what its fate was to be at the hands, or mouth, of this bright-eyed little man.

'Hairy' then drew a long piece of string from his pocket and tied one end of it to one of the rat's hind feet, and the other end he fastened to the nail in the centre of the table. The rat, which he then placed on the table, was free to run all round, but could not jump off.

The crowd of onlookers pressed closer round the table. Kelly took off his cap and stepped forward. The rat, now seemingly unconscious of the fact that it was becoming the centre of interest, was nonchalantly scratching one of its ears with its free hind foot. Kelly approached the table and leaned over with his face near the rat. Then began the 'fight'.

The rat ran, a grey-brown streak, all over the table, but everywhere it went Kelly's mouth followed it, waiting for an opportunity. Soon he managed to butt the rat over with his face, and hold it down on the table. But with a twist of its lithe body the rat turned over and leaped at Kelly's face. For one glorious moment, for the rat, Kelly's face was nipped, bitten and scratched, but it was only for a moment, for somehow Kelly managed to get the rat between his teeth, and, lifting his head triumphantly, shook it to death.

Throwing the limp body of the rodent on the table, he passed his cap round. I saw more than one woman, who had evidently enjoyed the show, open her purse and drop some money in the cap.

I spoke to Kelly afterwards. His face was bleeding in three places and he looked rather flushed. 'I'd challenge any dog there is', he said, 'to kill a rat' — he said 'rot' — 'quicker than me. I've won that' he continued, pointing to a penny, 'and from that up to £10 by killing rats quicker than a dog. I've had a rat and a ferret fighting in me shirt, and I've taken 'em both out dead. I started killing rats with me teeth when I was 16 — forty years ago. I was so quick with me 'ands, I could catch 'em as they come out of their holes, so I thought I might as well try to kill 'em too. And', he concluded, 'I'm the champion rat-catcher of the world'.

of Wellington, but known as Hell House. His daughter regularly acted as a second, and encouraged her man by shouting: 'Give 'im a red shirt, me bonny boy!' Local rivalries sometimes gave a contest a sharper edge. In 1835 Charley Hodge, the 'Brierley Hill Pet', easily defeated Gornal's champion, John Bate, the 'One-eyed Wonder'. Feeling ran high afterwards, and many a Gornalite and a Brierley Hiller came to blows. A young Gornal collier, Jem Hall, after beating the 'One-eyed Wonder', challenged Hodge to a return bout for £20 a side, winner to take all. Both fighters rigorously trained, and both were heavily backed, from well beyond the Black Country. The huge crowd which turned up for the fight on Kinver Edge in November 1836 included an unusually large number of women, many with babies in arms: they had come, it is said, because their husbands over several weeks had raided the housekeeping in order to place bets, and they wanted to be there to claim a share of the winnings. Jem Hall's wife, Maria, was a prominent and vociferous spectator. First the advantage went with the challenger, then with the champion, but after an hour and forty minutes (48 rounds) Hodge was unconscious, and his second threw in the sponge. Jem and Maria Hall were carried off in triumph by the Gornalites to the Gate Hangs well at Kinver. The Brierley Hillers stood in silence as the senseless Hodge received treatment from Dr Davidson, of whom a Bilstonian remarked, referring to his work on the body of a hanged man (for whom, see page 40): 'If the owd doctor can mek as good a job of puttin' Charley together as 'e did o' takin' Abel Hill to pieces, Charley ay got a lot to worry about'. Charley fought no more, but both he and Hall (after two more bouts in the case of the latter) remained keen on the ring, and acted as seconds until the 1850s. They became friends, and when Jem's son married Charley's daughter the wedding was celebrated in both Gornal and Brierley Hill.

Many Black Country fighters came to the notice of the outside world only briefly or not at all. W. Rollinson (born in 1825) recalled in 1911 that a week seldom passed at Brierley Hill without a match for stakes of from £1 to £5 a side. One contest in a field near the Whimsey Inn between a collier known as Lancashire Harry and 'a noted bruiser' from Stourbridge drew a crowd of some 10,000 people. Despite ending in a draw, with both fighters unable to come up to scratch, it was celebrated by the 'Brockmoor rhymer', Marshall Hadduck. Unfortunately, only one verse seems to have been recorded:

> Come hither, you bold colliers, and sit you down and sing,
> And let us all join chorus and make the place to ring.
> It is a song concerning (you may remember still)
> The fight between the collier lad and Cook at Brierley Hill.

Rollinson also remembered stand-up fights to settle differences at the back of the Old Star Inn.

Charles Perry of Lye, who died in 1907 at the age of 95, also had clear recollections of similar encounters:

> I have seen big fights down on the Green there — Baldwin's Green. I remember particularly one fight which I saw, two men fighting for a young woman. She married the man who won, and they went and kept a farm. But that wasn't such a big fight as the one between Joe 'Smacker' and Adam 'Puffer'. That took place in Hodge Hole, a proper fighting ring, near Wassell Grove. They were at it for two hours, and were so knocked about that they were in bed and had to be fed with spoons for weeks; they couldn't lift their arms up. In one fight at the Cross Walks I saw a man killed. He was carried away in a big chair. They didn't fight for money, but either because they had quarrelled, or to see who was the champion.

Other fighters acquired a national reputation, spread both by word of mouth and by widely-circulated accounts of their fights on printed ballad sheets. Tom Hickman (the 'Gas Light Man'), born in Dudley in 1785, falls into this category. He won many battles in periods as short as fifteen minutes but he was boastful, and his defeat by the Bristolian, Bill Neat, in 1821 inspired little sympathy. It was, incidentally, described by William Hazlitt in a famous essay, 'The Fight'. The ballad version, 'A new song on the late battle fought by the Bristol hero, Neat (now champion of England), and the Gaslight Man', with the jeering refrain, 'Huzza! Huzza! The Bristol hero Billy Neat,/The boasting gas-light man has beat', for some reason thought that Hickman was a Cockney.

'The Prize Fight, by Thomas Rowlandson, 1787

A moment from Bob Brettle's fight with Jem Mace

Robert ('Bob') Brettle (1833-72) was born at Portobello, Edinburgh, to parents who soon returned to their native Stourbridge. In due course he became a glass blower, and as late as the 1970s relatives still possessed a coloured glass walking stick he had made. (Was this a 'frigger'? See page 44). Brettle started fighting in 1854, under the sobriquet of the 'Wordsley Glassblower'. Having beaten one Malpass of Birmingham, he was for some reason adopted by his opponent's fans, and became known as the 'Birmingham Pet'. During a short career he defeated Jem Mace of Norwich (and also lost to him) and Tom Paddock of Redditch, but was bested in 1859 by Tom Sayers in what turned out to be his last fight (see illustration overleaf). By 1863 he was keeping the White Lion in Birmingham's Digbeth (on a site opposite the present police station), and used the rat pit at the rear of the premises for illegal cock fights. The business did not flourish, and Brettle left for what turned out to be another unsuccessful venture in the USA. Back in Birmingham, he returned to his trade of glassblowing, but died of consumption at the age of only 41. A whip-round among sympathisers realised only £28, of which 2s. 6d. remained after his funeral expenses had been paid.

The rags to riches to rags trajectory common to many fighters, before and since, was shared with William Perry, who, like Brettle, met nemesis at the fists of Tom Sayers. Perry (?1819/20-1880) started his working life at the age of seven on a narrow boat taking 'night soil' (a euphemism for human excrement) by canal from Tipton into the Staffordshire countryside. Five or six years later, despite a left leg crippled by childhood rickets, he was a strapping six-footer who enjoyed priority through locks for his employer's boat, thanks to the traditional Black Country skill of dominant fists. During a spell of navvying in London he fought and won his first professional fight at the age of 16. Back in his native Tipton, during a bout with Ben Spilsbury of Birmingham he used to devastating effect the right-arm swing which left him with the nickname of the 'Tipton Slasher', and his defeated opponent with broken ribs and jaw.

Perry's next challenger, Skim Skimmy, proposed fighting with stakes of a donkey and a bag of sand, 'Gornal fashion', meaning nothing barred but kicking and gouging, no division into rounds, and a contest ending only with one participant unconscious, disqualified, or crying 'enough'. After three hours on the day of the fight at Park Hall, Walsall, in 1837, the contestants adjourned until the morrow,

LINES ON THE

GREAT FIGHT

BETWEEN

TOM SAYERS,

Champion of England, and

BOB BRETTLE,

Of Birmingham.

FOR £600 AND A BET OF £200 TO £20.

You lovers of the pugelistic ring, attend with mirth and cheers,
Whilst I here pen down and will expound, the merits of Tom
He is the noble champion, who in honour does uphold. [Sayers,
The Belt of merry England, and her laurels tipt'd with gold.

His first battle was with Aby Crouch, in the year '49,
He polished of that hardy Son, in 13 minutes time; [score,
He fought next with Dan Collin's, and in rounds then full two
He thrashed his brave opponent, in minutes 84.

Next for 100 pounds, he fought the great renouned Jack Grant,
To face his man, Tom near was scan, nor neither was he daunt;
After three hard hours fighting, and rounds then 64,
Tom proved a finished workman, and the laurel again wore.

He fought next then with Jack Martin, and he fought with Georgy
He licked those two opponents and scattered all their tins; [Sims,
He fought with Harry Poulson, and he conquered Aron Jones,
And in victories most glorious the battles was Tom's own.

He fought the Tipton Slasher, and brought him to the dust,
And on the banks of Medway he emptied many a purse; [ditch,
He conquered the great Bill Bainge, and Tom Paddock of Red-
So brave a man as Tommy Sayers, ne'er came from proud Sussex.

And last he fought Bob Brettle, a man of courage bold,
Whoe's mighty deeds of manly art, the pages does unfold;
But from an accidental fall, Bob Brettle he must yield,
Leaving Tom Sayers the winner, and the victor of the field.

Now the praises of Tom Sayers, I could not full extol,
He's the champion of proud England, and the conquerer of all;
His manly determination, as in the ring he does appear,
Declare's him as the Champion, the Belt of England for to wear.

Street ballad, 'Lines on the Great Fight ...', 1859, between Sayers and Brettle

when, after two more hours, with Skimmy unconscious, the Slasher was declared the victor. As well as the donkey and 'lily-white sond', which he immediately sold, he won £25 in side bets. During the second afternoon of the fight, the Slasher, on top of Skimmy in heavy rain, reputedly asked: ''Ave yo 'ad enuff?' 'No, I ay', came the reply. 'Well', said the Slasher, 'yo con cum on top for a change. Ah'm getting' wet through up 'ere'. After losing a good deal of money on Skimmy the Gornalites put up Jem Scummer to fight the Slasher for £25 a side, this time under prize ring rules. In December 1837, after thirty-one rounds, again spread over two days (the first at Gornal Wood, the second at Kingswinford), the Slasher again won by a knock-out.

From this point on, his status was assured, but a chaotic career ensued. Established figures like Jem Bendigo, 'Deaf' Burke and Ben Caunt, the champion of England, refused to meet him at all. Other challengers defaulted, and forfeited their stake money. Fights that did take place were interrupted by police action or disqualifications for Slasher or an opponent. One of them, when he beat Tass ('Hazard') Parker of West Bromwich, in February 1844, went to 133 rounds. Eventually, after twenty-one years in the game, Slasher became champion, thanks to an opponent's failure to turn up. He then retired from the ring and set up a public house called the Champion of England, in Spon Lane, West Bromwich.

Perry enjoyed his fame. His likeness graced Madame Tussaud's in London, and also appeared in prints and paintings. He met one poet, Swinburne, and appeared in the verse of another, Browning, as part of a list of the fashionable bachelor's accoutrements:

> Or else there's no wife in the case,
> And the portrait's queen of the place,
> Alone 'mid the other spoils
>   Of youth — masks, gloves and foils,
> And pipe-sticks, rose, cherry-tree, jasmine,
>   And the long whip, the tandem-lasher,

THE GREAT FIGHT BETWEEN PADDOCK AND THE TIPTON SLASHER.

Ye sporting blades of England,
Come listen to my song,
And if you'll pay attention,
I'll not detain you long,
It is concerning a gallant fight,
The truth I will unfold,
In the prize ring of England
For £200 in gold.

CHORUS.

So here's success to Tipton Slasher
He has shown him British play,
And he has beat bold Paddock,
And bore the prize away.

On the Seventeenth of December,
These men came into the ring,
They toss'd up for the choice of ground
And Tipton he did win,
Then time being call'd these men did
And Paddock he did say, [strip,
I will bet twenty pounds,
That I will take the prize away.

These men they then came to the
Being eager of the game, [scratch
Tipton let fly with his right,
Paddock stopp'd it like a man,
Then they let fly both right and left,
To each other they did stand,
After a tremendous struggle,
Both men came to the ground.

At the commencement of the second
round,
These men they both look'd shy,
But Paddock he shot out his left
And cut the Slashers eye,

Then Slasher hit out right and left,
And the people round the ring,
Bet three to one on Tipton
For they was sure that he would win

When Tipton came to the scratch again
For mischief he was bent,
Paddock was not for to be gull'd,
At him left and right he went,
Paddock hit out and got away,
They cried its all a hoax,
Tipton with a tremendous blow
Cut Paddock's knowledge box.

These men they fac'd each other,
With courage stout and true,
Tipton with a well aimed blow,
Bold Paddock's claret drew,
Paddock returned the compliment,
With all speed so free,
With a left handed blow
On Tipton's box of ivory.

When Paddock he came up again,
He was weak and nearly done,
Tipton went in both right and left,
Broke Paddock's collar bone
Paddock he did try his best,
Bold Tipton for fling,
But Tipton with a heavy blow,
Knock'd Paddock out of time.

Then time being call'd
He was deaf unto their cry,
The referees they did declare,
Tipton had won the day,
Then the ring it was broken in,
The crowd did shout and sing,
Hurrah for brave Tipton
He his the Champion.

Now to conclude and make an end,
Of this my simple rhyme,
Success unto bold Tipton
When he does fight again,
And may he prove the Champion!
Of the British ring,
Like Ward, or bold Bendigo,
Or the veteran Tom Spring.

Street ballad, 1850

And the cast from a fist ("not, alas! mine,
  But my master's, the Tipton Slasher").
And the cards where pistol-balls mark ace,
And a satin shoe used for cigar case,
And the chamois horns ("shot in the Chablais"),
  And prints, Barey drumming on Cruiser,
  And Sayers, our champion, the bruiser,
And the little edition of Rabelais.

It is a measure of the Slasher's stature that six years of his retirement elapsed before a challenge came — from Tom Sayers — for his title as champion. Sayers, a bricklayer from Brighton, a lighter and smaller but also younger man, met the Slasher on the Isle of Grain near the River Medway in Kent on 16 June 1857. Early on, Sayers landed a heavy blow on Perry's temple, which may have exacerbated an earlier brain injury. Even so, the contest had run for an hour and 42 minutes, during which a single round lasted for a record 50 minutes, when the Slasher's seconds threw in the sponge. Four men had to hold down the defeated champion, who was unwilling to surrender, despite being concussed and also temporarily blinded by blood running into his eyes from cuts. Along with his title he lost his public house and its contents, and also his trophies, for he had backed himself to win with everything he possessed. Sympathisers bought him a beer house but 'this did not last long', wrote Tom Langley. 'His intelligence dulled and his physique ruined, he gradually went back to the canal boats and at one time was a night soil and stable manure contractor — taking boat loads between Tipton and Muckley Corner'.

The old Slasher surfaced from time to time. Once his boat and a Shropshire Union passenger craft were approaching a bridge from opposite directions. The 'flyboat' should have had precedence but the Slasher ordered the boy driving to go ahead. The two vessels were jammed together in the 'bridge hole'. One of the flyboat's crew jumped on to the tow path and told the Slasher what he would do to him if he had him on land. 'Stop a minute, my lad; I'll come to thee', said the Slasher, and jumped on to the path. The young man rushed at him, to be knocked back by a single blow. A second charge met a second blow, which deposited the attacker in the canal. As one of his mates helped him out of the water a passer-by called from the top of the bridge: 'You silly fools! Don't you know who that is? It's the Tipton Slasher'.

David Christie Murray (1847-1907), the novelist and journalist born at West Bromwich, was as a boy taught to defend himself by the Slasher, much to the disapproval of his parents:

> I have been soundly flogged time and time again for visiting him. ...
>
> I earned one of the soundest thrashings I ever got in my life by playing truant from school in order to follow the Slasher to a wretched

> little race meeting, held at a place called The Roughs, on the side of the Birmingham Road, in the parish of Handsworth. My hero was there in glory, followed about by an innumerable tag-rag and bobtail, and I am afraid that on two occasions at least he was tempted to swagger and 'show off', as children say. He shambled up to one of the 'try your strength' machines: the figure of a circus clown, with a buffer to punch at the neighbourhood of his midriff, and a dial on his chest to indicate the weight of the blow administered. The Slasher tossed a penny to the proprietor of the machine and waved him on one side; but the man stood in front of the contrivance and besought him pathetically not to strike. 'Not you, Mr Perry', he said humbly; 'oh, not you, Mr Perry'. The Slasher, with an 'Away, slight man' motion of the hand, said 'Gerrout!' and the fellow obeyed, seeing there was nothing else for it. Hercules spat upon his hand, clenched his fist, and smote. Crash went the whole machine into ruin, the wooden upright splintered, and the iron supports doubled into uselessness. The destroyer rolled on rejoicing; but the crowd made a subscription, and the owner of the machine stowed away his damaged property well pleased.

This kind of exploit was during the Slasher's prime. A later meeting of Murray's with him was much sadder:

> He was dying when I saw him again, and his vast chest and shoulders were shrunken and bowed, so that one wondered where the very framework of the giant man had fallen to. He was despised and forgotten and left alone, and he sat on the side of his bed with an aspect altogether dejected and heartless. In his better days he had liked what he used to call 'a stripe of white satin', which was the poetic for a glass of Old Tom gin. I carried a bottle of that liquor with me as a peace offering, and a quarter of a pound of bird's eye [variety of tobacco]. He did not know me, and there was no speculation in his look; but after a drink he brightened. …
>
> 'They mought ha' let me aloon. Tum's a good un. I've sin 'em all, an' I've niver sin a better. But he owed to ha' let me be. Theer was no credit to be got in hommerin' a man at my time o' life. All the same, mind ye, I thowt I should ha' trounced him. So I should if I could ha' got at him; but he fled hither an' he fled thither, and he was about me like a cooper a-walkin' round a cask. An' I was fule enough to lose temper, an' the crowd begun to laugh an' gibe at me, and I took to raacin' round after him, an' my wind went, an' wheer was I then? He knocked me down — fair an' square he did it. Th' ony time it iver chanced to me. I put everythin' I had o' that fight, an' here I bin'.

Perry died in 1880 on Christmas Eve in his house in Gibbet Lane, Bilston, and was buried in St John's churchyard at Kate's Hill, Dudley. He was one

Toll house at Gibbet Lane, Bilston, reputedly kept by the Tipton Slasher

of many Black Country prizefighters, of whom there was a particularly rich crop in the 1860s. Men like Jack ('Dollar') White of Halesowen, Joe Goss of Wolverhampton, Ned Hinish of Stourbridge, William ('Smoker') Evans and Josiah ('Sulphur') Jones of Dudley, and Thomas Farrell of Walsall, each had passionate supporters and backers at fights contested in such places as the Clent Hills, Delves Green, Hartlebury Common, Kinver Edge, Tividale and Wombourne, as well as further afield in Birmingham, Bristol, Nottingham and London. Sporting journalists, describing 'mills' sometimes running to several hours and over a hundred rounds, used elaborate language. 'Gallant rivals' or 'knights of the ring shied in their castors' (literally, threw their hats into the ring — hence the expression — to express their willingness to fight). The drawing of 'first blood' would be recorded; even better the man 'sent to Mother Earth' (knocked down) or, better still, having 'his dial plastered with carmine fluid'. For some reason, perhaps because he died fighting, the 'Rowley Bruiser', Ned Round by name, but known as Ned Brade, was remembered with particular affection. As the acknowledged champion of the village and the area, the winner of many fights, he confidently faced an opponent from West Bromwich by the name of Davis. However, after a particularly strenuous contest during which he took a sustained beating he fell to the ground with injuries which later proved to be fatal. He was buried in a remote corner of the churchyard of St Giles's at Rowley, next to his father, a quarryman.

The Tipton Slasher, though, was undoubtedly the most famous Black Country fighter. His grave at Kate's Hill was restored by public subscription in 1925. His portrait hangs in Tipton Library, and his statue stands in the town's Coronation Park, closed to where he lived and trained at the Fountain public house.

After the heyday of prizefighting in the 1850s and '60s attention began to turn to more pacific forms of entertainment such as association football, which has to this day retained a big following, with teams like Walsall, West Bromwich Albion and Wolverhampton Wanderers, not to mention many lesser but loyally supported teams. As early as 1863 pigeon flying was reported, 'if the weather is fine', as 'the favourite diversion' on a Sunday morning for Black Country miners:

> The sport is pursued in various ways: sometimes the bet turns on which of a rival pair of 'tumblers' makes the greatest number of summersets in the air; sometimes it is a race between two pigeons, turned out to fly to their usual feeding-place; or several are let loose at once, and the owner of the bird which first arrives at a designated spot pockets the stakes.

It became commonplace to see horse-drawn charabancs setting off from a pub with thirty or forty men, each clutching a basket of pigeons due for release. Racing pigeons were carefully trained and fed, an expensive business. According to Philip Solomon, poorer Black Country people usually kept tipplers or tumblers:

> Tipplers are birds of tremendous stamina, and I well remember one of my uncles telling me that his birds could fly up to sixteen hours non-stop, high in the sky, alternately flying, then suddenly pushing their wings up and gliding. Tumblers were tremendously popular and these birds would litter the sky of places like Willenhall, Bilston, Dudley, Tipton, and literally all over the Black Country. ... They could also fly very high, especially on sunny days, so much so, you could hardly see them. They could also suddenly stop in mid-flight and perform an acrobatic tumbling roll. Many tales would be told about a man's tumblers, or tossers, as we called them in Willenhall — stories of birds that flew so high that they went right through the clouds and were never seen again, or of a bird that was such a good roller it ended up in so and so's chimney.

Tom Langley (born 1907), who witnessed the popularity of pigeon flying when he was a boy, remembered a bird, Princess Irena, so well loved that it had a funeral:

Now this Princess Irena was a famous racing pigeon who flew in from Spain. It was first into the Black Country loft. Now, don't think I'm pulling your leg when I tell you this. When it landed it was covered in blood and it had got a hawk's head in its beak. They bred off the Princess Irena because long before the days of Mendel the old Black Country men knew all about line-breeding and in-breeding. They would ruthlessly sort out any misfits so that they would only breed off the best.

Now when they 'ad the funeral for the Princess Irena they 'ad a band and everybody turned out. I did as well because it was the death of a heroine. Then they never buried it. They went and 'ad it stuffed. Where it is now I don't know, but for many years that bird was in th' Uxbridge Arms at Chasetown, and people used to make a pilgrimage to see the Princess Irena.

Langley knew a tear-jerking song about the despairing wait of a dying man for his pigeon to come in, so that its winnings could keep his widow out of the workhouse:

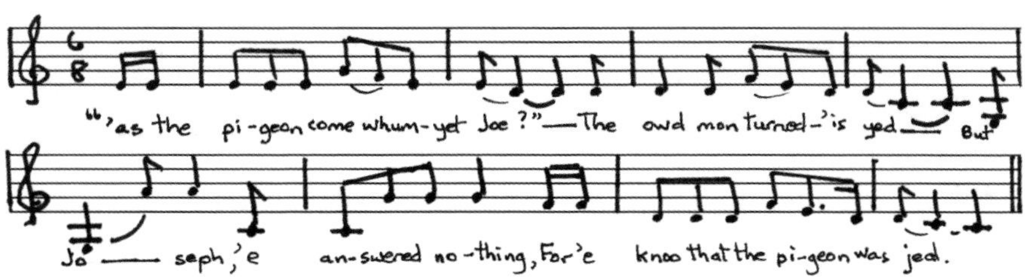

It was the owd mon's pride and joy,
This fan-tailed pigeon of 'is,
And the club money 'e wanted
To give to his owd gel, Liz.

The club money 'e wanted,
For the owd mon quite well knoo
That the workus 'ouse is no place
For a wife so trusted and true.

The owd gel, Lizzie, 'er blarted,
Then th' owd mon 'ad 'is say:
'Oh Joe, tell me, 'as the pigeon come whum?'
But Joseph 'e turned away.

Then Joseph 'e slowly turned,
'E turned to the bedside and said:
'Oh ferther, the pigeon who come'.
Then th' owd mon 'e fell back jed.

In a different death-bed scene a dying collier asks the attending clergyman: 'Shall we have wings in that next world yo talk about?' On being reassured that angels indeed have wings, he rejoined: 'Well, parson, if yo have wings and I have wings, when yo come up I'll fly yer for a quid'.

King's Head, Smethwick as seen on a postcard dated 1898

CHAPTER 10

Bears, Bulls and Gamecocks

A bloody history lies behind place names such as Bull Ring at Halesowen and Sedgley and Bull Stake at Darlaston. Wednesfield's Bull Ring disappeared beneath the embankment built for the canal by the Dog and Partridge Inn. Elsewhere, no formal name applied but there were traditional spaces where bulls and other animals were baited: at Willenhall, opposite the Baptist Chapel where Temple Bar joins the Wednesfield and Bloxwich Roads; at the Level, Brierley Hill. The activity was so popular at the Lye that the Cross, Lye Forge, Cross Walks, Stambermill and a field later covered by Spring Street, were all used. A traditional couplet celebrated another venue: 'The blood of a hundred bulls has been/Shed on the clinkers of Tipton Green'.

In the early 1900s eye-witness accounts of bull baiting in the century were still being taken down by journalists. Thomas Withers (born 1811) remembered the last bull baiting at his native West Bromwich. 'It took place in front of an

Bull Ring, Sedgley (from a postcard, c.*1905)*

Bull Stake, Darlaston (from a postcard, c.*1910)*

inn, which stood at the spot where the present police station now stands, and the bull, breaking loose, rushed into a cottage opposite, occupied by a sister of [mine]'. John Lawrence of Wordsley saw the last bull baiting at Brierley Hill

The Bull Bait, c.*1790*

in 1843. Interviewed in 1909, he gave few details, save that large numbers of smock-frocked farm labourers attended. Two years earlier, Charles Perry (born 1812) of Lye, asked: 'Did you ever see a bull fight?' replied: 'Lor's, yes, many a one', and added:

> People used to climb on the tops of houses and walls to watch the bull baiting. If a bull could catch a dog on his horn he would toss him high in the air. Often the dog would fall on the top of a house, or among us fellows, who were looking on. If he fell towards the road the people would run to catch him as he came down, so that he would not be hurt by the fall. If ever a dog pinned a bull's nose, his owner could get a pound or two for him in no time. I have seen the dogs bite an animal that badly that it was a pity to see. One bull I can remember well. They loosed two bull dogs at it, and it threw them off again and again. Then they put a third at him, and when he saw the third coming he dropped down and would fight no more. It had broken his heart, and they had to kill him.

In 1911 W. Rollinson (born in 1825) of Brierley Hill said 'Bull baiting was the popular sport in his early days; in addition, bear baiting and badger baiting were indulged in occasionally, whilst cock fighting was a very usual form of amusement among the masses'. He went on: 'The vacant land now in front of the Queen's Head, towards the bottom of Level Street, was the chief rendezvous of the bull baiters … Other bull baiting demonstrations took place near the Old Whimsey (then tenanted by a well-known character called Turley) …; others were held at the Horse Shoe Boiler Yard, and in Moor street'.Then he described the procedure:

> A strong stake in the ground held the bull by a chain, which being loose permitted the animal to face an opponent from whichever side it came. The colliers, puddlers, and other artisans would assemble for the ceremony — chiefly held at holidays or Mondays — with their bulldogs, and would pay some charge to let their dogs 'have a round at the bull'. The dogs, if well-trained and 'old hands at the job', would slip under the bull's body, and, passing between his front legs, 'pin' his nose. The infuriated beast would roar with pain. But in the case of dogs without experience the honours very frequently went to the bull, for the dogs, not knowing the risk, would 'bang' at the animal, and would be very quickly gored and tossed high in the air.

Bear baiting, Rollinson went on, was held at the Old Bell Inn, Bell Street, on the occasion of Brierley Hill Wake, the first Sunday after 19 September, when 'The bull dogs which most succeeded in escaping destruction by the bulls were specially chosen to "have a pop" at bruin'. The bear would have been muzzled, but would have been able 'to inflict heavy punishment upon

Right: Nottingham bear baiting jug of c.*1700*

his enemies by his claws and by the affectionate hugs which severely injured, and not infrequently killed the dog'. In about 1830 — presumably Rollinson must have been told this, since he would have been only five or so years old at the time — when a bear was being baited in a marl pit 'near to Messrs. Taylor's Chain Works, Brettell Lane', the stake came out of the soft ground and spectators had to flee. An official wearing 'the then fashionable white smock' fell in the mud as he tried to escape but the frightened animal ignored him, and was recaptured.

Rollinson adds:

> Badger-drawing was also a favourite sport in the Brierley Hill district in those times, and it would appear that even now it is not extinct, for we learn that as recently as last year [1910] a badger caught at Clent was brought to a spot not far from Delph, on the Lye side, and was there placed in a barrel for dogs to 'draw' him. ... In Brierley Hill the main centre for badger-drawing was just off the centre of High Street on land between the Town Hall and the old market. For years this place was known as Badger's Bank.

To return to bull baiting, there were undoubtedly occasions when a beast broke free and turned on its animal and human tormentors. There is also a tradition that in the 1830s a Primitive Methodist preacher with his bare hands uprooted a bull's stake and broke its chain during Tipton Wake. The bull then went with him 'like a lamb', and stood patiently in a field alongside Bull Lane while he preached a sermon directed against cruel sports. Such hostility, shared by many clergymen (see below), aroused

Left: Fighting cock lectern, Wednesbury Church

the ire and incredulity of defenders of what they saw as an old and cherished tradition.

Stourbridge records as early as 1570 show a bearward, Richard Harte. Jonathan Pyrke, the first landlord of the Talbot Hotel in Stourbridge, is known to have run a cockpit there between 1685 and 1695. G.T. Lawley found in some of the Bilston town documents what he took to be the earliest written reference in the Black Country to cock fighting — in 1690 (see panel below) — though there is earlier mute evidence in the shape of the fifteenth-century lectern in St Bartholomew's Church, Wednesbury, carved in the likeness of a fighting cock, which gave rise to a song known to Tom Langley:

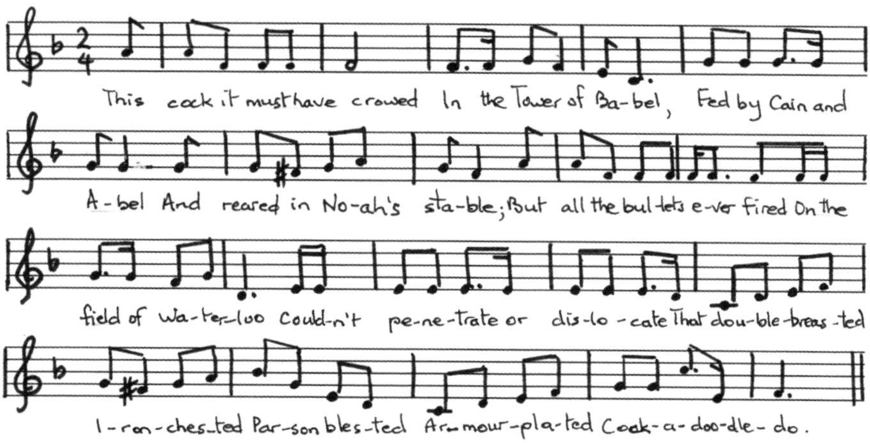

It is tempting to think that the Joe Willets mentioned in the 'Cock Fight at Wednesbury' (see panel below) was related to the Jack Willetts, Bilston's 'bullot' (master of ceremonies at bull baitings), who after serving as a soldier came back from Spain to his native town and officiated at the wake in 1743:

Cock Fight at Wednesbury

In 1690 there was a cock fight near unto Wednesbury, in a field called ye Holloway, between a certain red cock belonging to John Tomkyns, of Bilston, and a black red bird belonging to Thomas Horobin, of Wednesbury, for five guineas a side. There was a greate assemblinge of people from round about, and moch money was betted by ye friends of each bird. Y^e fighte lasted some time, but ye cocke belonging to Tomkyns was killed by ye other, whereat ye owner was so enrayged that he siezed hold of ye other birde and wrung off his head, before Horobin could stop him. This causede a greate commocion, and a general fighte between ye backers, which was not ended til manie persons had received moch injurie and detriment in property and body and John Tomkyns paid y^e vallie [value] of y^e cock. After which we all went peaceably together to Joe Willets' house, where y^e rest of y^e day was spent in festinge and drinkinge, and another match was made.

Game cocks fighting, after a print of 1831

'The bull, brightly bedecked with garlands and ribbons, was led to the stake by the town crier in his silver-laced coat and powdered wig. Jack Willetts himself, in what remained of his old military uniform and carrying a formidable Spanish sword, dominated the spectacle, which was completed by a company of local morris dancers and a band consisting of a wooden-legged fiddler and an asthmatical piper'.

After the pomp of the opening, things went badly wrong. The bull tossed several dogs, as well as a man who went after it with a club. Someone picked up the club and struck off one of the horns of the bull, which enraged it so much that it broke loose. According to a contemporary ballad:

> 'A lane, a lane', was all the cry,
> As fast they ran away,
> Leaving Jack Willetts there to die,
> Or live as best he may.

A bull breaks loose and tosses a dog

The Royal Cockpit, St James's Park, London, in the eighteenth century

In the event, though, Willetts killed the bull with his sword.

The respectability of cock fighting is shown by advertisements such as this, one of many, from Aris's *Birmingham Gazette*:

> On Monday, April 11, 1748, being Easter Monday, will be a match of cocks, weighed to fight the three following days, at Duddeston Hall, near Birmingham, each party to weigh 41 cocks for 10 guineas a battle, and 200 the main, and each party to weigh 20 cocks for bye battles, for 5 guineas a battle, each cock to give and take half an ounce. The gentlemen of Worcestershire and Herefordshire against the gentlemen of Warwickshire and Staffordshire.

Another, of February 1771, reads as follows:

> A main of cocks will be fought at the house of Thomas Rowley, known by the Sign of the Maypole in Pelsall on Midlent Monday, 11th March, between the Gentlemen of Walsall and the Gentlemen of Lichfield and Burntwood, to weigh 11 cocks on each side, two five pounds, two odd size ones; to begin to weigh at 8 a.m. and no-one to interfere in the Pit but the two Players: Gentlemen desired to attend by 11 a.m. Dinner will be ready at one. The main will be for Ten Guineas.

With high stakes at risk, birds were bred and fed with immense care. Feeders or trainers included Hadley of Wednesfield, illiterate, but 'a man of considerable experience in the training of game cocks, ... considered superior even to Tommy the Sweep [of Cheltenham] for his skill in trimming, spurring, and preparing them for battle'. The rules governing fights were precise, and a bird had to weigh within an ounce of its opponent. A Bilstonian, 'Cockie' Potter, left the pit where he had started work at the age of 11 to become a pot boy at the Britannia Inn, Moxley (a mile from Bilston). There he learned from the landlord the art of breeding and feeding cocks, and eventually became cockmaster to Lord Derby. He officiated at another big match at Duddeston Hall in 1824. E.J. Homeshaw mentions without naming him a celebrated cock trainer of Bloxwich, the favourite of whose many stories was 'when he was doorkeeping with John Somerfield at the Thatched House Tavern, he had the pleasure of refusing admission to two bishops because one of them had passed a bad "quid" on him at a previous main'.

John Freeth

John Freeth (1731-1808) of Birmingham wrote ballads celebrating both bull baiting and cock fighting. 'Bull Baiting' (1803) includes these verses:

Severn-bred fresh-water sailors,
O'er their cups who cheerly sing,
Leap for joy, like sturdy nailors,
At the sound, 'a ring, a ring'.

Bull-dogs now shall gain high credit;
They who prize them for their blood
Say the very best are bred at
Wyrley Bank and Dudley Wood.

'The Jovial Cockers', first published in 1766, was frequently reprinted. It lavished unqualified praise on the sport and its adherents:

When the time approaches nigh,
That there's sport ensuing,
To the PIT away we fly,
Fancy's will pursuing:
I hold a crown,
Before they're down,

Take of each your liking;
Standers by, loudly cry,
Odds the grey, wins the day,
But in a while, the ginger pile,
Foremost gets, now the bets
Turn about from side to side;
Panting, breathing, bleeding, dying,
There's a contest bravely try'd,
Grey was bottom [brave], tho' he dy'd,
And a true-bred chicken.

Another Birmingham man, the printer, Thomas Wood (at work 1802-27), issued a sheet entitled 'A New Song called Bloxwich Wake Bull-baiting' (see illustration overleaf) which relates how men from Bloxwich pawned a church bell so as to be able to buy a bull, only to have it spirited away to be baited by their Willenhall rivals. The tune prescribed (though not, of course, printed) was that of 'The Wednesbury Cocking' (see illustration overleaf), a ballad dating from the eighteenth century, later issued by Wood and others (see also chapter 12). It is a knockabout mock epic, far removed from the world of Lord Derby or Duddeston Hall (the seat of Sir Thomas Holte). The protagonists are colliers and nailers from Hampton, Bilston, Darlaston, Walsall, and Rowley, as well as Wednesbury, and much of the action involves their clumsy, brawling quarrels. Two of those mentioned can be identified. Ruff Moey (given as Ruff Morey in the text illustrated), was the nickname of Moses Whitehouse, a fighting man who kept the Mine Borer's Arms at Darlaston. The 'Old Spittle' of verse 6 may be Jonah Spittle, an eighteenth-century landlord of the Old Blue Ball at Hall End, Wednesbury.

The song undoubtedly contributed to Wednesbury's reputation as the place for rough, not to say cruel, sports. 'Wedgebury born and Birchmore bred/That cock'll fight until 'e's jed', ran one proverbial couplet. Birchmore is a tiny village between Polesworth and Tamworth: 'When I was a little chap', Tom Langley remembered, 'I've been on the carrier of my elder brother when 'e's cycled to go and fetch a cockerel from Birchmoor, where it's been fed, and bring it back'. From Wednesbury, Amy Lyons, the daughter of a former vicar of the town, quoted this verse:

In Wednesbury town, a town whose name
Is coupled with its cocking fame,
Was yearly held by custom's right
A wake where colliers met to fight,
Where bulls were baited, torn, abused,
And dogs were killed, which much amused
Those sturdy knights of coal and hammer,
Who scoff at peace and joy at clamour.

A NEW SONG

CALLED

BLOXWICH WAKE BULL-BAITING,

Tune—Wednesbury Cocking.

GOOD people I pray attend,
The truth to you I'll tell,
How the Bl—x—h men rais'd a Bull,
They were forced to p—n the Bell:
They p—n'd the Bell you know,
And gather'd to raise a new Steeple;
The Willenhall men ſtole their Bull,
And called them apiſh people.
Fal de ral, fal de ral, &c.

'he Bull ruffians, a council did call
Which way to keep him secure.
One said to the cord he'd be tied,
And another should lie at the door;
And when the council was o'er,
And they were fast asleep.
So softly into the ſtable,
Two Willenhall men did creep.

They said," Come Billy ariſe,"
From his neck the collar did take,
" To Willenhall you muſt go:
We mean to spoil Bl—w—h wake."
And when we had got him safe out,
And no one had us seen;
Fiddler was the dog,
That run him down the green.

And when to Willenhall we came,
There we made such a charm;
By five o'clock in the morn,
The Town we did alarm.
We run two dogs at a time,
And baited him up and down;
And then we all agreed,
To take him to Bilſton town.

And as we was going along,
Before we reach'd Bilſton lane,
O by the Bl—x—h apes,
There we was overta'en:
They got before the Bull,
And swore they would turn him back
We pitch't him into a ditch,
And their bones they went to rack.

And when to Bilſton we came,
Old Duffied said," For a rig,
O, I have never a dog,
My wife shall run the pig."
" A lane, a lane," she cry'd;
The pig-ſty tumbled down;
The old women got up in their smocks,
And followed us through the town.

To Willenhall we brought him back,
And bait him in a ditch;
And that was noble sport,
When Shut run his brinded bitch;
To see the bitch at his nose,
The apes went down of their knees;
They said," What can we do more,
Now, give us the Bull if you please.

They for the Conſtable sent,
All for to charge the peace;
And when he did come there,
He said," This noise muſt cease."
One of them to Buckett did say,
" You are sure to get in a scrape;"
He broke his head with a ſtick,
And call'd him a Bl—x—h ape.

And now for to conclude,
They say there's no offence;
If you will to Bl—x—h come,
And make us recompence;
For if you do not come,
And pay us all the coſt,
The Bell that we have p—n'd,
Will be for ever loſt.

They waited a week or more,
No Willenhall men to them came;
They said, for a warrant we'll go,
For on us they are making game;
And when they had swore a f—e oath,
And forced Powell to appear;
He made the apes pay the expence,
And set the Willenhall men clear.
Fal de ral, fal de ral, &c.

Wood, Printer, New Meeting-street, Birmingham.

Street ballad, 'A New Song called Bloxwich Wake Bull-Baiting'

THE

Wedneſbury Cocking.

AT Wedneſbury there was a cocking,
A match between Newton and Skrogging,
The colliers and nailers left work,
And all to Spittle's went jogging
To ſee this noble ſport;
Many noted men there reſorted,
And though they'd but little money,
Yet that they freely ſported.

There was Jeff'ry and Boburn, from Hampton,
And Duſty, from Bilſtone, was there,
Frumity he came from Darlaſton,
He was as rude as a bear;
And there was old Will from Walſal,
And Smacker from Weſt Bromwich came;
Blind Dobbin he came from Rowley,
And ſtaggering he went home.

Ruff Morey came limping along,
As though he'd ſome cripple been mocking,
To join the blackguard throng
That met at Wedneſbury cocking;
He borrow'd a trifle of Doll,
To back old Tavener's grey,
He laid fourpence-halfpenny to fourpence—
Loſt, and went broken away.

But ſoon he return'd to the pit,
For he'd borrow'd a trifle more money,
And ventur'd another bet
Along with blubber-mouth Coney;
When Coney demanded the money,
As was uſual upon ſuch occaſions,
He cried, Blaſt you if you don't hold your rattle,
I'll pay thee as Paul paid the Epheſians.

Skrogging's breeches were made of nankeen,
And wore very thin in the groin,
In ſtooping to handle his cock,
His b——ks hung out behind;
Beſides, his ſhirt tail was beſhit,
Which 'caſioned a great laughter;
Skrogging turn'd himſelf round in a pet,
And cried, Blaſt you, what's the matter?

The morning's ſport being over,
Old Spittle a dinner proclaim'd,
That each man ſhould dine for a groat,
If he grumbled he ought to be damn'd,
For there was plenty of beef,
But Spittle he ſwore by his troth,
The devil a man ſhould dine
Till he'd eaten his noggin of broth.

The beef it was old and tough,
Of a bull that was baited to death,
Bunny Hide got a lump in his throat
That had like to have ſtopped his breath.

The company fell in confuſion
To ſee poor Bunny Hide choak,
They took him into the kitchen,
And held his head over the ſmoke.

They held him ſo cloſe to the fire
That he frizzled juſt like a beef-ſteak,
Then threw him down on the floor,
And had like to have broken his neck;
One gave him a kick on the ſtomach,
Another a thump on the brow,
His wife cried, Throw him in the ſtable,
And he'll be better juſt now.

Then ſoon they return'd to the pit,
And the fighting went on again,
Six battles were won on each ſide,
The next was to decide the main,
For theſe were two famous cocks
As ever that country bred,
Skrogging's a duck-wing black,
And Newton's a ſhift-wing red.

The conflict was hard on each ſide,
Till braſſy wing blacky was choak'd,
The colliers were nationly vex'd,
And the nailers were all provok'd;
Peter Stephens ſwore a great oath
That Skrogging had play'd his cock foul,
Skrogging gave him a kick in the cod,
And cried, Yea, God damn thy ſoul.

The company roſe in diſorder,
A bloody fight enſued,
Kick, bollock and bite was the word,
Till the Walſal men ſubdued;
Ruff Morey bit off a man's noſe,
It's a wonder no one was ſlain,
They trampled both cocks to death,
And ſo they made a draw main.

The cock-pit was near to the church,
An ornament to the town,
On one ſide an old coal-pit,
The other was well goſs'd round;
Peter Hadley peep'd through the goſs,
In order to ſee them fight,
Spittle jobb'd his eye out with a fork,
And cried, Blaſt thee, it ſerv'd thee right.

Some people may think this is ſtrange
Who Wedneſbury never knew,
But thoſe who have ever been there,
Won't have the leaſt doubt but it's true;
For they are all ſavage by nature,
And guilty of deeds the moſt ſhocking,
Jack Baker whack'd his own father,
And ſo ended Wedneſbury cocking.

Street ballad, 'The Wednesbury Cocking'

G.T. Lawley in an article of 1923 quotes a lengthy account (see panel below) from a newspaper, which he does not identify, of a 'main of cocks' held in March 1817 'at the cockpit, in Old Meeting Street, to decide on a bet of one hundred guineas, between the gentlemen of Birmingham and the gentlemen of Wednesbury and district'.

Cock-fighting Paradise

Wednesbury is the very Paradise of cock-fighters. No lover of this old-fashioned old English sport was ever disappointed with his visit to that well-known town; and nowhere is the sport indulged in more heartily than here. The numerous patrons who assembled on the 17th ult. to witness the long contemplated match between Birmingham and Wednesbury veteran cockers, met with some capital sport; and the money that was betted was unusually large in amount. The odds all along were laid on the Wednesbury birds, and in the end, after a fair fight, they amply compensated their backers, numbering eight battles to five scored by their opponents.

Fight I. This encounter was between two fine red cocks, well matched, and weighing five pounds two ounces. The battle lasted eleven minutes, during which there was some hard hitting on both sides, when the Wednesbury champion sent his opponent to grass, dead.

Fight II. In this a black grey did battle for Birmingham, and a pyle did battle for Wednesbury. The former was the heavier bird, and on showing, the betting was five to three on the grey. A game struggle ensued, the pyle fighting like a Spartan, but after some slashing work he received his opponent's steel [spur], and died fighting. Time, nine minutes.

Fight III. A red pyle showed for Wednesbury, and was opposed by a blue pyle. The red had it all its own way, and proved the winner in four minutes. Betting on the main five to four on the Wednesbury birds.

Fight IV. This time Birmingham showed a red pyle, and Wednesbury pitted a black red. Both birds were very fine, and a furious fight ensued, going in flap for flap, and hit for hit in true style. The black red lost an eye, and was floored, but came up again to time, evidently bent on revenge. At it they went again like tigers, and a brain blow from the black-red secured the victory for Wednesbury. Time, ten minutes.

Fight V. These birds were a black-red for Wednesbury, and a light red for Birmingham. A good fight, but the Wednesbury bird got blinded and ran away. Time, four minutes.

Fight VI. Another black for Wednesbury was opposed by a grey pyle, but the latter proved little better than a dunghill bird, and after a flap or two, bolted. Time two minutes.

Fight VII. A duckwinged grey for Wednesbury and a dark red for Birmingham next toed the scratch, and another determined struggle ensued. Both the birds knew how to hold, and the feathers flew about the pit like snow flakes. First one then the other had the advantage, until the grey was floored, but not before the red had lost an eye, and was cut almost to mincemeat. Time, nine minutes.

Fight VIII. There was much excitement here, the game standing at four to three, but betting was slightly in favour of Wednesbury. Two fine birds were pitted, a black for Wednesbury, and a brown for Birmingham. The latter proved victor in six minutes, bring the game four to four.

Fight IX. Two fine reds were now shown, and showed rare metal. Money was betted freely on this fight, terms being about equal, but after some hard and bloody work the Birmingham bird was fit for cooking, the winner giving a loud 'cock-a-doodle-doo'. Time, seven and a half minutes.

Fight X. This time the Wednesbury gentlemen sent in a black, and it was evident their birds got no worse as the game progressed. A pyle showed for Birmingham. A good battle ensued, but the latter was over-matched, and was soon kicking. Time, five minutes.

Fight XI. The main was looking bad for Birmingham and odds against it went begging, but in this battle in which a brass black fought for Wednesbury, and a dark red for Birmingham, the fortune changed, and the latter scored a victory. Time, five minutes.

Fight XII. The duellists in this affair were a red pyle for Birmingham, and a blue pyle for Wednesbury, and on showing the former had the call of the betting. A sharp struggle ensued, however, proved the game qualities of the blue, and after some uphill work proved the victor. Time, eleven minutes.

Fight XIII. This fight was soon over, for the Wednesbury men sent in one of the finest birds of the match, having been kept back for any necessity, and, being opposed by one much inferior, had it all its own way. Time, four minutes.

A HEAVY SETTLING

This brought the affair to a termination, amid the ringing cheers of the Wednesbury patrons and a corresponding depression on the part of the Birmingham. The settling after was a heavy one; and several disturbances occurred during the day, in which one or two men were roughly handled.

Big events such as this, advertised in local newspapers, attracted sometimes hundreds of spectators. A number of towns had a recognised venue, such as the Townwell Fold at Wolverhampton. Individual pubs and hotels often had their own cock pits or held fights in a stable or a barn. Other contests took place in the open: at the Bug Hole in Bilston (a hollow between pit banks), on the Rowley Hills, or at the Saltwells, Brierley Hill, where, according to William Rollinson, 'A week without a cock-fight left a void in the calendar'. Cock Street at

The Wedgefield Wake

At Wednesfield at one village wake
The cockers all did meet
At Billy Lane's, the cock-fighter's,
To have a sporting treat.

For Charley Marson's spangled cock
Was matched to fight a red
That came from Will'n'all o'er the fields,
And belonged to 'Cheeky Ned'.

Two finer birds in any cock-pit
There never yet was seen,
Though the Wednesfield men declared
Their cock was sure to win.

The cocks fought well, and feathers fled
All round about the pit,
While blood from both of 'em did flow,
Yet ne'er un would submit.

At last the spangled Wedgefield bird
Began to show defeat,
When Billy Lane, he up and swore
The bird shouldn't be beat;
For he would fight the biggest mon

That came from Will'n'all town,
When on the word, old 'Cheeky Ned'
Got up and knocked him down.

To fight they went like bull-dogs,
As it is very well known,
Till 'Cheeky Ned' seized Billy's thumb,
And bit it to the bone.

At this the Wednesfield men begun
Their comrade's part to take,
And never was a fiercer fight
Fought at a village wake.

They beat the men from Will'n'all town
Back to their town again,
And long will they remember
This Wednesfield wake and main.

Darlaston and at Wolverhampton and Cock Heath near Moxley also signalled the place of fights.

At wakes and fairs (see also chapter 11), and after horse races, cock fights were often held in booths. During Wolverhampton Race Week in 1827 they took place every day after the racing in 'Adams's booth'. Willenhall came off worse in one encounter at a wake in Wednesfield which was celebrated in a ballad (see panel opposite).

Such brawls between the owners of birds were as commonplace as the cock fights themselves. The riotous scenes which often accompanied bull baitings and cock fights, even though some of the patrons were gentry or clergy, led to criticism which became sharper as notions of animal welfare developed. Magistrates, certain parsons, churchwardens and parish constables began what turned into a long-running campaign to restrain and ultimately to ban blood sports. At Wednesbury itself in 1750 this document was published:

> Notice, that on account of the many disorders and furious riots which occur in the alehouses of this town after cock-fights, all such persons who shall in future aid, encourage or abet in any way whatsoever or whomsoever in carrying-on cock-fighting, or any such sports, shall have their licences withdrawn; and all cockers who shall be caught stirring up or inciting any assembly to riot shall be whipped at the common whipping-post.

Similar moves were made in Darlaston and Bilston in the next two decades, and in 1789 the Walsall constables announced: 'Notice is hereby given, that on account of so many riots taking place at bullbaits, all publicans who shall in future encourage, aid or abet other persons in the brutal pastime, or shall aid or abet in any way whatsoever cockfighting, or assist cockers, shall have their licences withheld'.

Some clergymen stuck to the old ways. When Jonah Spittle was landlord of the Blue Ball at Wednesbury the vicar of St Bartholomew's is said to have slipped out during long hymns to place a bet on one of the cocks fighting in a pit in the churchyard. On one occasion, birds from Willenhall and Wednesbury were matched. The latter won, whereupon the Wednesbury parson wrung its neck. 'Whatever did you do that for? The cock won', complained his Willenhall colleague. 'Ar', was the reply, 'but I can truthfully say now that it never lost'. The clergymen are not named in the story, but Rev. William Moreton, vicar of St Giles's Church, Willenhall, from 1795 until 1834, was undoubtedly a cock fighting enthusiast, who had his own cockpit at Old Church House. He preached on Sundays with the church door open, and he would cut short the sermon if his cock fighting friends went past on their way to action in Darlaston Fields. Moreton went bankrupt in 1812, and afterwards scraped a living, reputedly sharing his beer with his pony (see chapter 3).

In 1831 when one minister declined to give a sermon against cock fighting some of his parishioners urged him:

> No more be seen to mount the sacred place,
> But deep in mines conceal and black thy face.
> Herd with bull-baiters and their deeds commend,
> Make him who fights a cock thy bosom friend.
>
> Dash from thy sight God's precious rule of good,
> And congregate with men who 'build with blood'.
> From cruelty and hell a pattern take,
> And head the devil's crew at Tipton Wake.

Lugubrious tales were told of awful fates for cock fighters. John Tregartha, a travelling preacher of the eighteenth century, in a curious book entitled *The Bank of Faith*, told how 'T.G.' of Sedgley, having bet and lost a large sum of money on a cock fight, swore that he would never fight another cock, and wished that the devil should take him if he ever did. Some two years later the man went to a cock fight at Wolverhampton, placed a bet, then threw down his hat and put his hand in his pocket for the money; but, 'awful to relate, he instantly fell – a ghastly corpse to the ground. Terrified at his sudden death, some who were present for ever desisted from this infamous sport; but others, hardened in iniquity, proceeded in the barbarous diversion as soon as the dead body was removed from the spot'. More omens followed. At the funeral, a few days later, a dog which ran beneath the coffin as it was being carried fell insensible, got up and ran beneath again, and fell dead. 'Those who conveyed the corpse were so terrified that they durst not for the present proceed to the churchyard, but proposed to leave the body on the spot; at length, however, resuming their courage, they conveyed him to the grave'.

During the cholera epidemic of 1832 a number of inhabitants petitioned the town constable to postpone Oldbury Wake, and he therefore gave notice 'that no *Bull, Bear, or Badger Baiting*' would be allowed. Five men apparently decided to go ahead with baiting a bull, 'but God frustrated their designs: the cholera attacked the whole party, and not one remained to execute their wicked purposes'. So wrote Abraham Smith, adding for good measure: 'I have seen a poor Bull, during divine service, on their wake sabbath, exhibited through their streets, followed by immense crowds, and bearing on his back a human monster, previous to his [the bull's] being baited on the following day! But how awful their visitation! The pestilence in a great measure emptied the town, and swept from the earth the promoters of this diabolical practice'. Smith was a schoolmaster in Birmingham, though he originated in the Black Country. His book, with the somewhat cumbersome title of *A Scriptural and Moral Catechism, designed chiefly to lead the minds of the rising generation to the love and practice of*

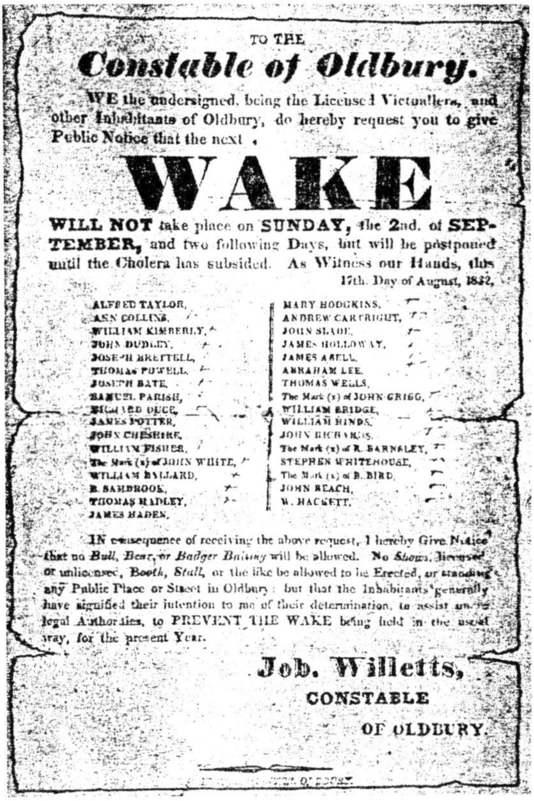

TO THE

Constable of Oldbury.

WE the undersigned, being the Licensed Victuallers, and other Inhabitants of Oldbury, do hereby request you to give Public Notice that the next

WAKE

WILL NOT take place on **SUNDAY,** the **2nd.** of **SEPTEMBER,** and two following Days, but will be postponed until the Cholera has subsided. As Witness our Hands, this 17th. Day of August, 1832,

ALFRED TAYLOR,	MARY HODGKINS,
ANN COLLINS,	ANDREW CARTRIGHT,
WILLIAM KIMBERLY,	JOHN SLADE,
JOHN DUDLEY,	JAMES HOLLOWAY,
JOSEPH BRETTELL,	JAMES ABELL,
THOMAS POWELL,	ABRAHAM LEE,
JOSEPH BATE,	THOMAS WELLS,
SAMUEL PARISH,	The Mark (x) of JOHN GRIGG,
RICHARD DUCE,	WILLIAM BRIDGE,
JAMES POTTER,	WILLIAM HINDS,
JOHN CHESHIRE,	JOHN RICHARDS,
WILLIAM FISHER,	The Mark (x) of R. BARNSLEY,
The Mark (x) of JOHN WHITE,	STEPHEN WHITEHOUSE,
WILLIAM BALLARD,	The Mark (x) of B. BIRD,
R. SAMBROOK,	JOHN BEACH,
THOMAS HADLEY,	W. HACKETT,
JAMES HADEN,	

IN consequence of receiving the above request, I hereby Give Notice that no *Bull, Bear, or Badger Baiting* will be allowed. No *Shows*, licensed or unlicensed, *Booth, Stall*, or the like be allowed to be Erected, or standing in any Public Place or Street in Oldbury: but that the Inhabitants generally have signified their intention to me of their determination, to assist [illegible] legal Authorities, to PREVENT THE WAKE being held in the usual way, for the present Year.

Job. Willetts,
CONSTABLE
OF OLDBURY.

Poster of 1832 for Oldbury Wake

mercy, and to expose the horrid nature & exceeding sinfulness of cruelty to the Dumb Creation, was dedicated to Princess (the future Queen) Victoria. He followed a number of clergymen, who decades earlier had declared their opposition to blood sports. For example, Rev. George Barrs, curate at Rowley Regis, noted in his journal on 15 September 1800: 'Felt much grieved and angry, when I saw great numbers of people engaged in that cruel and devilish sport, bull-baiting. Their shouts of pleasure resembled the horrid, triumphant yell which resounded through hell's dark caverns when Satan first betrayed our parents into sin. This being Wake Monday — Great God, have mercy on these beastly wretches and let them see how they are led captive and baited by Satan even as they chain and bait the bull'. A large congregation attended a service in the afternoon, and Barrs was appalled to hear 'the horrid yell of the bull-baiters, very near the church'.

Rev. John Howells campaigned in Tipton to such effect that by 1827 'Not a bull was to be found in the whole parish, kept for the purpose of being baited at the wake'. In neighbouring Horseley Heath, Rev. Richard Amner 'regularly preached a sermon to the youth of his congregation, against cruelty to animals, on the Sunday preceding Shrove Tuesday (a day particularly set apart for the horrid practice of cock-fighting)'. On Sunday, 4 November 1833, the day of Sedgely Wake, Rev. John Hill, minister of the independent chapel in Gornal, preached against cruelty to animals, especially bull baiting.

Such efforts were part of a groundswell of opinion which resulted in the Cruelty to Animals Act of 1835 and the Prevention of Cruelty to Animals Act of 1849. In the case of the former the constables of Wolverhampton took the trouble to issue a notice pointing out that one of its clauses brought in penalties for keeping or using any space 'for the purpose of *running, baiting, or fighting*

Bull Baiting,

COCK FIGHTING,

AND

DOG FIGHTING,

AT AN END

BY ACT OF PARLIAMENT.

In an Act of Parliament, passed on the 9th of September, 1835, is the following Clause:

" Whereas, Cruelties are greatly promoted and encouraged by Persons keeping Houses, Rooms, Pits, Grounds, or other Places, for the FIGHTING OR BAITING OF DOGS, BULLS, BEARS, or *other Animals*—and for FIGHTING COCKS—and by Persons *aiding or assisting therein;* and the same are great Nuisances and Annoyances to the Neighbourhood in which they are situate, and tend to demoralize those who frequent such places. Be it, therefore, enacted—that, from and after the passing of this Act, if any Person shall *keep or use any House, Room, Pit, Ground, or other Place,* for the purpose of *running, baiting, or fighting any Bull, Bear, Badger, Dog, or other Animal,* whether of domestic or wild nature or kind—*or for Cock Fighting—or in which any Bull, Bear, Badger, Dog, or other such Animal, shall be baited, run, or fought;*—every such Person shall be liable to a Penalty not exceeding FIVE POUNDS, nor less than TEN SHILLINGS, for every Day in which he shall so keep and use such House, Room, Pit, Ground, or Place, for any of the purposes aforesaid. —Provided always, that the Person who shall *act as the Manager* of any such House, Room, Pit, Ground, or other Place—or who shall *receive any Money* for the admission of any Person thereto—or who shall *assist in any such baiting, or fighting, or Bull-running,* shall be deemed and taken to be the Keeper of the same for the purposes of this Act, and be liable to all such Penalties as are by this Act imposed upon the Person who shall actually keep any such House, Room, Pit, Ground, or other Place, for the purposes aforesaid."

We, the undersigned Constables of Wolverhampton, beg to draw the attention of the Public to the above Act of Parliament.

WILLIAM SAVAGE,
HENRY CRUTCHLEY, } **Constables.**

Wolverhampton, October 12, 1835.

Printed by WILLIAM PARKE, Wolverhampton.

Poster of 1835

any Bull, Bear, Badger, Dog, or other Animal ... or for Cock Fighting' (see illustration opposite).

Bull baiting required a big open space, and was therefore difficult to hide. As a result it came to an end relatively soon after the act of 1835. One source suggested that the last such event in the Black Country took place at the Level, Brierley Hill, during the wake of 1843. Nigel Perry, the historian of Stourbridge, records a local view that the last bull baiting ever to be staged took place at Lye Waste, though he does not give a date.

Cock fighting could be, and was, conducted in clandestine fashion. A man interviewed anonymously in 1911 recalled having seen in the mid-nineteenth century 'hundreds of "battles"', of which one, encountered by Cradley Pool, remained vividly in his memory:

> There were a dozen or so men standing on the pool dam, and among the number were two engaged in marking out a circle with chalk, and on either side were two loops in which it was the custom to stand the birds before the conflict opened, and also to dress their injuries in the interval between the mains. In the meantime, ... the owners of the matched cocks were at the Horse Shoe Inn, High Street, spurring the birds in the orthodox fashion, with polished steel spurs. In time the birds were brought to the scene by their handlers – men versed in the handling of fighting cocks. They were beautiful birds...; one was a 'pile' and the other a 'brown red'. The last-named was the property of 'Old Batheram', a well-known Quarry Bank cocker. Both birds were of the 'real old Staffordshire strain', and the battle was as fierce as the most ardent cock fighter could wish. In the end Batheram's representative, which was the favourite in the betting, was rendered *hors de combat* by the 'pile' bird forcing one of its spurs clean through its neck. 'One might have thought, from the shouting and jumping that took place over the victory, that there were pounds at stake, whereas I found that these men had permitted lovely birds to be treated in this fashion for half-a-crown a side!'

Old Batheram staged cock fights in his walled yard at Quarry Bank, apparently with impunity, but on one occasion when some forty people were absorbed in a contest, the parish constable, from a position of vantage over a garden wall, noted all their names. The offenders were summoned to appear in the police court at Wordsley. Thinking one of their number had informed, they raised money to brief a Birmingham lawyer, but unanimously decided to plead guilty when they found that the constable was an eye-witness. One of the magistrates sitting was himself a noted cocker, and in another case he is said to have been lenient to a cock fighting butcher from Bilston called Johnny Thrupp, on the promise of an exchange of birds to improve the strain. Unfortunately, the butcher's birds did not live up to expectation, and when he appeared again before the same magistrate on a charge of furiously riding a horse he was fined the maximum amount possible.

Jack Giles (a pseudonym for John Collins) of Gornal worked as a collier for 57 years, and was a devotee of cock fighting from the age of ten, which he attained in 1846, nine years after the sport became illegal. He claimed that, over the years, parsons, lawyers, doctors and publicans, as well as colliers and puddlers, were also involved. They could take advantage of the horse fairs at Darlaston, Willenhall and Wolverhampton to meet for fights; at one fair he saw seventeen fights, and at another a country house near Wolverhampton was lost and won. 'Goodish Tuesday' (? Shrove Tuesday) signalled the start of the season in Gornal, where fights were held 'down the cinders' (derelict land near Furnace Row) and near the Crooked House. Jack Giles had never been 'cotched', he said, because 'In them days the pleece day trouble we: they wun as keen ter look on as the rest on we'.

In Edwardian Netherton, according to M.H.W. Fletcher, the landlord of the Star Inn on the corner of Spring Street not only bred bulldogs with which he baited badgers in a big washing tub in the brewery, but he had gamecocks which fought in an old barn and also in a hollow on Yew Tree Hills. However, 'If anyone should be foolish enough to broach the subject, he would say: "If thee's got owt t' say, keep thy trap shut"'. The Old Bush Hotel on the corner of High Street and Union Street in Dudley was, in the early nineteenth century, a meeting place for Radicals as well as being the place where stage coaches left for Birmingham (the *Tally-ho*), Worcester (the *Bang-up*) and Wolverhampton (the *Royal Perseverance*, the *Royal Mail* and the *Crown Prince*). It also had a cockpit which literally went underground when the sport became illegal: in 1929, during the demolition of the building, workmen discovered a secret pit with separate small pens in which the cocks waited to fight, reached through a hinged panel in the floor. Phil Drabble wrote that 'cocking was quite common' in the Black Country 'till just before the Great War and not unknown after'. George Dunn of Quarry Bank told me that it certainly continued until 1940. Tom Langley, some thirty years later, had this to say:

> Although it still goes on on Cannock Chase, there in the Staffordshire hills, it's so secret that nobody could get there. Some years ago I was asked if I could get a television camera to one. The producer was very anxious for the authentic thing. Well, I do know men who do cockfights, of course, and I told 'im the most that I can do - I don't want to watch it because it's a brutal, barbarous business, and I wouldn't want to be connected with it all, but if you do want to see it I can introduce you to a man who if 'e likes to take you any further, 'e will. And I did take 'im over and introduce 'im to this man. It was about six months after, I said: 'How did you get on?' He said: 'Well, I should have been all right, but they wouldn't trust you. Once a copper, always a copper, and although

you'd been brought up with 'em you were still a policeman, and that was that'.

I leave the last word to George Dunn, himself a one-time cock fighter, whose rejection of blood sports was as unequivocal as that of Tom Langley.

In the old times all the mining villages were cock fighters. They came from 'ere [Quarry Bank] and Gornal, 'Olly 'All [Holly Hall]. When the cocks were matched to fight they shouldn't be knocked about. Instead o' bein' spurred they were muffled: the spurs were wrapped up so they couldn't 'urt one another. Old English game — them were the fighters. There were the black-breasted red, the duck-wing grey ... There wasn't such a lot of fighting cocks about because they'd gotta be good and if they weren't good they weren't kept.

I'll tell yer a tale about one o' my cocks as I 'ad. One o' my neighbours, 'e raffled a gamecock off at the Sheffield Inn. Strange to relate, it's about the on'y thing I ever won in a raffle in all me life, an' I've 'ad scores o' tickets. 'E was a big un, a black-breasted red. They'm a nice bird, a gamecock is. 'E was about six pound and 'alf.

Another neighbour — 'e was a notorious character, 'e was, but it dae stop 'im bein' my neighbour, though — said, 'Bring 'im round, George, an' let 'im fight mine'. [He had] a little farm. They'd got plenty places, barns. 'E knowed I'd won this cock, and 'e'd got one that Jim Pegg bred. ('E kept the Elephant — 't ae very far from 'ere). I said, 'It isn't fair.

Fighting Cocks Inn, Dudley Road, Wolverhampton, now replaced by a supermarket

Yours is about five and a quarter [pounds] and 'e's a good six pound an' 'alf. 'E'll only kill 'im'. 'E says, 'Mine'll kill '*im*'.

When they fought cocks they gotta be weighed in, and ounces counted. 'E asked me several times and eventually I said, 'I'll bring 'im round'. There was a plenty big barn empty so I took the cock round. We put 'em down and they 'ad one flap. My big un 'e knocked the little un as far as from 'ere to the door, and 'e kicked 'im [his own bird]. I said, 'I told thee what it'd be'. 'E said, 'That's nothing. 'E can lick 'im. Let 'em 'ave one more flap'. I put the cock down again an' the same thing 'appened. 'E kicked 'im [his own bird] again. After 'e'd gi'n 'im another kick 'e said, 'Tek 'im off, or I'll kick 'is bloody liver out'. I towd 'im what'd 'appen. Yo cor fight six pounders wi' five pounders.

It was like the arena at Rome when the gladiators fought. They made it illegal. It wasn't illegal at one time, nor dog fighting, nor bull baiting. They were terrible cruel sports.

CHAPTER 11

Wakes, Feasts and Fairs

'He haunts Wakes, Fairs, and Beare-baitings': this is said in Shakespeare's play, *The Winter's Tale*, of one character, Autolycus, who would have been very much at home in the Black Country during one period of its history. Wakes originally celebrated the day of the saint to whom a church was dedicated, or rather the nearest Sunday. Sunday, chosen because it was the one day of leisure in the week, allowed a religious service, and then a secular jollification, the latter sometimes spilling into the days following. If a saint's day were deemed unsuitable for outdoor events, another would be chosen at a better time of year. Tipton Church is dedicated to St Martin, whose day falls on 11 November, but the town's wake was held on 4 July. Bilston's St Leonard has his day on 6 November, but parishioners preferred the end of July for their wake. Bloxwich parish church's dedication was changed at the Reformation from St Thomas the Martyr (29 December) to All Saints (1 November), but the inhabitants preferred the third week in August for their wake. The patron of Oldbury Church, St Nicolas, is celebrated on 6 December, but the local wake took place towards the end of August. On the other hand, West Bromwich's All Saints' Church chooses the due day, 1 November. The same dedication at Sedgley produced a wake on 12 November, Old All Saints' Day. Other towns' wakes followed the due dates: Brierley Hill and Tettenhall, 29 September (St Michael); Darlaston, 10 August (St Lawrence); Rowley Regis and Willenhall, both 1 September (St Giles); and Wednesbury, 24 August (St Bartholomew). Curiously, Walsall celebrated its wake (St Matthew, 21 September) very little, and Wolverhampton (St Peter, 29 June), even less, probably because they both had important fairs (see below). Perhaps for the same reason, Dudley, Halesowen and Stourbridge, all in the Worcestershire part of the Black Country, do not seem to have had wakes at all. In the case of the first-named, though, there was a wake at Kate's Hill, held at Midsummer: very popular and well attended between 1860 and 1880, and still going in 1914 although by then 'only a few stalls, and people do not trouble to attend'.

Climbing a greasy pole to win a ham

Ale drinking, ox roasting, dancing, and competitions such as climbing a greasy pole to win a ham, were once held in churchyards. The introductions of more boisterous and even violent activities, such as blood sports, caused wakes to move to wider spaces such as a market place or a convenient field. Some wakes came into being with no connection with a church at all. At Tettenhall Wake, which took place in 1812 at the Old Rose and Crown Inn, the list of sports on offer included:

1. A Blind Man's Match at Nine-pins.
2. Grinning through a Horse's Collar.
3. Jumping in Sacks from the Old Rose and Crown down the Hill to the Turnpike.
4. Hot Hasty Pudding Eating.
5. A Ladies' Sweepstake, the best of Three Heats, twice round the Green.

First Prize. – Three Balloon Tuckers. Second Prize. – Two Flannel Dickies. Third Prize. – A Black Velvet Reticule.

The anonymous author of *Down in Dingyshire, or, Sketches of Life in the Black Country*, published in 1873, claimed that 'every little cluster of houses in these parts has its feast', very much a modest kind of wake:

> Great preparations are made; houses are whitewashed and cleaned up (one advantage of the feast), new clothes are bought, barrels of beer and bottles of gin are laid in, and many pigs assiduously converted into pork. When the day comes, all the inhabitants of the surrounding parishes pour in by road and rail, the congregation at morning church is next to nothing, and the street, if the day is fine, is crowded with visitors and their friends. Why all this should be done has always been a mystery to me; for beyond eating and drinking far more than is usual or wholesome, and then general hanging about, nothing takes place. It is 'feast', however, and the Dingyshire mind reposes on that fact, and is satisfied. A week or two afterwards our people will go to some other village and repeat the process, and so until all the other places within reach shall have had their turn, and our turn comes round again.

There was certainly a good deal more than 'nothing' taking place at the Coppice Wake at Quarry Bank, on the first Sunday in May, by the Saltwells pub. It began in rousing fashion at 6 a.m. with three brass bands, and later in the day featured fights between dogs, and also their owners. 'Wake time was an especially aggressive and militant period, and often there was a fight for the very love of it', runs a comment of 1914. 'Just as long as a man could stick up, he kept at it, and the stakes were often a pot of beer. The only articles signed were: "I be as good as thee", and nobody ever paid a forfeit. They were gladiators in those days'.

Enville was famous for the luscious black cherries grown there, and every summer when they were ripe, held its Cherry Wake, which drew people from all over the Black Country, both for fruit and fun. The event, unfortunately renowned for drunkenness and rowdyism, involved bull baiting and cock fighting. In a single year up to thirty prize fights also took place.

Tipton, with its 'Slasher' associations (see chapter 9), was notorious for fights. In 1869 a tongue-in-cheek poster advertised that 'Flaming Gin, Sparkling Wine, Muddy Porter and Frothy Ale' would be at the wake, with each day ending 'in the usual way with Drunkenness, Brawling, Wife Beating, Empty Pockets and Aching Heads'. Again over several days, Bilston Wake featured sporting contests, side shows, theatrical performances and, of course, eating and drinking. Even shorn of bull baiting and the like, the event became too much for the authorities, who insisted, late in the nineteenth century, on suppressing it. An annual carnival, first held in June 1930, turned out to be a more acceptable substitute. Bloxwich Wake also became a carnival, the proceeds of which from 1919 until 1932 wemt to local hospitals. After a hiatus the event resumed in 1949, this time benefitting Old Age Pensioners.

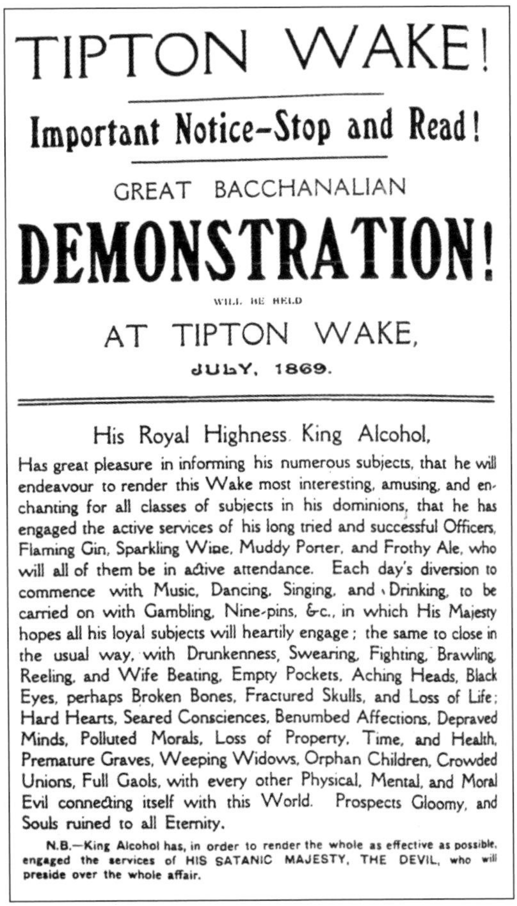

TIPTON WAKE!

Important Notice–Stop and Read!

GREAT BACCHANALIAN

DEMONSTRATION!

WILL BE HELD

AT TIPTON WAKE,

JULY, 1869.

His Royal Highness King Alcohol,

Has great pleasure in informing his numerous subjects, that he will endeavour to render this Wake most interesting, amusing, and enchanting for all classes of subjects in his dominions, that he has engaged the active services of his long tried and successful Officers, Flaming Gin, Sparkling Wine, Muddy Porter, and Frothy Ale, who will all of them be in active attendance. Each day's diversion to commence with Music, Dancing, Singing, and Drinking, to be carried on with Gambling, Nine-pins, &c., in which His Majesty hopes all his loyal subjects will heartily engage; the same to close in the usual way, with Drunkenness, Swearing, Fighting, Brawling, Reeling, and Wife Beating, Empty Pockets, Aching Heads, Black Eyes, perhaps Broken Bones, Fractured Skulls, and Loss of Life; Hard Hearts, Seared Consciences, Benumbed Affections, Depraved Minds, Polluted Morals, Loss of Property, Time, and Health, Premature Graves, Weeping Widows, Orphan Children, Crowded Unions, Full Gaols, with every other Physical, Mental, and Moral Evil connecting itself with this World. Prospects Gloomy, and Souls ruined to all Eternity.

N.B.—King Alcohol has, in order to render the whole as effective as possible, engaged the services of HIS SATANIC MAJESTY, THE DEVIL, who will preside over the whole affair.

Tipton Wake handbill of 1869

Crowning of Bloxwich Carnival Queen in 1953. The queen (front row, third from right) was Miss A. Edwards

Willenhall, too, had a record of violent sports to live down. According to an anonymous writer, the church weathercock, as it looked down on the wake, would have reflected:

The sun one morning fair did rise,
Turning the gray into golden skies.
The tip of my tail she turned to gold
And burnished it bright for men to behold.
Beneath me lay a rabble crowd
Of the hopeful young and the aged bowed;
A stake is driven in the greensward fast
And the bull is tied secure at last.
Shouts of the men and the bull's fierce roar,
The groans of the dog as he dies in his gore;
The shrieks of the women and the curses of men
Beggar description by mortal pen.

Darlaston Carnival, from a postcard of 1932

Left: The Neptune Inn, Willenhall

By the early twentieth century the event, according to Hackwood, had 'dwindled down to an assemblage of shows and roundabouts, shooting galleries, and gingerbread stalls'. On the same day, the club walks took place, processions of the friendly societies, preceded by a service at the church, and followed by feasting in the Neptune Inn. Back in the Georgian era, 'another wake custom was that of kissing the parson, a privilege of which the women were said to be very jealous'.

Of Wednesbury Wake, 'E.M.' wrote in the magazine, *Birmingham Iris*, in April 1839:

In Wednesbury Town, — a Town whose name
Is coupled with its Cocking fame,
Was yearly held, by CUSTOM'S RIGHT
A Wake, where Colliers came to fight,
Where Bulls were baited, torn, abused,
And Dogs were killed, which much amused
Those sturdy Knights of Coal and Hammer,
Who scoff at peace, and joy in clamour.

Amy Lyons gives a fuller picture in prose, which I summarise. The market place is lined with booths and stalls, all of which have paid a toll. Costermongers' carts arrive, drawn by dogs, and also stage coaches, bringing sporting men from all parts of England to see the bull-baiting. The Green Dragon and the Turk's Head provide accommodation. Little work is done during the week of the wake, and at the end of it many are penniless, after spending on food, drink, pleasure and gambling. Others paid out money wisely to lay in stocks of the merchandise and wares on display. The church beadle in his red and gold uniform, with streamers hanging from his hat and shoulders, leads the town band in procession from the market place, round the town, pausing for drinks at various taverns. Then they march up Church Hill to the Black Bull, and the bull baiting pit. Carriages bearing the well-to-do follow. Baiting continues for three days.

The wake outlasted the outlawing of blood sports, but it was still too rowdy in 1874 for the town's authorities, for on their petition the Home Secretary banished it from the market place. Even so, a watered-down version with

Wednesbury Wake in 1898

whippet racing and pigeon flying continued on private land for another fifty years or so.

Brierley Hill also had an unsavoury reputation to live down. A householder there, Mr A. Smith, composed an indignant letter to the editor of Aris's *Birmingham Gazette* on the 'thousands of people from distant parishes [who] congregated together to enjoy this feast of blood': 'Three bulls were baited on the Saturday evening previous to the Wake Sabbath, and for four successive days they were torn and lacerated for amusement, in a manner too shocking to relate'. The Horse Shoe Inn and the Queen's Head at the Level were popular during the wake, 'being noted', adds a writer of 1914, 'for a good bull and dogs that could be relied on to give plenty of sport'. He continues:

Brierley Hill, 'An old-fashioned wake'

> The finishing bait usually took place on the afternoon of the Wednesday in Wake week, and the bull was slaughtered next day, the joints being laid on boards outside the public house where the bait had been held, and sold at about 3d. per pound. It used, however, to be remarked that the bull's head was never exposed for sale, and the explanation generally accepted was that it accounted for all the customers being treated free to groaty pudding on the next Saturday evening. …

A further account was contributed in the same year by J.W. Clulow:

> So that earlier townsfolk should not suffer for lack of pleasure, Brierley Hill was always visited at Wake time, and occasionally at other times, by different kinds of shows. The earliest local venture of this kind was Lowe's Show, owned by a Brierley Hill man. The performance of this show comprised slack wire walking and tight rope dancing by Miss Lowe, who would conclude with conjuring tricks and fortune telling, assisted by a learned pony which she had taught to walk round and indicate the young men and women who were in love, and to point out with whom.
>
> About 1835 Mr Lowe converted his show into a theatre, and some time after he built a permanent wood and canvas erection in the top boiler yard, often wintering there with a fairly good company. His two principal assistants, Wesley and Potts, on a misunderstanding arising, left him, and commenced in the theatrical business on their own account, their Company afterwards becoming the well-known Bennett and Patch's Theatre, which later on had a rival in Holloway's.
>
> Other and varied amusements which visited Brierley Hill from time to time were the 'celebrated skeleton whale show, giants and giantesses, dwarfs, mummies, fat men and women, living skeletons and wild men; mermaids, sea lions, sea calves (all the same after a little doctoring up), peep shows, and breathing working waxworks, showing Solomon's wisdom in judging, and Daniel in the lions' den'. And last, but by far the greatest treat of all, the town was visited later by old Mr Wombwell's Wild Beast Show, with its famous band of musicians.
>
> Mountebanks often paid Brierley Hill a visit. This kind of entertainment required only a horse and a 'fool', who either walked on stilts, or, dressed up as a clown, rode the horse. A stage waggon was all the apparatus necessary. The performance usually took place in Mr Padgett's field adjoining the Mouth of the Nile.
>
> After tumbling and slack rope dancing, the manager would announce that prizes would be given away. These were mostly women's cotton gown pieces, with a grand first prize of a leg of mutton. The 'fool' rode among the audience, and disposed of tickets at 6d. each, which he afterwards collected, and in return gave the purchaser a round ball of paper, which took some time to unfold, and in which the holder found an intimation that he had either a blank or a prize. Those who held prizes went up to

> the waggon to receive them, and those who had blanks generally went straight home.
>
> About the middle of the performance care was taken to announce the next performance, and that the prizes would be on a more liberal scale, 'culminating on the Saturday evening with two legs of mutton, lady's long dress pieces, shawls, neckerchiefs, gentlemen's waistcoats, and pocket handerkerchiefs (all of which were spread out on view), and a first prize of a real silver watch, or £5 in money'. This bait generally took, and large crowds were attracted, there being much excitement. The crush for the prizes often upset the arrangements for their distribution, and the result was confusion worse confounded, and without a suspicion that it was cleverly manufactured by the mountebank, after a few prizes had been given away, to enable him and his 'fool' to sneak away from the place.
>
> Notwithstanding that drinking hours were not then limited, and licensed houses could keep open all night, drunkenness was not so prevalent as might have been expected. Mine host usually kept company with his customers, and, as in Tom O' Shanter's case, 'the landlord's laugh was ready chorus'. He often furnished a free table of bread and cheese, and seemed pleased with his customers' appetites in eating as well as drinking, which saved much drunkenness.
>
> The last bull to be baited at Brierley Hill was hired from Wednesbury, and baited at the Whimsey Inn, but as this did not meet with much encouragement, from this time [1839] bull baiting was discontinued. Shortly before then, considerable discredit had been occasioned by a man (Tom Bellison) for a foolish wager, riding in a nude condition a bull from the Old Bell Inn, through Brierley Hill, to the great annoyance and disgust of the inhabitants. ... The upshot was that Bellison was brought before the magistrates, and got six months' hard labour for his stupid folly.

Clulow adds that 'to keep up the Wake sports, a man with a fighting bear was engaged to visit the public houses, and to have his bear baited outside'. The dogs, though, showed a notable lack of enthusiasm for the contest.

The fortunes of the wake declined at Brierley Hill, so the event shifted to Wordsley. Mr Benjamin Greenfield of the Bush Inn, at the Level, on doubt with an eye to his takings, started pony races at wake time. The land used gradually extended, and became known as the Race Course Pits. Side shows followed, and then the full wake attractions returned from Wordsley, only for the whole thing eventually to peter out.

Horse racing was still a feature, indeed, the outstanding feature of Rowley Wake during the second half of the nineteenth century. The wake ground was at the top of Powke Lane, but the course covered a wide area, including parts of Old Hill and Blackheath. The owners of the horses, mainly local tradesmen, acted as their own jockeys, wearing silk hats and frock coats, and they backed

Colliers racing dogs during the coal strike of 1912, after a painting by Cyrus Cuneo

themselves heavily. 'People came from outlying districts to witness the event, which provided a local Derby, and few people worked on Rowley wake Saturday or Monday'.

In addition, whippets and also pigeons were raced. 'At the end of the festivities there were, of course, innumerable free fights, often between the owners of the losing birds or animals and the successful competitors. There was much inebriety, too, with the result that there were batches of offenders at the local police office in the following week, summoned for breach of the peace'. Even so, the showman, Pat Collins, on the basis of fifty years' experience of Black Country wakes, commented on the orderly conduct of the Rowley crowds, and contrasted it 'with the scenes of drunkenness and brawls which were associated with the wakes of olden days'. In the 1880s racecourse gangs operated a protection racket, refraining on payment of money from causing trouble for showmen. On one occasion at Tipton a gang of hooligans apparently took control of the entire wake ground.

Despite everything, ordinary people flocked to the wakes as one of the highlights of the year. Thomas Pinnock in 1893 claimed that the wakes were 'more popular than Christmas for family gatherings, and the heads of families who still remain in the native village usually keep open house for two or three days for the welcome of any even distant relative who may be drawn to visit the old spot'. According to a perhaps apocryphal tale, one candidate for confirmation, asked to name the three festivals of the church, replied 'Easter, Whitsun and Sedgley Wake' (see page 21). The elevation of the latter seems a little strange, in the light of this account from November 1892:

> The annual wake for the parish of Sedgley has been held this week. During the first three or four days, colliers and ironworkers in the district have been idle, in fact, there has been a general holiday. On Monday, the children at the various schools had a holiday, and the shooting galleries, gingerbread stalls, merry-go-rounds, round-a-bouts and swingboats near the Bull Ring, Sedgley, and at the Wake ground, Deepfields, were well patronised by the youngsters. The old custom of innkeepers distributing beef to their customers, was kept up and judging from the quantity supplied to the public houses in the district, the butchers must have done a roaring trade.

The wakes at Sedgley may well have been more exciting half a century or so earlier, but no first hand account seems to have come down.

Entertainments elsewhere, to say the least, were unsophisticated but also wide-ranging. Verses on Bloxwich Wake in the 1870s (see panel opposite) run through attractions and pitfalls, and provide a panoramic portrait of the fair-goers. The varied activities at Oldbury are described in good-humoured ballad (see panel on page 202) dating from before the First World War. From the same period come the comments of Rev. Frederic Willett, vicar of West Bromwich, though he disguises the place as 'Blackhampton': 'In Blackhampton the "Wakes", from time immemorial, have been, as they came round, an integral element in local life; they affected the routine of labour and trade, of family life and of local society generally; while they created an unlimited opportunity for money-making and money-spending. From my own experience, which was considerable, I may add that the "Wake" did not by any means always tend to be good'. Willett may have had in mind incidents of this kind: at one West Bromwich wake a man wagered that he, dog-fashion, could pin the bull's nose with his teeth. After a lengthy spell of manoeuvring he succeeded, but lost his front teeth when the animal flung up its head. Worse still, he was then knocked down and had a leg broken.

Willett went on to point out that people did not confine their attendance to a single wake: 'Wake would often follow Wake, and friends and relatives nothing loth, as being neighbourly, would keep the Wake in more parishes than one'. He was concerned with 'the inconvenience to trade': 'Men living in one parish kept the Wake in the parish they lived in, and working in another parish kept that also. Not infrequently works would stand idle for days, to the great loss of owners, and the injury physical, moral and financial of workmen. The only people who benefited were the public house keepers, showmen, and some few shopkeepers'.

However, the men in one mine (which Willett disguises as the 'Moorland Pit'), 'on conscientious and distinctly religious grounds … would have no part in the prevailing revelling and drunkenness'. During one wake sand suddenly poured in, and overwhelmed the workings, but by great good fortune, and indeed, as some thought, by the direct intervention of divine providence, not a man was in the mine. The workers had friends and relatives coming from some distance, one of them from America, to attend the wake; 'the butties, therefore, held a meeting, and under the circumstances agreed for once to play for this Wake; a special prayer meeting was called, at which they solemnly pledged themselves to keep from all wrong-doing, and induced the younger men to promise to resist the temptations they would have to meet'. Remarkable, but wholly untypical. Even so, by 1923 an observer could write: 'The Black Country wake is dying a natural death — at least the old-time observance of it'.

The Bloxidge Tallygraph

Edditid by a Bloxidge Mon.

No.1. Price One Penny.

The Edditors openin' remarks to his Inlighten'd Readers.

In starting the 'BLOXIDGE TALLYGRAPH' we dunner for won minnit pretend to say that our objeck is 'tu supply a want long felt by everybody', wich is yushully said when ennything fresh is bein' started. On the kontrary we don't mind telling yu right off that our objeck is, firstly, yure Pleshur, and nextly, our Profit, but principylly the latter. If it pays it ull go on, if it don't it won't; na that's a kandid an' strateforrard statemint.

Then with rispect tu our manner of spellin' and writin'. In the fust place we thought some on yu wud like tu see Black Country Dialect in print by way ov a kontrast tu good Queen's Inglish; in the second place, it's the langwidge spoken by about nine-tenths ov yu, konskwently yone be able to understand it better than enny uther style, it ull kum soo natteral, but no doubt all that ull be awter'd when the Skule Boord gets tu work, though I'm afeerd that at the rate they'm a getting on moost on yu wun be grey-yedded before that kums to pass.

Nextly we think it rite to say that we shall aim at causin' a little harmless mirth by tratin' local affairs an events in a yunerus manner, but shall strickly endevver tu avide giving needless offence tu ennywon. But if ennybody shud unfortunately get offended we shud advise hum to purchase sum Suthin Powders, an goo tu the sayside till he rekuvers!!!

An now for our first Article, which is mostly in Rhyme and kontains a discripshun ov what is generully to be seen at Bloxidge Wake, with reference tu a fu uther little matters. So here goos:

Tack Forgers an' Filers, Bit-makers an' yu
Butty Colliers an' Miners, all good men an' true,
Clodhoppers an' Farmers, Shopkeepers as well,
Come listen a minnit to wot I've tu tell.

It's consarnin' the Wake an' wot is tu be seen,
In the Streets, the Shop Winders, an' on the Big Green,
In the Beershops an' Publics, the Shows an' Theaters,
An' the fun that's provided for Wake-minded Craturs.

Down by the Sandhole as yo kum on the Green
The little Steam Hosses bin theer to be seen;
But they'm knocked out ov time by the Velocipedes,
A newfangled invention, rode by their own steeds.

(If yo luke tu the left, just across the green fields,
Yo con see wheer the Squoir lives, they call it the 'Hills'.
He's a good mon, God bless him, he thinks of the poor,
When they want enny help, or the Wolf's at the door.

Go, ye Rich, an' du likewise, an' be as kindhearted,
Then yore names wun be blessed wen yo bin departed;
If yo wish tu be happy, an' life tu enhance
Du sum good wi' yore munny while yone got the chance).

As yo goo further on theer's the Clown in his paint,
An' he tries hard tu mak yu believe that he ain't
Quite so much fule as knave, but he fails in soo doin',
If yore guidid by him, yone be guidid to ruin.

An' theer's Chep Jack — he's the biggist ode chate
That ever sode rubbish by way ov a trate;
He's charged menny Greenhorns a Bob an' a Tanner
For castiron Pocket knives, blowed if he hanner.

Then yore ears bin assail'd by the Voice of a Quack,
Who's fa filling his Puss by a most happy knack
Ov stuffin' the Geese who beleeve in his lies
With fizzick an' pills at a shocking 'low' price.

Tu forgers ov Tacks, an' tu makers of Locks
He's a selling his Pills, 'forty-three in a box',
Which, if you beleeve in his bare-faced crams,
Bin as 'sarchin' as tuth-combs an' mild as pet lambs'.

He sez that his Fizzick will give you release
From rhumatiz, Tewthake, an' ev'ry disease,
From Corns an' from Bunyuns, from Cough an' from Cold,
But if you buy from him yo'm bound tu be sold.

(Notey Beeney. — He'd be summut loike a mon if he'd cure the Butcher's Mate ov nein' soo dear, the Muzick Hall ov bein' soo dirty, the Highway Boord ov votin agen a Water Cart, the Skule Boord ov jawin' one another, the Rate Collector of cummin' round soo offen, an' the Church Clock ov bein' welly allus wrong).

Then the Methody Parson is heard tu complain:
'Them horrid Wake Folks bin a comin' again!
No rest con I get nayther night nor by day,
If it goes on much longer I'll run right away.

'For my residence is in the midst ov the fun,
An' the din is soo deffnin' I'm ommust undun,
I mun goo tu the Doctor an' tu him complain,
For I raly bin suffrin' from Wake on the Brain'.

Then theer's the Skulemeaster who lives on the Green,
He's welly druv mad with the horrible din,
An' he wishes the Shows an' the Stalls an' Steam 'osses
In a much warmer place — bekos he so cross is.

Now luke at the Fops an' the Dandies soo gay,
Who with pride fit to bust bin a comin' this way;
My eye! Don't they swagger an' give themsels airs,
With their brass Albert Chains an' their Penny Cigars.

Then theer's the Yung Wimmen, don't they cum it strong,
With their yeds in Chignon an' their Dresses soo lung;
But bless their sweet faces, we wo say no moor
Tu make them be loff'd at whom all men adoor.

An' all up an' down you wun see wi'out fail
Lots of Lurchers an' Riff-raff, Tag-rag an' Bobtail,
Fortune-tellers an' Gipsies, an' snakin' Pickpockets,
Who finger your Wipers an' Watches an' Lockets.

But if wi' small warnin' it sets on to rain
(It's done soo afore an' may du soo again),
Oh what a cummoshun theer is in the place,
For they set on tu run as if runnin' a race.

Now would it surprise you if I wos tu tell
That at Bloxidge the Cricketers know very well
How to get a chep Umpire when playin' a Match,
An' the price that is paid for a Run an' a Catch?

(Query. — May we be allowed tu ask whether it's a fact that at the last Match the allowance tu the Umpire inkluded a Bottle of Pop for every Wide, an' that in consekwence ov a lot of very wild Bowling the poor umpire was welly busted wi' Pop afore the Match wos half over?)

Now up in the Newsroom they'm playin' at Chess,
But yo cawn't understand it, it lukes such a mess;
Though they seem tu play at it wi soo much delight,
If the gas wonner turned off they'd stay theer all night.

They muve the Pawns one square, they muve the Knights three,
An' they move the Queen ennyhow — that puzzles me;
The Bishops muve crossways, the Castle muve strate,
An' the game is koncluded wi' Check and Checkmate.

All kommunikations for the Edditor tu be addressed 'To the Edditor ov the BLOXIDGE TALLYGRAPH, care of G. RAY, Bukseller, Bloxwidge'.

Oldbury Wake and Races

You can't forget when once you've been to Oldbury Wake and Races,
To see the women dressed so fine, and crushing in best places.
The word goes round that 'Smosh' is up, and clearing of the course,
His red coat suits him to a T when seated on his horse.

'The signal draps! They'm off, by gom! An' Keeton's chestnut's leadin'!*
Her'll win! Her'll win! I'll bet a quid, her's jom full up wi' breedin'!'
Twice round they go, the third's the time, 'Her tak's it 'asy, do' her?
Her comes in fust above five yard, an' could a won by more'.

*Branksome Lass.

See what a crowd hangs o'er the wall, right up the Birmingham Road,
And traps well filled women and men, a right Black Country load,
But some don't go to see the race, nor yet to see the shows,
But sit in Tip'on Slasher's booth with a quart jug under their nose.

It's 'How bist, Bill? I'm glad yo'm come, now sup, my lad, wi' me.
I'n had four quaerts, an' I bain't half full, I'm gooin' to have a spree.
What! Got no brass, well, I'n got some, I'n drawed at the guinea club;
Do' care for th' ale, we'll change it, lad – two glasses o' best rum shrub!'

And what a din outside the booth, with barrel organs playing,
Here's 'Tell yer height', here's 'Tell yer strength an'weight', a penny paying.
'A penny a shot, my dear', says one — a forty year-old tease,
'Yo've won! Well, rock or pudden'. He replies 'I'll tak' nuts, please'.

The puddings were such dainty ones, and made of fine boiled rice,
And upside down, with treacle round, and currants to make them nice.
The 'rock' was of the yellow kind, with stripes of brown and red,
But the lad he knew a thing or two when 'nuts' he gently said.

'Walk up! Walk up!' old Campbell cries, 'the side door there you'll find.
Three-pence, three-pence, about to begin — don't crush so there behind!'
The columbine performs a dance with Eldershaw, the clown,
And Mrs Latimer, finely dressed, walks grandly up and down.

Then Joey Barnett sings a song about a very 'saft place',
And Finch upon the tight rope shows how he can go the pace.
'About to begin! About to begin! Walk up and see the crime —
The Bilston Murder and Brandrick's Fate; walk up and be in time'.

'Hi! hi! hi! hi! — here, let 'em pass — the black mon's 'ating rots,
An' also see the lady fair, all kivered wi' jet black spots,
The skelington an' the fat lady — he's lately taken to court her —
You know her well, this virgin fair, her name it is Sall Orter'.

A band strikes up — why, Clapton's here, with moving figures, shewing
A storm at sea and a gallant ship right through the wild waves mowing.
We pay our coin, we go inside, the curtain's just drawn up;
It's soon all o'er, a lively tale about a poison cup.

We get among the crowd again, and steer for the 'over' boats,
The handle turns, up, up it goes, and in the air it floats.
Close by is the 'Leviathan', men pull, and soon it swings,
'O'er wi' it!' shout the men — the girls it soon to sickness brings.

The little horses, hoisted high, near by are ready found,
A penny apiece — you take your place — and lads beneath push round.
'I'm injiyin' myself, and do't yo think as I'm a gooin to clam' —
'Right, right you are, they're all a penny, fresh cut, a roll an' 'am'.

'What's all the fuss anunst the coorse? The crowd for long don't tarry;
He's welly done, he's earned his feed, blest if it a' saft Harry'.
With bag tied up right round his neck, he's jumped all round the town —
'Pull out your knife an' cut the string, an tak' 'im to the Crown'.

'He ain't won fairl' 'Then yo tak' that!' 'A fight!' 'Mind, Simmonds here'.
'What's up? What's up?' The Sergeant cries — 'Why, nothin', do't yo fear'.
And so the Wake was soon all o'er, it passed away too quick,
But the races begin again with the women to the 'Pop Shop', all next week.

Mrs Alfred Payne, writing of the Black Country in 1869, expressed this view: 'The dreary aspect of nature, so despoiled by man's works, may account perhaps, in some measure, for the multitude of fêtes, wakes, fairs, races, and club feasts, wherewith the people seek recreation'. By this time wakes and fairs were largely indistinguishable since for the most part they merely provided entertainment. However, fairs were originally annual gatherings for buying and selling commodities and animals, to which a pleasure element was added. For example, in 1769 Dudley had fairs on 8 May for the sale of cattle (which included horses), wool and cheese; 5 August, for lambs and cattle; and 2 October, for horses, horned cattle, wool and cheese. Even a place as small as Oldbury had fairs on 25 May and 5 October. Among the earliest charters for fairs in what became the Black Country were those granted to Hales and Walsall by Henry III in 1219/20. The abbot of Hales was accorded a weekly Wednesday market, together with a two-day annual fair starting on the feast of St Denis (9 October). Two years later this moved to the feast of St Kenelm (17 July), no doubt to attract some of the pilgrims visiting the nearby village of Clent. In 1344/5 a new charter from Edward III provided for a Friday market and a four-day fair at 'Hales Owenne', starting on the feast of St Barnabas (11 June). Walsall's fairs were revised under Charles I in 1627 to St Matthias's Day

(24 February) and the Tuesday before the feast of St Michael (29 September). By 1813 a Whit Tuesday fair had been added. Hackwood quotes these records from church registers:

1661.	Paid to 45 Clubmen yt. Walked ye Fair	7s. 6d.
1802.	Paid for Music, being Fair Day	7s. 0d.
	Paid H. Barber for Sergeants and Bellman's Cloaks	£13 8s. 7d.
1803.	Music, being Fair Day	7s. 0d.
1831.	Paid Deputy Constables in walking ye Fair	5s. 0d.

Until the 1870s Walsall's statute fairs were opened with due ceremony. At noon, the mayor, corporation, town clerk, police, firemen and two criers started from the town hall, and walked to the foot of the steps leading to the parish church at the top of the High Street. There, the clerk read the charter, then the procession continued down High Street and Digbeth, at the bottom of which the charter was read a second time, at which point the fair was deemed to be legally open. Then the procession returned to the town hall.

On the eve of Wolverhampton's great fair of 9 July (originally granted in 1258 for 28 June, the move of date caused by the reform of the calendar in 1752), men in antique armour paraded, preceded by musicians playing 'the fair tune' (which does not seem to have survived), and followed by the steward of the Deanery manor, the peace officers and prominent citizens. 'Tradition affirms', wrote Stebbing Shaw, 'that the ceremony originated when this town was a great

Walking the Fair (at Walsall), by Alfred Mudge (1859)

emporium of wool, and resorted to by merchants of the staple from all parts of England. The necessity of an armed force to keep peace and order during the fair, which is said to have lasted fourteen days, though the charter says only eight, is not improbable. This custom of *Walking the Fair* (as it was called) … was first omitted about the year 1789'. By the early nineteenth century the fair had become a more modest event, held on 10 July.

On the morning of Wednesbury's fairs (25 April and 23 July, becoming 6 May and 4 August after the change of calendar) the beadle appeared in the market place, carrying a bell and a pike. He then led a procession of worthies, with a band, through the town to the Elephant and Castle in High Bullen, where they all drank two tankards of ale. They then marched back to the market place for more ale, then lunch in one of the public houses. The costs were borne by parish funds.

Thanks to a case which reached the court of the Star Chamber in 1498, we know that a company of mummers from Wednesbury, Walsall and Wolverhampton went round local fairs to perform a Robin Hood play, with support from morris dancers and a pipe and tabor player. Money raised went to supporting the three parish churches. For some reason, bad feeling arose between the performers of the last two places. On the Wednesday before Trinity Sunday (which is the first Sunday after Whitsun), John Cradley of Wednesbury and a companion assaulted Thomas Rice of Walsall, and were then locked up, whereupon John Beaumont, lord of the manor of Wolverhampton, Robert Marshall of Wednesbury, and some two hundred others, armed with bows and arrows and other weapons, turned up at Walsall to free the prisoners and to destroy the town. The Walsall JPs not only made them back down, but also ordered 'the inhabitants of Walsall, Wednesbury, and of divers other towns, their adherents, that they should not assemble together out of the said town, and should not come to a Fair that should be holden at Wilnale [Willenhall] on Trinity Sunday'. Even so, some two hundred people from Wolverhampton and Wednesbury, wearing armour, led by William Milner (styling himself the Abbot of Marham, or Lord of Misrule), turned up at the fair with the intention of 'striking down' any men from Walsall. Fortunately, their intended victims had followed the magistrates' orders, and stayed away.

Only two years before these incidents, Stourbridge received from Henry VII the right to a weekly Friday market and annual fairs on the feasts of St Edward the Confessor (29 March) and St Augustine (8 September). These continued at least to the 1830s, by which time the town also had a perhaps unofficial Onion Fair in October. In addition a mart for horses occupied the week before the March fair. William Foxall of Wollaston (born in 1833, and a veteran of the Crimean War, during which he served in the marines) talked about this fair in 1914 to a journalist:

The Talbot (right) in Stourbridge in the early 1900s

His reminiscences of Stourbridge are exceedingly interesting. He can still picture Coventry Street in the old days when the Horse Fair was held there, and he used to take great interest in the doings of an old horse coper named 'Jerry', who used to come with a string of old crocks eight or nine days before the fair, and whose method of turning the poorest animals into fiery four year-olds was an education in privileged beholders. Coventry Street was the centre of the town in those days. Benny's Show used to pitch in Barlow's Yard, and the rest of the fair was spread out in the Market Place. 'We lads used to work the hobby horses for the sake of a ride before they used a pony, Mr Foxall says, 'for they had no steam then'.

The Market Place, Dudley

Some of the local markets, as we have seen, are as old as the fairs, and were almost as popular. Until 1914 Stourbridge had a bustling Friday market, where farmers' wives sold eggs, butter and poultry, while their husbands met corn dealers to sell grain, or attended auctions of land and property in the Talbot. Farmers drank in the same inn, where women were

Calendar for 1894 of Fairs and Wakes

Feb.	24:	Walsall Fair (St Matthias)
	26:	Shenstone Fair
Mar.	5:	Dudley Fair
May	6:	Wednesbury Fair
	7:	Dudley Fair
	14:	Bilston Fair
	15:	Walsall Fair
	17:	Birmingham Fair
July	10:	Wolverhampton Fair
	23:	Tipton Wake
	30:	Bilston Wake
Aug.	3:	Wednesbury Fair
	6:	Dudley Fair
	27:	Darlaston Wake
Sept.	10:	Wednesbury Wake
	24:	Bilston Fair
	25:	Walsall Fair
	27:	Birmingham Fair
Oct.	8:	Dudley Fair

(from Tom Brown's Black Country Annual, *1893)*

confined to a separate 'Market Room'. Often they would have the task of driving their husbands home, but if a 'market peart' farmer were alone he would be hoisted on his horse, which would be expected to find its own way back.

Dudley Market, still one of the liveliest in the Black Country, was described in verse (see panel overleaf) by the local collier-poet, Ben Boucher (1769-1851), said to be 'the best of poets and the worst of men'. Oldbury had markets on Tuesday mornings and Saturday afternoons. The market days at Wolverhampton were Wednesday and Saturday. On the latter the Parliamentary Children's Employment Commissioners commented in 1843:

> The great market-day, for working people, is of course, Saturday, because that is the day on which wages are paid; and there is, moreover, a general desire among the working classes to get rid of the greater part of their week's earnings in carousing on Saturday night, and in preparing profusely for Sunday. On the evening of Saturday the market, between seven and nine o'clock, becomes crowded like a fair. ... There are many fights and other street-rows towards midnight.

Oldbury Market, 1900

In between those hours there was a good deal of music, for which, see the next chapter.

Halesowen had a Sunday market which began almost 800 years ago by a cross in Cornbow. The event later moved to a specially built market house, and the cross moved to the churchyard. Apparently

Lines on Dudley Market

At Dudley Market, now I tell,
Most kind of articles they sell;
The women take the greatest care
To buy up crocks and earthenware,
Milkpans, and colliers' tots,
Coloured cups and chamber-pots.
Old shoes to sell, there stands close by,
With shabby strings — the same they tie;
If in thos shoes you walk about,
The bottoms soon will tumble out —
Hats, caps, and bonnets blue,
And trowsers wide enough for two, —
If you pop round the market place
There you may buy a farthing lace;
Besides penknives, for Jack and Jim,
And razors for the daddy's chin —
Rocking-chairs and wooden ladles. —
Kash from Walsall, kills the worms;
Judas brings a slave for corns;
Mind these men or you'll be bitten —
Black Jack's wife brings salve from Tipton —
At the top of the Shambles Sally stands,
She holds the basket in her hands:
'Now my good people don't be lacking,
Here you may find the best of blacking'.
Just below, the butchers there you'll find,
With shows of meat to please the mind;
From most parts these butchers come;
Mind the steelyard — twig the thumb. —
There's hares, rabbits, and partridges, and pheasants, too,
Some are shot by sportsmen, and some are hung by the neck, too —
There's butter, bacon, cheese, and eggs,
Sold by old Giles with crooked legs —
More than that if you just turn round,
There's gingerbread eightpence a pound!
Besides plum pudding, both rich and nice,
On the next stall twopence a slice. —
In Stoney Street there stands the swine,
Both right and left all in a line;
They sell these pigs so much per score,
So on that street I'll say no more. —
Come, to a tavern let us go,
There's some above and some below;
There's one that keeps good ale and pop,

Ben Boucher in 1847

He also keeps a liquor shop;
He sells roast beef down in Queen Street,
His house is always clean and neat –
Old nanny Mason comes in with her nuts,
And on the floor her baskt puts;
A curtsey drops, 'Kind sirs', says she,
'Mine age is nearly eighty-three'. –
Old Timms comes in, 'All hot', did cry,
And you may either toss or buy. –
There's one-armed Joe among the lot,
With mutton pies all smoking hot.

Please to remember what I have said:
You will never hear the like again.
Ben Boucher, 1827

alone among Black Country towns, Halesowen also had a fair or mop on the Monday nearest to 10 October for the hiring of farm workers and domestic servants. An anonymous writer contributed this account of the event to the *Stourbridge Express* in 1926, twenty-five years after it had ended:

> The mop achieved much fame and attracted many hundreds of people into the neighbourhood from outlying towns and villages. The farms and the nailshops were deserted for the day, and all roads led to Halesowen, visitors from afar making the journey in gigs, waggons, and by every method of propulsion known. … The streets of Halesowen were built on both sides with stalls and booths, and shows of all descriptions, exhibiting giant ladies, Tom Thumb men, five-legged cows, and all kinds of fake and genuine freaks.
>
> The chief happening of the day, however, was the roasting of the ox in the street. At Halesowen the fire was built up in the old Bull Ring, off Birmingham Street, and the ox, specially prepared, was placed on a spit over the flames. Crowds assembled to see the ceremony of turning the spit, and many of the old inhabitants considered it a great honour and a good omen if allowed to assist in the ceremony. Very soon the air was filled with a delicious savour, and by the time the ox was roasted to an appetising brown, a queue of moist-mouthed individuals had formed with dishes to obtain a portion of the beast. Few of the villagers missed having some of the ox, and there was always a rush for the first cut. It was something like being deprived of plum pudding at Christmas to be refused a portion of the mop beast. If an old resident went to live out of the district it was generally the custom to fetch the meat on Mop Monday, even if several miles had to be traversed in the process.

In the afternoon the ladies of the district who hired servants attended the mop, and all who wished to enter domestic service were assured of a position if they did likewise. Most of the agreements made between masters and men, and mistresses and maids, were for a period of twelve months, commencing and expiring on Mop Monday. Other agreements there were of course, which extended over several years, but they always expired on the day of the mop. Owing to this custom most of the servants who were paid annually had plenty of money to spend; in fact, it looks as though it might have been a subtle conspiracy between the stallholders, showmen, and the employers of domestic labour. However, no one restrained themselves, and the alehouses were generally well patronised by both sexes. It is said that the noise of the merrymakers was so great that it was the annual custom of Dr Offman, the village physician, to retire from the front to the back of his residence in order to enjoy a little quiet to prepare himself for the inevitable extra work which would result from the excessive eating or drinking, or both, of the residents.

The revelry continued without cessation throughout the night. The stalls and the streets were usually illuminated by flaming oil lamps, and in the inns no little effort was expended in entertaining the customers to be assured of the fullest extent of their patronage. It was impossible to sleep if anyone desired, for the streets resounded with the strains of concertinas and laughter of the visitors.

Market Place, Wednesbury, from a postcard, c.*1904*

CHAPTER 12

Music Makers

THE LAMENTATION

Of JOSEPH DACE,

WHO WAS EXECUTED

For House-breaking at Stafford Lent Assizes.

T Bloomer Printer Birmingham.

I'm Joseph Dace, now take my word,
From Bloxwich town I came,
My honest parents feared the Lord,
And brought me up the same.
They brought me up my God to fear,
And used me most tenderly;
But little did they think to hear,
Of my dying on the tree.
I was bound out an apprentice,
To learn an honest trade,
Belov'd by my master and mistress,
And never was dismay'd,
I was taken up on suspicion,
And ordered off to jail,
My parents try'd to release me,
By offering their bail,
Did not fear being ill treated,
My trial I did stand,
But soon I was convicted
By the jury of the land.
My father he doth sore lament,
And for me he doth grieve;
Yet all his tears in vain were sent,
They give me no relief.
If my mother had been living,
Distracted would have run,
To have parted with her darling,
Her own beloved son.
So now that I am going to die,
Of an independent death,
For what I ne'er transacted
Since e'er I drew breath,
I hope my blessed Redeemer
Will moderate my pain;
And I hope that all good people
Will freely say *Amen.*

Ballad sheet

'Amidst the throngs who are passing to and fro, there are many stationary groups, and one of these is not infrequently occasioned by a circle having been formed round a couple of colliers performing a dance. They always sing to their own dancing when no other music is at hand. They often however, enlist the service of a fiddler or a piper, and sometimes an Italian boy with his grinding spinet'. So wrote the Parliamentary commissioners in 1843 (see also previous chapter), of Wolverhampton's market on a Saturday night. 'Meantime', they added, songs and vociferations are heard in every beer-shop and small public house'.

Markets, wakes and fairs provided a splendid opportunity for the sellers of printed street ballads to hawk their wares, which often originated in Birmingham or even further afield. They catered for a strong interest in crime, the more violent the better. Theophilus Bloomer of Birmingham issued, some time between 1817 and 1827, a sheet (see illustration alongside) on the execution of a Bloxwich housebreaker at Stafford. In June 1852 Mary Robins of Oldswinford murdered her newly-born illegitimate child by throwing it down a pit shaft. She was 'saft', and had fits, but the judge at Worcester Assizes passed sentence of death on her. William Wright of Birmingham printed a ballad on the case (see panel opposite), putting a confession into the mouth of the woman. At the last minute her sentence was commuted to transportation for life to a penal colony in Australia.

Just a few months later Wright produced a further sheet, 'Verses on the Old Swinford Tragedy', which dealt with another murder:

In Oldswinford near to Stourbridge,
The Seven Stars is known full well,
One David Davies was the landlord,
Till now this deed of blood will tell:
On Monday last, the 9th of August
A dreadful row there did occur,
Between the neighbours and some navvies,
When Davies he did interfere.

He went upstairs and through the window
Fired off the fatal gun,
Poor Mary Pardoe was the victim!
Of this bad and wicked man;
He not content with this foul murder
He many times did fire the gunn,
And shot at random on the people
And sorely wounded several men.

At the trial Davis was ordered to be confined to a lunatic asylum, and his 14-year-old son to be imprisoned for two years for having repeatedly re-loaded the gun.

Another Birmingham printer, who claimed 'the Cheapest house in the Trade for Stationery, Ballads, Song Books, Children's Tale and other Books, Wholesale & Retail', issued 'A Copy of Verses on the Awful Murder at Willenhall' (see illustration overleaf). For the crime described, Christopher Edwards was hanged at Stafford in August 1872. Three years earlier, the bizarre murder of Eliza Bowen by William Hall came to the attention, probably via press reports, of a London printer, H. Disley, who issued 'Horrible and Atrocious Murder of a Woman at Wednesbury' (see illustration on page 215).

Sporting events provided another popular subject for ballads, as we saw in chapters 9 and 10. One of these, 'The Wednesbury Cocking' (see also chapter 10) had an extraordinary vogue. The earliest known version seems to be an eighteenth-century sheet without printer's name (see illustration on page 177) from the collection of the antiquarian, Francis Douce (1757-1834). The unfavourable portrayal of the cockers made it unpopular with them, and in

THE SORROWFUL LAMENTATION

Of Mary Robins, 25, under the Sentence of death in Worcester Gaol,
for the murder of her infant at Kingswinford, June 21st, 1852.

To tender-hearted Christians all, come listen unto me,
While I relate a tale of woe — which ends my misery.
Mary Robins is my name, and dreadful it is known:
For the murder of my infant child would melt a heart of stone.

Murder is my awful crime, and is denounced by Heaven,
And on my head my infant's blood, I hope to be forgiven.
So I was apprehended, to Worcester sent with speed,
And now I'm doomed to suffer all for this dreadful deed.

At the last Worcester Assizes I was placed at the bar,
That I was guilty of the deed the Jury did declare.
The Judge the sentence pass'd on me, and then to me did say —
'For the murder of your infant child, you must die upon the tree'.

In a dungeon dark, in irons bound, I bitterly do weep,
The midnight bell, the thoughts of death, deprive me of my sleep.
The ghastly form of my infant babe appears fresh before my sight,
Strikes terror to my guilty soul amidst the shades of night.

My life is forfeited to the Law for the deed that I have done,
Good people all – pray for me, when I am dead and gone.
May the Lord have Mercy on my soul, have mercy, Lord, I pray,
When I appear before thy throne on the Judgement Day.

about 1780, according to the Wednesbury historian, J.F. Ede, 'the guard of the mail coach *Nimrod* venturing on one occasion to give a few bars of the melody on his bugle while passing through the town, was attacked and savagely stoned for his pains'. Nevertheless, the tune was prescribed for other ballads, such as 'The Fight at Worcester' (1824) and 'The Windsor Election', the latter indicating that it had travelled south. In 'The Bullock Hanker's Medley', an account of a London bull running, printed by John Pitts, these lines occur:

Lord how you'd have laughed at the fun,
To see how he toss'd the poor whores.
Oh! Some up the streets was a running,
And some down the lane was a flocking,
Where he toss'd an old Birmingham turk,
That was singing about Wednesbury Cocking.

Bloomer of Birmingham reprinted this sheet, and no fewer than four of his colleagues issued their own editions of 'The Wednesbury Cocking', the author of which turned out to be a Birmingham man. Joshua Vernal published this account in 1859:

> I am old enough to remember the *furor* [*sic*] with which the song of 'Wednesbury Cocking' had used to be received. Although its wit is ribald and gross, yet its delineations of character are correct. Those who knew the 'black country' forty years ago, can bear testimony to its truth. How often has it been sung with a roaring chorus. How frequently did some

A COPY OF VERSES ON THE
AWFUL MURDER, AT WILLENHALL.

Come all good people give attention,
And listen to a dreadful tale;
Another sad and cruel murder,
Which all of us now do bewail,
On Tuesday was the deed committed,
At Church street in Willenhall Town,
One Christopher Edwards, slew his victim,
May the Lord have mercy on her soul,

Chorus.

Oh, Christopher Edwards, cruel Father.
Your dreadful deed had no control,
To deprive your Children of a tender mother,
May the Lord have mercy on her soul,

In my hand I carried the weapon,
Up stairs to do the dreadful deed;
And the murder I committed.
Which makes my wretched heart to bleed,
I aimed the blow at my poor victim;
As she lay upon the bed,
None was there but God to witness,
As I left my victim dead.

At Willenhall town where I resided,
And might have spent many an happy day,
With my wife and darling children,
But to the cursed drink I did give way,
The woman [illegible] cherish,
The day I made her my dear wife?
I beat her brains out with the poker,
And deprived her of her life.

No person was there for to rescue,
No friendly hand was there to save,
She is dead may the Lord have mercy on her,
She came to an untimely grave?
I gave her no time for repentance,
No time to say a single prayer,
She's gone to judgment I must follow,
Oh! God how shall I meet her there,

When I think of the deed that I've committed
I'm driven to grief and to despair,
To think I deprived my darling children,
Of fond mother's tender care,
I have broken the laws of my maker,
My wife she was murdered by me;
For which I soon shall have to suffer,
And end my days on the gallows tree.

Oh! men by me just take a warning,
To the cursed drink do not give way,
For by Satan I was tempted;
My darling wife all for to slay.
Oh, God look down upon my children,
To them be a father and a friend
And let no one ever upbraid them,
Or speak of their fathers untimely end.

Birmingham, Printed by J. BRUETON. 76 STAFFORD STREET. The Cheapest House in the Trade for Stationery, Ballads, Song books, Children's Tale and other Books, Wholesale & Retail of us old ones join in that chorus, and think it the best of songs, and as we drained the foaming tankard encore again and again. If the times have improved in decency and decorum, they have lost that wildness of mirth which made Old England merry. Who was the author of 'Wednesbury Cocking'? According to the enquiries I have made, he was a Birmingham gunmaker, living in Newton Street, and glorying in the name of Jack Probin. ... Being in the gun trade, he was in the habit of going to

HORRIBLE AND ATROCIOUS

Murder of a Woman

AT WEDNESBURY,

And Committal of William Hall, for the Murder.

Wm. Hall, was examined before the magistrates at Wednesbury, on the charge o murdering Eliza Bowen, on Sunday, under revolting circumstances. Superintendent Holland, proved that the prisoner was with deceased at three separate public houses on Saturday night, between 9.30 and 11.40, and he was with a woman at the spot where the murder was committed at ten minutes past on Sunday morning. He also produced a part af a muffler picked up by the body and the corresponding part was found in the prisoner's house. Mr. Kerr, surgeon, proved that death was caused through the insertion of stones into the body. He produced a large piece of brick and sixteen pieces of iron cinder, all of which were found imbedded in the corpse, at the time of the post-mortem examination. The prisoner was fully committed to take his trial for wilful murder.

Attend you feeling Christians,
One moment lend an ear,
Oh, listen to this dreadful deed,
Was done in Staffordshire.
Oh, such a barbarous cruel deed,
Before was never told,
Too horrible for to relate,
Too dreadful to unfold.

The murderer in a dismal cell,"
Lies trembling with fear,
For the dreadful deed at Wednesbury,
In the county of Staffordshire.

One poor Eliza Bowen,
Near Wednesbury did dwell,
At Darlaston, and the country round
There she was known full well!
Poor creature, she gave way to drink,
Which caused her untimely fate,
And she did not see her folly,
Until it was too late.

She went away to Wednesbury town,
Upon the Saturday night,
In company with a man named Hall,
And 'tis supposed he took her life.
She was plied with drink,abused,& slain
By a monster in disguise,
And as we can read this dreadful deed,
All classes did surprise.

Poor woman she was cruel killed,
Her body filled with stones,
And no one round did hear her cries,
Her sufferings, or her groans;
But the dreadful usage she received
No language can unfold,
Oh, such a dreadful murder
Before was never told.

William Hall was the victim's neighbour
Whom she was with that fatal night
And whom there is doubt, so cruel,
Took away her life;
He is a married man at Darlaston.
He does in angush lie,
Awaiting the assizes,
When a jury will him try..

There was never such excitement caused
As this has caused around,
Far and near for many miles,
From Wednesbury town;
This sad atrocious murderer,
Will meet with his downfall,
And Justice will find out the guilt,
Of the man named William H

H. Disley, Printer, 57, High Street, St. Giles, London.—W.C.

> Darlaston for gun locks. On one occasion stopping at Wednesbury, to see a fight of a main of cocks, the sport suggested to him to write the humours of 'Wednesbury Cocking'. If its wit had been more decent, it might have been more quotable, but it would not have been so accurate a delineation of the manner and customs of the times it describes. No matter: it was once as popular and effective as 'Lillibulero', or as 'Shall Trelawney Die?'

Vernal's last sentence implies that the song's popularity had waned. Yet in 1872 a remark on the subject by Michael Bass, MP for East Staffordshire, during the opening ceremony for Wednesbury's new town hall was, according to a local newspaper, very warmly received: 'In the … art of poetry he thought Wednesbury might be termed a distinguished place (laughter). He never knew a town with a more famous epic — although he should not like to quote it on that occasion — than the celebrated poem of the "Wednesbury Cocking" (loud laughter)'.

The text of the ballad appeared in 1881 in an appendix to Samuel Butler's book, *Alps and Sanctuaries*. Butler had it from his father, who learned it from his nurse, 'poor old Mrs Bromfield'. This, in fact expurgated version, was taken up by a string of twentieth-century anthologists, including Robert Graves (1957), Matthew Hodgart (1965) and Geoffrey Grigson (1975). Given such widespread publication, it is ironic that 'The Wednesbury Cocking' is no longer sung, for the reason that its original tune has not been found. A Mrs Rhoda Dawtry did prove in the 1960s to have a tune (see below), but it did not fit the original text, and may have applied to some kind of offshoot.

There were ballad printers in the Black Country, but the lurid crimes and spectacular sporting events seem to have been snapped up by their rivals further afield. Local men, often producing only a handful of ballads, included: Joseph Heming (at work from 1808 until 1832), of High Street, Stourbridge, bookseller, printer, stationer, and printer of the *Worcestershire and General Commercial Directory*; John Rann, born in Birmingham in 1785, (1819-39), of Hall Street, Dudley, bookseller, printer and stationer; George Walters (1817-47), of High Street, Dudley, bookbinder, bookseller, newspaper agent, seller of music and musical instruments, and stationer; and Joseph Smart, born at Rowley Regis in 1774, (1815-31), of High Street, Wolverhampton, bookbinder, bookseller, keeper of a stamp office, medicine vendor, music seller, printer, and proprietor of the *Wolverhampton Chronicle*. They leaned towards melodramatic tales such as 'The Oxfordshire Tragedy' (Rann), 'The Bristol Tragedy' and 'The Maiden's Tragedy' (both Smart). The last of these (see panel opposite) is set near Wolverhampton. There were also lighter items such as 'When this old hat was new' and 'Woodman, spare that tree' (both Walters), and 'The Windsor Miser Outwitted' (Smart). The journalist and antiquarian, William Hone, wrote

The Maiden's Tragedy,
Or,
A brief Account of a young Damsell near Wolverhampton,
who cut her throat in despair, because she could not have the man she loved.
To the tune of Russell's Farewell.

Near Wolverhampton liv'd a maid, who fell into despair,
Her yielding heart was soon betray'd, into Love's fatal snare:
A young man courted her we find, and seeming love did shew,
Yet after all he prov'd unkind, which wrought her overthrow.

Here do I languish in distress, the youthful damsel cried,
To see his most unfaithfulness, all round on every side:
I see nothing but clouds of grief, and storms of bitter woe,
It's death alone must yield relief, Love proves my overthrow.

False-hearted Thomas call to mind, the solemn vows you made,
That you would never prove unkind, and can you now degrade
Your loyal lover now at last, and fill my heart with woe,
Which will my life and glory blast, and prove my overthrow?

I courted was both day and night, at length I gave consent,
This done my love he straight did me slight, and leaves me to lament;
As if he took delight to see mine eyes like fountains flow,
Oh, most ungrateful man, said she, Love proves my overthrow.

Not long ago he did adore my very charms, he cried.
Was ever man so false before in all the world beside?
A harmless lover to deceive, and drown in tears of woe,
This world I am resolv'd to leave, Love proves my overthrow.

Thus being fill'd with discontent, she took a bloody knife,
In desperate sort resolv'd and bent to cut the thread of life;
Down from her throat the reeking gore in purple streams did flow,
And though she lay a week and more, it prov'd her overthrow.

With grief and sorrow compass'd round, she languish'd night and day,
At length her fatal bleeding wound did take her quite away;
And all along before she died, her eyes with tears did flow,
Likewise she wrung her hands and cried, Love proves my overthrow.

Though now at present he may have content, and pleasure find,
When I am sleeping in my grave, he then will call to mind
Who caus'd this present wretched state, and fill his heart with woe,
And then he may repent too late my dismal overthrow.

that he had seen the 'pleasant old song', 'A Carroll for a Wassell-bowl' (see chapter 13), 'in 1819, at the printing-office of Mr. Rann, at Dudley, printed by him for the Wassailers of Staffordshire and Warwickshire'. Rann also issued a sheet bearing both 'A Virgin Unspotted' and 'A New Carol for Christmas', and the former of these was among the fifty-eight carols in George Walters's *A Good Christmas Box*, published in 1847 (see chapter 14).

The Balladmonger, by George Cruikshank (1823)

Those hawking ballads in the streets and sometimes from door to door were very marginal figures. F.W. Hackwood tells the sad story, possibly dating from 1832, of a 'street ballad-monger' who 'after tramping through Wednesbury and Darlaston, dropped down in mortal agony in the streets of Bilston, while still giving vocal effect to his wares. … Ere set of sun the singer's corpse was carted away to the graveyard'. What he had been trying to sell was a ballad on the subject of cholera.

In the mid-nineteenth century an Irish ex-guardsman called Thomas Conway-Quinn wrote ballads which his partner, Catharine (Kate) Eddowes, helped him to sell in the pubs and on the streets. The couple often travelled to Warwick, Worcester or Stafford when executions were due to take place, so as to take advantage of those who would pay a penny for a sheet with an appropriate ballad. In a bizarre and almost unbelievable twist, Kate sold just such a composition at Stafford in January 1866 when her own cousin, Christopher Robinson, was hanged for the murder of his sweetheart at Wolverhampton. Conway-Quinn, his stock exhausted, ordered 400 more copies from Sam Sellman, a printer, of Church Street, Bilston. (Sellman appears in the trade directories of the time as a timber merchant; perhaps he had a small printing press as a sideline). Conway-Quinn and Kate later moved to London, where in 1888 she had the misfortune to become one of the victims of Jack the Ripper.

Tom Langley (born 1907) had a more cheerful memory of a ballad seller, in connection with 'A Poor Man's Work is Never Done': 'An old chap used to sing it round the Black Country when I was a boy. In the mornings he sang "A poor

The death of a different victim, Annie Chapman, at the hands of Jack the Ripper, from The Illustrated Police News *of 22 September, 1888*

woman's work is never done". My mother used to send me out with a halfpenny for him. "Give it to him. He never said a truer word". In the evenings he went round the pubs and sang "A poor man's work is never done", and my father was one who said, "Give him a pint of long pull. He never said a truer word"'.

From much the same period came H.T. Peplow's recollection of childhood days in Wolverhampton:

> The street-singers were plentiful, but those who got the most coppers worked in pairs, an elderly man and a youngish woman, obviously pregnant, or, better, still, she would be carrying a baby in her arms. Shabbily dressed, the man would be playing a cornet or accordion, while his wife (?) would be singing in a thin, reedy voice. Cold days when they looked really miserable, or if it were raining lightly, were the best times as people felt so sorry for them, and would give them pennies, while the 'musicians', looking as though they hadn't eaten for a week, shuffled slowly along, their pockets getting heavier all the time. At some point along the route they packed up and went home, but we never knew where they came from.

Street singers may well have been drawing material from the music hall, some of the stars of which performed in public houses. George Lashwood (1863-1942), who had a repertoire of over a hundred songs, sang at the old Crown at the Five Ways in Cradley Heath, and people flocked considerable distances to hear him. Another popular entertainer, somewhat strangely, was George Smith, the hangman, who appeared 'in most of the public houses between Dudley and Halesowen', where 'his dances and songs, many of his own construction and composition, greatly appealed to the sentiments of the villagers'.

There is a tradition that Vesta Tilley (1864-1952), a native of Worcester, whose repertoire ran to almost 200 songs, performed in her early days at the Horseshoe Hill, Brierley Hill. The young George Formby also appeared there, as did Jack Judge. Judge (1878-1938) was born in Oldbury and also died there: he is buried in Rood End cemetery. He started work at the age of nine, and five years later was pushing a fishmonger's barrow. He found he could write lyrics and poems, which he had printed, just like the old street ballads, and sold for a penny a time. He became a comedian and entertainer, and travelled the halls. The story goes that he was performing in the Grand Theatre at Stalybridge in January 1912, when he took a five shilling bet that he could write a new song within twenty-four hours. Having composed the text of 'It's a long, long way to Tipperary', he whistled a tune which his accompanist, Harry Williams, noted for him. Williams (1874-1924), another Oldbury man, played the piano in his parents' pub, the Malt Shovel. Towards the end of the First World War, he and they moved to the Plough at Mere End, Balsall Common, in Warwickshire, which they re-named the Tipperary. Williams maintained (and his relatives still maintain) that he had written the tune for 'Tipperary', not merely written it down; and it is not denied that he indeed wrote tunes for some other compositions by Judge. In 1933, though, Judge stated that he had given Williams a share of the 'Tipperary' royalties in return for earlier financial assistance, but that

Vesta Tilley

Left to right: Hary Williams (pianist), Bert Feldman (publisher) and Jack Judge

The Quarry Bank Mashers

Now last night to a ball we're invited,
To a ball, and two ladies were there;
Their cheeks were in bloom like the roses in June,
They were such a lovely pair.
We were dancing and singing till midnight,
We played as we had all the fun;
And after the dancing was over
We had whisky, bananas and rum.

(Chorus)
Singing tra la la la, etc.

Lucy Woodall

Williams did not write a single note or word of the song, which sold eight million copies during the First World War alone.

Music hall songs, with their strong melodies and clear narratives, had wide appeal. In 1971 Mr and Mrs Hadley of New Street, Quarry Bank, sang for me 'The Quarry Bank Mashers' (see panel previous page), a song which first appeared in the 1890s under the title of 'The Brothers Maloney'.

While working as a chainmaker, starting in 1912, Lucy Woodall (see also chapter 8) acquired a considerable repertoire of music hall songs, thanks to hearing her workmates singing then, and joining in herself. Several, including 'Two Sweethearts', 'The Volunteer Organist' (see panel opposite), 'An Old Man's Darling' and 'Break the News to Mother', dated from the 1890s; others, such as 'Tipperary', 'When I leave the world behind' and 'I'm for ever blowing bubbles', from the first two decades of the twentieth century.

A singer in a chain shop at Cradley Heath, drawn by Harold Piffard in the 1890s

The tradition of singing at work lasted well into the twentieth century. Joan Powderly, who grew up in Bilston was warned by her grandmother: 'Yo doh want to ever go to Bradley's. It's the last place God made'. Yet she spent sixteen years there, making mop buckets and ironing boards. She recalled in 1989:

> We always used to sing as we worked, although it drove the foreman mad. He used to say, 'For God's sake, shut up!' but we used to reply, 'That's the one thing you can't stop us doing. You can't stop us singing'. Then he used to reply, 'I wish I could!' But that was one way of getting rid of the boredom …

The Volunteer Organist

Each eye shed tears within that church; the strongest men grew pale;
The organist in melody had told his whole life's tale;
[The sermon of the preacher was no lesson to compare
With that of life's example, who sat in the organ chair.]
And when the sermon ended not a soul had left his seat,
Except the poor old organist who walked towards the street.
Along the aisle and out the door he slowly walked away.
The preacher rose and softly said: 'Good brethren, let us pray'.

The scene was one I'll ne'er forget as long as I may live,
And just to see it o'er again all earthly wealth I'd give:
The congregation all amazed, the preacher old and grey,
The organ and the organist who volunteered to play.

Original written in 1893 by W.B. Gray (words) and H. Lamb (music)

The story is an uncanny echo of an incident related a century earlier by Robert H. Sherard on a visit to a Cradley Heath chain shop when he saw a young girl at work: 'She was fourteen by the Factory Act, by paternity she was ten. I never saw such little arms, and her hands were made to cradle dolls. She was making links for chain-harrows, and as she worked the heavy Oliver she sang a song. And I also saw her owner approach with a clenched fist, and heard him say: "I'll give you some golden hair was hanging down her back! [A hit song of 1894.] Why don't you get on with your work?"'

When work was too strenuous, the workplace too noisy or simply unsuitable, people collectively relaxed with singing afterwards. One glassmakers' song runs:

> Bonny's backed the winner,
> We're on the booze today.
> We'll have a goose for dinner,
> And drink whisky in our tay.
> We'll line our coats with five pound notes,
> And drink our noses blue,
> For Bonny's backed the winner,
> And we don't care what we do.

'Music is generally cultivated among the colliers', wrote Mrs Alfred Payne in 1869, 'and may be heard at all seasons, sometimes in the sweet hymns of the schoolroom or the cottage meeting, but more often in the taproom or the dancing-saloon of the public-house'. J.W. Clulow believed that for miners their 'very favourite amusement' of dancing was one of the pursuits which took the place of bull baiting and cock fighting:

> At many of the public-houses in Brierley Hill and the adjoining villages the largest room, generally a club room, would be engaged, and as soon as it became known that a dance was to come off, the tickets of admission, for which the charge was from 2d. to 4d. each, would soon be disposed of. A fiddler would provide the necessary music at a fee of 5s. to 10s. for the occasion, according to his ability and the length of time the dancing continued, this being often till 3 or 4 o'clock in the morning.
>
> Another method was to hold dances, or routs — pronounced 'ruts' — at public-houses, where a stage or platform would be erected, and on these occasions two or three fiddlers would be requisitioned. The outside ground floor — in earlier times it would have been called the 'Pit' — was occupied by the throng and the dancers, who, if there were room, would form several sets at one time. A favourite 'rut' was held at Cornelius Plant's at Amblecote. The most popular one, however, for many years, was from time to time held at the Old Star Inn, Brierley Hill, where as early as 1825, on Easter Monday or May Day, a fiddler's platform used to be erected at

> the gable end of the stable, and the by no means 'deserted' village was at that time vocal with the gay shouts of the assembled crowd ...

Clulow adds that miners from Amblecote and Brierley Hill also excelled at solo hornpipe dancing, and that: 'A renowned dancer, Charlie Lee, from Dudley, very often was requisitioned to take part in these dancing matches in competition with Charlie Skelding, of the Delph, a miner who was a first-class hornpipe dancer and quite the expert of the locality'.

Singing features in many of the countless reminiscences of Black Country people's experiences as hop-pickers in Worcestershire and Herefordshire. As early as 1854 John Noake, describing a cart-load of Lye Wasters who stopped on the way back from hop-picking at a roadside public house, 'almost envied the hilarity of the happy female crew — laughing, squalling, chattering, singing, smoking'. Half a century later, Clifford Willetts (born 1896) wrote:

> The hop picking season was the highlight of the year for the poorer families. This was in September. School holidays coincided with the hop picking season. Otherwise the schools would have been half empty. Hundreds of Cradley families made the exodus to places like Leigh Court, Leigh Sinton, Bransford, Newnham Bridge, Tenbury, Knightwick, Whitbourne, Callow End, Bromyard and Hereford. These places were household names in Cradley. The pickers took with them cooking utensils of every size and shape. The most important was the 'hoppen box'. This was a tin trunk which held all the clothes. Prior to the season, the hop grower paid a visit to Cradley to choose a woman whose job it would be to marshal the pickers. These were paid a shilling hiring fee, which morally bound them to the grower. There was no legal contract as such, but the agreement was always honoured. On the great day, they made their way to Cradley Station to board the train for their destination. The train was so long that the phrase 'As long as a hoppen train' was coined. It took nearly the whole day to get to the required place, as the train was always shunted into a siding to make way for the regular trains. On arriving at the station, there was a stampede to the farm to get the best accommodation. At the best this was a stable, a cow shed or a loft, which had been whitewashed by the farmer. These people lived in poor conditions for a whole month, sleeping on straw beds and cooking their meals over stick fires. Strange though it may seem, they accepted these primitive conditions gladly. There were rewards. Orchards were raided and few returned without a good supply of fruit. There was the nightly visit to the pub, perhaps a mile away from the farm. The visitors, as they were called, relatives and friends, paid their visit on the second week. To hear them singing the popular songs of the day, as they walked along those country lanes, was an unforgettable experience. The hop pickers called it their holiday. It has its two fold purpose. It was a change from their environment and they claimed it built them up for the rigours of

Hop Pickers from Dudley at Munderfield Court, Herefordshire, c.*1909*

> winter. They also had what was to them a fabulous amount of money. This enabled them to buy new clothes and household articles, which otherwise they could not afford.

One of the agents mentioned was Flo Wothers of Wollescote, Stourbridge, who took pickers to the hop country for twenty years. She recalled:

> If you didn't go to the pub at night you sat outside the barracks [wooden huts] and warmed yourself by the 'devil' [brazier] and had a sing-song. On the last night everyone chipped in with as much money as they could afford, and the men went down to the pubs with enamel buckets to have them filled up with ale. The nearest pub was the Trumpet [near Ledbury]. When the beer was brought back you dipped your mug in and helped yourself. Some subbed and celebrated every night at the pub and they had nothing left to go home with.

Bessie Rock of Netherton, who started picking hops in 1919, remembered: 'It was two and a half mile walk from the farm to the Somers Arms in Leigh Sinton. One old lady, Granny Totley, she'd be 90, walked there for her half pint of beer of a night and had always done it. Maria Homer from Maybank was a character. I remember them wheeling her out in a pushchair, right into the middle of the pond, and she'd still be singing "Hands, knees and bumps-a-daisy"'. Mrs Mabel Field (born 1906) of Queen Street, Cradley Heath, first went out hopping at the age of four, and continued for eighty-three years: 'It

Hop Pickers from Tipton (from left to right, Lizzie, Irene, Bill and Andrew Morris) at Corbett's Farm, Leigh Sinton, Worcestershire, 1950

was the best times that I have ever had. In the day time we would sing songs and at night we'd go to the public house'. George Dunn (1887-1975) of Quarry Bank precisely echoed those views: 'On Saturday night we went to the pub and we 'ad a good spree, sing-song. … I've 'ad some good times down th' opyards. I 'ardly missed a year. It was the best o' my days'. As well as in the pub, he remembered singing both at work during the day and round cooking fires in the evening. The everlasting song, also sung by soldiers on the march, would sometimes go on 'for an hour at a time, singin' for killin' time':

> Oh she was so good and so kind to me,
> And all the rest of the family.
> I'll never forget my Mary Ann,
> She was, she was, she was so good and so kind to me,

And so on. George Dunn also sang traditional songs such as 'The Cruel Ship Carpenter' and 'Young Sailor Bold' in the hopyards.

He was a remarkable man who worked for fifty-nine years, mainly as a chainmaker (see chapter 8). He had a repertoire of over a hundred items: hymns, operatic arias, music hall numbers, and above all traditional songs. Many of them were learned from his father; as George's brother, Ernie, put it:

> My father worked from six till six — never was late and never 'ad a quarter till 'e was seventy. 'E dae come 'ome till it was seven o'clock.

> ’E’d wash ’im, sit in the chair, cut ’is bacca up, put it in ’is pipe, ’ouldn’t ’e? And then ’e’d sit. When the children was in after ’e’d ’ad ’is tea, about seven or eight o’clock, nothin’ at all to do: no readin’, no wireless; only the kettle a-goin’ woo-woo, the clock a-goin’ tick-tock, tick-tock. … When you’d all sit round we’d say: ‘Father, sing we a song. Sing we a song’.

George Dunn with his record, 1975

By 1971 George had been retired for twelve years. He was well known in Quarry Bank as a former chainmaker but his celebrity as a singer in public houses and at private parties was forty years behind him. Even his daughter, Mrs Valerie Chapman, had little inkling of the extent of his songs. Mrs Rhoma Bowdler, a mature student at Wolverhampton Day Training College for teachers, visited Quarry Bank in search of information on chainmaking, and was directed to George Dunn. She quickly realised that she was dealing with both a chainmaker and a singer, and she alerted Charles Parker, a BBC producer from Birmingham. I also became involved, and continued to visit George until his death in 1975. I was able to arrange for him to record an LP of thirteen of his songs, which he launched with immense gusto, deeply proud that his singing would be preserved for posterity. In 2002 I edited a two-CD collection of 51 of his songs, some fragmentary, but many in full versions, ranging from the music hall (‘The Stowaway’, ‘Don’t Go Down the Mine, Dad’, ‘Break the News to Mother’) to carols (‘Seven Joys of Mary’, ‘While Shepherds Were Watching’: see chapter 13) to rare versions of ancient ballads such as ‘Cold Blows the Wind’, ‘Henry’, ‘Broomfield Hill’ and ‘It was my Cruel Parents’ (see panel opposite). Not only was his repertoire of great interest, but he was a fine stylist, the best traditional singer ever recorded from the Black Country, and worthy to compare with any in England. All this at the age of over eighty.

There are tantalising glimpses of oral tradition from other sources. In the 1960s Mr H. Harper of West Hagley gave me this intriguing fragment:

Oh, it was my Cruel Parents

Oh, it's 'Hush, my dearest Nancy, oh, wait till we go to town.
I'll buy you a lady's bonnet, likewise a mus-e-lin gown;
There is no lady in the land your beauty can compare,
And I'll buy you a little lapdog to follow you everywhere'.

'I want none of your little lapdogs nor none of your gentle care;
It's a pity such an old man my beauty you should snare.
I am not sixteen years of age and scarcely in my bloom;
Oh, you are my cruel torment, both morning, night and noon'.

When he comes to bed at night he's as cold as any clay:
His feet as cold at midnight as corpse, I've heard them say;
His pipes are out of order and his old flute's never in tune:
Oh, I wish that he was dead and a young man in the room.

Now some they do persuade me to drown him in a well,
And others do persuade me to grind him in a mill.
I'd rather take my own advice and tie him to a stake,
And I'll get a big stick and wallop him well until his bones I break.

Come see the *Dolphin*'s anchor forged, 'tis at white heat now.
The bellows cease, the flames decrease, though on the forger's brow
Still flickering they do play. 'Hurrah', they shout, 'leap out, leap out'.
Bang, bang, the sledges go.

At the same period Miss Rhoda Dawtry of Tettenhall communicated three songs learned from her mother: 'Come all you blaids [blades] what's marryèd' (better known as 'Billy White and Nelly Green'), 'The Hampton Balloon', both of which are given in Jon Raven's book, *The Urban and Industrial Songs of the Black Country and Birmingham* (1977), and 'The Wedgbury Cockin'', of which she knew six four-line verses, with 'the chorus roared out, especially at Christmas, after some "'ot ale"':

To sing the original text of thirteen eight-line verses (see page 177) to this tune would unfortunately be very repetitive.

Miss Dawtry learned these songs from her mother, who in turn had them from her father, Mr John Marsh of West Bromwich:

> His business was the making of hames and all horse furniture. In the course of his trade he employed a number of local men and women in his 'blacking shop' to prepare the hames, etc. for going abroad. These people were rough in the ways but always happy to work for 'Mester Mash', and were fed from the house at mealtimes. They loved to sing and my grandfather collected a great many songs, but only these three remain and must, I feel, be part of much longer songs. The three workpeople principally responsible for teaching my grandfather rejoiced in the glorious nicknames of Black Bat, Lester Tum and Molly Tunky (the unfortunate lady having a resemblance to a tunky pig). One other person comes to mind, Ann Pit, who continually carried a small piece of coal round in her mouth, and had beautiful fine teeth.

Miss Dawtry also knew some children's singing games, including 'Sir Roger is Dead'. G.T. Lawley quotes this from his own childhood in Bilston:

There was a man, a man indeed,
Who sowed his garden full of seed.
When the seed began to grow,
It was like a garden full of snow.
When the snow began to fall,
'Twas like a bird upon a wall.
When the wall began to crack,
'Twas like a stick about my back.

When my back began to smart,
'Twas like an arrow to my heart.
When my heart began to bleed,
'Twas like a dying man in need.
Soon the poor man's pains are o'er,
And so I end, for I know no more.

He quotes a further rhyme, used by mothers to frighten children who stayed out of doors too long:

Raw head and bloody bones
Steals naughty children from their homes,
Takes them to his dirty den,
And they are never seen again.

He adds: 'The ghoul was supposed to haunt the village lanes at night and put all the children he caught in a black bag and carry them off to his den. In the place names of Bilston we have Rawbones Croft, which derived its name from this ancient superstition. When the wind howled at night children used to hide their faces under the bedclothes, for they were taught to believe that when they heard howlings in the night they were the cries of the demon as he passed down the street in search of victims'.

A sad though less nightmarish song, handed down through the family by her grandfather, was sung by Annette Smith, a pupil at Rood End School, Oldbury, in 1970:

A drun- ken man came home one night To
find his home with- out a light— He
went up- stairs to go to bed When a
sud- den thought came to his head.

He went into his daughter's room
And found her hanging from a beam.
He took his knife and cut her down,
And on her breast he readily found.

'Oh, father dear, I die in shame
To bear a child without a name,
So dig my grave and dig it deep,
And lay white lilies at my feet'.

So they dug her grave, they dug it deep,
And laid white lilies at her feet;
And on her breast they laid a stone
To show the world she died of love.

So all you maidens bear in mind:
A true love's very hard to find,
So if you find a love that's true,
Don't change the old love for the new.

Of all the musical instruments associated with the Black Country — and brass bands were once very widespread — perhaps the most notable, at least in quantity, was the jew's harp. One centre for its manufacture was Rowley Regis, where as a form of quality control every instrument had 'The Blue Danube' played on it before being passed fit for sale. Many thousands were exported until the jew's harp was overtaken by the mouth organ. John Barnsley of Netherton in the 1870s and '80s sent vast numbers to America, where, according to Horace Walpole, 'Maryland was bought from the Indian with a quantity of vermilion and a parcel of jaws [*sic*] harps'. As late as 1900 the instrument was still being made in a small workshop in Halesowen Street, Blackheath. Perhaps this was the last to survive.

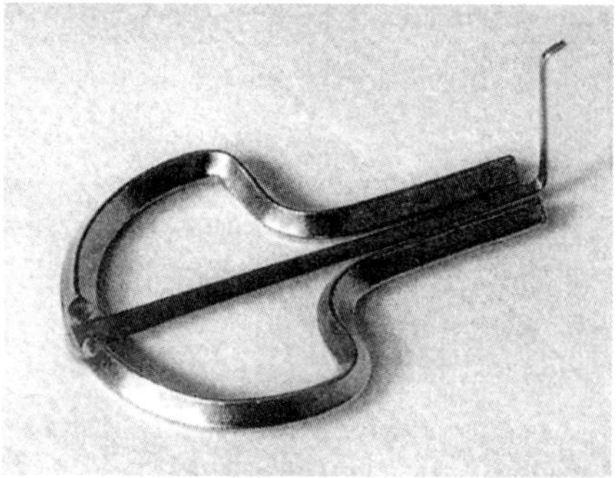

A Jew's harp

CHAPTER 13

Seasons and Shindigs, I: New Year to May Day

New Year

Bands played, bulls (factory hooters) boomed and hammers clashed on metal to salute the New Year in the Black Country. In some public houses a mock funeral was solemnly held for 'Old Tom', the year just gone. Groups of men or boys toured the houses to collect largesse. George Dunn (born 1887) as a boy sang a wassailing song (or 'wazlin', as he pronounced it) from door to door with a group of friends:

> We are not daily beggars that beg from door to door,
> But we are neighbours' children that you have seen before.
> (Chorus)

This is a completely different text from that seen by William Hone 'in 1819, at the printing-office of Mr. Rann, at Dudley, printed by him for the Wassailers of Staffordshire and Warwickshire' (see panel opposite), which went to the tune of 'Gallants come away'. It is very rare to see a mention of female wassailers, as here; and as early as 1851 John Noake recorded: 'Among the superstitions of Dudley is one very common, even with some of the more respectable classes — that is, of not allowing a *female* to be the first person to enter the house on a New year's morning, for fear of having bad luck all the year'. Seventy-five years later G.T. Lawley commented that even a fair-headed man would not do to let in the New Year: 'A dark man must be chosen, and … he must come in at the front door and go out at the back, and a lucky year is sure to follow. No member of the household must go out first on New Year's morning, about which they have this rhyme — "First in, then out/Good luck comes about"'. Lawley adds a cautionary tale told to him by a Black Country woman:

> One New Year's day my sister inadvertently opened the door to two females who were singing thereat, and who walked inside and began to sing a carol. I shall never forget the rage of the mater as she rushed downstairs and chased the obnoxious singers into the street. Now, it so happened that during the year several casualties occurred, two of the family were stricken down with fever, one dying, and the other recovering. Other minor misfortunes also presented themselves, and, as if to crown all, my sister, in the August of the same year, sailed with her two young children on board the ill-fated ship, *Ocean Monarch*, to join her husband in America. The vessel was destroyed by fire off the Welsh coast [in fact, off the Mersey, in 1848], with a loss of 170 lives. My sister, after being badly burnt, jumped overboard, with the youngest child in her arms, and after being in the water over an hour, holding her child with one arm, supporting herself with the other by clinging to a rope under the bows of the vessel, was rescued by a brave sailor, who took her child first and swam with it and put it on board a steamer, and then came back and fetched the mother, placing her on another boat by which she was taken back to Liverpool, and put in the Northern Hospital in a sad plight. The child was brought to her the same night. The second child was rescued by an old gentleman, to whom it had clung after losing sight of its mother. Thinking the child had lost its parents it was placed on a coasting steamer, by which it was kept away from Liverpool nearly a week, and then it was brought to the hospital to its mother. I should not have mentioned this occurrence only it had at the time a special interest in this part of the country, for a good number of people from these parts were passengers

A Carroll for a Wassell-Bowl

A jolly Wassel-Bowl,
A Wassel of good ale,
Well fare the butler's soul,
That setteth this for sale;
Our jolly Wassel.

Good Dame, here at your door
Our Wassel we begin,
We are all maidens poor,
We pray now let us in,
With our Wassel.

Our Wassel we do fill
With apples and with spice,
Then grant us your good will
To taste here once or twice
Of our good Wassel.

If any maidens be
Here dwelling in this house,
They kindly will agree
To take a full carouse
Of our Wassel.

But here they let us stand
All freezing in the cold;
Good master, give command,
To enter and be bold,
With our Wassel.

Much joy in this hall
With us is entered in,
Our master first of all,
We hope will now begin,
Of our Wassel.

Some bounty from your hands,
Our Wassel to maintain:
We'll buy no house nor lands
With that which we do gain,
With our Wassel.

This is our merry night
Of choosing King and Queen,
Then be it your delight
That something may be seen
In our Wassel

It is a noble part
To bear a liberal mind,
God bless our master's heart,
For here we comfort find,
With our Wassel.

And now we must be gone,
To seek our more good cheer;
Where bounty will be shown,
As we have found it here,
With our Wassel.

Much joy betide them all,
Our prayers shall be still,
We hope and ever shall,
For this your great good will,
To our Wassel.

on board the doomed ship. Now, my mother, although she lived to a good old age, always to her dying day, firmly believed that it was the female singers that brought about all these disasters.

Such strength of feeling makes readily understandable the care which people took to ensure the right caller. Thomas Pinnock wrote in 1893:

> Where a household consists entirely of the softer sex, and is situated far out of the way of the peripatetic benefactors who prowl about on New Year's Eve to perform, for a consideration, this annual rite, it is usual for the said ladies to make beforehand an arrangement with some male acquaintance to pay them a visit, and render them the necessary service. Sometimes a supper of bread and cheese, with hot coffee or mulled ale, awaits the harbinger of the infant year. But as the enjoyment of these good things, though very acceptable, occupies valuable time, and restricts the number of houses visited, and consequently the pecuniary results, it is usual to open the door, left unbolted for the purpose, shout a doggerel verse, and then call out the name of the benefactor as a means of recognition on the morrow, when the customary gifts are collected.

George Dunn and his companions, though, expected to be rewarded on the spot after singing:

Now Christmas is here we'll all have a drop of beer,
We wish you a merry Christmas and a happy New Year.

The roads are very dirty, the pocket very thin:
Please Mr. Master, chuck a penny in.

The cock sat up the rue [yew] tree, the hen came chuck-e-lin' by,
We wish you a merry Christmas and every day a pie.
A pie, a pie, a pie, a peppercorn.

Those who failed to make a contribution would be treated to a further verse:

> The cock sat up the rue tree, the hen come chuck-e-lin' by,
> I wish the cock'd drap a turd and drap it in yer eye.

After that, 'We'd got to flit then, we'd got to depart quick'. Similar verses, though without the cheeky coda, have been noted in Bilston, Dudley, Rowley Regis and Sedgley.

G.T. Lawley recorded Black Country people's prejudice against letting a neighbour have any fire or even a lighted candle on New Year's Day, though on any other day they would have been more than happy to oblige. 'Fire, on New Year's day, was regarded as sacred; hence it was religiously kept burning from 12 o'clock on New Year's Eve till midnight on New Year's day. If it went out, it was regarded as an omen that some one in the family would die during the year'. According to F.W. Hackwood, writing in 1924, 'Among the Black Country colliers superstition prevented them doing any work in the pits on New Year's Eve or on New Year's Day'.

Twelfth Night

The antiquarian, Robert Plot, related in 1686 the Walsall tradition, dating from over two hundred years earlier, that Thomas Moseley, walking in the town on Twelfth Eve (5 January), 'heard a *child* crying for *bread*', and made a vow that 'no person hereafter of what condition soever, should ever want for *bread* in that *Town* or *Liberties* on that day again'. In fact it seems that Moseley left money to be devoted to an *obit* (a perpetually burning candle) for his soul and that of his wife, Margaret, at Walsall parish church and Hales (Owen) Abbey. From the surplus, it seems that the town of Walsall provided 'a certain *dole* of one penny and no more on *Twelfth Eve* to all persons then residing within the Town or Burg of *Walshall* [*sic*]; and in all the *Villages* and *Hamlets* belonging thereunto; *viz. Walshall-wood*, *Shellfield*, Great and Little *Bloxwich*, *Harding*, *Goscot*, *Woodend*, *Caldmore*, *Bescot*, the *Pleck*, and *Burch-hills*, which they called the *foraigne* ...'. The custom continued until the early nineteenth century, when penny loaves were distributed instead of cash. Then, in 1825, the money was diverted to building and the upkeep of eleven almshouses.

Valentine's Day

Pinnock described both this day (15 February) and Mid-Lent Sunday (see below) as being 'of general but waning observance'. Over a century later, thanks to more affluent times and also vigorous commercial promotion, the former at least remains ubiquitous.

Shrove Tuesday

Depending on the date of Easter, Shrove Tuesday can fall any time between 3 February and 11 March. It is the last day before Lent, which runs for forty days (excluding Sundays) and ends on Easter Saturday. People were confessed or 'shriven' on Shrove Tuesday (hence its name), and until the 1890s at Halesowen parish church 'a curious custom prevailed of "shriving" the bells ..., anciently intended to call the people to confession'.

More popular, perhaps, were the bells rung at 11 a.m. to remind cooks and housewives to start preparing pancakes. Children that morning, expecting the traditional half holiday, sang on their way to and from school:

St John's Church, Halesowen, from a nineteenth-century engraving

Pancake day is a very happy day.
If they don't give us holiday we'll all play away.

There were different renderings of the bells' messages; at Wolverhampton:

Pancakes and fritters say the bells of St Peter's;
Let them fast who will, we'll have our fill.

at Willenhall:

You can hear we miles, say the bells of St Giles;
The frying pan's on and the pancake's done.
Pan on.

and at Wednesbury:

The pancake swells say the Wedgbury bells,
Ding dong, ding dong, ding dong, ding dong.

As well as children, servants once looked forward to Shrove Tuesday: in their case they could 'lay abed' and have a pancake brought to them. They had to be up so as to receive it, though, or it would be stuck to the front door as a sign of disapproval. G.T. Lawley treasured this story from when he was twelve years old:

> I remember seeing this curious custom put into practice in the year 1857. The pancake was carried on a plate by a middle-aged woman … accompanied by all the 'ladies' of the locality who, as was their wont, castigated the unfortunate 'lye-abed' with a cataract of offensive epithets, being encouraged to 'keep it up' by a bodyguard of vagabond boys with tin cans, kettles and old pieces of iron, which they beat unmercifully with sticks, and added to the hubbub by shouting to the utmost capacity of their leathern lungs. On which occasion a riot nearly ensued through some of the 'lye-abed's' acquaintances taking her part; during which hubbub the precious pancake disappeared.

Mothering Sunday

On Mid-Lent Sunday (the fourth in Lent, which can fall between 1 March and 4 April), otherwise known as Mothering Sunday, young people made their way to the parental home, where they were fed on roast veal and rice pudding. In some districts, including Sedgley, the visitors took a simnel cake as a present.

At Wolverhampton until the 1930s the roast veal would sometimes be accompanied by a sauce made of salt fish and egg, and followed by custard pudding or 'laid' pudding, the latter so called because of its layers of fruits and other ingredients. Another favourite dish for Mothering Sunday in the Black Country was 'grey pays and bacon':

> Peas and bacon in a pot,
> Stewed till they be tender got;
> Served up on a trencher wide
> To match the room in yo'r inside,
> Bin very poor for hungry men
> When Motherin' Sunday comes again.

Butty colliers once shared a toast in ale with all the men employed in their pits, and feasted apprentices on beans and bacon. The occasion has now been almost entirely submerged in the modern and highly commercialised Mother's Day introduced from America.

Good Friday

E.A. Underhill noted of Sedgley in 1942 that Good Friday (the penultimate day of Lent) was known by the children as Hot Cross Bun Day, and commemorated by the song:

One a penny poker, two a penny tongs,
Three a penny fire-irons, hot cross buns,
One a penny, two a penny, hot cross buns.
Give one for our sister, give one for our brother,
One for our father, and one for our mother,
One a penny, two a penny, hot cross buns.

Later in the same decade, according to Jon Raven, children at Christ Church primary school, Tettenhall Wood, Wolverhampton, sang:

Hot cross buns, hot cross buns,
One a penny, two a penny, hot cross buns.
If you have no daughters, give them to your sons,
One a penny, two a penny, hot cross buns.

Hot cross buns, once a rare and short-lived treat, said to commemorate the crucifixion, are now on sale in supermarkets all the year round. Fish was favoured for a Good Friday meal, and bread baked that day was thought to be capable of keeping for a year. According to Pinnock, there was 'no general cessation for work, for the gigantic plants engaged in collieries and ironworks cannot economically be put to stand idle for an occasional day'. All suds and slops from domestic work were retained indoors, to be thrown away the following morning, because of the belief that 'a woman of Jerusalem threw suds on our Lord as he walked towards Calvary'.

Pinnock also remarked on the custom of annual gatherings at Dudley Castle on Good Friday: 'No matter how cold or wet the weather may be, some hundreds of lads and lasses are sure to appear at the noted rendezvous'. The event seems to have subsided into a gathering at which girls skipped, and this in turn came to an end in 1937 when the zoo was opened. However, large numbers of people assembled at Dudley Castle on other occasions (see below and chapter 14).

Easter

Easter, once 'a popular season for marriages' in the Black Country, falls between 21 March and 25 April. As late as 1930, T.V. Shaw's glossary of Black Country words and phrases still carried this entry: '*Aive*, heave, lift. Easter Monday is "aivin day", when men have the privilege of lifting women, perhaps as a crude reminder of the Resurrection'. Over a century earlier, in 1826, William Hone's *Every-day Book* noted the prevalence of '*heaving* or *lifting* at Easter-tide ... in Lancashire, Staffordshire, Warwickshire, and some other parts of England'. Twelve years after this a writer described walking with a friend in Wolverhampton on Easter Tuesday:

> Not bearing in mind the season of the year we ventured on a short cut to Darlington Street through the Townwell Fold. Until half way there were no signs of danger, but once fairly in the net, out pounced a bevy of 'Nymphs' who debarred further passage and one of the most stalwart seized and fairly 'heaved' us off the ground and claimed the silver guerdon [reward] demanded for the practice.

In about 1850 at West Bromwich Heath toll gate 'a band of sturdy viragos actually stretched a rope across the road to stop all vehicles, from which the male passengers were compelled to alight and submit to be blackmailed on the approved Easter Tuesday plan'. The custom clearly remained strong in 1863, when an anonymous commentator wrote:

> The pit-girls are not less fond of holidays than their fathers, and much they enjoy two days of saturnalia when, by immemorial custom, the field of labour is turned into a scene of general riot. On Easter Monday, the men roam about the colliery in gangs, and claim the privilege of heaving, as they call it, every female whom they meet, — that is to say, of lifting her up as high as they can, and saluting her in her descent. On Easter Tuesday the ladies have their revenge — and in their hands this strange horse-play acquires redoubled energy. Neither age nor rank are respected; not even the greatest of men, the manager himself, would be secure from attack; and those who will not enter into the fun must purchase exemption by a ransom proportionate to their station.

F.W. Hackwood, writing in 1924, offers a personal memory of an 'Easter Tuesday scene in Wednesbury upwards of fifty years ago': 'It was in the narrowest part of the High Street near to Rollasons-fold that a band of brawny pit-bank wenches took up their position for levying blackmail on all male passers-by. And the narrow-mouthed Fold serving them well as a place of ambush, their raids on unsuspecting male strangers proved invariably successful, and much backsheesh was collected for the afternoon's entertainment'.

C.H. Poole supplies the detail that the 'process is performed by two strong men or women joining their hands across each other's wrists, then, making the person to be heaved sit down on their arms, they lift him or her aloft two or three times, and often carry him several yards along a street'. Underhill points out that 'a great slapping kiss' accompanied the lifting.

The custom led at times to incidents which reached the magistrates' courts, and D.C. Woods has turned up a number of these in local newspapers. In 1861 two Irishmen in a Wolverhampton public house heaved each other's wife, then became jealous and fought each other with pokers. In 1893 Theresa Evans of Hill Top, West Bromwich, attempted to heave the police officer who found her lying drunk in the middle of the road, in the hope that he would treat her to a

Heaving Days

Easter Monday and Tuesday were always kept as 'play days' by the colliers and ironworkers, and early on Easter Monday groups of men might be seen strolling about the streets, and they seemed to be eagerly scanning the roads, as though looking for someone.

As it was a bright sunshiny day, the vicar's niece, Kate Hamilton, leaving her uncle (the Rev. J. Lydbury) deep in his books, and Mrs. Japp busy in her kitchen, started for a walk, and, after walking about the churchyard for a time looking at the quaint and curious epitaphs on some of the old tombstones, sauntered down the hill, passing Ben Sheppard's house. At that moment Mrs. Ben, with duster in hand, was looking through the window into the street.

'Marcy on us, if tha vicar's missie isna abroad! Hur dunna knaw, I guess, an' hur 'ull sure tow be cotched. Theer knows, wha' dow I tells thee, mother! 'ere be Josh, Joe, and two ither lads a-cummin'!'

Both women looked eagerly through the window, and saw what they expected: these stalwart young colliers rushed towards Kate, and Josh, being the first, picked her up in his strong arms, and ran about twenty yards with her; then, setting her on her feet, he gave her a good sounding 'buss' (kiss).

Kate, recovering her presence of mind, twisted herself out of his arms before the others could reach her (for they all meant to have their turn), and ran like a hunted deer back up the hill, the colliers in full pursuit. The two women had rushed to their door, and as she was passing Mrs. Ben stepped in front of her, flung her arms around her waist, and dragged her into the house, shutting and bolting the door in the disappointed young colliers' faces.

Kate, recognising Mrs. Ben, felt decidedly safer. Old Mrs. Sheppard remarked severely: 'Dunno yo' knaw as this be Heaving Monday, when the men lifts the wummen, an' tha allus bides whum? For tha men allus busses the pretty uns, an' tha men alllus mak's tha ode and ugly uns pay a shilling instead. Tha ode vicar dinna ought tow a let thee cum out today'. Kate shook her head, still too short of breath to speak.

'Wull, wull, tow think o' thatten!' said Mrs. Ben; 'it shows as tho bist a stranger; an' I suppose yo dunna knaw as tomorrow tha wummen allus heaves tha men. Why, laws! Tomorrow being as 'ow it be Easter Tuesday, tha men wull all bide a whum, or tha 'as sum wark tow dodge 'em. I minds one toime as Mr. Stephen's father 'ad a pritty run onct. Two fat ode wummen seed un a-cumming, an' tha started tow cotch 'im; he sees 'em jest i' toime, an' jumps o'er a wall, ne'er looking wheer he wor a-goin', an' plump he drops intow a barrel o' pig-wesh. My! 'ow tha wummen did roar; tha laughed fit tow split theer sides! Tha cudna run wi' laughin' when he got out, cuvered an' stinkin' o' pig-wesh; an' he runs whum wi' about twenty wummen ater 'im, but tha cudna run fast for laughing, soo he got whum safe without gettin' heaved. I guess he ne'er went out agen on a Easter Tuesday. Sometimes', she said, laughing, 'it takes four wummen tow heave a big mon'.

'I see', said Kate, 'it was entirely my own fault. It looked as if I had gone out on purpose. I have been so accustomed to go about alone all my life that I never feel afraid, and of course I never thought of this odious custom. I really dare not go back to the vicarage yet'.

Amy Lyons, 1901

quart of beer. Unable to pay her fine of 11s. 6d., she went to prison for fourteen days. On Easter Monday in 1896 at the Black Horse Inn at Walsall Herbert Hancox attempted to heave Esther Heap, and to 'kiss her and have a quart of ale'. She declined; he insisted, and in the struggle she fell over several times, and bit his finger in retaliation. He was fined 20s., with costs. More hazards, this time in Wednesbury, are described by Amy Lyons (see panel opposite).

By the end of the nineteenth century the custom, according to Hackwood, had died out in Wednesbury, though it remained 'prevalent in Sedgley parish, not only amongst the men and women, but particularly so amongst the lads and lasses'. 'It was a common sight' (on Easter Tuesday), added Underhill, 'to see the women and girls from the brickyard or other work lying in wait for any gentleman, to catch him unaware, heave him, not only for the fun of the thing, but for the treat, which he was expected to find, as a reward on the occasion'. Pinnock noted: 'A gentleman well known to the writer — an ironworks cashier, of some pretensions to dignity — would walk on that particular morning [Easter Tuesday] two miles further than usual along unfrequented lanes, and across miry pit banks, to avoid the Nemesis, which would after all sometimes overtake him in the person of the Amazonian brickmakers or pit bankswomen'. In the judgement of D.C. Woods, heaving moved 'almost exclusively' to public houses, but 'was slowly dying out and it did not survive long into the twentieth century in the Black Country'.

Easter was also the time for church clipping (see chapter 3) and for all kinds of sport and entertainment. On Easter Monday at the Mounts, an open space

Brickyard wenches, c.*1900*

in Wednesbury, young people simply enjoyed rolling down grassy slopes. (A similar custom at Birmingham's Newhall Hill inspired this comment in a song: 'At Easter time girls fair and brown used to come roly-poly down,/And showed their legs to half the town, the good old sights of Brummagem'). Hackwood, reflecting the opinion of the time, tartly comments: 'However unobjectionable such a pastime might be for young men, it was scarcely suitable for young women clothed in skirts and petticoats to engage in; so as times progressed and manners became less coarse, this old-time revel was gradually frowned out of existence, and we hear no more of it after 1830'.

An alternative for young people on Easter Monday was a trip to Dudley Castle, where both sexes would skip in the courtyard. Cliff Willetts (born 1896) records that 'At Easter and Whitsuntide, whatever the weather, it was a ritual to go to Clent':

> We took a packed lunch with such as our parents could afford. There was always a 'noggin' of bread pudding, which would see us through, and a bottle of water. At most we rarely had more than 1d. to spend. We started early and arrived before dinner. By afternoon the hills were crowded with people from all over the midlands. That 1d. represented problems which an affluent society never knew. We were rent between a choice of spending it on something to eat or a cane. You could have a link of sausage between two pieces of lickered [?liquored] bread or a cane for the same amount. A cane was a status symbol. It lasted longer and was a reminder that you had been to Clent. As it was no new experience to be hungry, the cane usually won the day. We stayed on until evening watching what was to us the affluent society going round the specially made track on donkeys and horses. It was 1s. 5d. for a donkey and 3d.

Riding on donkeys at Clent (from a postcard franked in 1914)

for a horse. We watched with envy those who went round and perhaps wondered if ever we should enjoy the experience. To most, like myself, it remained an unrealized dream. It did enable Black Country people to coin a song, still [1977] enjoyed by the Cradley Sons of Rest on their outings, and which I have heard described as the chainmakers' anthem: 'We all went on the donkeys when we went to Clent'. I recorded the song from Frank Billingham of Halesowen in 1974 [see panel below].

We all went on the donkeys when we went to Clent

We all went on the swingboats …

We all went in a horse and brake …

We all had pop and ice cream …

We all went in the ferns again …

Rogationtide

More festivals depend on the date of Easter. Ascension Day (a Thursday) follows, forty days on, and the three days before that (which can fall any time between 27/29 April and 31 May/2 June) are known as Rogationtide (see also chapter 3). On these days it was customary to beat the parish bounds. In Wolverhampton, where this was known as 'processioning', on both the Monday and the Tuesday, sacrist, resident prebendaries, 'charity children' with long poles garlanded with flowers, assorted clergymen, and choirboys in surplices, paraded with suitably 'grave and appropriate melodies', pausing for bible readings at Gospel Trees. This ceremony came to an end in 1765, but rather less elaborate bound beatings continued until 1824. The churchwardens' accounts from Wolverhampton show payments to bell ringers on the three days of Rogationtide, to 'Charity Boys and Processioners' and to 'divers of ye Parishioners and Inhabitants ... who attended ye Minister in ye Perambulation'.

At Walsall a third of the bounds was beaten each year at Rogationtide. The first year started at Shavers End and covered Walsall Wood and its neighbourhood; the second went from Butts Gate (near the centre of what is now the Arboretum) through Bloxwich and Bentley to James Bridge; and the third from James Bridge to Bescot, Barr, Longwood, and then back to Butts Gate. These perambulations ended in 1807 but at Wednesbury they continued rather longer. At Tame Bridge, where the three parishes of Wednesbury, Walsall and West Bromwich came together, boys were thrown into the river: it was considered that by this means the boundary would be indelibly imprinted on their memories. Administering the bumps was also thought to achieve this result. Boys no doubt submitted in order to take advantage of the refreshments which followed in the shape

Walsall Arboretum (from a postcard franked in 1926)

of bread, cheese and beer. When there was a dispute about Wolverhampton's boundaries in 1775 an old man, Walter Gough, gave his testimony, based on the recollection that at 'fifteen years old he was thrown by the parish clerk into a heap of nettles that grew near, … and in consequence of the same stinging had to be in bed for two days afterwards'. A Stourbridge man, J.M. Gething, who died in 1919 at the age of 90, recalled beating the bounds at Wolverley as a boy, and being thrown into a gorse bush during the procession. The proceedings at Codsall in the early 1920s is described by Hackwood (see panel below).

Bound Beating at Codsall

Within recent times the boundaries of Codsall parish were perambulated in quite modern style by the Vicar, Churchwardens, Overseers and parish officers, who assembled at the church-gates on the Rogation Tuesday, where a photograph of the party was taken before they started. At Gunstone Bridge they were joined by the Assistant Overseer of the adjoining parish of Brewood in which was recorded an account of a similar 'walking' in 1861, and who accompanied them along the line of the common boundary. At Bilbrook, where a cottage and outbuildings stood across the line of boundary between the parishes of Brewood and Tettenhall, the younger members of the party climbed over the roofs, followed by a director of the route, a County Council surveyor, who carried a chart of reference. Thence the route followed was by Dam Mill, along the brook side to the Wergs, and along the turnpike road to Wrottesley Lodge. After another photograph had been taken in Wrottesley Park the walk was resumed round Wrottesley Observatory, and then by way of the Junction Inn to Kingswood Church. Refreshments were then served to the party in the adjoining schoolroom. *F.W. Hackwood, 1924*

May

It is possible that the name of Mayer's Green at West Bromwich reflects the ancient custom by which men and women went out into the woods to find greenery, and perhaps a maypole, too, to bring back on May Day in the morning. 'For ye gathering of ye May, Maypoles and for Ringers as was usual … 15s. 9d.', says an entry of 1665 in the Wolverhampton churchwarden's accounts. As a local rhyme put it:

> Waaken chaps and wenches gay,
> An' off t' country to gather may!

Miners and ironworkers took rum on the expedition, to which they added milk obtained from farms, and called the resulting drink 'whey'. Perhaps they toasted each other with these traditional words:

May Queen at Cradley Wesleyan Church, c.*1900*

Here's a health to the merry month,
The merry month of May;
Drink deep, and pledge it in a cup
To drive dull care away.
Pledge it all, both great and small,
Pledge it now, come one and all,
Hurray, hurray, hurray!

They took back with them blossoms and green boughs with which they decorated pitheads and factories, a custom which lingered until the end of the nineteenth century, in some cases transferring to Oak Apple Day. The folklorist, Charlotte Burne, wrote: 'I travelled by rail through the Staffordshire Black Country on May 29th, 1883, and noticed that all the engines and many of the sheds and signal-boxes, were furnished with boughs of oak'.

G.T. Lawley adds, in what must surely be a reference to morris dancing:

> It was usual fifty years ago for colliers out of work, or on strike, to go [on May Day] in bands of about a dozen, decorated with ribbons, and armed with stout staves, accompanied by a fiddler, to the sound of whose music the band went through a curious kind of dance. The men stood opposite each other in groups of four, and, at a particular part of the tune, struck each other's staves one, two, three, crossing from side to side as they did

so. … The dancers all wore ribbons in their caps, as did also the man with the collecting box, which was fastened at the end of a long stick, and occasionally received a good shaking, as a spur to the liberality of the crowd, or as an accompaniment to the music.

Maypole dancing at Etheridge School, Bilston, 1953

In 1914 T.E. Lones was still able to write of Dudley people that 'Going into the country on May Sunday is the chief outing of the year'.

Maypoles, as with many customs, became part of children's rather than adults' traditions. It may be, though, that the rhymes preserved by Lawley are survivors from an earlier era, though it is difficult to imagine the second one below as having been sung by Bilston miners:

Up with the maypole, high let it be.
If none say me nay I'll now christen thee.
The maypole, the maypole, thy name it shall be,
Now all you good folk, come shout with me,
Hurrah! Hurrah!

Now I've got my Nancy to trundle on my knee.
Oh! My lovely Nancy, she's the girl for me.
She hops and she skips while the tabors play.
It's well for the shepherds on the first of May.
First come the buttercups, then come the daisies,
Then come the gentles, then come the ladies.
So all round the maypole here we trot,
From the very bottom to the very top.

Among other days in May and later in the summer, May Day was often chosen by clubs and friendly societies for their walk, a public procession of members with banners flying, led by their officers in full regalia, for a church service followed by dinner in a public house. Before the introduction by Lloyd George in 1911 of Britain's first comprehensive health and unemployment scheme, those who fell ill, retired from work, or became unemployed, had recourse only to public or private charity and the workhouse. Many joined clubs, paying a small weekly contribution, and receiving modest sickness and unemployment benefit. Weekly meetings were held in whichever public house a club had chosen as its base, but they were very tightly organised. The walk, sometimes jointly with other clubs, and feast were notable events. Berrow's *Worcester Journal* reported on 27 May 1779:

St Mary's Church, Oldwinsford

On Monday last was held, at the Golden Cross Inn in Oldswinford, near Stourbridge, the annual feast of that Charitable and Laudable Society of gentlemen, tradesmen, artificers, and others, which commenced in the year 1752, and hath flourished ever since under the patronage and encouragement of most of the principal gentlemen of that place and Stourbridge. About 10 o'clock they began their procession from the inn, attended by a select band of music, and, joined by seven more societies of the same kind, to the amount of 520 people, proceeded to the parish church. After service each society repaired to its respective inn. At the Golden Cross, a most superb and magnificent entertainment was provided. The evening was spent with the greatest harmony and festivity.

By the 1870s benefit clubs were widespread. Some were local branches of national organisations. For example, H. Jack Haden tells us that the Ancient Order of Foresters was represented at Wolverhampton (by fifteen branches), West Bromwich (nine), Brierley Hill (eight), Wednesbury (five), Walsall (four), Bilston, Dudley, Darlaston and Tipton (three each), Willenhall (two), and Cradley Heath, Daisy Bank, Lower Gornal, Kingswinford, Quarry Bank, Pensnett, Princes End, Rowley Regis, Wallheath and Wordsley (one each). Haden goes on: 'The Manchester Unity of Odd Fellows had the "Eagle" Society at Great Bridge, the "Navarino" and "Miners'" societies at Horsley Heath, three societies at Smethwick, ten at Tipton, including the "Navarino", the "Invincible", the "True Briton", the "Princess Royal" and "Britannia's Pride", six at Wednesbury with nearly 300 members, at at Wallheath the "Sir Stephen Glynne"' — better known as the Crooked House. On the other hand, there were small independent bodies such as the 'Who Would Have Thought It Friendly Society' at Brierley Hill, with 37 members and funds of £153; the 'Bush Inn

F.S.' at Cradley Heath (87 and £586); the 'Locomotive, Steam Enginemen and Firemen's F.S.' at Walsall (34 and £142); and the 'Sick, Medical and Burial Society' at Willenhall (1,211 and £2,536).

The Amicable Society, founded in 1778, the first of its kind in Bloxwich, meeting at the Old King's Arms, Wallington Heath, had 140 members by 1813, 90 men and 50 women. A rival Amicable Society, founded in 1785, had its headquarters at the Bull's Head, which was also favoured by a third club, with 260 members. This paid 10s. 6d. a week to members unable to work because of sickness or an accident, at a time when the weekly wage was 18s. 6d. By the early twentieth century Bloxwich people could turn to the Caledonians, with branches at the Red Lion, Beehive, Station Hotel, Lamp Tavern and Royal Exchange; the Free Gardeners, with lodges at the Bell and the George; the Foresters at the Bull's Head; George's Glory at the Canal Tavern, Little Bloxwich, and the Royal George (favoured by miners) at the Queens Head; the Oddfellows at the King's Arms; and the Rechabites at the Methodist Chapel.

A similar proliferation was to be found in many places, including Edwardian Netherton (see panel below).

May Day Walk

They paraded round Netherton, gathering as they went the Odd Fellows, Free Gardeners, the Druids, Foresters, and bedecked in their regalias and bright ribbons, and at 12 o'clock they arrived at church for the annual May Day sermon, afterwards going to their own headquarters for a dinner.

At night the officers all met at the Star Hotel, Hampton Street, to supper served by mine host, Dicky Daykins. James Mackay was their leader, and I was told by one who attended these suppers and afterwards became their leader, long since gone to rest, the following: 'here was a round of beef, a leg of mutton, a boiled home-fed ham for the sandwiches which appeared at the meeting later. A thirty-six [pint barrel] of the best and a nine of old ale with the necessary bottles of brandy, etc. for the toasts'.

There was only one constable stationed in Netherton, Old Joe: he was invited 'to keep the peace'. The village priest was there, by virtue of his office and the sermon; the parish clerk and the parish sexton too. Before the cloth was drawn each diner was regaled with a glass of neat brandy, known as 'the oden down pin'. The business was interspersed with songs, trumpet solos, flute solos, etc. The sandwiches handed round and the liquid refreshments flowed fast and free. At 11.30 from a nod by mine host a wheelbarrow well lined with straw would be brought to the door and the village policeman would be lifted gently into it, and he would be wheeled down and just round the corner of the National Schools to his home, lifted on to 'the squab', and his boots taken off. He was due to meet the sergeant over the 'Firey Banks' at 4.30 and mine host knew as a keeper of the peace that he was best at home.

Some time later the priest and clerk would be got to their feet and given a start for home; the latter was mine host of the Druids Tavern (two doors below

> Mr. Walker's hairdresser's shop) and the priest's home was down the opening, now the Loving Lamb Inn. At 3 o'clock, the wheelbarrow being otherwise engaged, the chairman would be taken home on a shutter, and those that were left who had not slipped under the table would stand up to pay homage to our sovereign lady the queen. Mine host would slip round and snuff the candles out, bolt the doors, and get down on the hearthrug for forty winks: he had not time to go to bed, as he had to be up and off at 4.30 as he worked at Noah's [Hingley's] on big chains.
>
> *M.H.W. Fletcher, written in 1946*

W. Morgan, writing in 1909, described the annual club walk at Oldbury, on '*the* day of the year for the Green', its flowers and garlands recalling the may-gathering of much earlier times: 'This was the only day, saving weddings and funerals, on which the family tall hat was brought into daylight, and the black suit with velvet collar taken out of the trunk or box. At daybreak scaffold poles were erected in front of the club houses, and women were busy making garlands of greenery and flowers, the clothes lines coming in handy, and the men climbing hand over hand to fasten crowns on the top and garlands from pole to pole, and entwining them round and round as well'.

Although some clubs were wound up immediately after 1912, others lingered until as late as the 1950s to supplement state benefits. Dr Francis Maylett Smith, who worked as a general practitioner in the Black Country from 1915 until his retirement in 1933, gained two-fifths of his income from clubs, into which each family paid 1s. 6d. per quarter for medical care. Payments were passed on to the doctor annually, in February or March, by the clubs, of which there were at least a dozen in his area. 'The two largest', he wrote, 'were efficiently run by Nonconformist chapels, but the management of the others was in the hands of uneducated women, whose conduct was not always above suspicious'. He found to his embarrassment that he was expected to attend a meeting of each club at its rendezvous — the Cottage in the Bower, the Pilgrim's Cottage, the Gate Hangs Well, the Maypole Inn, the Cottage in Spring — to answer any complaints and to collect his money. At the first of these, 'The members were seated at bench tables in a barely furnished loft, each with a mug of beer in front of her. Having learnt with relief that there were no complaints, I was set the invidious task of publicly picking up my money'. Then he found that he needed to offer a gratuity to the officers, and finally, 'I hurried off with my spoils in a canvas bag, having been left in no doubt that the members considered me a lucky and a happy man'. He then decided that from then on the money would have to be brought to him: 'Such a break with tradition would, I was told, be deeply resented, but I stuck to my guns and eventually got my way'. Perhaps the good doctor would have been happier if he had thrown aside reserve, and joined in like the parson and policeman from Netherton, and gone home in a wheelbarrow.

CHAPTER 14

Seasons and Shindigs, II: Whitsun to Christmas

Whitsuntide

Whit Sunday is the seventh Sunday after Easter. Whit Monday became a bank holiday in 1871, and remained so for a century until it was superseded by the spring bank holiday (the last Monday in May). Whitsuntide was traditionally a time for buying new clothes, and this may have reflected the custom of decorating churches at the same time with flowers and greenery such as birch boughs. Celebrations included Whitsun ales and also morris dancing. The Black Country miners, known to be enthusiastic morris dancers, may or may not have resembled those in the famous Betley window from the north of Staffordshire, once thought to date from about 1500 but now known to be early seventeenth century. The women nailers who took over the colliers' dance to raise money when they were on strike certainly had long streaming coloured ribbons from their bonnets and their arms.'The last of these dances by Lye girls on strike', wrote W.J. Clulow in 1914, 'happened about 1856, when, as they were too poor to employ a fiddler, a youth whistled the morris dance

The Betley window
(for details see overleaf)

tune, the girls themselves assisted in chanting it, and they kept time in striking their staves together'.

From the 1850s onwards a three-day Whitsuntide fête was held at Dudley Castle. As many as 20,000 people attended, some from as far afield as

Details from the panels in the Betley window

Dudley Castle fête (from a postcard franked in 1908). The object in the left foreground is a balloon

Birmingham, and they were allowed to go to the top of the castle keep on payment of one penny each. The war of 1914-18 brought an end to this event, though Good Friday skipping (see above) continued until 1937.

Whit Monday was one of the times favoured by clubs (see also previous chapter) for their walks. One account dated 1843 paints a picture of decline:

> Never was such a Whit-Monday as the last seen in Stourbridge: no clubs walking to church, accompanied with bands of music, flags and banners streaming; no jolly pageant, bearing of high wreaths of flowers sufficient to deck a ballroom; no feasting at the club houses. No, the clubmen cannot afford to dine together, except in one instance, that of the Old Bell Club. A few years ago on this day, twenty or more sick clubs might have been seen, dressed in their best, matching to church and parading of each society; but their ranks are now broken. Some of the numbers of honest industrious men, who in better times paid in hope that, when old age and sickness overtook them, they should have support, are doomed to receive from the parish what they anticipated they were providing for themselves.

Hospital parade entering Dudley Castle grounds. The banner is that of the Dudley United Friendly Societies (1932)

Part of the same hospital parade as shown in the previous illustration gathers in Dudley Market Place

The setback does not seem to have been permanent. F.W. Hackwood wrote in 1924: 'in many places to the present day advantage is taken of the favourable weather reasonably to be expected at this time of year by the village clubs and friendly societies to make an annual parade of the streets with flags and bands, every member decked with his badge of office, and resplendent in the regalia of the order to which he subscribes'.

At Wednesbury, not only did clubs walk on Whit Monday but the town's Sunday schools jointly attended a church service, then marched to the market place. After this the scholars were given buns in a convenient field or hall. Dudley's United Friendly Societies, starting in 1872 and continuing for at least sixty years (though not always on Whit Monday), organised an annual 'hospital parade' from the market place to the castle. Photographs of 1932 show over 300 people taking part.

Such gatherings were very decorous, compared with the wild scenes of an earlier era during the wakes (see chapter 11) and the midsummer bonfires. According to Lawley there are 'many references' to bonfires on St John's Day (24 June), including this from St Leonard's, Bilston, in 1665: 'For three loads of coal for the watch, 1s. 5d.'. Churches were decorated at Midsummer, as well as at Whitsuntide, with birch and broom preferred.

August Bank Holiday

Like the Whit Monday bank holiday, this was instituted in 1871, initially only for banks, but soon adopted generally, on (originally) the first Monday in

August Bank Holiday crowds at Dudley castle in the early 1950s

August. Dudley Castle strongly featured as a desirable destination on that day, and also (after 1937) the zoo. The Corbett Hospital near Stourbridge opened in August 1893 with a fête and parade of friendly societies. The fund-raising fête

A fête and parade of Friendly Societies was an annual fund-raising event for the Corbett Hospital at Stourbridge. The float shown here took part in 1927

continued annually on August bank holiday Monday, with up to 30,000 people attending. Cliff Willetts described the attractions of the day:

> We watched the tight rope walkers, clowns, Punch and Judy. For the gardeners there was a vegetable and flower show. The highlight was a huge gas-filled balloon, and we watched it with the same fascination as today's [1977] children watch Concorde. We had an afternoon and evening's enjoyment for 1s. 5d. We started back at dusk to get back to see the firework display at 10 p.m. People for many miles round went to their bedrooms and other vantage points to see the grandeur of the display.

All Saints', St Clement's, St Catherine's and St Thomas's Days

All Saints' Day (1 November) was also known as All Hallows, the eve of which is Hallowe'en. The profusion of witches' hats and brooms, devils' masks and tridents, together with extravagant parties and trick or treating, leading up to and at Hallowe'en, are innovations of the last decade or so. It is worth remembering, though, that trick or treating, castigated as an alien importation from America, originally crossed the Atlantic from these islands in the other direction.

On All Saints' or All Souls' (2 November) Days a custom called 'souling' took place, when groups of people went from door to door singing and asking originally for the 'soul' cakes specially baked for the occasion, and also fruit. Later, the special cakes were made no more, though the begging songs retained the appeal for:

The custom, widespread in Cheshire and Shropshire, obtained only in parts of Staffordshire, and in the Black Country seems to have been recorded only at Walsall and Bilston. In the latter G.T. Lawley heard as a schooboy in 1857 a fuller version of the song which seems to hark back to pre-Reformation theology:

Soul day, soul day,
We be come a-souling;
Pray, good people, remember the poor,
And give us all a soul cake.
Soul day, soul day,
One for Peter, two for Paul,
Three for him who made us all.
An apple, a pear, a plum or a cherry,
Or any good thing to make us merry.
Soul day, soul day,
We have all been praying
For the soul departed:
So, pray, good people, give us a cake,
For we are all poor people,
Well known to you before;
So give us a cake for charity's sake,
And our blessing we'll leave at your door.
Soul, soul, for an apple or two,
If you have no apples pears will do;
If pears are scarce then cakes from your pan,
Give us our souling and we'll be gone.

Souling was the first of a number of occasions in the autumn and early winter when poorer people were traditionally permitted a ritual request for assistance, in kind and in money, from their more affluent neighbours. 'Clementing' and 'catterning' came next, and took their names from St Clement's and St Catherine's Days (23 and 25 November respectively). As early as 1686 Robert Plot, the historian of Staffordshire, noted that in a clog almanac (a perpetual calendar inscribed on a length of wood or other material, 'still in use here amongst the meanest sort of people'; see illustration overleaf), 'a *pot* [marked] against the 23 of *Novemb.* for the Feast of St *Clement*, from the ancient custom of going about that night, to begg drink to make merry with'. He does not say whether the revellers chanted or sang, but children collecting on St Clement's Day certainly did. A correspondent from Worcestershire sent a set of words to William Hone for his *Every-day Book* in 1827, and Rev. Edward Bradley ('Cuthbert Bede') recorded another thirty years later at Enville, where in December 1912 children were still singing:

Clemeny, clemeny, year by year,
Some of your apple and some of your pear;
Apple or pear, plum or cherry,
Any good thing to make us merry.
One for Peter, one for Paul,
Three for the merry man under the wall.

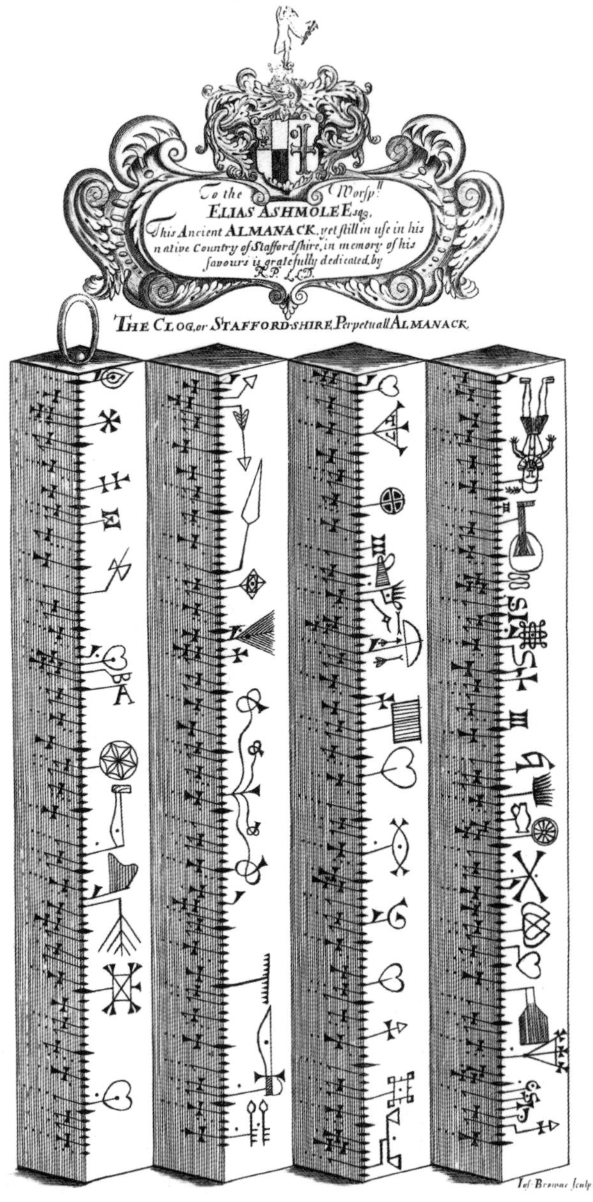

'THE CLOG, or STAFFORD-SHIRE, Perpetuall ALMANACK'. Plot presented the example shown to Elias Ashmole, and it is now in the Ashmolean Museum, Oxford. Two others are in the William Salt Library, Stafford. The pot indicating St Clement's Day is in the lower part of the right-hand column, and St Catherine's Day, two notches later, is marked by a wheel. Christmas Day, according to Plot, is signalled by 'a Horn; the ancient vessel in which the Danes *use to* Waysale, *or drink healths; signifying that this is the time we ought to rejoyce and make merry'*

Butler, butler, fill your bowl.
If you fill it of the best,
God will send your soul to rest;
If you fill it of the small,
Down will come butler, bowl and all.

Pray good mistress and master sitting by the fire,
Here we come clemening year by year all around the mire.
Up a long ladder and down a short pole,
Give us an apple and we'll be gone.
Hip, hip, hooray.

Clemening or clementing also took place at Kingswinford, Oldbury, Penn, Walsall, Wolverhampton, and no doubt elsewhere. In his book, *The Folklore of Staffordshire*, Jon Raven relates how in response to a newspaper appeal in 1965 a Mr W.H. Hickman came forward to say that over seventy years earlier he gone round the streets of Wolverhampton with other children, singing a version of the clemeny words to 'a see-sawing chant of no particular musical merit'. He added that they 'performed for the edification of the gentry, for you may be sure we chose only the houses which, outwardly at least, looked as though there was likely to be a welcome response'.

St Clement, who had to work as a miner for a time, and was reputedly martyred by being tied to an anchor and thrown into the sea, seems to have been viewed sympathetically by Black Country colliers and metalworkers. He was the patron saint of blacksmiths, who knew him affectionately as Old Clem. West Bromwich Old Church is dedicated to him. His day, as well as for clemening, was known for games with apples, and for that reason called Bite-apple Day. In Bilston, Wednesbury and neighbouring areas participants with hands kept rigorously behind backs tried to take bites out of apples suspended on strings from a nail or hook in the ceiling. Sometimes, though, they were allowed the use of a fork with which to impale the fruit. A variation on the game was to have hanging from a string a lath with an apple fixed at one end and a lighted candle at the other. In trying to take a bite of the apple a player often encountered the flame of the candle. At Sedgley, E.A. Underhill, whose family called the occasion 'apple and candle night', had the additional game of trying 'to bite at apples thrown into a jowl of water'. His version of the 'old ditty sung on that day' runs:

Clemeny, clemeny, clemeny mine,
A good red apple and a pint of wine,
Some of your mutton and some of your veal;
If it is good pray give me a deal:
If it is not pray give me some salt.

Butler, butler, fill you bowl;
If thou fillest of the best,
The Lord'll send your soul to rest.
If thou fillest it of the small,
Down goes butler, bowl and all.
Apple, pear, plum or cherry,
And good thing to make us merry;
A bouncing buck and a velvet chair,
Clement comes but once a year:
Off with the pot and on with the pan,
A good red apple and I'll be gone.

At Walsall until the mid-nineteenth century there was another apple custom on St Clement's Day. Boys from the grammar school were allowed into the sessions courtroom at the Guildhall, where they scrambled for apples thrown from the magistrates' bench. At the same time nuts and also heated copper coins were thrown to the crowd outside by the town crier. The town's accounts were audited on the same day. Before the church at Walsall was pulled down and rebuilt in 1820 it had four chapels, dedicated respectively to St Mary, St Nicholas, St Clement and St Catherine. At Brierley Hill, Netherton, Wollaston, and perhaps other places, the collecting of apples was done on St Catherine's Day, two days after St Clement's, with similar chants, changing clemening to catterning. Catherine's connections with the Black Country seem much more tenuous than those of Clement.

St Catherine, who was tortured by being broken on a wheel (shown in the illustration), and so gave her name to the modern firework

A last chance before Christmas for the poor to seek some help was provided by St Thomas's Day (21 December), when people went round 'thomasing' or 'gooding'. A correspondent in the periodical, *Notes and Queries*, noted in 1857 that in many parts of Staffordshire representatives of every poor household in the parish sought alms: 'The clergyman is expected to give a shilling to each person, and at all the houses a subsidy is looked for, either in money or in kind'. The custom was also recorded from Oldbury in Worcestershire.

Some forty years later the *Bilston Mercury* reported this local rhyme (which, as it happens, was shared with Darlaston and Wednesbury):

Well a day, well a day,
St Thomas goes too soon away,
Then your gooding we do pray,
For the good time will not stay.
St Thomas grey, St Thomas grey,
The longest night and the shortest day.
Please to remember St Thomas's Day.

A shorter version at Rowley Regis simply said: 'Please to remember St Thomas's Day,/And do not turn the poor away'. Underhill at Sedgley remembered: 'The longest night and the shortest day,/ Please remember St Thomas's Day'. As late as 1927 a local newspaper reported:

> On St Thomas's Day, this week, as in preceding years, the aged people in Rowley Regis and Halesowen made a tour of the district with the oft-heard cry: 'Please to spare a copper [coin], it's St Thomas's Day'. Shopkeepers anticipate the visit, and in districts where people are so jealous of and conformable to the maintenance of old customs, genuine 'Thomases' are rarely refused. … The memory of this custom [which, according to the writer, dated back to the seventeenth century, when penny and twopenny loaves, 'together with other charities', were distributed each year on St Thomas's Day] naturally lingers with those who are able to benefit by it, and probably its fortunate, and not altogether coincident, proximity to Christmas has a lot to do with its survival.

Christmas

A curious preliminary was featured in the early 1870s in the *Wolverhampton Chronicle's* 'Notes and Queries':

> It was usual fifty years ago, and continued for many years after that time, for working boys, during the four or five weeks before Christmas, to join in parties of about four, five, six, or seven, to start out each weekday morning at about four or five o'clock, with tin kettles or old iron pans, and to beat them as hard as they could along the streets. The more noise they made the better it was considered, as their object was to awaken the sleepers in order that they might rise early to begin work. Many boys who were awakened by the earliest 'tin kettlers', as they were called, formed themselves into parties and went through a few streets, 'beating up'. If the old watchmen had not left their rounds they sometimes dispersed these inharmonious musicians, but many working men considered the custom a valuable one. I do not know how early, or rather, how much earlier than my own recollection this 'tin kettling' began.

The rough music was clearly welcomed by fellow workers at a time of year when waking up in the morning for those who may not have had watches or clocks was particularly difficult.

A week or two before Christmas in about 1900, preparations at Sedgley, Wednesbury and neighbouring parishes began with the killing of a fatted pig, from which pork pies and pig's puddings would be made. The housewife's next tasks would be to prepare mince pies and plum puddings.

G.T. Lawley (born in 1845) saw in his youth on Christmas Eve this elaborate spectacle:

> Another custom no longer celebrated was what was once known as the 'sword dance'. It was performed on Christmas Eve, before the residence of the principal inhabitants, by bands of colliers, sometimes as many as twenty in a band. Decorated with sprigs of holly and mistletoe, and armed with wooden swords. Two of their number, called Tommy and Bessy, were usually dressed in skins and masks of the most grotesque fashions, making them look not unlike some of the fantastic figures in Saxon mummeries. They were accompanied by a fiddler or musician of some kind, and two or three lads, also fantastically dressed, carrying lanterns made of immense swedes, hollowed out and cut to represent grim human faces, to give this group as grotesque an appearance as possible. They proceeded at first slowly to cross their wooden swords, changing their position to the music of a fiddle. While the dance was proceeding the speed of their movements was gradually increased until they seemed to be engaged in mortal combat. Their proceedings were accompanied by the singing of a carol, which they timed to end with the dance. Tommy and Bessy meanwhile went through a dance on their own account, putting themselves into a variety of ridiculous postures to rouse the mirth and liberality of the spectators. The carol, sung on this occasion, the present writer took down at the time, and it ran as follows:
>
> Christmas comes but once a year,
> Give us of your beef and beer.
> If the beer is getting low,
> And the beef is gone also,
> Wine and mince pies give instead,
> Or money, that we may be fed.
> Merry is the Christmas time,
> Merry is our simple rhyme,
> A 'Merry Christmas' to you all.

A rather more gentle appeal for contributions survives from 1819 in the shape of an appeal, printed by Joseph Heming (for whom, see page 216), which was probably left at suitable houses to prepare the way for a later personal call (see panel opposite).

The Stourbridge Lamplighter's Address

Chill blustering winds, nor driving rain,
Hail, Frost, nor Snow, do me restrain;
Anxious my willing feet are ever
Resolv'd to travel in all sorts of weather,
Lighting your paths, when bright SOL [the sun] is down,
Each night with pleasure, I go thro' the town,
Since you, my friends, my willing labours crown.

Pray then, my patrons, who dispos'd may be,
Remember 'tis Christmas time — and think of me.
I will your approbation strive to gain,
Contrive to have my lamps well trimm'd and clean,
Expecting your kind favours to obtain.

On Christmas Eve mistletoe placed on the altar at Wolverhampton's collegiate church (St Peter's) was then blessed and given to the members of the congregation, who prized it for its medicinal properties. Lawley, who says the practice continued at least until 1900 adds that it was considered unlucky to take down mistletoe hung up at Christmas until the Christmas Eve following: 'in some houses the old mistletoe bush is still to be seen hanging from the ceiling, dry and dusty, but sacred until its purpose is served'. Church registers from Bilston and Darlaston also record expenditure for holly and mistletoe at Christmas. The same three churches show payments to ringers for peals heralding the arrival of Christmas Day.

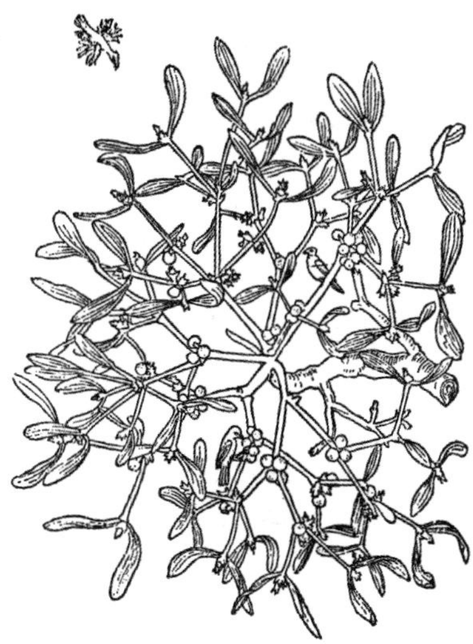

*Mistletoe (*Viscum album*)*

'No one who has passed through the district when the Christmas show of meat, game, and poultry were on view', wrote F.W. Hackwood in 1898, 'would for a moment doubt the loyalty of the people to King Christmas'. Amy Lyons wrote that 'Black Country people, colliers, ironworkers, and those of the labouring class, washed down their Christmas fare of tripe and onions, liver and bacon, cow heels, etc., with a bountiful supply of home brewed beer'. Some of the beer was set on the hob to warm, some, known as a nob, left to stay cool on a table. Lyons suggests that the question, 'Wut have a hob or a nob?' may have led to the expression, 'hob-nobbing'. Slang dictionaries, though, say that it meant drinking together, and then simply having an intimate conversation.

The huge gulf in the Black Country of the past between the poverty of the many and the wealth of the few is dramatically illustrated by different stories of Christmas cheer. For Cliff Willetts at Cradley Heath 'it was just another break from school. We really did hang our stockings up, usually over the fireguard. Even then, the stocking was big enough to hold our presents. It never varied. It was an apple, orange, nuts and a new penny. I don't know how our parents managed to get that new penny every year. Perhaps an understanding mint struck them specially for poor children. The only variation was a 'sucker [? sugar] pig' which cost a halfpenny'.

In 1819, some seventy-five years before Willetts's birth, Viscount Dudley and Ward, 'the rich man's model and the poor man's friend', kept open house at Himley Hall for the twelve days of Christmas:

> The boar's head was receiving final touches in the enormous vaulted kitchen, with ovens large enough to bake the enormous quantities of bread made from ten sacks of flour weekly, and given away to the poor nailers of Sedgley and Himley. Huge turkeys were revolving on the smoke jacks. The long passages, with curious beams and boarded ceilings, were lighted only be deep circular holes, covered with thick glass, but originally horn. At the far distant end was a slaughter-house, a very necessary apartment when a home farm was an adjunct of every nobleman's establishment. At no great distance was the brewery, with enormous vats and ladling jars; one beer barrel so large, it was named 'Big Ben'. Vaulted and cloistered passages led to the wine cellars and muniment room, where were kept the deeds and hatchments in use at funerals. Still rooms, in which her ladyship's elderwater, perfumes and salves were prepared, were close to the servants' hall, above the fireplace of which was the axiom, 'Waste not, want not; repeat no idle tales'. Ancient retainers, in picturesque garb, waited at the festive board. Large branches of yew adorned the high mantelpiece carved with the family arms. On the completion of the feast the company adjourned to the music room, where songs and dances were played on the earl's new organ.

In the servants' hall, when supper of groaty pudding and mulled ale was ready, the waits were ushered in, and sang:

> The cock sot up in the yew tree,
> And the hen come chatterin' by.
> I wish you a merry Christmas
> And a good fat pig in the sty.

The waits were originally paid municipal musicians, but the word seems to have been used in the Black Country to mean any instrumentalists and singers doing the rounds during the Christmas season, as in this passage by Hackwood, referring to Sedgley in the first minutes of Christmas Day:

> The practice of the 'carol singers' in the Black Country is for them to wait until the bells have ended their 'merry midnight peal' before they sally forth, and then to commence their carols at the houses of those most likely to bestow 'largesse' in honour of the season. Some people sit up to receive them liberally with 'cakes and ale'. Generally, however, after singing a carol 'the waits' pass on, and call again for the customary donation when the household is astir next day preparing for the Christmas dinner.

Amy Lyons, mentioning waits at Wednesbury, comments: 'Windows and doors would be thrown open, and the merry-making folk would stop their merriment to listen to the singing of these quaint old carols'.

Of course, as well as listening to the waits, people sang themselves. 'They gathered around the harmonium or organ', wrote J. Wilson Jones, 'and sang the local carols, mainly composed by a Rowley Regis nailmaker, Mr Joseph Parkes'. One of Parkes's tunes, which he called 'Rowley Regis', became well known as an alternative melody for the carol, 'Brightest and best'. Another of his compositions, 'Come again, Christmas', was sung until her death in 1979 by Lucy Woodall of Old Hill.

Some of the carols claimed to be local were jealously guarded versions of items in fact widely known. For example, the so-called 'Gornal Nailmakers' Carol', beginning 'O the Jews they crucified him/And nailed him to a tree', was known in much of England and as far afield as Newfoundland. Willenhall was noted for carol singing; as early as 1860 William White noted: 'Neither in Willenhall, or its suburb, called New Invention, must you look for loveliness;

but of good bread and meat, rabbits and poultry, you will see abundance; shops of booksellers also, one stored with Wesleyan books and religious stories; the other with light reading — *The Willenhall News* — *The Gipsey* [*sic*] *Bride* — *The Bandit Chief* — and Christmas carols' — though he then quoted lines from a wassail song: 'Call up the butler of this house, put on his golden ring,/ Let him bring up a glass of beer, and the better we shall sing'.

Hackwood, remarking that 'the repertory of a Black Country band of carol singers was a wonderful assortment of Christmas lyrics, crude of language and quaint in expression', goes on to mention 'a Willenhall collection' which included not only 'universal favourites' such as 'While shepherds watched', 'Lo, the eastern Magi' and 'Crown him Lord of all', but 'local curiosities' like 'Dives and Lazarus', 'The Creation o' the World' and 'The Cock o' th' Dish'. Of 'Dives' he says it 'took twenty minutes to sing', though in fact it consists of fifteen short verses only. He may be on firmer ground with 'The Creation', for which he estimates forty minutes, partly because it runs to forty-four verses of four lines, and partly because of the manner in which it was sung '… by two voices, line by line alternately, and two lines repeated in unison. It was sung andante, with a pause on the last note of the line; and the invariable custom was that if a mistake was made the singers had to begin it all over again, a custom fruitful of much liveliness in a Christmas tavern sing-song'. The only known sighting (or rather hearing) of the tune (the original follows) was in a small town, Staceyville, in Maine, USA, where in 1942 M. Olney recorded a version from Mr Jack McNally which he had learned from his father, an officer in the British army stationed in Canada. The tune perfectly fits the words, two verses at a time, from the Dudley publication, *A Good Christmas Box* (see below), of a century earlier. I quote the first section only of this, with McNally's melody.

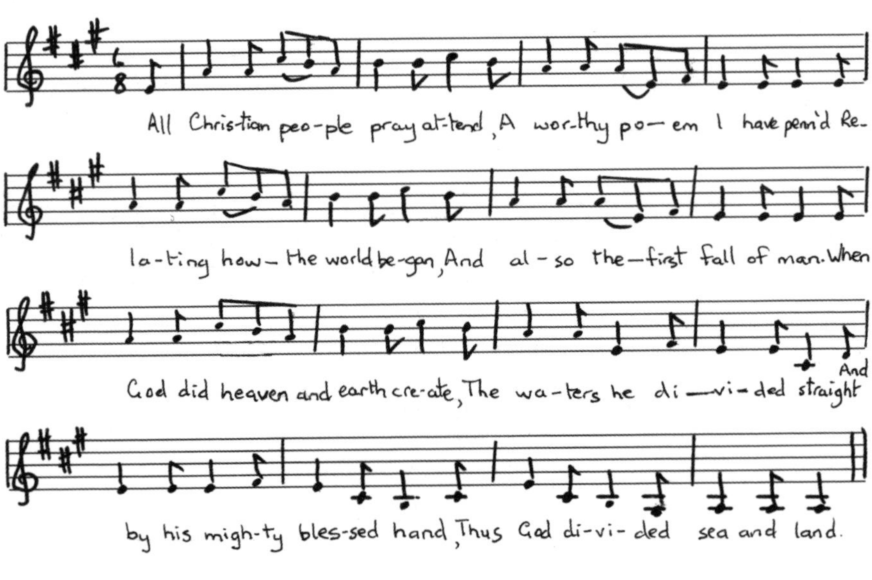

God gave command and there was light,
The sun by day, the moon by night,
The stars and planets too withal,
Was placed within this spcious ball.
The cattle, beasts, and birds with wings,
And every kind of creeping things;
All fruits and herbs of yielding seed,
Was by the hand of God decreed.

He saw 'twas good and lik'ed it well,
As we from holy writ may tell;
And in six days we understand,
Perform'd the work he took in hand.
For when the sixth day was began,
God said, come let us now make man;
In our own image he shall be,
To glorify our majesty.

The normally impeccable Hackwood goes on to describe 'The Cock o' th' Dish' as 'a relic of the old cock fighting days' and 'an ancient monkish composition', containing 'many phrases that were unadulterated blasphemy', of which he can bring himself to quote only two lines: 'The roasted cock that lies i' the dish/ Shall crow full fences three'. In reality, this is a fragment from a lengthy ballad, 'The Carnal [crow] and the Crane', listed by William Hone in 1823 as one of the 'Christms Carols now annually Printed'. It is full of biblical tales, some apocryphal, dealing with the birth and early days of Jesus, the threat of Herod, the flight into Egypt and the massacre of the innocents. In a short sequence, sung separately as 'The Cock i' th' Dish', a roasted bird miraculously comes back to life:

[Tune from Warwickshire].

The wise men soon espy'd it,
And told the king on high,
A Princely Babe was born that night
No king should e'er destroy.

If this be true King Herod said
As thou tellest unto me:
This roasted cock that lies in the dish
Shall crow full fences three.

The cock soon freshly feather'd was
By the work of God's own hand,
And then three fences crowed he,
In the dish where he did stand.

The miracle is somewhat counter-productive, since Herod sees it as proof of a rival, and gives orders for all boys up to the age of two to be killed.

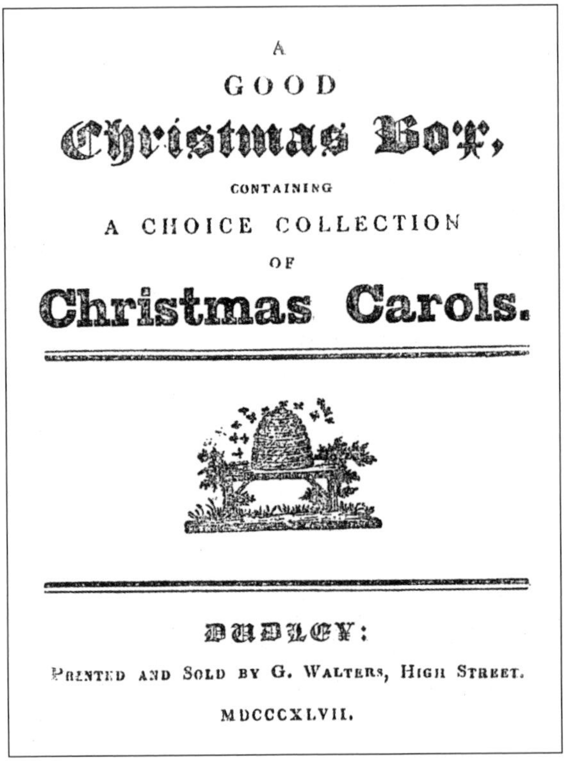
A
GOOD
Christmas Box,
CONTAINING
A CHOICE COLLECTION
OF
Christmas Carols.

DUDLEY:
PRINTED AND SOLD BY G. WALTERS, HIGH STREET.
MDCCCXLVII.

The Title Page of A Good Christmas Box

It is possible to be clear about the three carols discussed by Hackwood because they all appear, in company with over fifty others, not in a Willenhall collection, but in *A Good Christmas Box*, printed by George Walters (for whom, see also chapter 12) of Dudley in 1847. 'It is a type of book', wrote 'H. W. S.' in 1927, 'which at one time was suspended on string in little shops during the Christmas season, or sold by ballad singers'. With perhaps the solitary exception of 'While shepherds watched', its contents were sung, not in churches and chapels, but in pubs and public spaces. Other printers, especially in Birmingham, but also in the Black Country, issued single sheets with the texts of one or two carols. J. Rann (for whom, see also chapter 12) of Dudley, for example, printed two items later included in *A Good Christmas Box*, 'The Virgin Unspotted' (see panel opposite) and 'A New Carol for Christmas', of which the latter turns out to be 'While shepherds' — new in fact in 1700 when it was written by Nahum Tate.

The Virgin Unspotted

A Virgin unspotted the prophets foretold,
should bring forth a saviour, which now we behold;
to be our Redeemer from death, hell, and sin,
which Adam's transgression involved us in.

[Chorus]
Therefore let's be merry, cast sorrow away,
our Saviour Christ Jesus was born on this day.

Through Bethlehem city, in Judea it was,
that Joseph and Mary together did pass;
and for to be taxed wherever they came,
since Caesar Augustus commanded the same.

But Mary's full time being come, as we find,
she brought forth her first-born, to save all mankind,
the inn being full, for this heavenly guest,
no place could be found to lay him to rest.

But Mary, blest Mary, so meek and so mild
soon wrapped in swaddlings this heavenly child,
contented she laid him where oxen were fed,
the great God of mercy approved the deed.

To teach us humility all this was done,
then learn we from hence all imprudence to shun,
a manger his cradle, who came from above,
the great God of mercy, of peace, and of love.

Then presently after the shepherds did spy,
vast numbers of angels to stand in the sky,
all happy their converse, so sweet they did sing
all glory and praise to our heavenly king.

Despite such evidence of the circulation of traditional carols in the Black Country, finding someone who sang some of them proved difficult until George Dunn (see also chapter 12) of Quarry Bank was discovered. Then, at last, some of the texts were matched with tunes. He knew the melody of 'The Seven Joys of Mary' but did not remember all the words given by Hackwood, who called it 'a Wednesbury Carol', 'of which the crudities of language and of religious sentiment … testify to the genuineness of its antiquity' (see panel overleaf).

The Seven Joys of Mary

The first great joy that Ma-ry had, It was the joy of one. To
see her own son, Je-sus Christ a — suc-king at her breast-bone, A-
suc-king at her breast-bone, my boys, O hap-py 'may we be! Praise
Fa-ther, Son and Ho-ly Ghost to all e-ter-ni-ty

The second great joy that Mary had,
It was the joy of two,
To see her own son Jesus Christ
A-making the lame to goo,
A-making the lame, etc.

The third great joy that Mary had,
It was the joy of three,
To see her own son Jesus Christ
A-making the blind to see,
A-making, etc.

The fourth great joy that Mary had,
It was the joy of four,
To see her own son Jesus Christ
A-preaching to the poor,
A-preaching, etc.

The fifth great joy that Mary had,
It was the joy of five,
To see her own son Jesus Christ
A-making the dead alive,
A-making, etc.

The sixth great joy that Mary had,
It was the joy of six,
To see her own son Jesus Christ
Raised on the crucifix,
Raised on, etc.

The seventh great joy that Mary had,
It was the joy of seven,
To see her own son Jesus Christ
Ascending up into heaven,
Ascending, etc.

George Dunn also knew two different versions, tune and words, of 'While shepherds'. Many of the oral tunes once well known in the Black Country are now irrecoverably lost. 'H. W. S.', quoted earlier, explained that he spent many years searching for an item called 'The Little Room', and that 'many aged Black Country people ... said ... that they had heard this carol many times, but they could not remember the words'. He was delighted to find the words in *A Good Christmas Box*, but for a tune we should have to go out of the Black Country to a Shropshire or Herefordshire source.

One other feature of the Christmas scene was the mumming play which survived into the twentieth century at Cradley Heath, Darlaston, Pelsall and Walsall Wood, and were also reported from Smethwick, Wednesbury and Wednesfield. Phil Drabble, who says it was put on either on Bonfire Night or at Christmas by lads calling themselves guisers, who blacked their faces, begged or borrowed costumes appropriate to the characters they played (Little Billy Wittle, squire's son, stranger and doctor), and toured likely houses looking for contributions to their collection. In a letter of 1962 to Christopher Cawte Drabble adds that the guisers, from a range of places running from Pelsall to Cradley Heath, were commonly children, performing at Christmas for mince pies and money, until 1939. Drabble prints only a few minutes' worth of dialogue, but Hackwood gives a much fuller version, heard 'in the bar parlour of a Wednesbury tavern in 1879':

Good St George and the Bold Hector

Enter, after a loud knock at the door, Open-the-door
OPEN-THE-DOOR
The first that doth step in is good old Open-the-door,
And, lads, if you'll believe me well, I've opened many a score.
With sly wink and gesture at this, he next proceeds to clear an open space for the other actors, who have now followed him in, but leave him the centre of the stage.
Give room, give room, in this gallant hall, give us room to play,
And you shall see a right merry masque upon this happy Christmas Day.
So shift the chairs and make a good wide ring,
That you may see us well, both act and dance and sing.
Silence, brave gents and lovely ladies fair! Now give an eye
To see and hear our queer, quaint comico-tragedy.
He retires. St George takes centre of stage.
ST GEORGE
Here come I, St George, approved of old,
A knight of valour and virtue, stout and bold.
Many the gallant deeds that I have done,
Clean victories, both east and west, that I have won.
In deadly marsh, and eke on sandy plain,
Giants, griffins and rocs in swarms I've slain.

'Twas I that brought the famed dreaded dragon to slaughter,
For which I gained the Egyptian monarch's handsome daughter.
Enter to him Bold Hector.
HECTOR
Who's this that boasts in Hector's hearing?
Of all braves and braggarts I'll soon make a clearing!
I am bold Hector! Bold Hector is my name,
And with my trusty sword I always win the game!
Enter, smartly, Slasher.
SLASHER
The game, sir? What game, sir? This game's not in your power,
The brave St George will slash and slay you dead within the hour!
Enter, stately, the Black Prince.
PRINCE
Not so fast, my gallant lads and heroes all!
Fair's fair, brave's brave, but when you try a fall,
Sides and chances equal, for Englishmen is reckoned —
So to see all things square, I'll act for one as second.
SLASHER
Well said, most noble prince. To make the combat square,
You second good St George, and I will see Bold Hector fair.
The two principals and two seconds prepare their arms. Enter, deliberately, Safety Sam.
SAM
Hear one last word for peace from Safety Sam of Staffordshire!
Peace is a noble thing, though it may be bought too dear.
So ere to mortal strife these noble gallants do repair,
'May God defend the right!' be our one and only prayer.
Enter, with roguish sliding shuffle, Beelzebub.
BEELZEBUB
Here comes I, sly old Beelzebub!
Over my shoulder I carries my club,
And in my hand a frying pan —
So don't you think I'm a jolly old man?
If you think I'm cutting it rather fat,
Just drop a penny in the old man's hat —
A useful penny it is you'll then lay out,
If you want to see the whole of our fine play out.
Enter, impishly and perkily, the little Blue Dwarf.
DWARF
Stand off, stand off! I've fought ten thousand duels on the Delves [area between Walsall and West Bromwich],
And all you knaves that want to fight had best defend yourselves.
No foe stands up but I'll hash and smash him as small as flies,
And sell his vile carcase to make nice mince pies —
Mince pies hot, mince pies cold,

Good mince pies at ten days old!

Black Prince coolly lifts him up bodily, throws him into the arms of Beelzebub, and carries him out. The two champions, St George and Bold Hector, and their seconds, Black Prince and Slasher, take the centre, and the combat begins. The fencing is done with much dancing round the ring, loud clashing of swords, and the excited shouts of the other actors. After many fierce lunges and rapid parries, and cracks on the head and legs with the flat of the swords, Hector is stabbed and falls prone.

SLASHER

O champion saint, O holy George! What hast thou done?
Thou hast gone and slain my dear, my only son!
He was indeed my first-born, and my true-begotten heir —
I cannot, will not, idly stand and see him bleeding there!
A doctor, a doctor! I'll give ten thousand pound
If but a good and learned doctor can be found!

Enter, slowly and sedately, the Doctor.

DOCTOR

Here come I, the great and learned Doctor Brown,
The cleverest, safest doctor in all the town.
Crutches for lame ducks make I, and spectacles for poor blind bats,
Also barber-leech I am, to shave and bleed all pussy cats.
I've travelled far, in Italy, Titaly, Dudley Port and Old Spain,
But right glad am I to be once more in Wednesbury again.

SLASHER

What diseases, sir, are they you cure?

DOCTOR

Why, all diseases known, you may be sure:
The gout, the scurvy and the phtysic,
And all of them without a drop of physic.
So *(taking Hector gravely and skilfully by the hand)* you get up, sir, and sing that fine old song
Of one who's not been dead for very long.

HECTOR (rising to his feet again)

Once I was dead but now I am alive,
God bless the doctor who made me to survive!
Through his great art I was not dead for very long,
And so to prove his skill, let me sing to you a live man's song!

Sings some popular song of the day, which has a chorus in which all can join.

BEELZEBUB

Our play is played and now we've done,
We hope we've given you lots of simple fun.
So if you think at all it's really funny
You'll fill our empty pokes with lots of money.
Send us away, please, now all is calm,
And sly old Beelzebub'll do you no harm.

Take notice that we've got no leathern bottle,
And nothing was poured down the dead man's throttle.
For your fun 'twas he fought and get himself slain,
For your money he'll rise and fight his battles o'er again.
We hope this nonsense your spirits will joyful rouse,
So we bid you good day and peace be on this noble house!
All join hands to dance round, to the accompaniment of some other popular song, which at the end is changed to one which they march out, Beelzebub collecting the largesse in his frying pan.

'The bells ring out joyously both on Christmas Eve and New Year's Eve', wrote Amy Lyons. 'Forgetting in social pleasures the dangers incidental to their perilous calling, the colliers and their families keep up the Christmas trade of merriment and feasting in right good style'. The people of Rowley Regis believed that they had to remain awake on New Year's Eve until the old year had gone, since otherwise they would begin the new with six months' bad luck. To make doubly sure of good luck, on New Year's Day they ate Christmas pudding made at least seven days earlier. At Cradley Heath housewives would not sweep their floors before noon on New Year's Day lest they sweep their luck away.

Bibliography

Abbreviations

BCB	*Black Country Bugle*
BCM	*The Blackcountryman*
BGA	*Black Country Bugle Annual*
DUD	'Dudleiana' (see under Palfrey)
nd	no date of publication shown
np	no place of publication shown
NQ	*Notes and Queries*
STO	'Stourbridgeiana' (see under Palfrey)
TWAS	*Transactions of the Worcestershire Archaeological Society*
WHC	Worcestershire History Centre
WRO	Worcestershire Record Office
WWL	*Warwickshire and Worcestershire Life*

Note

All books were published in London unless otherwise stated

Allen, Walter *Black Country* 1946

Allies, Jabez *The British, Roman, and Saxon Antiquities and Folk-lore of Worcestershire* 2nd ed., 1856 (orig. 1852)

Anon. *Around the Town, Views from Walsall Local History Centre* (Walsall, 1991)

'The Black Country', *Edinburgh Review* (April, 1863), 406-443

'The Crusading Curate of Rowley: the Rev. George Barrs', BGA (1979), 22-24

Down in Dingyshire, or, Sketches of Life in the Black Country 1873

'The Halesowen Nailers', BGA (1979), 39-40

'A Pretty Girl sings of a Drunken Man', BCM 3:4 (1970), 36-37

A Short History of West Bromwich West Bromwich, 1964

'Some old Bilston Quacks and Medicine Men', BGA (1979), 37-38

'Some Warlocks, Witches & Wizards of old Hell Lane', BGA (1995), 89

'Witchcraft in the Black Country. Strange Stories of Ancient Superstitions. Modern Beliefs in Good and Evil Omens', DUD VII (30.1.1926)

Barnsby, George J. *Social Conditions in the Black Country, 1800-1900* Wolverhampton, 1980

Socialism in Birmingham and the Black Country, 1850-1939 Wolverhampton, 1998

Barnsley, Peter *A Cradley Album* West Hagley, 1994

'An esteemed Black Country Woman – Lucy Woodall', BCM 4:4 (1971), 6-8

Bell, David *Ghosts and Legends of Staffordshire and the Black Country* Newbury, 1994

Bentley, Josiah *Bentley's History, Gazetteer, Directory and Statistics of Worcestershire* Birmingham, [1841]

Bentley's History and Guide to Dudley Birmingham, [1843]

Betjeman, John (ed.) *Collins Guide to English Parish Churches* 1959

Bibby, Bob *Grey Paes and Bacon. From the Heart of the Black Country* Bridgnorth, 2001

Bird, Vivian *Staffordshire* 1974

Bloomer, Edgar 'Black Country Chainmakers', STO XII (10.2.1917)

Booth, Geoffrey *The Midlands – Industrial Archaeology* 1973
Bott, Ian M. *Britain in Old Photographs: Wednesbury Revisited* Stroud, 1998
Bradford, Anne, and Roberts, Barrie *Midland Ghosts and Hauntings* Birmingham, 1994
Brailsford, Denis *Bareknuckles. A Social History of Prize-fighting* Cambridge, 1988
Brand, John *Observations on Popular Antiquities* 1877 (orig. 1777)
Brew, Alec *Wolverhampton Pubs* Stroud, 2004
Brockway, A. Fenner *Hungry England* 1932
Brown, Tom [? pseudonym for Thomas Pinnock, q.v.] 'Black Country Dialect', DUD I (7.8.1909)
'More Black Country Nicknames', DUD I (15.8.1910)
'The Black Country. I. Its Dialect compared with Chaucerian English', *Leisure Hour* (1893), 31-33
Tom Brown's Black Country Annual Wednesbury, 1893
Bubb, Geoffrey 'Jack Judge – a Retrospective', BCM 31:4 (1998), 50-51
Burne, Charlotte Sophia *Shropshire Folk-lore* 1883
'Souling, Clementing and Catterning. Three November Customs of the Western Midlands', *Folk-lore* 25 (1914), 285-299
Burritt, Elihu *Walks in the Black Country and its Green Borderland* Kineton, 1976 (orig. 1868)
Butler, Archie '"Monkey Island" and other Heath Town Curiosities', BGA (1985), 13-14
Cawte, E.C., Helm, Alex, and Peacock, N. *English Ritual Dance* 1967
C.E.B. 'Cradley Heath 60 Years Ago. Some Recollections', three articles, STO XXVI (26.6.1929-20.7.1929)
Chamberlain, Mary *Old Wives' Tales. The History of Remedies, Charms and Spells* Stroud, 2006
Chance, Hugh 'The Glass Makers of Smethwick', WWL 6:12 (Feb.1960), 445-447
Chandler, G., and Hannah, I.C. *Dudley as it was and as it is* 1949
Chapman, N.A. *A History of Coal Mining Around Halesowen* np, 1999
Chinn, Carl *Black Country Memories* Studley, 2004
Black Country Memories, 2 Studley, 2005
Chitham, Edward *The Black Country* 1972
Rowley Regis. A History Chichester, 2006
Clark, C.F.G. *The Curiosities of Dudley and the Black Country* Birmingham, 1881
Clarke, Bob, and Reuter, Michael *Britain in old Photographs: Stourbridge, Wollaston & Amblecote* Stroud, 1997
Britain in old Photographs: Wollaston & Amblecote. A Second Selection Stroud, 2000
Clulow, J. Walter *'Brierley Hill a Hundred Years Ago'*, DUD II (14.3.1914)
Coleridge, Samuel Taylor *Table Talk* 1917 (orig. 1812)
Court, W.H.B. *The Rise of the Midland Industries, 1600-1838* 1938
Craig, Sarah E. *'The Ghost of Sparrows Forge Lane'*, BGA (1984), 78
Dickens, Charles *The Old Curiosity Shop* 1840-1
Disraeli, Benjamin *Sybil, or, The Two Nations* 1845
Douglas, Alton, and Moore, Dennis (eds) *The Black Country Remembered* Wolverhampton, 1996
Memories of the Black Country Wolverhampton, 1985
Memories of Dudley Studley, 1999
Memories of Walsall Wolverhampton, 1990
Memories of West Bromwich Wolverhampton, 1990
Memories of Wolverhampton Wolverhampton, 1989
Drabble, Phil *Black Country* 1952
Staffordshire 1949
D.R.G. 'A Ballad of Brierley Hill', DUD III (11.11.1916)

'A Little Song on Place Names', DUD III (28.10.1916)
Dudley, Dud *Metallum Martis: or, Iron made with Pit-coale, Sea-coale, &c.* 1665 (reprinted in Clark, q.v.)
Duignan, W.H. 'The Dudley Riots', *Dudley Post* (Jan. 1881)
Ede, J.F. *History of Wednesbury* Wednesbury, 1962
Elmes, Simon *Talking for Britain. A Journey through the Nation's Dialects* 2005
Ellis, Jason *Glassmakers of Stourbridge and Dudley, 1612-2002* Harrogate, 2002
Elwell, C.J.L. 'Frederick William Hackwood. Historian or Journalistic Bohemian?' BCM 26:3 (1993), 16-21
'Robert Blatchford on the Cradley Heath Chainmakers and Samuel Butler on the ballad of Wedgbury Cocking', BCM 8:3 (1975), 12-17
'William Cobbett in the Black Country', BCM 32:1 (1998/9), 52-5
E.M. 'Wednesbury Wake', *Birmingham Iris* (Apr. 1839), 223-224
Engels, Frederick *The Condition of the Working Class in England* 1845 (reprinted in *Karl Marx and Frederick Engels on Britain* Moscow and London, 1953)
Faulkner, Christine *Hops and Hop-pickers* Brierley Hill, nd
Fletcher, Kate 'Living with Dialect', BCM 18:4 (1985), 30-1
Fletcher, M.H.W. *Netherton – Edward I to Edward VIII* Dudley, 1969 (orig. 1946)
Fraser, Antonia *The Gunpowder Plot* 1996
Goode, Dilys J. *Black Country Life, 1830-1880* Upton-on-Severn, 1994
Goodyear, G.H. *Stourbridge Old and New* Stourbridge, 1908
Gordon, John F. *The Staffordshire Bull Terrier Owner's Encyclopaedia* np, nd
Gough, G.H. *Black Country Stories* 5 vols, Dudley, 1934-1939 (omnibus edition, Birmingham, nd)
Griffith, George *Reminiscences and Records during Ten Years' Residence in the Midland Counties* Bewdley and Madeley, 1880
Griffiths, Stanley A. *Black Dots. Stories of the Midlands* Birmingham, 1943
More Black Dots Birmingham, 1944
Green, G. Harry 'Old Stourbridge', STO X (15.2.1913 and 22.2.1913)
Guttery, D.R. *From Broad-glass to Cut Crystal. A History of the Stourbridge Glass Industry* 1956
Gwilliam, H.W. 'Old Worcestershire Inns and Taverns', typescript, nd, in WHC
Worcestershire's Hidden Past Bromsgrove, 1991
Hackwood, F. W. *The Annals of Willenhall* Wolverhampton, 1908
Oldbury and Round About Wolverhampton and Birmingham, 1915
Sedgley Researches Dudley, 1898
Staffordshire Customs, Superstitions and Folklore East Ardsley, 1974 (orig. Lichfield, 1924)
Staffordshire Stories, historical and legendary; a miscellany of county lore and anecdote Stafford and Birmingham, 1906
The Story of the Black Country Wolverhampton, nd [1892]
Wednesbury Workshops Wednesbury, 1889
Haden, H. Jack 'Black Country Friendly Societies', BCM 6:2 (1973), 38-43
Notes on the Stourbridge Glass Trade Dudley, 1949
The 'Stourbridge Glass' Industry in the Nineteenth Century Tipton, 1971
Hatton, Charles *Black Country Folk* Birmingham, 1945
Hickling, A.J.M. *Black Country Pits* np, 1989
Homeshaw, E.J. *The Story of Bloxwich* Bloxwich, 1955
Hone, William (ed.) *The Every-day Book* vol.2, 1827
Hope, Robert Charles *The Legendary Lore of the Holy Wells of England, including Rivers, Lakes, Fountains, and Springs* 1893

Horne, J.S. 'Staffordshire Clog Almanacs', *North Staffordshire Field Club Transactions* 83 (1949), 13-28
Hoskins, W.G. *Chilterns to Black Country* 1951
Hunt, Julian *A History of Halesowen* Chichester, 2004
Hutton, William *A History of Birmingham* 1782
H.W.S. '"The Little Room": a Rare Carol', DUD VIII (13.12.1927)
Jackson, N.A. 'The hand-made Nail Industry in the Black Country and District', typescript, nd, in WHC
Jeavons, S.A. *The Monumental Effigies of Staffordshire* Oxford, 1955
J.M.F. 'Women in the Nail and Chain Trade', BCM 5:3 (1972), 55-8
Jones, Jim Williams 'One Man's Bilston', WWL 27:2 (apr. 1980), 32-33; 35
'One Man's Smethwick', WWL 27:10 (Dec.1980), 32-33; 35; 37
'The Spirit of the Black Country', WWL 25:12 (Feb. 1979), 48-49; 26:4 (June 1979), 94-95; 26:6 (Aug. 1979), 62-63; 26:7 (Sept. 1979), 64-65; 26:9 (Nov. 1979), 60-61
Jones, J. Wilson *History of the Black Country* Birmingham, nd [1950] (repr. Halesowen, nd)
Jones, R.G. *Family Almanack* Lye, 1877
Langford, J.L., et al. *Staffordshire and Warwickshire, Past and Present* 4 vols, nd [1884]
Langley, Tom *Tales of Puddingbag* np, 1978
The Tipton Slasher. His Life and Times np, nd [1971]
Lawley, G.T. 'The Black Country', DUD V (27.1.1923)
'The Black Country Dialect', DUD V (10.3.1923, 7.4.1923, 14.7.1923)
'Black Country Stories', DUD V (26.6.1923)
'Christening Customs and Superstitions', DUD V (9.12.1922)
A History of Bilston, in the County of Stafford, a Record of its Archaeology, Ecclesiology, Parochialia, Folklore, and Bibliography Bilston, 1893
'John Wilkinson, the Great Ironmaster', DUD V (17.3.1923)
'Local Burial Customs', DUD V (26.5.1923)
'Local Marriage Customs', DUD V (7.4.1923)
'Local Nursery Rhymes', DUD V (22.4.1922)
'New Year Customs', DUD IV (1.1.1921)
'South Staffordshire Stories. Cock Fighting as a Local Sport', DUD V (22.9.1923; 29.9.1923; 7.10.1923; 13.10.1923; 20.10.1923; 27.10.1923)
'South Staffordshire Stories. Midsummer Eve Superstitions', DUD III (26.6.1920)
'South Staffordshire Stories. Wife Selling', DUD V (6.8.1921)
'Whitsuntide Customs', DUD V (3.6.1922)
Lees-Milne, James *Worcestershire. A Shell Guide* 1964
Lewis, Marilyn (ed.) *Walsall Chronicle. An Oral History of Walsall* no.5, np, 1985
Lines, Charles 'The Fate of Haden Hall', WWL 21:8 (Oct. 1974), 82-84
Lones. T.E. *A History of Mining in the Black Country* Dudley, 1898
'Scraps of English Folklore: Worcestershire', *Folklore* 36 (1925), 85-88
'Worcestershire Folklore', *Folklore* 25 (1914), 370
Lyons, Amy *Black Country Sketches. A Series of Character Stories illustrating the Life of the Black Country District* 1901
Malcolmson, Robert W. *Popular Recreations in English Society, 1700-1850* Cambridge, 1973
McKean, Henry (ed.) *Picturesque Oldbury Past and Present; also, the Legend of St Brade* Oldbury, 1900 (repr. Halesowen, nd)
Meachem, Roger Clive *Victorian Hamstead – its People, its Colliery* Studley, 1988
Menefee, S.P. *Wives for Sale* Oxford, 1981
Miller, Hugh *First Impressions of England and its People* 1846
Moore, Gilbert 'The Black Acres', *Warwickshire and Worcestershire Magazine* (Jul. 1956), 194-195

Morgan, W. *Our Anuk, and Other Black Country Stories* Oldbury, 1909
Moss, Ron *Chain & Anchor Making in the Black Country* Stroud, 2006
Chainmaking in the Black Country Brierley Hill, nd
Murray, David Christie *A Capful o' Nails* 1896 (repr. np, 1973)
The Making of a Novelist. An Experiment in Autobiography 1894
Noake, John *Notes and Queries for Worcestershire* 1856
The Rambler in Worcestershire vol.1, Worcester, 1848; vol.2, London, 1851
Northall, G.F. *English Folk-rhymes* 1892
Norton, John 'In Praise of Woden's Town', WWL 26:3 (May 1979), 40-41; 43; 45
Opie, Iona and Peter *The Lore and Language of Schoolchildren* Oxford, 1959
Palfrey, H.E.(comp.) 'Dudleiana: newspaper cuttings related to all aspects of Dudley and district' 29 vols, 1890-1955, in WRO
'Foleys of Stourbridge', TWAS new ser. 21 (1945), 7-15
'Notes on the Early History of Stourbridge', STO XIV (14.2.1920; 21.2.1920; 13.3.1920; 20.3.1920; 27.3.1920; 3.4.19220; 10.4.1920; 17.4.1920)
'Stourbridgeiana: newspaper cuttings related to all aspects of Stourbridge and district' 76 vols, 1904-1956, in WRO
Palmer, F.P., and Crowquill, Arthur *The Wanderings of a Pen and Pencil* 1846
Palmer, Roy 'Black Country Stories', *English Dance and Song* 44:2 (1982), 6
(ed.) *George Dunn, the Minstrel of Quarry Bank. Reminiscences & Songs* Dudley, 1984
'George Dunn: 'Twenty-one Songs and Fragments', *Folk Music Journal* 2:4 (1973), 275-296
(ed.) *Poverty Knock. A Picture of Industrial Life in the Nineteenth Century through Songs, Ballads and Contemporary Accounts* Cambridge, 1974
The Folklore of Shropshire Logaston, 2004
Folklore of Warwickshire Stroud, 2004
The Folklore of Worcestershire Logaston, 2005
(ed., with Pamela Bishop and Katharine Thomson) *Songs of the Midlands* East Ardsley, 1972
Parsons, Harold *The Black Country* 1986
Murder and Mystery in the Black Country 1989
Payne, Mrs Alfred *Pits and Furnaces; or, Life in the Black Country* 1869
Peplow, H.T. 'Wolverhampton Street Scenes and Characters from Long Ago', BGA (1979), 11-12
Perks, Francis *A Selection of Poetry* Birmingham, 1853
Perry, Nigel *A History of Stourbridge* Chichester, 2001
Pike, E.R. (ed.) *Human Documents of the Industrial Revolution 1966*
Pinnock, Thomas 'The Black Country. II: Queer Customs'; 'The Black Country. III: Its Nicknames'; 'The Black Country. IV: Its Superstitions', *Leisure Hour* (1893), 112-114; 260-262; 340-341 respectively
Pitt, William *A Topographical History of Staffordshire* Newcastle-under-Lyne, 1817
Plot, Robert *The Natural History of Stafford-shire* Oxford, 1686
Poole, Charles Henry *Customs, Superstitions and Legends of the County of Stafford* nd [1875]
Priestley, J.B. *English Journey* 1934
Prince, H.H. *Old West Bromwich. The Story of Long Ago* West Bromwich, 1924
Quaestor [W. Byford Jones] *Vagabonding through the Midlands* 1935
Radford, Peter 'More about the Ballad of Wedgebury Cocking', BCM 9:1 (1976), 28-30
Raven, Jon *The Book of the Black Country* Wolverhampton, 1988
Stories, Customs, Superstitions, Tales & Folklore of the Black Country and Staffordshire Wolverhampton, 1986
The Folklore of Staffordshire 1978

The Urban and Industrial Songs of the Black Country and Birmingham Wolverhampton, 1977
Raven, Michael *Black Country Towns and Villages* Wolverhampton, 1991
A Guide to Staffordshire and the Black Country, the Potteries and the Peak Market Drayton, 2005
Raven, Michael and Jon (eds) *Folklore and Songs of the Black Country* Wolverhampton, 1965
Folklore and Songs of the Black Country and West Midlands Wolverhampton, 1966
Folklore and Songs of the Black Country and West Midlands vol. 3, Wolverhampton, 1967
Rees, Elizabeth A. (comp.) *Bilston in old Photographs* Stroud, 1988
Richards, D.H. 'Old-time Black Country Collieries and Colliers', BCM 13:2 (1980), 55-56; 60; 62-63
Richardson, Ruth *Death, Dissection and the Destitute* 1989
Rollinson, W. 'In the Days of our Grandfathers. Reminiscences of old Brierley Hill', DUD II (14.10.1911)
'In the Days of our Grandfathers. More Reminiscences of Old Brierley Hill', DUD II (28.10.1911 and 11.11.1911)
Rolt, L.T.C. *Worcestershire* 1949
Roud, Steve *The English Year* 2006
Rowlands, M.B. 'Foley Family', article in the *Oxford Dictionary of National Biography Oxford, 2004*
Schwarz, Hans and Lena *The Halesowen Story* np, 1955
Scott, W. *Stourbridge and its Vicinity* Stourbridge, 1832
Shaw, Stebbing *The History and Antiquities of Staffordshire* 2 vols, 1798-1801
Shaw, T.V. *A Glossary of Black Country Words and Phrases* Birmingham, 1930
Shepherd, A.P. *The Story of the Parish Church of St Thomas, Dudley* Dudley, 1979
Simpson, Jacqueline, and Roud, Steve *A Dictionary of English Folklore* Oxford, 2000
Smiles, Samuel *Self-help* 1859
Smith, Abraham *A Scriptural and Moral Catechism, designed chiefly to lead the Minds of the rising Generation to the Love and Practice of Mercy, and to expose the horrid Nature & exceeding Sinfulness of Cruelty to the dumb Creatures* Birmingham, 2nd ed., nd [? 1834]
Smith, Francis Maylett *A G.P.'s Progress to the Black Country* Hythe, 1984
Solomon, Philip *Black Country Ways in Bygone Days* Willenhall, 1992
Somers, F. and K.M. *Halas Hales Hales Owen* Halesowen, 1932
Spittal, C.J. 'Some literary and historical reflections on "Wednesbury Cocking"', BCM 15:1 (1982), 14-18
Staffordiensis 'A Black Country Legend', NQ 4th ser. 7 (1871), 71
Starkey, Eva M. 'Black Country Dialect', BCM 3:1 (1970), 14-17
Taylor, David *Images in Wood. The Medieval Misericord Carvings of St Matthew's Church, Walsall* Halesowen, 2006
Taylor, Walter H. 'The Nail Shop. Memories of Halesowen', BCB (14 Feb. 1978)
Tregartha, John *The Bank of Faith* Manchester, nd [18th. Century]
Underhill, E.A. *The Story of the Ancient Manor of Sedgley* Tipton, 1942
Vance, William Ford *Sermons; with A Voice from Mines and Furnaces* Wolverhampton and London, 1853
Vernal, Joseph 'The Author of "Wednesbury Cocking"', *Birmingham Daily Post* (24 Aug. 1859)
Vodden, David F. *The Parish Church of St Matthew, Walsall. An Illustrated Guide and History* Walsall, 1995
'The Myth and Legend of a Midland Church [St Matthew's, Walsall], WWL 27:1 (Mar. 1980), 64-65

Wadsworth, Edward *The Black Country: a Book of 20 Drawings*, with an introduction by Arnold Bennett 1920
Walker, Ted *Black Country Graveyards* Wednesbury, nd
Webb, Geoff 'The Story of Eliza Tinsley – Nail Mistress', BCM 15:3 (1982), 43-46
Westwood, James *Our Black Country – Its Past and Future* np, nd [1945]
Westwood, J., and Simpson, J. *The Lore of the Land. A Guide to England's Legends* 2005
White, Walter *All Round the Wrekin* 1860
Whitehouse, John *Worcestershire Inn Tokens* Colwall, 1988
W[illett], F[rederic] *Osney Foss* Brighton and London, 1908
Willetts, Arthur *The Black Country Nail Trade* Dudley, 1987
Willetts, Cliff *When I was a boy* 2 vols, Dudley, 1977
Williams, H.H. *The Story of Old Swinford Church* Gloucester, nd
Williams, Ned *Black Country Chapels* Stroud, 2004
Black Country Folk at Werk [sic] Wolverhampton, 1989
A Century of the Black Country Stroud, 1999
Netherton Stroud, 2006
Woodall, R.D. *West Bromwich Yesterdays* Streetly, nd
Woods, D.C. 'The Custom of Heaving in the Black Country', BCM 12:2 (1979), 8-9
Woolley, Eric *The Black Country. A Portrait in Old Picture Postcards* Market Drayton, 1988
Wright, Alan *Tom Sayers* Lewes, 1994

Note on Sound Recordings

My own recordings, including those of George Dunn and Lucy Woodall, are part of the Roy Palmer Collection in the National Sound Archive at the British Library. *George Dunn: Chainmaker*, a double CD with a 32 page booklet, was issued by Musical Traditions Records (MTCD317-8) of Stroud in 2002. Lucy Woodall has one track on each of two CDs, *It was on a market day: English traditional folk singers*, issued by Veteran (VT6CD and VT7CD) of Haughley, Stowmarket, Suffolk, in 2005 and 2006 respectively.

Index

Also from Logaston Press

The Folklore of Shropshire

by Roy Palmer

Shropshire's folklore is presented in a series of themed chapters that encompass landscape, buildings, beliefs, work, seasons, people, music and drama. In the eleven chapters the county's rich store of folklore unfolds in a way that allows you to dip into what most intrigues, or to read from start to finish. Here are stories of mark stones, stone circles, giants, tunnels, dragons, rivers, meres, pools, hills, church sites changed by the devil, vengeful spirits, bull and bear baiting, cockfighting, fairs, herbal remedies and stories of peculiar activities, minstrels, histriones, waits, charmers and 'cunning folk', ghosts, witches, bountiful cows; accounts of characters such as the early saints, Caratacus, Edric the Wild, Humphrey Kynaston, Jack Mytton and even recent folklore surrounding Hilda Murrell; tales of the Civil War and of Hopton Quarter, of celebrations and customs surrounding times such as Easter, Christmas, All Souls' Eve, Ascension Day and Palm Sunday along with the likes of 'burning the mawkin', 'tin panning' and wife selling, of rhymes that link villages; and ballads that tell of events in the county's past, of folk plays and mummers—to mention just some of what is included.

Paperback, 320 pages with over 250 black and white illustrations
ISBN 1 904396 16 X Price £12.95

Herefordshire Folklore

by Roy Palmer

This follows a similar format to the above, but for the county of Herefordshire.

Paperback, 240 pages with over 135 black and white illustrations
ISBN 1 873827 58 X Price £12.95

Also from Logaston Press

Churches of Worcestershire

by Tim Bridges

Introductory chapters tell of the spread of Christianity across Worcestershire and detail the early development of churches. The major events that affected church building in the county — from new architectural fashions to political upheavals — are detailed to provide a background to the gazetteer that follows. Likewise a history of the changes in internal layout, and of the architects and craftsmen in furnishing, design, carving and stained glass is given.

The core of the book is a gazetteer to the Anglican churches of Worcestershire — some 270 in total — allowing this book to be used as a guide when exploring the county. Each entry places the church in its setting, describes the church, gives its building history and details the main decorations, monuments, glass and any notable external features such as lychgates and crosses. As such it is an invaluable aid to exploring what you are seeing — and for ensuring that you don't miss anything on your visit.

Paperback, 288 pages with over 200 black and white illustrations
ISBN 1 904396 39 9 Price: £14.95

Also from Logaston Press

The Folklore of Worcestershire

by Roy Palmer

Roy Palmer presents the folklore of the county as a series of themes that embrace landscape, buildings, beliefs, work, seasons, people, sport, dance, drama and music. In so doing, ten chapters are crafted that can stand alone or be read as a whole, each full of snippets of insight into the county's past in a way that adds to anyone's enjoyment of Worcestershire. After a reading of the book, features of the landscape, for example, will appear as landmarks associated with certain folk beliefs adding to their interest and to one's own sense of 'belonging' to the county.

The volume contains a great deal of information on the various customs of the county, on its music, drama and dance, together with the cryptic and not so cryptic tales of life recorded on gravestones, as well as various spectral apparitions. In addition some 'customs' have been revived or even created, whilst others, not long re-established, have once again gone out of fashion.

Roy Palmer has written on the folklore of many counties in the west midlands and along the Welsh border as well as compiling a number of anthologies of traditional songs, and a study of songs of social comment, *The Sound of History*.

Paperback, 368 pages with over 200 black and white illustrations

ISBN 1 904396 40 2 Price: £12.95

Also from Logaston Press

The Mercian Maquis

The Secret Resistance Organization in Herefordshire and Worcestershire during World War II

by Bernard Lowry & Mick Wilks

For decades after the end of the Second World War little was known about the secretive organisation known as the Auxiliary Units. Formed in 1940, at the same time as the Home Guard, its members were recruited from amongst a tightly-knit farming community and from those in other reserved occupations. Organised into patrols of about half a dozen men and knowing their locality intimately, their role would have been to carry out acts of sabotage and terror behind the German invader's lines whilst the Regular Army regrouped for counter offensives.

Whilst the bulk of the patrols covered the coastal areas, this book details the Units' most inland operational area. The establishment, operation and function of the 12 patrols formed in Herefordshire and Worcestershire are fully explained, together with information on the even more shadowy world of the Special Duties spies and urban saboteurs.

From carefully camouflaged underground Operational Bases liberally supplied with explosives and arms and constructed in woodland on high ground, patrol members would have set out at night to harry the invader. This was to be done in the knowledge that they and their families risked summary execution if captured.

This book covers a period of little known local history now revealed through research of the few remaining documents and by interviewing surviving patrol members. Over a period of several years the authors have found or identified Operational Bases near Dinmore, Dinedor, Credenhill, Ross, Ledbury and Bromyard Downs in Herefordshire, and near Alfrick, Broadheath, Claines, Crowle, The Lenches and Overbury in Worcestershire.

Paperback, 160 pages, 70 drawings, plans and photographs

ISBN 1 873827 97 0 Price £7.95

Also from Logaston Press

Flying for Fun in the southern Marches

by Tony Hobbs

This book looks at the early history of manned flight in the southern Marches, from ballooning, through gliding and parachuting to flying. In doing so it considers the question as to whether the earliest manned flight in Britain was actually made in Shropshire; abortive attempts at flying in Ross, the engine and propeller of the machine eventually being attached to a water craft to make a more successful speed boat; the contribution to ballooning made by Charles Rolls; the unscheduled stops of early aircraft in fields around the counties; and an individual who helped in the testing of parachutes.

More recent claims to fame and activities are also detailed, from a commercial airfield at Hereford, to the developments at Tilstock (Shropshire), Shobdon (Herefordshire) and Staverton (Gloucestershire), the Gliding Clubs at Shobdon, in the Black Mountains and on the Long Mynd; Ian Ashpole's attempts at a variety of ballooning and allied records; the development of hang gliding, paragliding, microlight flying, and helicopter and flying enterprises.

Each of these activities Tony Hobbs also attempts in his own right in the spirit of the early pioneers, meeting today's enthusiasts in the hope it may encourage others to also 'have a go' — though, in at least one case, with less self harm resulting!

Paperback, 160 pages, 70 drawings, plans and photographs
ISBN 1 873827 97 0 Price £9.95

Also from Logaston Press

The Defence of Worcestershire
and the southern approaches to Birmingham
in World War II

by Mick Wilks

In the summer of 1940, an invasion of Britain by the apparently invincible forces of the Third Reich was widely expected. In the time-honoured fashion of the British, preparations to meet the invasion were left almost to the last moment. Profusely illustrated with over 60 drawings and maps and over 150 photographs, this book attempts to tell the story of how Worcestershire was prepared for defence against both ground and air attack by the enemy. Worcestershire was the chosen location for both the Government and Royal Family had it been necessary to evacuate them from London, and the county occupies a crucial location on the southern approaches to Birmingham and the Black Country, whose industries were then busily producing aircraft and munitions for the home forces.

The book deals in some detail with the defence of airfields, munitions works, petrol stores and communications within the county, as well as providing an explanation of the methods of defence to be used against the German blitzkrieg techniques that had been so ably demonstrated beforehand in Scandinavia and continental Europe. The book assesses the military forces available for defence, and includes a summary of the formation, arming and role of the Worcestershire Home Guard. An entirely different picture to that portrayed by the popular TV series, *Dad's Army*, is put forward, describing a serious and dedicated body of men numbering about 19,000, a good proportion of whom had already fought the Germans 20 years before and were determined to beat the old enemy again.

After a career in town planning, but now retired and working as a part-time volunteer researcher with the County Archaeological Service, Mick Wilks has been researching and recording modern defence sites in Worcestershire for over 12 years.

Paperback, 160 pages, 70 drawings, plans and photographs

ISBN 1 873827 97 0 Price £14.95